STATE and LOCAL
POLITICS and POLICY

STATE and LOCAL POLITICS and POLICY:

CHANGE and REFORM

Michael J. Ross
University of San Diego

PRENTICE-HALL, INC., ENGLEWOOD CLIFFS, NEW JERSEY 07632

Library of Congress Cataloging-in-Publication Data

Ross, Michael J., [date]
   State and local politics and policy.

   Bibliography: p. 307
   Includes index.
   1. State governments. 2. Local government—United
States. I. Title.
JK2408.R59 1987   320.8'0973   86-91478
ISBN 0-13-843384-4

Editorial supervision and interior design: Serena Hoffman
Cover design: Wanda Lubelska
Manufacturing buyer: Barbara Kelly Kittle

© 1987 by Prentice-Hall, Inc.
A Division of Simon & Schuster
Englewood Cliffs, New Jersey 07632

PRINTED IN THE UNITED STATES OF AMERICA

10 9 8 7 6 5 4 3 2 1

ISBN 0-13-843384-4 01

Prentice-Hall International (UK) Limited, *London*
Prentice-Hall of Australia Pty. Limited, *Sydney*
Prentice-Hall Canada Inc., *Toronto*
Prentice-Hall Hispanoamericana, S.A., *Mexico*
Prentice-Hall of India Private Limited, *New Delhi*
Prentice-Hall of Japan, Inc., *Tokyo*
Prentice-Hall of Southeast Asia Pte. Ltd., *Singapore*
Editora Prentice-Hall do Brasil, Ltda., *Rio de Janeiro*

For Josiane,

who made it all worthwhile.

Contents

Part III: *Local Government*

Part IV: *Outputs*

chapter 11   **POLICY AREAS: SOCIAL SERVICES   228**

chapter 12   **POLICY AREAS:
SYSTEM-MAINTENANCE SERVICES   271**

EPILOGUE   305

SUGGESTED READINGS   307

NAME INDEX   311

SUBJECT INDEX   315

Preface

The theme of this book is change and reform: the content of various proposed reforms, how they worked in practice, and whether they affected the public policies adopted by state and local governments.

Subnational governments have long been the focus of reform attempts because many of them are said to lag behind the federal government, which is usually taken to be the model for reform. We shall consider the assets and liabilities of various reform proposals and whether their implementation resulted in the anticipated consequences. It may come as a surprise that reforming an institution—for example, the state legislature or the courts—sometimes does not have much effect on the decisions made by policy makers.

Part I sets the stage for much of the material that follows. In it we consider how states vary, particularly in terms of political culture, and how the federal government influences state and local decisions. President Reagan's attempts to alter the federal system and to reorder federal, state, and local spending priorities will be noted here and throughout the book. Another way that states vary is in terms of interparty competition. Some have a rough balance of party strength, but others lean toward one political party, usually the Democrats. Finally, we shall consider interest groups, noting their strategies and how their activities are regulated by the states. Important weapons of interest groups—the direct-democracy devices of initiative, referendum, and recall—will be described.

Part II begins with a discussion of the governor and other elected executives, as well as appointed administrators. In recent years, state administrative branches have been substantially reorganized, and governors have been given increased powers. State legislatures too have changed and are now more capable of discharging their constitutional responsibilities. State courts have shown a new activism.

Part III deals directly with local governments—their forms of government, their elected officials, their fiscal problems, and their political response to budgetary woes. Different theories of community power will be explored, as will the much discussed "flight to the suburbs."

State taxes and expenditures, as well as the state and local services provided by those expenditures, are studied in Part IV. Reforming the tax system so that some individuals pay more and others pay less is a constant topic in state capitals. How much the states spend on different policies is affected by both economic and political factors; the politics-versus-economics debate will be addressed, and perhaps resolved. Finally, ten different policies in the areas of social services and system-maintenance services will be considered.

I want to thank the many people who helped me write this book. My academic reviewers pointed out numerous gaps, errors, and overstatements: Susan Welch, University of Nebraska-Lincoln; Frank T. Colon, Lehigh University; Joseph B. Tucker, Ohio University; Bradley R. Rice, Clayton Junior College; Edward I. Sidlow, Miami University; Raymond Tatalovich, Loyola University; Conrad Joyner, University of Arizona; and Jill Clark, University of Texas-Arlington. Copy editor Bruce Fulton turned many of my clumsy sentences into precise ones, which was a humbling experience for me. Serena Hoffman of Prentice-Hall expertly guided the book along the stages of production.

Finally, I would like especially to acknowledge the role of my wife, Josiane, in completing this project. There were many times that I was tempted to quit, but her love and encouragement gave me the incentive to see it through to conclusion.

Michael J. Ross

STATE and LOCAL POLITICS and POLICY

chapter 1

Introduction

If asked "When someone mentions government or politics, what level of government do you think of?" most Americans would probably answer "The federal government." This tendency to be preoccupied with Washington, D.C., is unfortunate because, as this book will show, state and local governments provide many important services for the public and are a fascinating subject for academic study. States or their local governments regulate family relations (especially in such matters as divorce), supply education from preschools to postdoctorate fellowships, define the vast majority of crimes, and provide law enforcement. Moreover, they attempt to meet the needs of the public in such areas as health, welfare, and transportation. With varying degrees of thoroughness, states protect the environment and regulate economic activities, including the ownership of private property. In fact, as the Reagan administration has sought to decrease the influence of the national government on the environment and business regulation, state and local governments have become an increasingly important means for resolving conflicts in these two areas.

Eighty-two thousand state and local governments have become big business, whether we measure them in terms of expenditures, employment, or taxes. If we count federal grants-in-aid as spending by state and local governments, the federal sector and the state-local sector are about equal in spending for domestic purposes.[1] However, since state and local employment is labor-intensive, there are many more subnational employees than federal employees. About 58 percent of all government employees in this country work for local governments (as teachers, police and fire fighters, sanitation workers, and so on), 23 percent are employed by state governments, and only 18 percent were hired by the federal government.

Employment growth over the last three decades has clearly been in the state-local sector. However, the federal government helps to pay for many of the services actually delivered by lower levels. In terms of tax revenues collected, the states are clearly gaining at the expense of the federal government, which now garners only about half of all taxes (see Table 1-1).

Interestingly, a case can also be made that state and local governments have various devices for making them more responsive to the public than the federal government.[2] The national government has no election of judges or administrative department heads; no recall of elected officials; no provision for voters to pass laws or constitutional amendments by means of the initiative process; no referendum to challenge laws passed by the legislature; and no provision for voters to directly approve or reject bond issues, tax increases, governmental reorganizations, or constitutional amendments passed by the legislature. (Each of these devices will be considered in later chapters.) On the other hand, the public knows less about events in their state capitals than events in Washington, partly because there is much more media coverage of the nation's capital.[3] Public opinion polls have enabled political scientists to study the extent to which public policy reflects public opinion at the state level. They have found that it varies not only from state to state but from issue to issue. Idaho, Nevada, and New York especially follow the preferences of their citizens; Maine, Vermont, and Maryland generally do not.[4] Public policies on aid to church schools, right-to-work laws, welfare, liquor and gambling, and capital punishment show much higher congruence with state public opinion than do policies on firearms control or motor-vehicle regulation. When asked in 1984, "From which level of government do you feel you get the most for your money—federal, state, or local?" the U.S. public answered 35 percent for local government, 27 percent for state government, and 24 percent for the federal government; 14 percent did not know.[5]

TABLE 1-1 Tax Revenue Collected*

Fiscal Year	Federal	State	Local
1957	70.8%	14.7%	14.5%
1984	56.3%	26.8%	16.9%

SOURCE: Advisory Commission on Intergovernmental Relations, *Significant Features of Fiscal Federalism, 1984 Edition* (Washington, D.C.: ACIR, 1985), Table 32.

* Excludes fees paid for services such as water, garbage collection, or admission to government facilities, utility and liquor-store revenue, and all social-insurance contributions.

THE CHANGING NATURE
OF STATE AND LOCAL GOVERNMENT

Criticism of state and local governments, especially the former, has been a long-standing practice of many journalists and political scientists. Writing in 1949, Robert Allen said, "State government is the tawdriest, most incompetent, and most stultifying unit of the nation's political structure. In state government are to be found in their most extreme and vicious forms all the worst evils of misrule in the country."[6] In the 1960s, Roscoe Martin charged state leaders with having a "rural orientation, provincial outlook, commitment to a strict moral code, . . . and intermittent and imperfect contact with the realities of the modern world."[7] The demise of the states has long been expected—for example, by Luther Gulick, who said in 1933, "The American State is finished. I do not predict that the States will go, but affirm that they have gone."[8] More recently, James Stever has asserted that "we are presently facing the extinction of states and localities as meaningful political entities."[9]

It is altogether true that state and local governments have, in some instances, not improved their reputation. Some recent examples of misbehavior include the revelation by a Massachusetts special investigating commission that corruption in government construction was "a way of life" in the 1960s and 1970s and that "the state was for sale"[10]; the three-year prison sentence given former Tennessee governor Ray Blanton for fixing the state Alcoholic Beverage Commission so that his political supporters were issued liquor licenses; the conviction of the president pro tem of the Mississippi Senate for attempting to extort fifty thousand dollars on a proposed bill; and the suspension of the chief justice of the Rhode Island Supreme Court for friendship with reputed mobsters. (Corruption as a special kind of crime will be treated in Chapter 11.)

But condemnation of state and local governments frequently misses the important reforms and improvements that they have instituted in the last three decades. A key theme of this book will be that subnational governments "ain't like they used to be." State constitutions have been substantially updated. Governors today nearly always serve four-year terms (rather than two-year terms, as before) and can succeed themselves, have increased budgetary powers, and have gained greater control over management of the executive branch as a result of reductions in the number of other separately elected executive officials. The proportion of state employees covered by some form of a civil service system has increased dramatically. State legislatures have been reapportioned in accordance with the "one person, one vote" principle, meet more frequently and for longer periods, have a streamlined committee structure and a larger professional staff, and have established higher salaries to attract more competent members. State-local court systems have become more integrated, have established judicial qualifications commissions to handle disciplining and removal of judges, and are increasingly willing to take an activist role—for example, by extending personal rights beyond those recognized by federal law. State revenue systems have been overhauled, becoming more productive and broad-based. For example, forty states have broad personal income taxes, and forty-five have corporation income taxes. The increased revenue generated by these reformed tax systems has been used for expanded services in such areas as education, welfare, health, and transportation, and also for local aid and tax relief. Regional differences in wealth have declined, especially as the Southeast (historically the nation's poorest region) has moved closer to the national average. Between 1960 and 1980 alone, black voter registration doubled in the eleven southern states. Moreover, liberal and minority groups once shut out of state capitals are becoming increasingly effective. For example, as the next chapter shows, these groups were able to persuade many state governments to restore spending for social programs cut by the Reagan administration.[11]

The roots of reformism are many and various. Some reformers have wished to change the structure of state and local government, others have sought to alter the policies these governments enact, and many have wanted to do both. Structural reformers will be emphasized in Parts I, II, and III of this book; policy reformers, who usually act on the basis of liberal or conservative principles, will be noted in Part IV. The movement to alter the structure of state and local government has proceeded in fits and starts throughout this century. It is an attempt to "streamline," "professionalize," or "modernize" subnational governments so that they will operate according to an idealized model of how the federal government runs. In addition to working to weed out corruption, such good-government groups as the League of Women Voters and the National Municipal League want to "bring state and local governments into the twentieth century" so that these governments can more forcefully meet their constitutional responsibilities and serve the needs of their people. Structural reformers laboring in a particular state may be able to professionalize only a part of state government (for example, the governorship or the legislature). Even so, the result is usually a more powerful and activist form of government. Changed structures usually lead to changed policies, but that is not always the case, as this book will document. Many reformers seek to modernize state and local governments because they believe that only a powerful and activist government can introduce significant social change and can redistribute economic resources to poor and disadvantaged people. Other reformers may care little for the intricacies of government structure and may direct their energies toward changing and molding government policies to reflect their philosophical or moral principles. Groups seeking to redirect state-local policies are usually thought of as

liberal groups, but they also include the Moral Majority, led by fundamentalist Protestant television preacher Jerry Falwell, who describes his
policy agenda as "pro-God and pro-family" and anti-abortion and anti-
homosexuality. The net result of all the energetic activity intended to alter
and reform state-local structure and policy is fifty state governments and
eighty-two thousand local governments, which have changed considerably
in recent years and will undoubtedly change more in the years to come.

STATE VARIATIONS

The American states, although sharing many features, also exhibit numerous interesting and peculiar variations. One of these is population
gain or loss. The 1980 census revealed clearly what had been surmised
for some time: national population movement has been south and west,
away from the Frostbelt and toward the Sunbelt. The nation's population
center has become DeSoto, Missouri—the first time this point has been
west of the Mississippi River. States adding seats in the U.S. House of
Representatives as a result of population gain included Florida (four
seats), Texas (three), and California (two). Gaining one seat each were
Oregon, Washington, Arizona, Nevada, Colorado, Utah, New Mexico, and
Tennessee. Among the states losing House seats—a bitter pill to swallow—
were New York (five) and Ohio, Pennsylvania, and Illinois (two each).
Missouri, Indiana, Michigan, South Dakota, Massachusetts, and New Jersey
each lost one. Population change for each state is depicted in Table 1-2
and Figure 1-1.

An extraordinary revelation of the 1980 census was that "for the
first time since 1820, rural areas and small towns are growing faster than
the nation's metropolitan areas"—in fact, at a rate 1.5 times faster than
the national average.[12] Such *reverse migration* is especially pronounced in
the West. Ironically, this movement does not signal a return to the nation's
farms, because the number of farm workers is declining. Rather, it reflects
relocation of industries, businesses, and colleges to once-remote areas;
long-distance commuting, which has been made easier by expressways;
the growth of recreational and retirement communities in rural areas;
and dissatisfaction with urban and suburban living. Reverse migration
reminds us that there are differences not only *between* states but *within*
states as well.

States vary not only in population and rate of population growth,
but in many other significant ways as well—a key theme of this book. For
example, as Table 1-3 shows, personal income is twice as high in Connecticut as in Mississippi. The same table also shows the Southeast to be
the poorest region of the country, but this disparity is lessening, as we
noted earlier.

TABLE 1-2   1980 State Populations (in thousands) and Population Change since 1970

Northeast	54,585	+0.5	**South**	69,900	+21.4
New England	12,348	+4.2	South Atlantic	31,494	+23.7
Maine	1,125	+13.2	Virginia	5,346	+14.9
New Hampshire	921	+24.8	West Virginia	1,950	+11.8
Vermont	511	+15.0	North Carolina	5,874	+15.5
Massachusetts	5,737	+0.8	South Carolina	3,119	+20.4
Rhode Island	947	−0.3	Georgia	5,464	+19.1
Connecticut	3,108	+2.5	Florida	9,740	+43.4
Middle Atlantic	42,237	−0.5	East South Central	14,663	+14.5
New York	17,557	−3.8	Kentucky	3,661	+13.7
New Jersey	7,364	+2.7	Tennessee	4,591	+16.9
Pennsylvania	11,867	+0.6	Alabama	3,890	+12.9
Delaware	595	+8.6	Mississippi	2,521	+13.7
Maryland	4,216	+7.5	West South Central	23,743	+22.9
D.C.	638	−15.7	Arkansas	2,286	+18.8
			Louisiana	4,204	+15.3
			Oklahoma	3,025	+18.2
			Texas	14,228	+27.1
Midwest	58,854	+4.0	**West**	43,165	+23.9
Great Lakes	41,670	+3.5	Mountain	11,368	+37.1
Ohio	10,797	+1.3	Montana	787	+13.3
Indiana	5,490	+5.7	Idaho	944	+32.4
Illinois	11,418	+2.8	Wyoming	471	+41.6
Michigan	9,258	+4.2	Colorado	2,889	+30.7
Wisconsin	4,705	+6.5	New Mexico	1,300	+27.8
Great Plains	17,184	+5.2	Arizona	2,718	+53.1
Minnesota	4,077	+7.1	Utah	1,461	+37.9
Iowa	2,913	+3.1	Nevada	799	+63.5
Missouri	4,917	+5.1	Pacific	31,797	+19.8
North Dakota	653	+5.6	Washington	4,130	+21.0
South Dakota	690	+3.6	Oregon	2,633	+25.9
Nebraska	1,570	+5.7	California	23,669	+18.5
Kansas	2,363	+5.1	Alaska	400	+32.4
			Hawaii	965	+21.7
Total				226,505	+11.4

SOURCE: "States and Regions," *National Journal*, November 14, 1981, p. 2019.

States differ in other obvious ways as well: Alaska is about 550 times as large in land area as Rhode Island—and its population density is over 1200 percent less! Some states rely on manufacturing, others on agriculture, still others on tourism. Some states exhibit wide racial, ethnic, or religious diversity; others are more homogeneous.

No doubt the many changes in state and local governments mentioned earlier have made the states less dissimilar, but one key differentiating variable is political values such as liberalism and conservatism. David Klingman and William Lammers have developed an index of general

FIGURE 1-1   State Population Gains

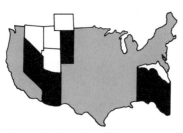

Growth Greater Than
Three Times National Average

Arizona   Utah
Florida   Wyoming
Nevada

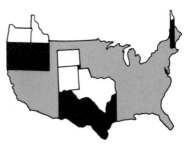

Growth Greater Than
Two Times National Average

Alaska   New Hampshire
Colorado   New Mexico
Hawaii   Oregon
Idaho   Texas

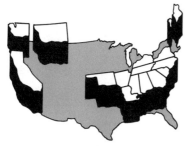

Growth Greater Than
National Average

Alabama   Maine   South Carolina
Arkansas   Mississippi   Tennessee
California   Montana   Vermont
Georgia   North Carolina Virginia
Kentucky   Oklahoma   Washington
Louisiana   Puerto Rico

Growth Less Than
National Average

Delaware   North Dakota
Maryland   West Virginia
Minnesota   Wisconsin

Growth Less Than
One-half National Average

Indiana   Missouri
Iowa   Nebraska
Kansas   South Dakota
Michigan

Growth Less Than
One-quarter National Average

Connecticut   New York (Loss)
D.C. (Loss)   Ohio
Illinois   Pennsylvania
Massachusetts   Rhode Island (Loss)
New Jersey

SOURCE: *New York Times*, December 25, 1980, p. 9. Copyright © 1980 by The New York Times Company.
Reprinted by permission.

policy liberalism that indicates how extensively a state is willing to use the public sector to deal with problems. The index includes such factors as consumer protection laws; social services spending, including welfare; ratification of the Equal Rights Amendment; and overall policy innovativeness.[13] As Table 1-4 indicates, the most liberal states are generally nonsouthern coastal states or Great Lakes states (the Frostbelt); the least liberal are southern, border, or southwestern states (the Sunbelt). Liberal states tend to exhibit the following features: an urban population, racial and religious diversity, greater wealth, a developed but stagnating economy, higher voter turnout, a reformed legislature and governorship, and especially a loss of population. Ideas have consequences. As we shall see in our discussion of public policy (Chapters 11 and 12), liberal states' policies are different from those of states with contrasting values. In the next chapter we will note that the ability of states to determine most of their own policies is one of the assets of a federal system.

TABLE 1-3   Per Capita Personal Income, 1984

Alaska	$17,155	Ohio	$12,314
Dist. of Columbia	$16,845	Wisconsin	$12,309
Connecticut	$16,369	Nebraska	$12,280
New Jersey	$15,282	Missouri	$12,129
Massachusetts	$14,574	Iowa	$12,090
California	$14,344	Indiana	$11,799
New York	$14,121	Oklahoma	$11,745
Maryland	$14,111	Arizona	$11,629
Colorado	$13,742	Oregon	$11,582
Illinois	$13,728	Georgia	$11,441
Delaware	$13,545	South Dakota	$11,049
Kansas	$13,319	Louisiana	$10,850
Minnesota	$13,219	North Carolina	$10,758
Nevada	$13,216	Vermont	$10,692
New Hampshire	$13,148	Maine	$10,678
Virginia	$13,067	Tennessee	$10,400
Hawaii	$12,761	Kentucky	$10,374
Rhode Island	$12,730	New Mexico	$10,330
Washington	$12,728	Montana	$10,216
U.S. average	**$12,707**	Idaho	$10,174
Texas	$12,636	South Carolina	$10,075
Wyoming	$12,586	Alabama	$9,981
Florida	$12,553	West Virginia	$9,846
Michigan	$12,518	Arkansas	$9,724
North Dakota	$12,461	Utah	$9,719
Pennsylvania	$12,343	Mississippi	$8,857

SOURCE: *U.S. News & World Report,* May 20, 1985, p. 6. Copyright 1985, U.S. News & World Report, Inc.

TABLE 1-4 State Liberalism

Rank	State*	Score	Rank	State*	Score
1	New York	1.862	25	Wyoming	−0.081
2	Massachusetts	1.805	26	North Dakota	−0.110
3	New Jersey	1.518	27	New Mexico	−0.146
4	California	1.464	28	Nebraska	−0.251
5	Connecticut	1.453	29	Kentucky	−0.304
6	Oregon	1.436	30	Texas	−0.389
7	Wisconsin	1.378	31	Florida	−0.481
8	Minnesota	1.227	32	South Dakota	−0.582
9	Colorado	1.121	33	Utah	−0.584
10	Michigan	1.100	34	West Virginia	−0.608
11	Pennsylvania	1.060	35	Indiana	−0.615
12	Rhode Island	0.871	36	Louisiana	−0.668
13	Washington	0.576	37	Virginia	−0.738
14	Illinois	0.539	38	Oklahoma	−0.860
15	Maryland	0.393	39	Missouri	−0.895
16	New Hampshire	0.386	40	North Carolina	−0.923
17	Vermont	0.352	41	Georgia	−0.933
18	Iowa	0.303	42	Nevada	−1.170
19	Kansas	0.207	43	Tennessee	−1.209
20	Ohio	0.145	44	Alabama	−1.285
21	Idaho	0.138	45	Arizona	−1.403
22	Maine	0.119	46	South Carolina	−1.491
23	Montana	0.107	47	Arkansas	−1.863
24	Delaware	0.090	48	Mississippi	−2.061

SOURCE: David Klingman and William Lammers, "The 'General Policy Liberalism' Factor in American State Politics," *American Journal of Political Science,* 28 (August 1984), 602–3. By permission of the University of Texas Press.

* Alaska and Hawaii omitted because of missing data.

POLITICAL CULTURE

Another important difference among the states, one that takes into account liberalism versus conservatism and numerous other matters, is their political culture. Daniel Elazar writes that two political concepts, sometimes conflicting and sometimes complementing each other, have always influenced Americans' understanding of government and politics.[14] The first is that public life is a marketplace in which individuals and groups bargain in order to promote their self-interest. The second, in contrast, is that society is a commonwealth dedicated to implementing shared moral principles. The interaction of these two concepts produces three distinct political cultures that are found in nearly every state.

The *individualistic* political culture embraces the marketplace idea: politics is a means individuals can use to better their economic or social position. Those people engaged in politics supply the governmental services the public demands, and expect to be adequately compensated in return. In this political culture, private concerns are paramount; hence, governmental or nongovernmental interference in private affairs is limited. Mutual obligations are important, and strong political parties provide the organization and norms for harnessing the energies of office seekers. Party loyalty is essential in this culture in which politicians pursue office as a means of manipulating the distribution of the favors and rewards of government, rather than as a means of using the power of government to implement a political philosophy or a conception of the public interest. This political culture is clearly not ideological. The idea of a politically neutral civil service is suspect, for the role of the bureaucracy is to dispense the favors and quid pro quos lying at the heart of the individualistic culture. Politics is viewed as a grimy business best left to the professional politicians who are willing to engage in this kind of morally compromising activity. A moderate amount of corruption—viewed as the necessary cost of transacting the public's business—is tolerated. Two particularly individualistic states are Nevada and Pennsylvania.

In sharp contrast to the view that politics can be used as a means of private economic enrichment is the *moralistic* political culture, which sees politics as the means to create a good society. Those politicians who want to improve the commonwealth may or may not be religious people, but their most important characteristic is a belief that government is a valued means for promoting the general welfare. Government should intervene in the economic and social life of the community, whether to end sexual discrimination, or to protect the environment, or to control pornography. The just society that politicians seek can be either a liberal one or a conservative one, depending on their point of view. Needless to say, philosophical and ideological issues are the main political currency of a moralistic culture. Party loyalty is less important in this political culture; in fact, candidates and voters can switch parties or form third parties or choose a nonpartisan system, if any of these will promote their political beliefs. Every person is encouraged to participate in political life because politics is not limited to political professionals. Good examples of states with a moralistic political culture are Minnesota and Oregon.

The *traditionalistic* political culture seeks to maintain the existing order, in which those persons at the top of the social hierarchy play the dominant role in government. A small and self-perpetuating group of leaders have inherited their right to govern by means of family ties or social position. Politics consists of personal factions grouped around upper-status leaders who compete with one another. Either political parties are not important or, as in many southern states, one party overwhelmingly dominates. New Mexico and Mississippi are states with a traditionalistic political culture.

Some states exhibit one of these three political cultures in pure form.

Most, though, have a mixture of the three, or else different cultures dominate different parts of the state. The geographical distribution of these three cultures is depicted in Figure 1-2.

Elazar presents further evidence of diversity when he notes the cultural differences found within many states. These cleavages (which have strong overtones of religious, racial, or ethnic conflict) are described in the terms used in the states in question:

Rednecks versus Lowlanders (Alabama, Florida, Mississippi, South Carolina)

Hillbillies versus Lowlanders (Arkansas, Kentucky, North Carolina, Tennessee)

Whites versus Eskimos or Indians (Alaska, Arizona)

Anglos versus Orientals (Hawaii)

Mormons versus Gentiles (Arizona, Idaho, Utah)

Northerners versus Southerners (Illinois, Indiana, Kansas, Missouri, Ohio)

Old Stock versus Ethnics (Connecticut, Illinois, Maine, Massachusetts, New Jersey, New York, Pennsylvania, Rhode Island)

Anglo-Protestants versus French Catholics (Louisiana, Maine, New Hampshire, Vermont)

Protestants versus Catholics (Iowa, Wisconsin)

Fundamentalists versus Open-life-style Advocates (California)

Elazar's significant concept of political culture has prompted a vast outpouring of studies in which political scientists seek either to confirm empirically or reject it, or to apply it to their particular state. Despite being subjected to many different research methodologies and partially disconfirmed by some studies, the theory has stood up surprisingly well.[15]

STATE CONSTITUTIONS

Daniel Elazar has written that state constitutions have three functions: as overall frames of government for political systems (which are, in most states, better developed than most of the world's nations), practical public expressions of the purposes of government, and reflections of public conceptions of the proper role of government.[16] Although Americans share the same legal and constitutional theory—the English common law tradition—state constitutions are similar in some respects and widely dissimilar in others, as are the states themselves.[17]

> Though no two state constitutions are alike in all details, all of them conform roughly to a common pattern. First there is a preamble, repeating in rather stock phrases certain first principles regarding the nature and purposes of government. Then there is a bill of rights, spelling out in familiar language the basic rights of conscience and of property and the rights of persons accused of crime. The next three articles usually deal with the legislative, executive, and judicial branches of the state government, in that order,

FIGURE 1-2 Political Culture

M: Moralistic
I: Individualistic
T: Traditionalistic

Note: Two letters juxtaposed indicates either a
synthesis of two subcultures, or the
existence of two separate subcultural
communities in the same area, with the
first dominant and the second secondary.

SOURCE: Daniel Elazar, American Federalism: A View from the States, 3rd ed. (New York: Harper & Row Pub. 1984) pp. 124–25. Copyright © 1984 by Harper & Row.

describing their structure, powers, and limitations. At the end is an article dealing with the methods of constitutional amendment or revision and a schedule for the transition to the new dispensation. In addition, most state constitutions have articles of varying length and detail on a wide variety of additional subjects, notably education, local government, the suffrage, public finance, corporations, and other business organizations.[18]

The oldest state constitution is the Massachusetts Constitution of 1780; the newest is Georgia's 1983 document. (The latter constitution, however, is really a major revision of previous specific provisions and not a truly new document that has significantly changed the basic structure of Georgia's government.) Both the Massachusetts and the New Hampshire constitutions predate the U.S. Constitution. Louisiana has had eleven constitutions, Georgia ten, and South Carolina seven.

Although the United States Constitution has been amended only 26 times in nearly 200 years, the California Constitution has been amended over 450 times in almost 110 years and the Alabama Constitution over 440 times in 85 years. Five states have constitutions shorter than the U.S. Constitution, and eight state constitutions are about equal in length to the national document.

State constitutions are sometimes faulted for being overly long, detailed, and specific, for containing much outdated material, and for taking up matters best left to ordinary legislation. David Fellman describes the problem of excessive detail:

> It solidifies the entrenchment of vested interests. It makes temporary matters permanent. It deprives state legislatures and local governments of desirable flexibility and diminishes their sense of responsibility. It encourages the search for methods of evading constitutional provisions and thus tends to debase our sense of constitutional morality. It makes frequent recourse to the amending processes inevitable.[19]

Many state constitutions were written in the 1800s and reflect that century's experience with venal and corrupt state legislatures. Popular distrust of the legislature prompted constitution writers to insert commands in order to guarantee that the legislature do certain things. Therefore the documents are overly specific and must be frequently amended, which in turn makes them even longer. But the key point to remember is that constitutions confer advantages on some people and disadvantages on others. In certain respects, a state's basic law has at least one thing in common with national party platforms: it is "a picture of who is up and who is down in the struggle for dominance" among interest groups and ideological organizations, and "a sign of who has made bargains with whom."[20] That a state's fundamental law is viewed in such a light is perhaps unfortunate, but it is also possibly inevitable, since state constitutions are much harder to change than ordinary laws. If some interest can get favored treatment written into the state's basic law, that group may receive benefits for some time to come. It is well known that the highway lobby has succeeded in state after state in securing the constitutional earmarking of the gas tax for building and maintaining roads.[21] Lewis Froman found that states with a strong interest-group system have longer (hence, more detailed and specific) constitutions, a greater number of constitutional amendments proposed each year, and a greater number of amendments adopted.[22]

Since detailed and comprehensive constitutions touch a wide variety of interests, it is not surprising that the numerous provisions of such constitutions must be contested in court. Courts in these states will play a key role in distributing political burdens and benefits. More will be said later in this chapter about the role of the courts in constitutional interpretation.

TABLE 1-5   Summary of National Municipal League's Model State Constitution

Provision	Characteristics
Preamble	Succinct statement of purpose of constitution
Declaration of Rights	Sparse; modeled after federal constitution
Enumeration of Powers	Explicit statement that constitution is a grant, not a limitation on state
Legislature	
Form	Unicameral
Size	Set by statute
Term of Office	Two years, lower house; six years, upper house
Type of district	Single-member
Compensation	Set by statute
Sessions (length)	Flexible
Procedure	Unspecified
Postaudit	Specifically under legislative control
Executive	
Time of election	Odd-numbered years
Term	Four years, no limit
Elected state offices	None
Administrative organization	Consolidated
Succession	Explicitly provided for
Judiciary	
Organization	Unified
Selection	According to Missouri Plan
Administration	Centralized
Minor Officials	Eliminated
Finance	Broad local autonomy
Education	Specific grant
Intergovernmental relations	Free from obstacles to cooperation
Civil service	Specific grant
Constitutional change	Liberal rather than cumbersome procedure

SOURCE: Elmer E. Cornwell, Jr., Jay S. Goodman, and Wayne R. Swanson *State Constitutional Conventions.* Copyright © 1975 Praeger Publishers. Reprinted by permission of Praeger Publishers.

What are the characteristics of a superior constitution? According to Fellman, "Certainly, the first requisite is brevity. . . . It should do no more than set down fundamental and enduring first principles." Another important quality is "readability, for one of its central purposes is to educate the public in first principles. . . . In short, the constitution should be intelligible to ordinary people, if it is to command confidence and, indeed, general reverence."[23] It is clear that Fellman, and numerous other writers, do not view the state constitution as merely another arena in which the state's contending interest groups battle for power and preference.

Generally, most authorities contend that constitutions should be basic documents that briefly outline the division of powers among the state's executive, legislative, and judicial branches and local governments. They should also include a bill of rights specifying citizens' basic liberties, and a means for amending the document or calling a constitutional convention. The National Municipal League has drafted a model state constitution and recommended it to the states; it is summarized in Table 1-5. This document reflects a "good government," reform perspective favoring a centralized, powerful, and activist state government.

CONSTITUTIONAL CHANGE

Between 1970 and 1984, 3011 proposals to change state constitutions were submitted to the voters, and 2062, or 68.4 percent, were adopted. By far the largest number, 92.0 percent, were constitutional amendments voted by the state legislature and submitted to the voters for their approval.[24] However, there were also a substantial number of initiative constitutional amendments, and proposals submitted by constitutional conventions. We will now consider these formal methods of constitutional change, plus the informal means of court interpretation, custom, and usage. During the period mentioned, nearly every state was involved in formal constitutional change, and all were affected by the informal means.

Legislative Constitutional Amendments

In twenty states, constitutional amendments may be proposed by a two-thirds vote of the legislature—the same requirement under which the U.S. Congress proposes constitutional amendments. Connecticut mandates a three-fourths vote in each chamber in one session, or a majority vote in each chamber in each of two sessions. Of the remaining states, nineteen demand only a majority vote of the legislature, and ten a three-fifths vote, either of which is a more lenient requirement than the one under which Congress operates. In fifteen states, many of which have a majority-vote requirement, constitutional amendments must pass the legislature twice.

As for the *electorate*, usually only a majority vote on the amendment is necessary. However, four states require a majority of those who have voted in the election. These four states have a very strict requirement: let's say 800,000 people voted in the election; therefore, at least 400,001 must vote "yes" on the amendment for it to pass. Roll-off makes the so-called "majority" in the election difficult to obtain. Because of *roll-off*— more people voting on matters at the top of the ballot (such as the office of governor or president) than on matters farther down—such a majority can be hard to attain.

Constitutional change by means of amendment is typically piecemeal and ad hoc: an article or section is added here, another is dropped there. *Individually*, these changes may not amount to much. But, over the years, amendments may *cumulatively* alter the constitution in basic ways.

Revision Commissions

To change substantial amounts of the state constitution at one time, a constitutional revision commission is often used. This "blue-ribbon" commission of distinguished citizens and legislators is selected by the governor, legislative leaders, or the chief justice of the supreme court. It meets at length, and its recommendations must be forwarded to the state legislature before being submitted to the voters. The legislature can approve, alter, or reject the recommendations.[25] Legislators prefer revision commissions to constitutional conventions because the former are easier to control. The leading authority on the subject describes revision commissions as "auxiliary staff arms" of the legislature.[26] Interests having influence in the state legislature may not want to entrust their benefits embedded in the state constitution (for example, earmarked funds) to the vagaries of a convention. The changes recommended by revision commissions can range from a series of proposed amendments to an entirely new constitution.

Constitutional Conventions

Fourteen states have a constitutional provision that the question of whether or not to have a constitutional convention shall be periodically presented to the voters. In eight states it is submitted every twenty years, in Michigan every sixteen years, and in five states every ten years. The theory behind such requirements was stated by a former governor of Virginia, Thomas Jefferson:

> [Since] manners and opinions change with the circumstances, institutions must advance also and keep pace with the times. . . . Each generation is as independent of the one preceding as that was of all which had gone before. It has then, like them, a right to choose for itself the form of government it believes most promotive of its own happiness, consequently, to accommodate to the circumstances in which it finds itself that received from its predecessors;

and it is for the peace and good of mankind that a solemn opportunity of doing this every nineteen or twenty years should be provided by the constitution, so that it may be handed on, with periodical repairs, from generation to generation. . . .[27]

In states lacking such a provision, it appears that a crisis is necessary before the issue becomes a salient political concern. For example, severe revenue problems in Illinois during the late 1960s prompted the calling of a constitutional convention.[28] A convention composed of elected delegates commands more respect than one appointed by incumbent officeholders (who may have played a role in precipitating the crisis). A key point that the legislature must determine when putting the convention call on the ballot is whether the convention should be limited or unlimited. *Limited* conventions may deal only with named subject matters, but *unlimited* conventions are free of state restrictions. Another restriction on constitution writers is that all state constitutions and laws must not conflict with the U.S. Constitution, federal laws, treaties, or court decisions.

There are three models of how constitutional conventions go about their task.[29] In the *statesman* model favored by reformers and good-government groups, delegates place themselves "above" grubby politics and contemplate nothing but the long-term interests of the state. Whether this school of thought has any axes to grind may be discerned from Table 1-5. The *political* model affirms the view that conventions must take note of political considerations because they are a part of state government, which certainly makes note of such considerations. Finally, in the *partisan-legislative* model, political parties and their leaders manage the convention in the same manner that they guide the legislature. They decide issues in a partisan vein and frankly acknowledge how the largess is being divided. Although the second model can easily deteriorate into the third, delegates guided by it have a much more honest and realistic view of what they are doing than delegates who profess adherence to the first model.

Delegates themselves can be classified to six types:

> Stand-patters are office holders at middle or upper-middle levels of state or local government (legislators, judges, state bureaucrats) who enter the convention to protect a present position in the governmental structure. They are sufficiently far along, in age and in career development, to perceive change as threatening. Their behavior on issues is likely to be a consistent opposition to change in the existing arrangement.
>
> Stand-ins are older individuals who hold low public office or small party position, and who seek neighborhood recognition and notoriety. They enter the convention to satisfy these ego needs. Selection to the convention is a reward for various kinds of political loyalty, and is given to the Stand-ins by local political magnates or office holders who find it inadvisable to seek the office themselves. The Stand-in, whose presence depends upon partisan district electoral arrangements, is expected to follow the advice of those who provide him with the nomination—for whom he is a "stand-in." They are

likely to be supporters of the status quo, backing the anti-reform positions of the Stand-patters.

Statesmen have held position in high public office (governors, judges, congressmen) or in some cases presently hold "terminal" judicial positions or the like. They enter the convention for the public prestige of capping prior careers through being constitution-makers. Because of their past positions, Statesmen may generate some following in the convention but this will be restricted by their lack of present political power. Their behavior on issues is likely to be fluid, with some potential for reform support.

Chieftains are individuals with a large existing power base in state politics, or great and immediate potential for achieving such a position. They enter the convention for career advancement. Because they have such a base outside the convention (as governors or potential governors, legislative leaders, mayors) they are in a position to exercise considerable internal convention leadership. Although their behavior on issues is likely to be fluid, there is considerable potential for reform support.

Aspirants are young professionals, often lawyers, on the political make. Many have held some party or civic position prior to convention office; the convention is a stepping off point to further political activity—their motive for entering is therefore career advancement. Their voting behavior is likely to be fluid, but they go preponderantly in the direction of whatever is the majority block in the convention. Thus there is both standpat and reform potential here.

Reformers often have been active in civic organizations including citizen's commissions and the League of Women Voters, though few have held office in government. They are likely to be highly educated professionals from middle and upper-middle social strata who enter the convention to change the established order. On issues they will vote uniformly for change in the direction of "good government" provisions.[30]

The methods of selecting delegates are very important. Partisan rather than nonpartisan races for delegate posts tend to increase the number of political party activists and members of the state legislature who are selected. Partisan election of delegates also favors the stand-in type of delegate, but nonpartisan systems reward reformers. An eight-state study found that "in many ways . . . the ratio of stand-ins to reformers establishes the balance of power within the convention."[31] Stand-ins, in alliance with Stand-patters, may be able to prevail over reformers. In addition to conflict between reformers and defenders of the status quo, recent conventions have seen rivalries between legislator delegates and nonlegislator delegates, Democrats and Republicans, and urban delegates and rural delegates.

Whatever the cleavages within the convention hall, the delegates must sell their product to the people outside the hall—the public. This fact is a powerful force for moderation during the convention: delegates who leave the hall to campaign against the constitution can prevent its ratification by the voters. Ratification supporters have a peculiar problem: they must sell the document as a whole. The opponents of the constitution, on the other hand, can follow a different strategy. They can concentrate their criticism on particular articles of the constitution, claiming, for example, that one article will increase taxes, another will allow public aid to church-related schools, and still another will do something else objectionable. Their hope is to piece together different minorities opposed to various provisions into a majority in opposition. To counter such a strategy, supporters of the constitution may allow controversial provisions to be voted upon separately from the main body of the constitution. This approach was successful for Illinois, Louisiana, and Montana in the 1970s. A majority vote on the convention's proposal is usually sufficient for ratification, but four states require a majority of all those voting in the previous election, or a three-fifths vote, or even a two-thirds vote. It is not surprising that none of these four states has adopted a new constitution in this century.

Constitutional Change through Informal Means

Constitutions do not interpret themselves. That is, no constitution says what its words mean in every specific situation. This crucial function is performed by the courts in a common-law country like the United States. In applying the words of a very old document to a modern situation, judges must of necessity use their own judgment and their beliefs concerning what is good public policy. For example, the Kentucky Constitution states the salary of the governor and various mayors. As time has passed and the ravages of inflation have taken their toll, the stated amounts have become intolerable. Finally, the Kentucky Court of Appeal held that the salaries could be "adjusted" to reflect the increased cost of living in order to retain the same purchasing power they had when they were established. In a similar vein, the Kentucky Constitution requires "that *every* bill be read at length in each house at least once before passage."[32] This unworkable provision is dispensed with by legislative leaders. Unfortunately, such practices "debase our sense of constitutional morality," to use Fellman's phrase. But if constitutions are exceedingly difficult to revise formally or to amend, informal means may provide something of an answer.

Contributions of State Constitutions

There appear to be eight key contributions that state constitutions have made to constitutional theory and constitutional government:

1. Constitutions should be written documents "which establish the principal organs of government, distribute the powers of government among them, and define the relationships that shall exist between the government and the people."
2. "Constitutions are distinct from and superior to ordinary statute law."
3. Fundamental law should be made by popularly elected constitutional conventions and later ratified by the people; statute law is made by legislatures.

4. Judicial review of statute law insures its conformity with the constitution.
5. Separation of powers
6. Bills of rights that guarantee basic liberties
7. Initiative and referendum (see Chapter 4)
8. "the federal state, in which the functions of government are distributed through the fundamental law between a national or central government and local or state governments"[33]

We might also note that state constitutions have enumerated some rights not explicitly protected by the federal Bill of Rights. For example, the Illinois Constitution forbids discrimination against physically or mentally handicapped persons in housing and employment (Article I, Section 19), and the New Hampshire Constitution provides for freedom from monopolies (Part II, Article 83) and even a right of revolution (Part I, Article 10).

SUMMARY

This introductory chapter has considered a number of key themes that will recur throughout the book. The states and localities are significant units of government with important duties to perform. Moreover, they have undergone marked change and reform in recent years. States vary in many ways; one of the key variations is in political culture. Not only a state's political culture, but the struggle of interest groups, will be reflected in the state's constitution. States do not act in isolation; they must all interact with the federal government, which is sometimes a partner, sometimes an antagonist. Federalism is the topic of the next chapter.

NOTES

1. Roy Bahl, *Financing State and Local Government in the 1980s* (New York: Oxford University Press, 1984), pp. 9 and 206. Federal domestic expenditures are defined as spending for purposes other than defense, international affairs, space research, and interest attributable to these functions.

2. Robert Fried, *Performance in American Bureaucracy* (Boston: Little, Brown, 1976), p. 356.

3. Donald Songer, "Government Closest to the People: Constituent Knowledge of State and National Politics," *Polity*, 17 (Winter 1984), 387–95.

4. Richard Sutton, "The States and the People: Measuring and Accounting for 'State Representativeness,'" *Polity*, 5 (Summer 1973), 460–61; and Ronald Weber, *Public Policy Preferences in the States* (Bloomington: Indiana University Institute of Public Administration, 1971), pp. 107–9.

5. Advisory Commission on Intergovernmental Relations, *Significant Features of Fiscal Federalism, 1984 Edition* (Washington, D.C.: ACIR, 1985), Table 87.

6. Robert S. Allen, ed., *Our Sovereign State* (New York: Vanguard, 1949), p. vii.

7. Roscoe C. Martin, *The Cities and the Federal System* (New York: Atherton, 1965), p. 77.

8. Luther C. Gulick, "The Reorganization of the State," *Civil Engineering*, August 1933, pp. 420–21.

9. James Stever, *Diversity and Order in State and Local Politics* (Columbia: University of South Carolina Press, 1980), p. xv.

10. "The Nation," *Los Angeles Times*, January 1, 1981, pt. I, p. 2; June 24, 1984, pt. I, p. 2; June 5, 1985, pt. I, p. 2; June 22, 1985, pt. I, p. 2.

11. Jerry Hagstrom, "Liberal and Minority Coalitions Pleading Their Cases in State Capitals," *National Journal*, February 23, 1985, pp. 426–28. For more details on state-local reforms and improvements, see Carl Stenberg, "Federalism in Transition," *Intergovernmental Perspective*, Winter 1980, p. 10; David B. Walker, "State Institutions 1960 and Today," *Intergovernmental Perspective*, Fall 1980, p. 7; and Richard Leach, "Federalism and the Constitution," *University of Virginia Institute of Government Newsletter*, December 1984, p. 24.

12. John Herbers, "Nation's Rural Areas Grow Faster than Cities, Ending 160-Year Tide," *New York Times*, March 3, 1981, p. 1.

13. David Klingman and William Lammers, "The 'General Policy Liberalism' Factor in American State Politics," *American Journal of Political Science*, 24 (August 1984), 598–610.

14. Daniel J. Elazar, *American Federalism: A View from the States*, 3rd ed. (New York: Harper & Row, Pub., 1984), pp. 112–20, 219. The discussion of political culture that follows is based on Elazar's insightful book.

15. For only a small sampling of the huge literature dealing with political culture, see Ira Sharkansky, "The Utility of Elazar's Political Culture," *Polity*, 2 (Fall 1969), 66–83; Charles A. Johnson, "Political Culture in American States," *American Journal of Political Science*, 20 (August 1976), 491–509; Timothy Schiltz and R. Lee Rainey, "The Geographic Distribution of Elazar's Political Subcultures among the Mass Population," *Western Political Quarterly*, 31 (September 1978), 410–15; Richard Joslyn and Dennis Ricci, "The Relationship between Public Opinion and Public Policy across the States" (paper presented at the annual meeting of the Midwest Political Science Association, Chicago, 1980); John Kincaid, "Political Culture and the Quality of Urban Life," *Publius*, 10 (Spring 1980), 89–110; Raymond Wolfinger and Steven Rosenstone, *Who Votes?* (New Haven: Yale University Press, 1980), p. 100; and David Lowery and Lee Sigelman, "Political Culture and State Public Policy: The Missing Link," *Western Political Quarterly*, 35 (September 1982), 376–84.

16. Daniel Elazar, "The Principles and Traditions Underlying State Constitutions," *Publius*, 12 (Winter 1982), 11.

17. Louisiana, however, reflects French legal practice.

18. David B. Fellman, "What Should a State Constitution Contain?" in *Major Problems in State Constitutional Revision*, ed. W. Brooke Graves (Chicago: Public Administration Service, 1960), p. 139.

19. Ibid., 146.

20. Herbert Agar, *The Price of Union* (Boston: Houghton Mifflin, 1950), p. 346; see also John Goldbach and Michael J. Ross, *Politics, Parties, and Power* (Pacific Palisades, Calif.: Palisades Publishers, 1980), chap. 16.

21. The problem, though, with any earmarking scheme—for example, hunting- and fishing-license fees going to support only a Department of Fish and Game—is that the state legislature cannot put the revenue generated to a better use *and* the earmarked function may not need the amount of money generated.

22. Lewis A. Froman, Jr., "Some Effects of Interest Group Strength in State Politics," *American Political Science Review*, 60 (December 1966) 1952–62. Froman relied on a 1954 survey of the impressions of interest group strength given by political scientists from different states.

23. Fellman, "What Should a State Constitution Contain?" p. 156.

24. Only Delaware allows the legislature to change the state constitution without voter approval.

25. Only in Florida may the commission submit amendments to the electorate without going through the legislature.

26. Albert L. Sturm, "State Constitutions and Constitutional Revision," in *Book of the States, 1978–79*, ed. Council of State Governments (Lexington, Ky.: Council of State Governments, 1978), pp. 198–99.

27. Letter to Samuel Kercheval, July 12, 1816, in *The Political Writings of Thomas Jefferson*, ed. Edward Dumbauld (Indianapolis: Bobbs-Merrill, 1955), p. 124. Possibly Jefferson's view *degenerated* into the view that constitutions have a status only slightly removed from political-party platforms. The opposing view that constitutions should not be tampered with is espoused by James Madison throughout *The Federalist*.

28. Elmer E. Cornwell, Jr., Jay S. Goodman, and Wayne R. Swanson, *State Constitutional Conventions* (New York: Praeger, 1975), p. 26. In three states, the people may call a constitutional convention if enough of them sign petitions.

29. Ibid., pp. 33–35.

30. Elmer E. Cornwell, Jr., Jay S. Goodman, and Wayne R. Swanson, "State Constitutional Conventions: Delegates, Roll Calls, and Issues," *Midwest Journal of Political Science*, Vol. 14, No. 1 (February 1970), 108–9. By permission of the University of Texas Press.

31. Cornwell, Goodman, and Swanson, *State Constitutional Conventions*, p. 71. See also pp. 67–72, 90.

32. John Reeves, *Kentucky Government*, 5th ed. (Lexington: Bureau of Government Research, University of Kentucky, 1966), pp. 15–16 (emphasis added).

33. Harvey Walker, "Myth and Reality in State Constitutional Development," in *Major Problems in State Constitutional Revision*, ed. Graves, pp. 10–12.

chapter 2

Federalism

Reforming federalism has been a key theme of Ronald Reagan's presidency—and a very controversial one at that. On the other hand, federalism has always been controversial in America. One can easily get a sense of how controversy might arise by noting that *federalism* is a way of distributing governmental power between a central (or federal) government and the states into which the country is divided.[1] Moreover, both the central government and the state governments operate directly on the people and are regarded as supreme within their own spheres of authority. Any time that power is distributed between units of government or between politicians, friction and jostling will surely result. If both levels of government are supreme within their spheres of authority, what are the outer limits of those spheres? Indeed, how can both be supreme if each operates directly on the people?

SIX PHASES OF FEDERALISM

Americans' attempts to resolve these questions can be described as occurring in six overlapping but different phases: (1) conflict (1930s and before); (2) cooperative (1930s to 1950s); (3) concentrated (1940s to 1960s); (4) creative (1950s and 1960s); (5) competitive (1960s and 1970s); and (6) calculative (1970s and 1980s).[2]

In the *conflict phase* of the 1930s and earlier, officials at the federal and state-local levels viewed each other as adversaries as each group sought to define and expand the boundaries of its power. Adding fuel to the fire was the belief that these boundaries should be mutually exclusive.

The Depression and World War II ushered in a period of *cooperative* federalism (1930s to 1950s): officials were more likely to collaborate in

the face of serious domestic and international threats. Federal administrators began to distribute money in the form of formula grants-in-aid
(discussed later in this chapter) to state and local governments for health
and welfare purposes.

From the 1940s to the 1960s, these federal grants became more
specific or *concentrated*. Federal administrators now required extensive
reporting and performance standards from their counterparts at lower
levels as a condition of granting money for such areas as highway or
hospital construction, slum clearance, or waste-water treatment plants.
Thus targeted to specific purposes, these monies were called *categorical
grants*.

A *creative* period ensued in the 1950s and 1960s. It was characterized
by federal requirements for comprehensive statewide or areawide planning
before the receipt of federal money; *project grants*, in which local governments submitted extensive requests for funds for a particular project; and
federal requirements for participation by the public, especially poor
people, in program operations. The number of federal grant programs
increased dramatically in this period.

In the *competitive* phase of the 1960s and 1970s, tension and rivalry
between federal and state-local officials again increased as the latter
demanded more flexible fiscal mechanisms such as consolidation of grants
and revenue sharing (discussed later in the chapter). Criticism of the
alleged ineffectiveness of programs and their purported lack of coordination and accomplishments became the center of public debate.

The *calculative* phase of the late 1970s and 1980s is characterized by
debates over the proper role of the federal government and by lessened
public confidence in government in general, by charges that the intergovernmental system for delivering public services is overloaded, and by
claims that certain regions of the country (such as the Sunbelt) are receiving
a disproportionate share of federal funds.

ASSETS AND LIABILITIES OF FEDERALISM

The virtues of federalism were capably described by Nelson Rockefeller:
"The federal idea fosters diversity within unity" because it allows the states
"to resolve their own problems in their own way."[3] Therefore, policies
for many heterogeneous states with many different needs are not cut out
of the same mold. Federalism is an arrangement whereby Americans can
agree to disagree. Furthermore,

> the federal idea permits and encourages creativity, imagination, and inno-
> vation in meeting the needs of the people. . . . It gives scope to many energies,
> many beliefs, many initiatives, and enlists them for the welfare of the people.[4]

Another former governor, Thomas Jefferson, wrote:

> What has destroyed liberty and the rights of man in every government which
> has ever existed under the sun? The generalizing and concentrating all cares
> and powers into one body. . . ."[5]

The existence of smaller-scale governments, rather than a large single
government, furthers another Jeffersonian ideal: citizen control. A remote,
centralized leviathan is far more difficult to control and is less likely to be
attuned to popular sentiments than are local units of more manageable
size.[6]

Finally, federalism has certain beneficial effects on the practice of
politics. State political parties in a federal system can take positions at
variance with the national party's position. By this means, party appeals
can be tailored to local needs, and thus both parties can compete throughout the nation. Furthermore, state parties in a federal system can provide
a haven when political tides have swept the national party from office.
State officeholders in the party's areas of greatest strength may survive
such tides and provide the nucleus for the party's return to power.

Some of the drawbacks of federalism are presented in Reading 2-1
by Gladwin Hill, former national environmental correspondent for the
New York Times.

Whatever the strengths or weaknesses of the theoretical arguments
advanced by each side in this dispute, the legal-constitutional relationship
between the federal government and the states is as follows: the latter
possess all powers *not* delegated, expressly or implicitly, by the United
States Constitution to the federal government. The states may not exercise
powers prohibited to them by the U. S. Constitution or by their state
constitution. The governmental power wielded by the states is usually
referred to as the *police power,* or the power to pass all laws promoting the
health, safety, welfare, and morals of the people. It is obvious that this
power, by its very nature, is quite broad and encompassing; hence it is
the duty of state and federal courts to determine if the police power is
being exercised properly. State legislatures are the branch of government
employing this power the most frequently, and we will note specific
applications of it in Chapter 6. The resolution of disputes regarding the
proper scope of the police power, which is a major source of state court
cases, is explained in Chapter 7. States may delegate the police power to
local governments, and Part III shows how cities and counties seek to
promote the health, safety, welfare, and morals of their residents.

The United States Constitution does not give the federal government
a police power, but Congress attempts to achieve much the same result
by resorting to other powers that they do possess. For example, Congress
has complete power to regulate interstate commerce and all intrastate

READING 2-1   The Case against Federalism

Current disclosures of the managerial mess in the Environmental Protection Agency may be construed by some, including President Reagan, to lend support to his aim of shifting environmental authority "back to the states—closer to the people."

That notion has the appealing ring of states' rights, local autonomy and other buzz-phrases that are associated with self-determination, democracy and freedom.

The trouble is that as far as environmental values are concerned the notion is demonstrably wrong.

We *had* states' rights and local autonomy in environmental management for nearly 200 years. And where did it get us? It got us into the dreadful mess that, in the late 1960s, precipitated the Environmental Revolution and the establishment under the Nixon Administration of federal authority to rectify conditions.

Let's just glance back at how things were only a couple of decades ago. Nearly every state had its air- and water-pollution control boards, commissions or whatnot—and the air and water were generally horrible. As surveys at the time documented, these boards and commissions—including some in California—were loaded with polluters and representatives of polluters. It took federal laws and regulations to purge these panels of conflicts of interest that in many cases had thwarted public pressures for reform.

Nearly half the water pollution in the country could, as of 1970, be traced to inadequate municipal sewage systems. There was hardly a community that had a really adequate system. Sewer systems were the patsy of local politicians. Fifty thousand dollars spent on a village bandstand would bring more votes than $50,000 allocated to improving a sewage plant that citizens seldom laid eyes on.

It took federal action—setting standards for water quality and sewage treatment, and allocating grants to help communities upgrade their systems—to bring about improvement.

Drinking water was another matter that had been left to the sovereign authority of states and localities. And it became a national scandal. Outbreaks of water-borne diseases were chronic.

Water systems were an obscure item of community overhead, and politicians squeezed annual capital expenditures for this most vital of public services down to a few cents per capita on the average—until many systems could not meet the minimal standards of purity that the federal government set for travelers on interstate buses. It took the federal Safe Drinking Water Act of 1974 to ameliorate this example of states' rights gone wrong.

Similarly for solid waste. Politicians try whenever they can to bury the costs of collection in water/sewer charges, or sneak the money from general funds, and then to dispose of the refuse as cheaply as possible by dumping it on the edge of town, the way cavemen did. As for what a factory did with its waste products—out of sight, of of mind. The result: possibly hundreds of Love Canals that festered for generations all too "close to the people" until the federal government began investigating the chemical plague and moving against it.

Local self-government is a fine principle that is a foundation stone of this country's weal. But it is not suited to many current environmental problems for several reasons.

It's too easy for special interests, with state and local political clout, to obstruct environmental reform. State environmental administrators, as opposed to politicians, were pathetically grateful when the federal government stepped into the pollution picture and forced them to take action. It got them off the hook of being pressed by citizens for improvements only to be balked by political wire-pulling.

Then, too, the major environmental problems are not local or even state-level, but regional and national. They demand across-the-board solutions, with uniform standards of federal origin, if only in the name of fairness. Otherwise we'd have the anarchy of each area concocting its own criteria, with an eye on self-interest rather than on the general welfare.

Although industry chafes at federal regulation, its more enlightened quarters saw the benefit of uniform federal ground rules for problems like water pollution, in place of a 50-state rat race in which competitive advantage went to the least scrupulous.

Granted that federal intervention has engendered a big bureaucracy with its concomitants of excessive paperwork and wheel-spinning. Granted that "some guy at a desk in Washington" is less familiar with local environmental problems and possible solutions than are people on the scene.

But there is a middle ground. Standards need to be nationally uniform and therefore federal, and enforcement often has to be federal. But figuring out ways to meet these standards, in accordance with federal guidelines, manifestly is something that people at the area level probably can manage much better than "some guy at a desk in Washington," and they should be allowed to do so.

That is the sensible division of effort, rather than trying to turn back the environmental clock with demagogic cant about returning all "power to the people." We've tried that, and it wasn't good.

SOURCE: Gladwin Hill, "Environment: Too Important for Localities," *Los Angeles Times*, March 10, 1983, p. II-9.

---

commerce affecting it. This provides the basis for federal regulation of local business activity. Through the postal power, Congress can prohibit the mailing of objects it deems dangerous to public safety (for example, the pistols known as "Saturday night specials") or materials thought to be harmful to public morals, such as child pornography. Through its power to tax and to spend federal money, Congress is able to achieve social objectives favorable to federal officials.

When state and local governments go to court to challenge actions taken by federal officials, the disputes often end up in the U.S. Supreme Court, with the subnational governments the losers. The latter suffered a serious defeat in the 1985 U.S. Supreme Court decision in *Garcia* v. *San Antonio Metropolitan Transit Authority*, 83 L. Ed. 2d 1016. The court reversed a five-to-four decision it had issued only nine years earlier, *National League of Cities* v. *Usery,* 426 U.S. 833. In the prior case, the Supreme Court had ruled that the Tenth Amendment to the U.S. Constitution bars Congress from legislating on the traditional or integral functions of state and local governments. In *Garcia,* the Court decided that it is too difficult for judges to determine which are the traditional functions of state and local governments. If subnational governments dislike the laws Congress has passed to regulate them, their recourse is through the political processes of lobbying Congress or of electing new House members and Senators. Dissenting justices in the case charged that the decision substantially alters the federal system and could lead to an emasculation of the powers of the states. Conceivably, Congress could expand widely its control of such cases as law enforcement, education, and consumer protection. The dissenters pointed out that the *Garcia* case was also a five-to-four decision and that any of President Reagan's future Supreme Court appointees would surely favor their point of view. An examination of President Reagan's federalism reform program will bear out this contention.

REAGAN'S REFORM PROGRAM

President Reagan's plan for reforming American federalism is daring, comprehensive, and controversial. Advancing on various fronts, Reagan would increase the number of block grants, end revenue sharing, "swap" programs and tax sources between the federal government and the states, and significantly cut back the amount of money spent on grant programs.

An Increase in Block Grants

Since *block grants* consist of various related categorical grants that have been combined, we must first understand categorical grants. There are nearly four hundred categorical grant programs, but only about a dozen block grants. Categoricals finance some specific endeavor, such as a construction project. They can be classified as formula or project grants. *Formula grants* provide money according to an established formula, which is applied uniformly to all state and local governments that apply for the money. Such grants limit the discretion of the federal administrators who provide the funds. *Project grants,* on the other hand, provide money for specific state-local projects, which federal officials may or may not approve. Approximately two thirds of all grant programs are project grants, but project grants account for only one third of all grant money. State officals or local officials submit a grant application to federal administrators requesting money for a specific project (sewage treatment plant, mass transit). Since there is never enough money to fund every request, federal officials can pick and choose among projects. This type of grant increases their power.

Project grants negate one of the key purposes of the entire grant-in-aid system: redistributing resources from wealthier areas to poorer ones. Those jurisdictions that can prepare the most professional grant applications—with the aid of staff people called *grantsmen*—are more likely to get the money, but they may not be the ones that need the money the most. Moreover, categorical grants of either type maximize the influence of the nonelected public officials who must administer these programs. These *program specialists,* whether at the federal, state, or local level, may have more in common or feel a greater sympathy toward one another than toward the *generalists* at their level of government, whether these generalists are members of Congress, governors, or city council members. Block grants, on the other hand, may allow generalists a predominant influence in determining how the money will be spent, because they are intended to achieve a more comprehensive goal.

Early in his first term, President Reagan persuaded Congress to combine fifty-four categorical grants into nine block grants, primarily in the areas of health and education. Governors had eagerly sought these changes because they believed the flexibility of block grants would lead to greater efficiency, even if funds for the programs were cut by 10 percent or more. In fact, Reagan asked Congress to cut the programs by 25 percent and Congress agreed to reductions of 13 percent. Arizona's Democratic governor Bruce Babbitt, who had long favored block grants, was led to remark that blocks had now become "a tactical weapon to cut the federal budget while deputizing the governors to hand out the bad news."[7] In any event, the combining of categorical grants into block grants has probably spent its course, because of the fairly large number that have already been combined, and because the process is politically difficult. Richard Nathan of Princeton, who worked in the federal Office of Management and Budget during the late 1960s, describes the process:

> The Administration proposed consolidating several narrow library grants. The Congress resisted, and the reason was simple. It can be expressed quantitatively; 99.99% of the public is not interested in library grant reform. Of the 0.01% who are interested, all are librarians and oppose it.[8]

An End to Revenue Sharing

Another flexible program, but one that Reagan wants to end as an economy move, is revenue sharing. Created in 1972 and renewed in 1976, 1980, and 1983, revenue sharing provides $4.6 billion per year to thirty-nine thousand local governments; very few conditions or guidelines are attached. Cities and counties do not even have to apply for the money—the checks come automatically and are calculated by a congressionally enacted formula. In the years since the program was established, local governments have come to depend on the money for day-to-day expenses. Under ideal circumstances, they would put the money only into nonessential services or one-time-only expenses. However, considering the financial straits of local governments (80 percent of the cities belonging to the National League of Cities are taxing at their legal limit), circumstances are far from ideal. President Reagan and key members of Congress oppose revenue sharing because the federal government has a massive deficit, and many local governments are running surpluses. From their point of view, the program is not revenue sharing but "deficit sharing." What they neglect to mention is that most local governments are required to balance their budgets and cannot legally run a deficit. To be safe, they must have at least a modest surplus. Moreover, local governments employ any surplus funds the following year. As New York City mayor Ed Koch testified before Congress, "You think when we use the word 'surplus' we've got the money in the bank and someday, maybe 20 years from now, we'll take it and go to Brazil."[9] In addition to the positive feature that local governments can spend the money for whatever purpose best suits local needs—a feature that categorical grants may lack—revenue sharing has not created a large federal bureaucracy, and costs only one tenth of 1 percent of its budget to be administered. President Reagan's opposition to the program can only be explained by his desire to reduce the federal deficit. Apart from that, revenue sharing clearly furthers his goal of returning power to grassroots governments.

The "Swap" Plan

Early in his first term, President Reagan proposed a massive swap. The federal government would turn over to the states approximately thirty programs, the most prominent being Aid to Families with Dependent Children (AFDC). In return, the federal government would pay all the costs of Medicaid. The president claimed that the plan would not raise the states' expenses: the states would be granted increased power to levy various taxes to pay for the programs. Congress proved to be a major stumbling block: members of Congress did not want to give up the power to set standards for important programs. Moreover, the intended beneficiaries of the swap plan, officials at the state, county, and local levels, gave the plan only lukewarm support. Furthermore, lobbyists for the programs to be delegated are skilled at influencing legislators and administrators in a single location (Washington, D.C.). They did not relish the idea of having to labor in fifty different state capitols. Eventually, Reagan had to shelve the AFDC-for-Medicaid swap idea.

The whole affair is reminiscent of something that happened many years before. President Eisenhower also favored this approach, and he appointed a committee of distinguished persons to study which federal functions could be turned over to the states. After two years of work, the committee could find only two relatively minor programs for the states to assume. Opposition from state and local officials and from interest groups concerned about lowered funding for the two programs killed Eisenhower's very modest plan.

Cuts in Grant Programs

Although advertised not as a strategy to reform the federal system but rather as a way to lower the deficit, cutting back dramatically the amount of money spent for federal grants is a final Reagan reform tactic. The biggest cuts have been made in entitlement programs such as welfare, food stamps, unemployment insurance, and Medicaid, and have fallen the most heavily on the working poor. Existing programs in social-service areas such as education, job training, public health, and day care have also been substantially reduced, but carryovers from previous categorical programs have cushioned the effects of these cuts.[10] In a seven-hundred page study of the Reagan reform strategy in fourteen states and forty localities, Richard Nathan and his associates at Princeton found that the effects of the Reagan program reductions have been more limited than originally thought: Congress has restored many of the cuts, and the states replaced significant amounts of lost federal money when programs were put under their control. This action by the states resulted from the fact that the interest groups that had helped to establish the federal programs in the first place shifted their lobbying to the state level and were effective. Another by-product of the Reagan strategy was that power shifted from local governments to state government.[11]

All of the Reagan initiatives would restructure the federal system in important ways, and all (with the possible exception of the ill-fated swap program) save the federal government money. The Princeton research team argues that the Reagan strategy will have permanent effects, even if the Reagan administration is followed by a pro-spending Democratic administration. This is because the 1981 Reagan tax cuts and his massive deficits have produced such a fiscal gap that future tax increases will not be large enough to close it. The federal deficits will hamstring pro-spending forces, "cut them off at the pocketbook," and deny them "the fiscal flexibility to reverse this flow of influence and responsibility to the states."[12]

AUSTERITY FEDERALISM

The intergovernmental fiscal system has clearly passed from one of affluent federalism to one of austere federalism. Federal grants-in-aid as a percentage of state and local receipts from their own sources was 11.8 percent in 1955 and rose steadily to a high of 31.7 percent in 1978, but fell to 23.7 percent in 1984.[13] Cities were especially dependent on this aid, for state and local spending grew at a faster rate than the economy or federal spending itself. Federal aid came to be the fastest-growing element in state and local budgets. Figure 2-1 reveals some of these trends. In the halcyon days of affluent federalism, hardly any activity at the subnational levels of government was ineligible for federal assistance, including such presumably local concerns as urban gardening, noise control, snow removal, rat control, rural fire protection, and school security.

State and local governments are well organized to defend their interests in a time of austerity federalism. In addition to U.S. House members and senators from each state, there are five major state and local government lobbying organizations, usually referred to as public interest groups (or PIGs for short). The National Governors Association represents the governors of the fifty states and maintains a staff of almost 80 lobbyists and researchers in its Washington office. The National Conference of State Legislatures represents the nation's 7500 state legislators and has a staff of 35 in Washington and another 90 in its Denver headquarters. The U.S. Conference of Mayors, with a staff of 70, lobbys for mayors of large cities, most of whom are Democrats and rely heavily on federal aid. The National League of Cities, on the other hand, looks

FIGURE 2-1   The Rise and Decline of Federal Aid*

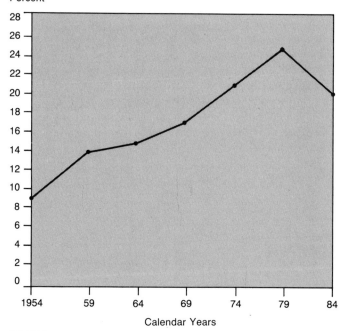

Percent

Calendar Years

SOURCE: John Shannon, "Not a Good Fiscal Year for Big Brother," *Intergovernmental Perspective,* 11 (Winter 1985), 5.

* Federal aid as a percentage of state-local expenditures after transfers.

after the interests of mayors and council members from 15,000 cities that are mostly small or medium-sized. Viewed as more conservative than the Conference of Mayors, the League of Cities has over 100 employees. The National Association of Counties (NACO) employs 130 people to further the interests of counties. In addition, there are the International City Management Association, the Council of State Governments, the National Association of Towns and Townships, and a whole host of associations representing specialized state and local functions, such as the Council of Chief State School Officers, the National Association of State Budget Officers, and the Council of State Housing Agencies.[14] The thrust of all of these groups is to protect, if not expand, programs that benefit them.

In addition to lobbying, elected officials and administrators at lower levels of government can influence federal officals by continuous inter-action through common interests such as joint projects or membership in political party organizations. They are aided in this effort by the fact that many decision makers now serving at the federal level once served at state and local levels and still maintain sympathies acquired earlier. For example, both of California's U.S. senators and over two thirds of its House members are former elected officials at the state and/or local levels.

Moreover, the national government may imitate successful policies pioneered at the state level. The states are often described as the labora-tories of federalism: one state may experiment with a particular policy, and if it works well, other states or the federal government are encouraged to adopt it. If it works poorly, only the residents of that state suffer. If the federal government experiments with an untried policy and it fails, all Americans will suffer. Some recently adopted state policies that the federal government has copied or might copy are sunset laws, zero-based budgeting, publicly financed legislative elections, lifeline utility rates, no-fault automobile insurance, and televised trials. A high-ranking official in the U.S. Department of Energy has admitted, "We've stolen a lot of our legislation from the states, especially California."[15]

Concern about the amount of forthcoming federal aid is supple-mented by concern about the regional distribution of that spending. This is the much-discussed Sunbelt-versus-Frostbelt controversy, the dimensions of which are revealed in Table 2-1. The table shows some regions to be winners and others losers in the race for federal dollars: states classified as South Atlantic, South Central, or Mountain are gaining at the expense of the Mid-Atlantic and Midwest states.

Information such as that in Table 2-1 has sparked bitter regional disputes in Congress over such issues as aid for housing and community development, welfare and food stamps, education, and other services. There are numerous reasons for these regional disparities. The Sunbelt (the South and the West) has been gaining in population, while the Frostbelt (the Northeast and the Midwest) has been losing. Population gain has meant that Sunbelt states receive not only greater payments to

TABLE 2-1   The Flow of Federal Funds*

Northeast		South		West	
New England		South Atlantic		Mountain	
Maine	1.30	Delaware	0.83	Montana	1.07
New Hampshire	0.98	Maryland	1.27	Idaho	1.13
Vermont	1.10	Virginia	1.52	Wyoming	0.75
Massachusetts	1.10	West Virginia	1.07	Colorado	0.91
Rhode Island	1.05	North Carolina	0.95	Utah	1.27
Connecticut	1.02	South Carolina	1.25	Nevada	0.92
Mid-Atlantic		Georgia	1.09	Arizona	1.14
New York	0.92	Florida	1.09	New Mexico	1.80
New Jersey	0.70	South Central		Pacific	
Pennsylvania	0.96	Kentucky	1.10	California	1.09
Midwest		Tennessee	1.20	Oregon	0.89
Great Lakes		Alabama	1.29	Washington	1.09
Ohio	0.85	Mississippi	1.61	Alaska	1.01
Indiana	0.83	Louisiana	0.90	Hawaii	1.38
Illinois	0.70	Arkansas	1.27		
Michigan	0.78	Oklahoma	0.88		
Wisconsin	0.82	Texas	0.78	**Total United States**	**1.00**
Great Plains					
Minnesota	0.85				
Iowa	0.80				
Missouri	1.43				
Kansas	1.02				
Nebraska	0.95				
South Dakota	1.24				
North Dakota	1.06				

SOURCE: "The Flow of Federal Funds," *Intergovernmental Perspective*, 11 (Spring-Summer 1985), 19.
* Total federal spending per person divided by the federal tax burden per person. This is the average for fiscal years 1982 to 1984.

individuals but increased voting power in the U.S. House of Representatives and the Electoral College, especially for such states as Florida, Texas, and California. Because of the milder climate in the West and the long-standing political clout of the South in Congress, many military bases are located in these regions. Defense contracts and defense salaries clearly boost western totals and ratios for southern states such as Mississippi (Table 2-1). Mountain states receive substantial amounts of aid for highway construction. That nearly half of the nation's poor people live in the South means that the federal tax burden is lighter there while federal spending is higher. Finally, retired persons receiving Social Security or military and railroad pensions, as well as federal civil-service retirees, prefer the warmer climates of the South and West.

As we shall see in Chapters 10 and 12, the Frostbelt not only regrets its loss of population and political power, it believes that the Sunbelt is stealing jobs and charging unfairly for energy exports. To make matters worse, almost all federal grants are calculated on the basis of per capita income. The South has a lower per capita income *and* lower energy, housing, and tax costs than the North. However, population gains are a mixed blessing for the Sunbelt. In addition to their possible environmental impacts, migrants may increase expenditure demands because they have come from the Frostbelt, which has higher levels of public services. On the other hand, these migrants are better prepared to pay the taxes that finance these services.[16]

NATIONAL-LOCAL RELATIONS

Special mention should be made of national-local relations, because federalism is frequently thought of as primarily a relationship between the federal government and the states. Federal-local relations blossomed during the Great Society of President Lyndon Johnson and continued to grow into the mid 1970s.

As we shall see in Chapter 8, local governments are legally "creatures of the state." This legal status, however, has not stopped the federal government from bypassing the states to deal directly with local governments. The reasons for this development can be found at both the national and the local levels. Congress felt that critical urban needs were not being met, and that it was its duty to step in and remedy the situation. Moreover, local governments (particularly cities) felt that getting federal money was easier and less politically risky than either raising local taxes to pay for higher services or seeking the funds from the state government. The public interest groups mentioned earlier, especially the U.S. Conference of Mayors, sought federal aid. But even small communities realized that they could band together to get their "fair share" of the federal largess through the National League of Cities or the National Association of Towns and Townships. President Johnson especially sought to stimulate local governments to support federal urban initiatives as more and more programs received federal assistance. During his administration such seemingly local responsibilities as rat control and rural fire protection came to receive federal funds.

Local reliance on national money grew rapidly, at least during the period of affluent federalism: city revenue from the federal government expressed as a percentage of revenue from its own sources grew from 2.8 percent in 1960 to a high of 25.8 percent in 1978, but then dropped to 16.4 percent in 1983. Affluent federalism saw Frostbelt cities such as Buffalo, Cleveland, Newark, Philadelphia, Detroit, and St. Louis receive fifty cents or more in direct federal aid for every dollar they raised themselves.[17] As we shall see in the next section, such federal money also came with increasingly intrusive federal regulations.

But affluent federalism was succeeded by austere federalism as President Reagan sought to reduce both federal aid and federal red tape. Much of his program to reform federalism was also intended to strengthen the state governments vis-à-vis local governments.

REGULATORY FEDERALISM

The previous description of federalism has generally shown the federal government following a "carrot" approach: state and local governments are induced to do what the federal government wants in order to receive a financial reward. To receive the money, subnational governments must fill out extensive paperwork and agree to audit requirements and planning procedures—on balance, not overly onerous stipulations. But in recent years, a "stick" has been added to the traditional carrot. The Advisory Commission on Intergovernmental Relations has identified four coercive regulatory techniques: direct orders, crosscutting requirements, crossover sanctions, and partial preemption.[18]

Direct Orders

Under threat of civil or criminal penalties, the federal government can simply order that something be done or not be done. For example, the Marine Protection Research and Sanctuaries Act Amendments of 1977 prohibit cities from disposing of sewage sludge through ocean dumping. Wage and hour requirements imposed on transit authorities under the Fair Labor Standards Act were upheld in *Garcia* v. *San Antonio,* mentioned earlier. Because of the heavy-handedness associated with this strategy, Congress seldom uses it.

Crosscutting Requirements

Far more common are the crosscutting requirements attached to nearly all grants as a means of furthering *national* social or economic goals. Regardless of the actual purpose of a grant, Congress attaches requirements relating to endangered species, historic-sites preservation, protection of the handicapped or the elderly, and many other matters. There are at least sixty crosscutting requirements; some local governments receiving federal aid may not be aware that all apply to them.

Crossover Sanctions

These are fiscal sanctions in one program area that influence state and local policy in another area. For example, the Emergency Highway Conservation Act of 1974 prohibited the secretary of transportation from approving highway construction projects in states having a speed limit over fifty-five miles per hour. More recently, Congress passed a law providing for reduced federal highway funds for any states with a minimum drinking age of less than twenty-one. President Reagan, who originally opposed forcing the states to change their drinking laws, switched sides on this issue after being lobbied by Mothers Against Drunk Drivers (MADD), who claimed that the legislation would reduce highway fatalities.

There is evidence that this approach is not very effective. After being coerced into passing the law that Congress wants, the states may not seriously enforce it. Moreover, the federal administrators who have the authority to withhold funds "are often reluctant to apply the severe penalties that Congress mandates."[19] Although Congress may have authorized the withholding of funds from all states that do not comply, the point at which federal enforcers start to move against a particular state is also the point at which that state's House members and senators will rally to protect it. Because state officials have protested strongly that it is unfair to reduce funds for program A because Congress does not like state action regarding unrelated program B, the federal government has used this approach sparingly.

Partial Preemption

This technique is employed extensively in making environmental policy. Rather than totally preempt a certain activity, the federal government establishes the basic policy but delegates to state and local governments the responsibility of administering the law, subject to federal standards and conditions. For example, the Clear Air Act Amendments of 1970 set national air-quality standards but required the states to implement and enforce them.

The reform program of the Reagan administration has sought to curtail regulatory federalism. Catherine Lovell reports that the administration has attempted to change (1) the laws on which the regulations are based (a *statutory* approach), (2) the administering agency's interpretation of the law's intent (an *administrative* approach), and (3) the agency's enforcement policy (a *behavioral* approach).[20] The merging of categorical grants into block grants is the prime statutory strategy. Lovell notes that although the intent of the block grants was to increase flexibility for state and local officials, the Reagan administration actually tightened regulations and imposed more controls in the areas of welfare, food stamps, school lunches, and Medicaid as a way of saving money. The administrative approach was pursued by empowering the federal Office of Management and Budget (OMB) to review all proposed regulations before they are published in the *Federal Register*. Following a behavioral strategy, the administration has persuaded various federal departments to delay or not enforce crosscutting requirements. The latter may be the most successful of the three approaches.

Some observers argue that when business interests square off against the states, the Reagan administration sides with business.[21] They point to the administration's efforts to prevent Connecticut from banning double-length trailers from its highways, and the Occupational Safety and Health Administration's issuance of a relatively weak regulatory standard preempting stronger state laws requiring disclosure of workplace toxics.

The greatest complaint of state and local officials regarding regulatory federalism is its cost: if the federal government wants something done, then it should provide the money. In addition, many federal regulations are seen as overly rigid and intrusive. The Advisory Commission on Intergovernmental Relations has suggested that the U.S. Supreme Court reconsider its historic ruling in *Massachusetts* v. *Mellon*, 262 U.S. 447 (1923), the case in which the Court decided that grants-in-aid are voluntary contractual agreements that state and local governments may reject if they do not like the conditions attached. When the decision was issued, over sixty years ago, there were few grant programs and any attached strings were relatively simple. Today, there are about four hundred grant programs, with stringent conditions such as crosscutting requirements and crossover sanctions.[22]

SUMMARY

An influential book written just before Ronald Reagan assumed the presidency found the American intergovernmental system to be "overloaded."[23] Between 1968 and 1979, federal aid to state and local governments doubled *in inflation-adjusted dollars*. The number of grant programs proliferated dramatically, with federal dollars going for many activities that only a short time earlier were considered strictly state and local responsibilities (such as juvenile justice, libraries, and solid-waste disposal). A "creeping conditionalism"—requirements for citizen participation, access for the handicapped, and historic-sites preservation, to mention only a few—became intricate, intrusive, and pervasive. This conditionalism is especially burdensome for smaller governmental jurisdictions.

The Reagan reform program has sought to improve this situation. As we have seen, it has succeeded in some areas, failed in others, and actually *contributed* to the woes of state and local governments in still other areas by decreasing funding and increasing regulations. Whether or not a pro-spending liberal presidential administration could restore affluent federalism would perhaps be determined by the huge federal deficit. Clearly there are factors that will keep the federal government's role in state and local operations a dominant one.[24] Pressures from interest groups, from alliances of administrators at the federal, state, and local levels, and from intergovernmental lobbyists will keep substantial numbers of dollars in the federal pipeline. Presidential committments, congressional entrepreneurship, and Supreme Court decisions will set limits to any substantial winding down of the system. The inadequacy of local revenue sources and the reluctance of some states to assist local governments, the regional nature of many problems, and federal desires to stimulate state and local spending for purposes favored by the federal government all point to a key role for Washington in the activities of over eighty-two thousand state and local governments.

NOTES

1. Richard H. Leach, "Federalism and the Constitution," *University of Virginia Institute of Government Newsletter,* 61 (December 1984), 1.

2. Deil S. Wright, *Understanding Intergovernmental Relations,* 2nd ed. (Monterey, Calif.: Brooks/Cole, 1982), chap. 3. Wright employs the term *intergovernmental relations* rather than *federalism.* The former includes state-local relations in addition to national-state and national-local relations. State relations with local governments are discussed in Chapter 8 of the present book.

3. Nelson A. Rockefeller, *The Future of Federalism* (Cambridge, Mass.: Harvard University Press, 1962), pp. 7–8.

4. Ibid., pp. 8–9.

5. Letter to Joseph Cabell, February 2, 1816, in *The Political Writings of Thomas Jefferson,* ed. Edward Dumbauld (Indianapolis: Bobbs-Merrill, 1955), p. 99.

6. This argument is not rebutted by the fact that turnout is lower in state and local elections than in national elections. The activities and leaders of the former receive much less media attention than do those of the latter.

7. Quoted in Rochelle Stanfield, "For The States, It's Time to Put Up or Shut Up on Federal Block Grants," *National Journal,* October 10, 1981, p. 1800.

8. Quoted in "Is Major Change Necessary?" *Intergovernmental Perspective,* Summer 1982, p. 13.

9. Quoted in "39,000 Local Officials Await Decision on Revenue Sharing," *Congressional Quarterly Weekly Report,* March 2, 1985, p. 395. State governments originally received money from the program but were dropped in 1980.

10. Richard Nathan and Fred C. Doolittle, "The Untold Story of Reagan's 'New Federalism,'" *Public Interest,* Fall 1984, p. 98.

11. Reported in "Study Finds States Pick Up Slack When Programs Lose Federal Aid," *San Diego Union,* June 10, 1984, p. A-1. For an earlier report on this research, see Richard Nathan and Fred C. Doolittle, *The Consequences of Cuts* (Princeton, N.J.: Princeton University Press, 1983).

12. Nathan and Doolittle, "The Untold Story," p. 105.

13. Advisory Commission on Intergovernmental Relations, *Significant Features of Fiscal Federalism, 1984 Edition* (Washington, D.C.: ACIR, 1985), Tables 8 and 42. See also John Shannon, "1984: Not a Good Fiscal Year for Big Brother," *Intergovernmental Perspective,* 11 (Winter 1985), 4–7; and David B. Walker, *Toward a Functioning Federalism* (Cambridge, Mass.: Winthrop, 1981), pp. 175–76.

14. Rochelle Stanfield, "Reagan's Policies Bring Cities, States Together in a Marriage of Convenience," *National Journal,* December 19, 1981, p. 2228; "State, Local Lobbying Groups Suffering Withdrawal Pangs under Reagan's Federalism," *Congressional Quarterly Weekly Report,* October 31, 1981, p. 2109.

15. Quoted in "Tail Wags Dog as States Lead U.S. in Energy Programs," *Los Angeles Times,* May 18, 1980, p. VI-1. The classic description of the states as the laboratories of federalism is given by Justice Louis Brandeis in *New State Ice Co.* v. *Liebmann,* 285 U.S. 262, 311 (1934). See also Charles Adrian, *State and Local Governments,* 4th ed. (New York: McGraw-Hill, 1976), p. 52.

16. Roy Bahl, *Financing State and Local Government in the 1980s* (New York: Oxford University Press, 1984), pp. 147–71.

17. Parris Glendening and Mavis Mann Reeves, *Pragmatic Federalism,* 2nd ed. (Pacific Palisades, Calif.: Palisades Publishers, 1984), pp. 171–89. See also Advisory Commission on Intergovernmental Relations, *Significant Features of Fiscal Federalism, 1984 Edition* (Washington, D.C.: ACIR, 1985), Table 42.

18. Advisory Commission on Intergovernmental Relations, *Regulatory Federalism* (Washington, D.C.: ACIR, 1984).

19. Ann Cooper, "When the Federal Carrot Doesn't Work, Congress Is Ready to Use the Stick," *National Journal,* June 30, 1984, p. 1261.

20. Catherine H. Lovell, "The 'Deregulation' of Intergovernmental Programs," *University of California at Berkeley Public Affairs Report,* 25 (April 1984), 2–3.

21. Art Levine, "Easing of State-Local Regulatory Burden Leaves Some Pleased, Others Grumbling," *National Journal,* August 4, 1984, pp. 1464–69.

22. ACIR, *Regulatory Federalism,* chap. 2.

23. Walker, *Toward a Functioning Federalism,* pp. 3–16, 173–76, 251–55.

24. Grover Starling, *Managing the Pubic Sector,* rev. ed. (Homewood, Ill.: Dorsey Press, 1982), p. 76.

chapter 3

Parties and Elections

Before we describe the policy-making institutions of state government, such as the governorship, the legislature, and the courts, it is necessary to note the political processes through which these policy makers are selected and the political considerations to which they respond. This chapter will assess the relative strength of the Democratic party and the Republican party at the state level, the procedure for drawing legislative-district lines, political party organization, voter registration and turnout, election campaigns, and campaign finance.

INTERPARTY COMPETITION

We noted in Chapter 1 that states vary in many different ways, and that one of these is partisan preference. State voters may have a long-standing preference for one party, or be fairly evenly split in their allegiances. Since almost all elected officials are either Democrats or Republicans, the extent of interparty competition is extremely important. (Judges in many states, as well as Nebraska legislators, run on a nonpartisan basis; many local elected officials are officially nonpartisan.)

Almost everyone has some notion that his or her state is a Democratic state or a Republican state or a competitive state. What are the facts of the matter? Table 3-1 classifies the fifty states in terms of their partisan tendencies. The predominant strength of the Democrats is evident: over half of the states are at least strongly Democratic. No states are one-party Republican and only North Dakota is strongly Republican. The Democrats have been increasingly successful in recent years in state elections. On the basis of the classification system used in Table 3-1, in which an overall index of .5000 indicates perfect two-party competition and an index in

TABLE 3-1   Classification of the States According to Degree of Interparty Competition, 1974–80*

One-party Democratic	Modified One-party Democratic	Two-party	Modified One-party Republican
Alabama (.9438)	South Carolina (.8034)	Montana (.6259)	North Dakota (.3374)
Georgia (.8849)	West Virginia (.8032)	Michigan (.6125)	
Louisiana (.8762)	Texas (.7993)	Ohio (.5916)	
Mississippi (.8673)	Massachusetts (.7916)	Washington (.5806)	
Arkansas (.8630)	Kentucky (.7907)	Alaska (.5771)	
North Carolina (.8555)	Oklahoma (.7841)	Pennsylvania (.5574)	
Maryland (.8509)	Nevada (.7593)	Delaware (.5490)	
Rhode Island (.8506)	Hawaii (.7547)	New York (.5390)	
	Florida (.7524)	Illinois (.5384)	
	Connecticut (.7336)	Nebraska (.5166)	
	New Jersey (.7330)	Maine (.5164)	
	Virginia (.7162)	Kansas (.4671)	
	New Mexico (.7113)	Utah (.4653)	
	California (.7081)	Iowa (.4539)	
	Oregon (.6954)	Arizona (.4482)	
	Missouri (.6932)	Colorado (.4429)	
	Minnesota (.6680)	Indiana (.4145)	
	Tennessee (.6648)	New Hampshire (.3916)	
	Wisconsin (.6634)	Idaho (.3898)	
		Wyoming (.3879)	
		Vermont (.3612)	
		South Dakota (.3512)	

SOURCE: John F. Bibby et al., "Parties in State Politics," in *Politics in the American States: A Comparative Analysis,* 4th ed., ed. Virginia Gray, Herbert Jacob, and Kenneth N. Vines, p. 66. Copyright © 1983 by John F. Bibby, Cornelius P. Cotter, James L. Gibson, and Robert Huckshorn. Reprinted by permission of Little, Brown and Company.

* An index of .8500 or higher is one-party Democratic.
  .6500 to .8499 is modified one-party Democratic.
  .3500 to .6499 is two-party competitive.
  .1500 to .3499 is modified one-party Republican.
  .0000 to .1499 is one-party Republican.
The index is based on the percentage of votes won by each party in gubernatorial elections and the percentage of seats won by each party in each house of the legislature; on the length of time each party controlled the governorship and/or the legislature; and on the proportion of time in which control of the governorship and legislature was divided between the parties.

excess of .5000 represents a Democratic tendency, the mean was .5435 for 1946–62, .5845 for 1962–73, but .6430 for 1974–80. In the 1946–62 period, there were seventeen one-party Democratic or modified one-party Democratic states and eight modified one-party Republican states. For 1974–80, there were twenty-seven Democratic states but only one Republican state.[1]

Many two-party states and modified one-party Democratic states are urbanized states with higher incomes, more extensive union memberships, larger black populations, and fewer farmers. Since the Democratic party and the Republican party tend to appeal to different socioeconomic groups, these cleavages form the basis for partisan politics. As more states move from the two-party column to the modified one-party Democratic column, the social and economic differences that once existed between the two categories of states begin to fade. Moreover, many of the one-party Democratic or modified one-party Democratic states are Sunbelt (southern or border) states that have received extensive migration. This population movement, and the emergence of the Republican party in the South, may lessen allegiance to the Democratic party and increase competition between the parties.[2]

DISTRICTING

The drawing of legislative-district lines is usually politically motivated, and has been nicknamed *gerrymandering*. Districts are drawn in such a way as to reduce interparty competition significantly. The process begins after each decade's U.S. census, when the state legislature must redraw its own district lines and those of the state's delegation to the U.S. House of Representatives. The only legal restrictions on the legislature are that districts must have approximately equal population (the U.S. Supreme Court's one-person-one-vote rule) and that there must not be either the intention or the effect of diluting the voting strength of minority groups.

The political party that controls the legislature proceeds to draw district lines that will protect majority-party incumbents and result in the election of even more majority-party candidates. District lines are often tailored so that a local official or other aspiring politician can move up to legislative office. Sometimes two or three minority-party incumbents are placed in the same district so that they will kill each other off. The strategy employed by the majority party is to force the minority party to waste its votes. Minority-party voters can be split up in so many districts that they constitute a threat in only a few districts, or they can be consolidated into a few districts so that they waste their strength by electing their party's candidates with 80 percent or 90 percent majorities. The result of these strategies is the creation of many lopsided districts in which the minority-party candidate has little or no hope of winning election. (In situations of divided control, as when the governor and the legislature belong to different parties or when the chambers of the legislature are controlled by different parties, the legislature will pass a bill protecting incumbents of both parties from losing office as a result of districting. Such an *incumbent gerrymander* is different from the *partisan gerrymander* described here.)

Since most state legislatures are controlled by one party (see Chapter 6), the districting process sets off a contest between factions within the majority party. Liberals, middle-of-the-roaders, and conservatives all struggle to gain control of the party in the legislature, as happens in Texas and New Hampshire. Rural legislators may square off against urbanites in a state such as Kansas. Or it may be east versus west, as in South Dakota, or "upstate" vs "low-state," as in South Carolina.[3]

The importance of the gerrymander for legislative elections cannot be stressed too much. By carefully drawing district lines, the majority party rigs most general-election contests. The party that draws up the districts at the beginning of the decade can heavily influence the outcome of legislative elections for much of the rest of the decade.

There are, however, some factors that can upset the best-laid plans of gerrymanderers. In some parts of some states, the homes of Democratic voters and Republican voters may be so intermingled that it is impossible to draw noncompetitive districts. Unforeseen events can sweep into office minority-party candidates, even in lopsided districts: the majority party can be caught in a scandal; electoral tides or significant issues such as taxes or crime may be running against the majority party; the minority-party ticket may be led by an exceptionally popular presidential or gubernatorial candidate. In any case, the primary election of the majority party is usually a more significant political event than the November election, because November's winner was probably chosen in the spring or summer primary of the majority party. However, most incumbent legislators do not face primary election challengers, and many more voters choose to vote in the November general election than in the primary. The ramifications of these two characteristics of state elections will be discussed later in the chapter.

The gerrymander is clearly an unfair political device because the majority party has stacked the deck before the game has begun. But to expect *either* the Democrats or the Republicans *not* to act in their political self-interest is to make unrealistic assumptions about human nature. Moreover, the gerrymander is in some sense undemocratic, because it intensifies the Matthew Effect: "To him who has, more will be given, and he will have an abundance; but from him who has not, even what he has will be taken away" (Matthew 13:12). A political party winning at least a plurality of the statewide vote gets more seats than its percentage of the vote would dictate, and the minority party receives proportionately less seats than its share of the vote. By manipulating district lines, the majority party can get 10 percent more of the seats than its percentage of the vote.

According to Alan Heslop, an authority on the gerrymander, this device decreases compromise and consensus in state politics because it pushes political parties to extremes.[4] Candidates running in noncompetitive districts do not need to broaden their appeal or to court independent voters or members of the opposition party.

The liberal reform group Common Cause has long favored an innovative plan to create a bipartisan reapportionment commission to draw district lines. The commission would consist of five members. The Democratic and Republican leaders in each chamber of the legislature would each select one person who is not an elected official. The first four members would then select the fifth person. The commission would be bound by standards intended to inhibit gerrymandering. For example, city and county boundaries would have to be followed as much as possible. This requirement would make it less likely that cities would be split up to "waste" their votes. Furthermore, districts would have to be compact, a requirement intended to eliminate some of the bizarre configurations chosen by gerrymanderers to achieve their objectives. Critics of the Common Cause plan argue that the reapportionment commission would take too long to select the crucial fifth member and would probably deadlock in selecting a plan; the issue would thus be thrown into the courts, which would end up selecting the plan.

The director of California Common Cause argues that in terms of meeting court tests and legal standards, reapportionment commissions have been far more successful than state legislators in creating reapportionment plans.[5] Less than 15 percent of the reapportionment-commission plans drawn up during the 1980s were rejected by the courts, as opposed to 41 percent of the plans created by state legislatures.

PARTY ORGANIZATION

The City Level

Party committees are found at the precinct or city level, the county level, and the state level. In many cities, parties are organized either on the basis of *precincts* (small voting districts) or on the basis of councilmanic *wards*. This lowest rung of the party organization ladder is most likely to be found in those parts of the country with vigorous parties, such as the Midwest. In other parts of the country, precincts or ward organizations either exist only during elections or are present year-round only for the majority party.

The County Level

The chairpersons of the precinct or ward committees usually constitute the county party committee, which is probably the most significant of the three levels of party organization. The county is important because it is the basis for many electoral districts, such as those for the state legislature. Moreover, county government is still a reliable source of patronage (jobs and construction contracts) in most states. Finally, state election laws usually recognize the county and county committee as an important electoral unit. In many parts of the country, the Democratic or Republican county chair in a key county is a political force to be reckoned with. It is standard political protocol for governors and even presidents traveling near the county of a long-powerful chair to pay at least a courtesy call.

The State Level

Although the political party is growing weaker in terms of voter allegiance (more people now consider themselves independents rather than Democrats or Republicans, and there is more ticket splitting than before), the party organization at the state level appears to be gaining strength.[6] Nearly all state parties have a permanent headquarters, usually located in the state capital. (In the past, the party organization operated out of the home or business office of the person who happened to be state chair at the time.) Nearly two thirds of the state headquarters have at least five staff members, and nearly one fourth have ten or more. This number allows each person to specialize in such duties as public relations, issue research, voter registration, or fund raising. Almost all state organizations have a full-time salaried chairperson (to be described shortly).

In terms of services provided, over two thirds of the state parties engage in ongoing programs of voter identification and registration, and launch get-out-the-vote drives that benefit all party candidates. One third even engage in opinion polling in nonelection years. State parties make contributions to candidates for governor, state legislature, and other offices. Eighty-nine percent of the state headquarters run campaign seminars for state legislative candidates, and two thirds actually recruit candidates to run for the legislature. Finally, state party organizations make either formal or informal preprimary endorsements in an attempt to influence the nomination of party candidates. Interestingly, the Republican party, which showed such electoral weakness in Table 3-1, is organizationally stronger than the Democrats in all regions of the country.[7]

A significant figure in state party organization is the state chairperson, particularly the chair of the party that does not control the governorship. The chair is selected by the state central committee or the state convention, usually with the support of the incumbent governor if he or she is of the chair's party. The state chairperson tries to create a favorable public image for the party. In states in which the party does not control the governorship, he or she may be the state spokesperson for the party. The state party chair also engages in raising funds, recruiting candidates, influencing federal and state patronage decisions, and especially building the party organization at the local level.

Incentives for Political Activism

It is important to understand why people devote countless hours to a party organization or a candidate's campaign, because without these volunteers American politics would be far different from what we know it as today. The incentives for political activism are usually considered to be material, solidary, or normative.[8]

Material incentives include patronage (the "spoils" of politics), government contracts, and the opportunity to make more business contacts. Some people begin their political career by walking precincts for a local party organization because they hope this will be the first step to the governor's mansion.

Solidary incentives are personal and psychological satisfactions—the social aspects of politics. For many people, political activity provides fun, excitement, friendships. To understand this, one need only stand in a party headquarters on election night—anticipation and electricity are in the air. Even in defeat there is consolation: "we" fought a good fight, "we" will beat them next time, etc. A person can easily be swept up in the social life of a political party. For some, it can become a way of life, or even an opportunity to project one's aggressions in socially acceptable ways.

Increasing in importance are the *normative* incentives to activism. Recall our discussion of the moralistic political culture in Chapter 1. People are willing to work long hours for a party or candidate because they believe in certain issues, principles, causes, or ideologies. Liberalism, conservatism, environmentalism, feminism, nuclear power and nuclear weapons, abortion, the Equal Rights Amendment, and civil rights are only a few of the concerns that attract people to political activity. Working for a favored cause can give a deeper meaning to what for many people is a rather mundane existence.

Third Parties

A concern for issues provides the *raison d'être* of third parties. The Liberals, the Conservatives, and the Right to Life party are on the ballot in New York, and the Libertarians, the Socialist Workers party, and others are found on many state ballots. Third parties have not been very successful in electing their members at the state level, although one Libertarian was elected to the Alaska legislature, the 1978 Libertarian candidate for governor in California (running as an independent) got 378,000 votes, and the 1978 Right to Life candidate for governor got 120,000 votes in New York. Seldom do third-party candidates get more votes than the difference between the Republican and Democratic candidates, which is usually said to be the margin needed for affecting an election outcome. The strong suit of third parties is the dedication of their members, who are fed up with the "politics as usual" style of the Democrats and Republicans. The liabilities of third parties, in addition to their small number of adherents, are that mainstream voters are reluctant to "throw away their vote" on a protest candidate and that the Democrats and Republicans make it as difficult as possible for third parties to get on the ballot. In any event, these parties provide a safety valve for unhappy people and even extremists. Indeed, third parties often raise issues having great popular appeal—which are then immediately stolen by the Republicans and Democrats. In politics, there is no way to patent good political ideas.

REGISTRATION AND TURNOUT

The *suffrage,* or the right to vote, is regulated by the states, subject to the U.S. Constitution and its amendments. For example, states decide if prospective voters must register in order to vote, and if so, how and when it should be done. They also determine if candidate nomination is to be accomplished by primary or convention (or some combination of the two), and what form it shall take, along with its date. The form of the ballot differs from state to state. Strictly speaking, there are no federal elections in this country; there are only federal officials selected in state-conducted elections. In fact, even the president is selected in simultaneous elections held in the fifty states and the District of Columbia.

With the exception of North Dakota, all states require people to register before they can vote. However, some states require registration only in urban areas; Minnesota, Wisconsin, Maine, and Oregon allow registration on election day. Registration by mail is more convenient for prospective voters but, by itself, does not necessarily increase the number of persons registered.[9] Registration usually closes thirty days or less before election day, but the U.S. Supreme Court has allowed Arizona fifty days for state and local elections; New Mexico has forty-two days.

Studies based on voter turnout in the 1960 election and the registration laws then in effect show that level of registration had by far the greatest influence on the percentage of the population who voted.[10] However, federal and state laws, constitutional amendments, and court decisions since that time have made registration and voting much easier. A newer study using more recent data has found that eliminating the thirty-day closing date for registration, keeping registration offices open during the normal forty-hour business week and on evenings and Saturdays, and allowing absentee registration for the sick, disabled, and those away from home would increase turnout by 9 percent.[11] However, this expanded electorate would be very similar to the present electorate in demographic, partisan, and attitudinal characteristics.

Ironically, the following provisions have *little or no* effect on voting: providing more deputy registrars, allowing people to register in their own neighborhood rather than at city hall or county offices, and allowing citizens who fail to vote for eight years to remain on the voting rolls rather than purging them as was customary after four years. Strange as it may seem, this last procedure has little or no effect on voting; that is, it does not increase the percentage of people who vote.

Certain kinds of people are more likely to vote than others: the key variable is education.[12] Education improves a person's ability to deal with abstract matters such as politics; it increases interest in politics, which leads one to seek out more political information; it causes people to have a higher sense of civic duty to vote; and it enables people to deal better with the bureaucratic aspects of registration and voting, such as filling out forms and meeting deadlines. Education clearly has the most influence on who votes; it is more important than such factors as income, occupation, urban residence, and amount of free time. Some kinds of people are 20 percent *less* likely to vote than others: people with only an elementary school education, very poor people, Puerto Ricans, Mexican-Americans, nonstudents aged eighteen to twenty-four, people older than seventy-nine, and those who have moved in the last two years.[13] Other people with unusually low turnout rates are southerners, blacks, and the unemployed.

In explaining the difference in turnout among states, we must consider differing registration laws and socioeconomic composition along with political factors such as differences in interparty competition among the states. Close election contests increase media coverage of elections, voter interest, and the parties' efforts to get out the vote. Turnout is highest in presidential elections and in off-year elections when the governorship is on the ballot.

Surprisingly, voter turnout has been declining since the early 1960s, which is something of a paradox since education levels have been increasing and registration laws have been relaxed. The poll tax has been abolished, postcard registration is frequently allowed, racial discrimination at polling places is less likely, and bilingual ballots are available. On the other hand, reducing the voting age to eighteen has enfranchised a group of people who have exhibited lower rates of turnout. Differing levels of turnout for different states in different types of election years are revealed in Table 3-2. Note that the average turnout for the 1984 presidential election (52.9 percent) is considerably higher than that for the 1982 off-year elections (38.7 percent), and that some states have consistently high (or low) turnout regardless of the offices being contested. Maine, Minnesota, and South Dakota, perhaps reflecting a moralistic political culture, exhibit much higher voter turnout than traditionalistic Georgia and South Carolina.

It might be appropriate to end this section with a note of caution on confusing the quantity of democracy with the quality of democracy:

> Frequently, campaigns are conducted by politically interested groups to encourage people to register and vote. The motives behind such activities are praiseworthy, but the result may be a mixed blessing. Everything possible should be done to remind the citizenry that an election is approaching and to encourage people to qualify themselves to cast ballots. At the same time it should be remembered that little is gained when uninformed, ordinarily disinterested people are encouraged to vote simply for the sake of voting.

TABLE 3-2   **Percentage of the Voting–Age Population Voting in 1982 and in the 1984 Presidential Election**

State	1982*	1984	State	1982*	1984
Alabama	40.1	48.9	Montana	56.4	60.0
Alaska	67.9	48.3	Nebraska	47.9	54.5
Arizona	35.2	46.3	Nevada	36.3	40.1
Arkansas	47.8	51.6	New Hampshire	40.8	52.9
California	43.0	48.1	New Jersey	39.5	55.5
Colorado	42.9	51.3	New Mexico	43.4	51.2
Connecticut	45.5	60.1	New York	39.7	50.6
Delaware	43.1	55.2	North Carolina	29.9	47.5
Florida	32.9	46.6	North Dakota	55.3	62.0
Georgia	28.9	42.1	Ohio	43.5	56.9
Hawaii	43.5	44.2	Oklahoma	38.4	51.2
Idaho	49.4	59.5	Oregon	53.3	59.0
Illinois	44.2	56.6	Pennsylvania	41.4	53.3
Indiana	46.5	54.1	Rhode Island	47.2	54.1
Iowa	49.5	61.6	South Carolina	29.3	37.2
Kansas	43.3	56.4	South Dakota	57.8	63.5
Kentucky	26.7	50.2	Tennessee	37.3	49.1
Louisiana	17.0	53.3	Texas	29.5	46.3
Maine	55.3	64.7	Utah	53.8	60.1
Maryland	35.7	49.1	Vermont	44.5	58.9
Massachusetts	46.6	57.1	Virginia	34.6	50.8
Michigan	46.3	58.0	Washington	43.3	52.5
Minnesota	60.4	67.9	West Virginia	40.1	50.7
Mississippi	36.9	51.3	Wisconsin	45.6	63.4
Missouri	42.4	57.2	Wyoming	47.7	51.4
			National average	**38.7**	**52.9**

SOURCES: Council of State Governments, *Book of the States, 1984–85* (Lexington, Ky.: Council of State Governments, 1984), p. 209; and *State Legislatures* (published by the National Conference of State Legislatures), January 1985, p. 19.

* The 1982 figure is for the office voted on by the highest percentage of the voting-age population.

It may reasonably be said that an uninformed vote is as bad, if not worse, than no vote at all. Since nonvoting appears to be most prevalent among those least informed, efforts by civic-minded individuals and groups to get out the vote would be more meritorious if directed at *informing* nonvoters on issues and candidates and then prompting them to vote.[14]

ELECTIONS

The Primary

Until the early 1900s, party nominations were made in party meetings or conventions dominated by the party organization and party machine. Reacting to the back-room deals, heavy-handed tactics, boss rule, and corruption of these meetings, a group of reformers known as the Progressives sought to open up the process by having nominations made by all party members voting in a primary election. One authority has described the primary as "the most radical of all the party reforms adopted in the whole course of American history" because it greatly weakened political parties.[15] Parties still have some role in the nominating process. For example, in Connecticut and Utah, the only way for a candidate to get on the primary ballot is to first obtain a certain percentage of the vote at the party's convention. In Colorado, New Mexico, North Dakota, New York, Delaware, and Rhode Island, candidates usually seek the endorsement of the convention before contesting the primary. In Massachusetts, Minnesota, Illinois, and other states, party organizations make informal endorsements prior to the party primary.[16]

Although the primary has replaced the convention as the principal state nominating device, it is not without its own drawbacks.[17] Because the primary in a carefully gerrymandered district or a one-party state may be more important than the general election, the defects of the primary are especially serious. Long-term incumbents are unlikely to encounter serious primary competition, while the minority party in the state or district may have to conscript someone to run. Only about 3 percent of incumbent state legislators are defeated in primaries.[18] On the other hand, in a competitive district the parties may discourage a primary contest for fear of losing the seat.

However, there are circumstances under which primary competition is increased. *Open seats,* those in which no incumbent is seeking renomination, are almost sure to be contested in a primary by the majority party. (But the decreased turnover in state legislatures—see Chapter 6—and the increased tenure for governors—see Chapter 5—have resulted in fewer open seats.) Factions within each party may be unable to settle their disputes over patronage or ideology or power, and will battle it out in the primary. The incumbent may have been involved in a scandal. Incumbents can become so old that they are vulnerable to aggressive young challengers. Conversely, incumbents may be seeking renomination for the first time and may have not established themselves in their districts, which can also prompt primary contests. Finally, district lines can be altered through reapportionment, which puts unfamiliar territory in an incumbent's district, in addition to a new crop of ambitious potential challengers.[19]

There may be not only a shortage of primary contestants, but also a shortage of primary voters. The Progressives had hoped that the primary would spur widespread popular participation, but only about half as many people turn out for the primary as for the general election. This smaller primary electorate can pose serious problems for party strategists if it is unrepresentative of the party as a whole—for example, if it is dominated by strong liberals or strong conservatives, by voters in a particular city or region of the state, or by one ethnic group or occupational group. The party's fear is that a candidate with such limited appeal will be nominated that he or she cannot win the general election. This is especially a problem for the minority party, which must appeal across party lines to get a majority. However, a sample survey administered to 1970 Democratic primary voters and to Democratic general-election voters revealed "no significant differences between the groups in age, sex, educational level, political participation and occupation."[20] There was also no difference in party loyalty or attitudes toward issues, and, contrary to expectations, general-election voters had *more* political information.

Primaries further weaken political parties in that mavericks or ideological nonconformists, rather than party loyalists, can get the nomination as long as they can secure at least a plurality of votes on primary day. Since party leaders have not given governors and legislators the nomination, they cannot take it away. The primary is a major reason for the lack of party cohesion in state legislatures. Moreover, political parties can be torn asunder as party factions go after each other. Since the primary is a fight within the family, it is often more bitter than the general election. Many primary battles are struggles over legitimacy, over who is the "true" Democrat or the "true" Republican. The combatants may not be inclined to take any prisoners. Of course, issues raised against a primary opponent, along with any mud thrown, can be used with devastating effect by the other party in November.

Finally, primaries exacerbate the long-ballot problem, although they did not create it. Americans prefer to elect (rather than have appointed) an immense number of officeholders. These people not only have to run in a general election, but probably had to run in a primary as well.

Types of Primaries

There are four different types of state primaries: closed, open, blanket, and nonpartisan.[21] In the *closed primary,* which is found in thirty-eight states, the voter must reveal a party preference so that he or she will be given the ballot of his or her party. In the nine *open-primary* states, the voter is given the ballots of all parties, only one of which may be marked in secret. The distinction between closed- and open-primary states is blurred considerably by those closed-primary states that do not require prior registration *by party*: in those states, the voter simply declares a party affiliation on primary day before receiving the requested ballot.

Closed primaries without prior registration by party and open primaries can further seriously weaken the minority party in a one-party state or district. Voters like to go where the action is, which is almost always the primary of the majority party. People who might otherwise favor the minority party may choose to exercise a short-run, balance-of-power strategy and vote in the majority-party primary. By doing this, they neglect the tortuous, long-term process of building up their own party.

Republican voters in those one-party Democratic states listed in Table 3-1 are likely to follow this route.

In an open-primary state or in any state without registration by party, *crossover voting* will occur: members of one party vote in the other party's primary. Crossover (as opposed to raiding) is found when one's party has no exciting races this year but the other party does. Party leaders dislike crossover because their party members may feel some residual commitment to vote in November for the person they favored in the primary, and because today's crossover voter may eventually become a member of the other party. *Raiding*, on the other hand, is voting in the other party's primary in order to nominate the weakest candidate. There have been few, if any, documented instances of large-scale raiding because most primary voters are not strong enough partisans to engage in this kind of political sabotage. In any event, a fear of crossovers and raiding has prompted the national Democratic party to refuse to seat any national convention delegates selected in open-primary states. Many voters, however, feel that their privacy is protected in open-primary states because they do not have to reveal a party preference.

Alaska and Washington use the *blanket primary,* in which there is a single consolidated ballot on which all parties appear. A voter can choose, for example, to nominate a Republican for governor, then a Democrat for the state senate, and then a Republican for the state house of representatives. The blanket primary weakens political parties and gives considerable power to independent and middle-of-the-road voters, who can pick and choose between parties for each office. It also maximizes the campaign contributions of interest groups.[22]

Louisiana has a *nonpartisan primary,* in which the candidates of all parties are listed on a single ballot. Should any candidate receive more than 50 percent of the vote, he or she is elected in the primary. In the likely event that no one carries a majority in the primary, the two highest vote-getters, regardless of party, have a runoff in November.

In the blanket primary, each candidate's party affiliation is listed on the consolidated ballot. In the nonpartisan primary, no party affiliations appear on the ballot. Moreover, *only* the nonpartisan primary allows a candidate to be elected in the primary by getting more than 50 percent of the vote.

Types of Ballots

The general-election ballot form used in most states is the *party-column ballot.* All of the Democratic candidates are listed in one column, all of the Republican candidates are listed in the next column, and so on for third parties. The visual impression given by this ballot is that all the members of one party are members of a team; the voter may feel a little guilty if he or she "jumps ship" to vote for a member of the opposing party in the other column. To encourage straight-ticket voting, a circle is placed at the top of each column: one can vote for all of a party's candidates simply by making a single mark in the circle. Use of the party column ballot is symptomatic of a strong-party state. Political parties in strong-party states campaign as a team and view the other party collectively as an "enemy."

A minority of states use the *office-block ballot,* in which all the candidates for the same office are grouped together. The voter must make a decision among *these* candidates for *this* office before moving on to the next block of candidates for the next office. We can speculate that voters now emphasize offices or individual candidates more than political parties, and that this facilitates ticket splitting.

What Influences Voters?

Numerous factors influence voting in state general elections.[23] Perhaps the most important is the traditional distribution of party loyalties in the state. We noted regarding Table 3-1 that there are more Democratic states than Republican states, and that formerly two-party states are becoming more Democratic. A trend in the other direction, also noted earlier, is that Republican party organizations are stronger and more effective than Democratic ones. Although almost every recent study of voting behavior has shown an increase in voter independence and a decrease in voter partisanship, the distribution of party registration and the results of recent elections are still the best guides to predicting future election results in any particular state.

But political trends sweeping the whole nation affect election outcomes in a specific state as well. In 1980, Republican national tides swept into office many state candidates, but two years later, the political currents were flowing in a Democratic direction. The party-column ballot clearly ties state and local candidates to national trends.

Incumbents, especially those of the majority party, usually do well in state elections. This is especially the case for low-visibility offices, such as the state legislature. The gerrymander assists majority party candidates, and the voters are more inclined to vote their party affiliation in a low-visibility election in which they know little about the candidates. The assets and liabilities of incumbent governors seeking reelection, and those of their challengers, will be discussed in Chapter 5. Voter information may vary with level of office, but the kinds of candidate characteristics (in addition to party affiliation) that can swing an election are experience, record, personality, and image. Salient issues such as corruption or taxes may be important as well.

If we want to explain a particular state election, we will have to start with aggregate voting results. Which counties did the winner carry? Which were the winner's best cities, and which ones put him or her "over the top"? Public opinion polls are important because they can tell us how the voters evaluated the candidates and which issues were important. Finally, we need to look at the conduct of the campaign itself. How well did the candidates campaign? In the case of gubernatorial candidates, did their media consultants and campaign management firms produce effective television and radio commercials and direct-mail pieces? What did the candidates say? Did anyone have foot-in-mouth disease? How much money did the candidates spend? What kind of media coverage of the campaign was there? Inadequate? Biased? If we can answer these various questions, we can probably explain a particular election. Yet again, we may only know for sure who won and who lost.

CAMPAIGN FINANCE

The states have clearly fulfilled their role as the "laboratories of federalism" in the area of regulating campaign finance. Fifteen states provide for partial or full funding of campaigns, all states except North Dakota require disclosure of the names of campaign contributors, half of the states limit the amount of money an individual can give to a candidate, and eight limit how much money candidates can spend.

When elections are financed in whole or in part by public funds, those who design the program must answer four key questions: How should the money be raised? Who should administer the program? Which elections should be subsidized? Who should receive the money?[24]

Massachusetts, Maine, Maryland, and Montana have systems through which taxpayers can indicate on their income tax form that a small additional tax be earmarked for supporting election campaigns. Few people avail themselves of the opportunity, and little money is raised. The rest of the states use an income tax checkoff system similar to the federal government's, in which taxpayers indicate that a small amount of their normal tax liability be used for campaigns. Participation ranges from 7.5 percent in North Carolina to 41 percent in New Jersey, and averages 22 percent among all the states that use this plan. The highest percentage of people ever participating in the federal checkoff plan was 29 percent.[25] Checkoff participation varies according to a state's political culture, the amount of effort expended by public officials and party leaders in publicizing the program, and where on the state income tax form the checkoff system is located.

Most states have created an agency to administer and enforce the campaign finance law; other states, such as Oregon and Utah, entrust this responsibility to the secretary of state.

The money can be given to gubernatorial candidates only, to candidates for all major statewide positions, to state legislative candidates, or to some combination of them. New Jersey, Massachusetts, Michigan, and

Hawaii fund not only general elections but primaries as well. We noted earlier that the primary in a gerrymandered district or a one-party state may be more important than the general election. The funding of primary elections is particularly significant, but it can also lead to the situation of the 1981 New Jersey gubernatorial primary, in which twenty-one candidates qualified for public funds. As the number of publicly financed candidates goes up, the chances of any candidate receiving a majority of the votes goes down. Some procedure to distinguish legitimate from frivolous candidacies is clearly required. For example, Michigan requires gubernatorial candidates to raise $50,000 in contributions of $100 or less. In Massachusetts it is $75,000 in amounts of $250 or less. If money is to be disbursed in both primary and general elections *and* to candidates running for numerous different offices, the amount of money that each candidate receives is necessarily reduced.

A key consideration is whether the money should be given to political parties, to individual candidates, or, as is done in Oklahoma, to both. All of the states giving money exclusively to political parties allow the taxpayer to designate a party. If the money is given to political parties, state party organizations are strengthened; if the funds are disbursed to individual candidates, their independence is enhanced and power in state politics is dispersed.

Any discussion of publicly financed elections that does not consider whether such a system has a partisan bias or an incumbent bias is a naive discussion indeed. Ruth S. Jones has concluded that "most public finance programs tend to favor the dominant (usually Democratic) party . . . in states that collect and allocate strictly on the basis of taxpayer party designations."[26] However, the advantage is not significantly greater than the majority party's share of the party-affiliated registered voters.

In addition to requiring the disclosure of the names of major contributors, many states prohibit or limit cash contributions or anonymous contributions, forbid contributing money in the name of another person, require the disclosure of the original source of a contribution, and require that election officials be notified of contributions made right before an election.[27] A person who has nothing to hide should not mind having a campaign contribution disclosed publicly. Even so, disclosure laws may make certain people or interest groups reluctant to contribute to the campaign of the challenger to a powerful incumbent. Incumbents can always use governmental power to injure the interests of those persons or groups who have made their life more difficult. More than thirty states require that officeholders disclose their personal finances; some extend this to the officeholder's spouse and children as well. This provision is intended to prevent contributions from being concealed as business transactions. Finally, candidates in some states must reveal how they spent their campaign funds.

There are also limits on contributions *to* candidates and expenditures *by* candidates. Citizens are limited in how much they can give to favored candidates—for example, $1000 per election in West Virginia or $1500 per election per candidate in Arkansas. Eight states restrict how much candidates may spend. In these eight states, challengers may not spend more money than their better-known incumbent opponents, who also have the perquisites of office. Here as elsewhere, election laws are written by incumbents, not challengers.

A little-noticed, unprecedented occurrence in the area of campaign finance is the extraordinary efforts of the *national* Republican party to aid state and local candidates in the 1978, 1980, and 1982 elections. In 1978, the Republican National Committee (RNC) spent $2 million, and in 1980, $2.9 million; this sort of thing has never been done before. The Republicans wanted to capture as many state legislative chambers as possible in order to minimize a Democratic gerrymander after the 1980 census. In 1982, the GOP was trying to improve the candidate base of the party, and the RNC spent $600,000. An additional half-million dollars was distributed by GOPAC, an independent political action committee set up by Republicans. Aware that only about one third of all state legislators are Republicans, the party felt it was weak at its base and had too small a pool from which eventually to recruit United States House of Representatives candidates. In addition to cash contributions, some of the services provided were campaign managers, public opinion polling, advice on media advertising, preparation of direct-mail pieces, targeting of precincts and counties, setting up and operating of telephone banks, candidate seminars, and candidate recruitment. This unprecedented national effort also included intervention in gubernatorial primaries in Wisconsin and Nevada.[28] We can assume that should such national support become institutionalized, it will offset some of the Democratic party dominance shown in Table 3-1.

SUMMARY

An important theme of this chapter has been interparty competition. We have found that most states are Democratic, but we have also noted some factors that have been increasing Republican competitiveness. Among the latter are strong Republican party organizations, the migration of northerners into the South, and financial assistance from the national Republican party. The gerrymander remains an important tool for dissipating the strength of the minority party. Registration laws and election turnout vary from state to state, but the key determinant of whether a person will vote is the amount of his or her education. Factors that influence voting in state elections have been examined, and the importance of the often-neglected primary has been stressed. Finally, we have considered how some states provide public money for elections and how states regulate the role of private money in elections.

NOTES

1. John Bibby et al., "Parties in State Politics," in *Politics in the American States: A Comparative Analysis*, 4th ed., ed. Virginia Gray, Herbert Jacob, and Kenneth N. Vines (Boston: Little, Brown, 1983), p. 67; Austin Ranney, "Parties in State Politics," in *Politics in the American States*, ed. Herbert Jacob and Kenneth Vines (Boston: Little, Brown, 1965), p. 65.

2. Bibby et al., "Parties in State Politics," pp. 68–69.

3. Leroy Hardy, Alan Heslop, and Stuart Anderson, eds., *Reapportionment Politics: The History of Redistricting in the 50 States* (Beverly Hills, Calif.: Sage Publications, Inc., 1981), p. 23.

4. "Computer Technology Is New Political Force," *Los Angeles Times*, March 16, 1984, p. II-6.

5. Walter Zelman, "Fair Reapportionment," *Sacramento Bee*, February 21, 1985, p. B15.

6. James L. Gibson et al., "Assessing Party Organizational Strength," *American Journal of Political Science*, 27 (May 1983), 193–222.

7. Ibid., p. 206. See also Cornelius Cotter et al., *Party Organizations in American Politics* (New York: Praeger, 1984).

8. John Goldbach and Michael J. Ross, *Politics, Parties, and Power* (Pacific Palisades, Calif.: Palisades Publishers, 1980), pp. 16–17, 205–8.

9. Richard Smolka, *Registering Voters by Mail* (Washington, D.C.: American Enterprise Institute for Public Policy Research, 1975), p. 82. This study also found greater potential for vote fraud under mail registration (rather than in-person registration), especially when it is combined with absentee voting.

10. Stanley Kelley, Jr., Richard Ayres, and William Bowen, "Registration and Voting: Putting First Things First," *American Political Science Review*, 61 (June 1967), 359–77.

11. Steven Rosenstone and Raymond Wolfinger, "The Effect of Registration Laws on Voter Turnout," *American Political Science Review*, 72 (March 1978), 33, 38.

12. Raymond Wolfinger and Steven Rosenstone, *Who Votes?* (New Haven: Yale University Press, 1980), chap. 2.

13. Ibid., chap. 6.

14. Russell Maddox and Robert Fuquay, *State and Local Government*, 4th ed. (Monterey, Calif.: Brooks/Cole, 1981), p. 137. Emphasis in original.

15. Austin Ranney, *Curing the Mischiefs of Faction: Party Reform in America* (Berkeley: University of California Press, 1975), p. 121.

16. Malcolm Jewell, "The Impact of State Political Parties on the Nominating Process" (paper presented at the annual meeting of the Midwest Political Science Association, Chicago, 1983), pp. 3–5.

17. Primary elections are described in Goldbach and Ross, *Politics, Parties, and Power*, chap. 10.

18. Craig H. Grau, "Competition in State Legislative Primaries" (paper presented at the annual meeting of the Southern Political Science Association, Gatlinburg, Tennessee, 1979), p. 14.

19. V. O. Key, Jr., *Politics, Parties, and Pressure Groups*, 5th ed. (New York: Thomas Y. Crowell, 1964), pp. 451–52.

20. Andrew DiNitto and William Smithers, "The Representativeness of the Direct Primary: A Further Test of V. O. Key's Thesis," *Polity*, 5 (Winter 1972), 211–21.

21. Some Democratic parties in the South also have runoff primaries for the two top vote-getters of the initial primary in the event no one got a majority.

22. Richard C. Kelly and Sara Jane Weir, "Unwrapping the Blanket Primary," *Washington Public Policy Notes,* 9 (Summer 1981), 2.

23. See Malcolm Jewell and David M. Olson, *American State Political Parties and Elections,* rev. ed. (Homewood, Ill.: Dorsey, 1982), chap. 6.

24. Ruth S. Jones, "State Public Financing and the State Parties," in *Parties, Interest Groups, and Campaign Finance Laws,* ed. Michael Malbin (Washington, D.C.: American Enterprise Institute for Public Policy Research, 1980), pp. 283–303. In Hawaii and Maryland, the public financing law extends to local level elections as well. The city of Seattle, but not the state of Washington, has publicly financed elections.

25. Herbert Alexander and Jennifer Frutig, *Public Financing of State Elections* (Los Angeles: Citizens' Research Foundation, 1982), p. 6. In New Jersey, the state legislature funds elections through a regular legislative appropriation, which is then reimbursed from the checkoff fund. Michigan matches checkoff fund money with money appropriated from the state's general fund.

26. Ruth S. Jones, "State Public Campaign Finance: Implications for Partisan Politics," *American Journal of Political Science,* 25 (May 1981), 352, 354.

27. Karen J. Fling, "The States as Laboratories of Reform," in *Political Finance,* ed. Herbert Alexander (Beverly Hills, Calif.: Sage Publications, Inc., 1979), pp. 250–52, 263.

28. John Bibby, "Political Parties and Federalism: The Republican National Committee Involvement in Gubernatorial and Legislative Elections," *Publius,* 9 (Winter 1979), 231–35.

chapter 4

Participation in State Politics: Interest Groups, Direct Democracy

In the last chapter, we saw that citizens participate in state politics by voting for political candidates, volunteering to work for candidates or political parties, and making campaign contributions. Americans can also express their political beliefs by forming or joining interest groups and by participating in initiative, referendum, and recall campaigns (direct democracy).

Interest groups are similar in many respects to political parties. For example, they sometimes recruit candidates to run for office, help finance election campaigns, and attempt to rally the public to their point of view. However, they do not contest elections in their own name—a key difference. Interest groups are *exclusive*: those who do not agree with the group's main objectives are excluded from membership. Political parties, on the other hand, are *inclusive*: they seek to include as many people as possible, regardless of their interest or ideology. Interest groups are *programmatic* because they have a public policy program they would like to have enacted. In contrast, parties are *pragmatic* because they are concerned primarily with winning elections. Parties usually espouse programs that will win them votes and drop issues that turn voters away. Finally, interest groups usually have a tighter, more hierarchical structure than political parties. Interest groups that are particularly effective, such as the National Rifle Association (NRA), are structured so that leadership can mobilize members quickly and pressure specific policy makers. As we saw in the last chapter, seldom does a state party chairperson or a state party committee have the power to issue orders that will be obeyed by subordinates.

Interest groups are active in state politics because they want to advance the welfare of their membership. The Big Three of business, labor, and agriculture come readily to mind. There are also groups at the state capital representing professional organizations such as the state medical association; public utilities (electric companies, railroads, the telephone company, and so on); and racial and ethnic groups. Some groups do not always seek strictly economic benefits. Many people spend long hours lobbying for causes of all sorts: religion, ideologies, "good government" and other reform, the environment, senior citizens, the consumer, women's liberation, or gay liberation.

THE SETTING

The groups active in a state capital reflect both the state's history and its unique characteristics. Past battles set the stage for present struggles. The existence of powerful institutions in certain states, such as the Mormon church in Utah and the Catholic church in Massachusetts, also affects the struggles among groups. States with close two-party competition in which legislative leaders can enforce party-line voting are usually thought to be better able to withstand the pressure of interest groups. On the other hand, the need for campaign contributions by parties and candidates in such states may help make them subservient to interest groups. The extent of a state's complexity, as measured by industrialization and income distribution, is closely related to the strength of interest groups in the state: states that are *more* complex have *weaker* interest groups.[1] Perhaps as the number of competing demands increases in a complex state, party and legislative leaders are better able to play off the demands of one group against those of another. On the other hand, in the relative absence of complexity, a lone, dominant interest will find few barriers to working its will. Many southern states fit this pattern. In addition, poorer states tend to have more powerful groups, whereas wealthier states have weaker ones.

 Zeigler and van Dalen find four patterns of group conflict in states with strong interest groups.[2] The first is an *alliance of dominant groups*: in states with nonindustrial, fairly undiversified economies, little party competition, and low legislative cohesion, a few prominent economic interests control public policy. Maine and many southern states fit this pattern. Second, a *single dominant interest*, such as Anaconda Copper in Montana, can prevail in a state with an undiversified economy, moderately high interparty competition, and moderately high cohesion in the state legislature. Third, a *conflict between two dominant groups* takes place in a different kind of undiversified setting. Urban, industrial Michigan has strong and competitive parties that generally do battle on behalf of auto workers (the Democrats) or the automobile companies (the Republicans). Finally, the more complex pattern of a diversified economy, party competition, and low cohesion in the state legislature can lead to a *triumph of many interests*. California generally fits this pattern.

Which interests are most influential in state politics? Wayne Francis questioned 838 state legislators across the country and got the answers shown in Table 4-1. The predominance of business interests is evident; an industry such as Du Pont in Delaware or the oil companies in Texas can loom exceedingly large in a state's politics. However, the picture can sometimes be overdrawn. "With so much weight to throw around, the giants are afraid of a public display of strength.[3] One study of business activity concluded: "A business can be too big to be politically effective along some lines."[4] Another study found that the weaker the interest groups in a state, the weaker the influence of business in that state.[5] On the other hand, the clout of business rests on its ability to make campaign contributions and to threaten to move out of state if officials take actions adverse to its welfare.

The assumption that "business" is a monolithic force marching toward a common goal is mistaken. Two observers have written that "most business influence is expended in internal warfare; i.e., business groups spend more time, money, and energy fighting each other than anyone else."[6] For example, Greyhound may exert more effort in struggling with Trailways over choice bus routes than in competing with trains, truckers, employee unions, or the state highway department.

TABLE 4-1   Powerful Interest Groups

Type of Group	Percentage of State Legislators Saying Group Is Powerful
Business: manufacturers, utilities, truck and bus companies, liquor interests, oil interests, financial institutions, Chamber of Commerce, railroads, insurance interests, etc.	43
Professional: education groups such as teachers' association, medical association, bar association, etc.	18
Labor: unions such as the AFL–CIO and government employees, etc.	16
Farm: Farm Bureau, REA co-ops, cattlemen's association, Farm Union, etc.	12
Public Agency or Officials: municipal associations, county and township officials, etc.	5
Other: religious groups, taxpayers' association, civil rights groups, health groups, sportsmen, etc.	6

SOURCE: Adapted from Wayne Francis, "A Profile of Legislator Perceptions of Interest Group Behavior Relating to Legislative Issues in the States," *Western Political Quarterly*, 24 (December 1971), Tables 1–3.

TABLE 4-2 **Union Membership as a Percentage of the Voting-Age Population, 1984**

Alaska	30.0	Maryland	9.4
New York	19.9	Utah*	8.7
Michigan	19.1	Wyoming*	8.5
Ohio	17.4	Kentucky	8.4
Hawaii	16.6	Tennessee*	8.0
Illinois	15.8	Alabama*	7.6
Washington	15.4	Nebraska*	7.6
Pennsylvania	14.9	Vermont	7.3
Missouri	14.1	Idaho	7.2
Nevada*	13.3	Louisiana*	6.9
California	13.1	Texas*	6.8
Minnesota	13.0	Georgia*	6.5
Oregon	13.0	North Dakota*	6.5
Wisconsin	12.6	New Hampshire	6.3
Indiana	12.4	Arizona*	6.2
Colorado	12.2	Oklahoma	5.9
West Virginia	11.6	New Mexico	5.8
Delaware	11.2	Kansas*	5.6
Rhode Island	11.1	Arkansas*	5.2
Massachusetts	11.0	Virginia*	5.2
Connecticut	10.9	Florida*	4.3
Iowa*	10.7	North Carolina*	4.2
Maine	10.6	Mississippi*	4.0
Montana	10.2	South Dakota*	4.0
New Jersey	10.1	South Carolina*	2.6

SOURCE: *U.S. News & World Report,* July 30, 1984. Copyright 1984, U.S. News & World Report, Inc.

* This state has a right-to-work law.

What about labor, the traditional adversary of business? According to one estimate, organized labor "may be in a position to exercise greater influence in state legislatures than in Congress."[7] As business influence in a state declines, labor influence increases. Zeigler argues that labor increases in strength as groups in general get weaker.[8] However, this position is not supported by Table 4-2, which shows labor union membership to be lowest in the southern states, which generally have the strongest interest group systems.

Generally speaking, union membership and hence union power are greatest in the larger, more diversified states. Union influence rests not only on vote power but on campaign contributions and other campaign assistance for candidates. However, labor union membership dropped in the late 1970s and early 1980s. With the exceptions of Nevada and Iowa, right-to-work laws are found only in states in which less than 10 percent of the voting-age population are union members. *Right-to-work laws,* discussed in Chapter 12, provide that employees cannot be required to join a union, and thus are bitterly opposed by labor unions. Right-to-work states are generally located in the Sunbelt areas of the West, the South, and the upper Plains states.

LOBBYISTS

The men and women who speak on behalf of interest groups in the state capital are called *lobbyists*. (Interest groups at the local level will be considered in Chapter 9.) Most lobby only part-time, while the legislature is in session. At other times, they hold a full-time position with a business or trade organization, or a labor union. Many are lawyers. Finally, lobbyists usually have spent much more time in the state capital than the legislators whom they are attempting to influence.

Lobbyists generally view themselves as having three roles. As *contact persons*, they rely on personal friendships and acquaintances with legislators to present directly their group's case. As *informants* they keep legislators informed, especially through testimony at committee hearings. And as *watchdogs* they monitor the legislature, particularly legislative calendars, for developments affecting their employers.[9]

One lobbyist described his work day in the following terms:

> I will get down to the capitol regularly at seven fifteen or seven thirty in the morning and will have breakfast in the capitol coffeeshop. There will usually be some legislators there and I will sit with them and we will talk. Quite often they will be members of one of my committees that will meet at eight o'clock. I will go to the committee meetings whether or not I testify. I cover all the committee hearings as far as I can to be able to answer questions. That period will be over about nine thirty and we'll go back to the coffeeshop with a different group of people and sit down with them. They will go upstairs at ten o'clock to sit through the session. I will go upstairs and call the office, talk to some other lobbyists and go down and have another cup of coffee with some other lobbyists. We will compare notes. The session adjourns at a quarter to twelve. I will pick up a couple of legislators and take them out to lunch in the coffeeshop or somewhere else.
>
> Quite often I will have a one o'clock hearing. If not, by this time the doors to the floor are open. Let us assume that it is early in the session and they aren't meeting afternoons. I will talk to many legislators on the floor, stand around and wait for them, quite often because they are being called to the phone or someone else is talking to them, and you line up back there and it looks like a bull ring or something. I also will check the bills that were introduced or printed the day before. You will pick up those that apply to you. If you have time, then you will start doing some research or I will go down to the three o'clock hearing if there is one. If not, then I will spend my time on the floor of the Senate or the House.
>
> Five o'clock or five thirty you will leave. I will go up to the apartment, sit down and have a drink and, if I am taking someone out to dinner I get dressed for dinner and we go out. If not, we run what we call the track-line, which is running the bars to see who is out with whom. Quite often there is a legislator out by himself. You see who is with whom. Notice how the alliances are building up. About midnight or one o'clock I call it a day and go home.[10]

INTEREST GROUP STRATEGIES

In order to achieve their objectives, interest groups employ a wide variety of strategies. Probably the foremost of these is making campaign contributions. In populous, competitive states such as New York and California, it takes a great deal of money to run for the governorship or the state legislature. Candidates come to rely on interest group money. In sparsely populated states, money can also be put to good use because there are fewer people to reach (but they are also farther apart). Endorsements and favorable publicity in interest group publications are valuable in any state. Campaign contributions go overwhelmingly to incumbents rather than challengers because incumbents are more likely to win (as a result of gerrymandered districts and higher name identification with the voters) and because they have a record that political action committees (PACs) can evaluate. Later in this chapter, we will see that interest groups are also the prime financiers of initiative and referendum campaigns in those states that have these direct-democracy devices.

As we have just seen, interest groups and their lobbyists "work" the legislature. Testimony at committee hearings is important because so many crucial decisions are made at this stage of the legislative process. Lobbyists try to get legislators friendly to their interests assigned to committees likely to hear bills of importance to their group. Because so many state lawmakers are amateur legislators or are new to the job, interest groups may have their greatest influence in the least professional legislatures. Frequently, these are the less wealthy states, which we already noted as having strong interest group systems. Lobbyists can tell the novice or poorly informed legislator the effects of a bill, how it will work in practice. But this information is usually couched in terms favorable to the interest group. Most lobbying efforts are directed at legislators who already lean toward the group's point of view; the purpose is not conversion of opponents but reinforcement of friends. Appeals are also made to any uncommitted legislators.

A study of interest group activity in three state legislatures examined a number of bills. A large number of bills (between 38 and 45 percent) were favored by coalitions of various interest groups. In a smaller number (between 23 and 33 percent), interest groups squared off against each other.[11] In fact, groups generally favor rather than oppose bills. This is not unrelated to the fact that many bills are actually drawn up by lobbyists and later introduced into the legislature by legislators.

Formal interest group interaction with legislators is supplemented by the informal meetings occurring along the "track-line" mentioned earlier. By entertaining legislators, lobbyists hope to establish favorable social relationships with them. The extent of this activity is strongly affected by a state's political culture. In an individualistic political culture, politics is the means people use to further their economic position. Since politics is already viewed as a morally compromising activity, the sight of lobbyists and legislators "whooping it up" in the capital's watering holes is not a particularly disturbing sight. In a moralistic political culture seeking to create a just commonwealth, such activity is frowned upon. In this as in so many other respects, states can vary widely: Pennsylvania is a long way from Oregon in more ways than one.

Assuming that a bill of interest to a group has made it through the legislative process, the group will attempt to persuade the governor to sign it (or to veto it if they are opposed). Civil servants, who must administer the laws, usually have a great deal of discretion in carrying them out. Therefore, they too will become the focus of group attention.

In some instances, interest groups are actually empowered to engage in what amounts to self-regulation. For example, the state of New York licenses or certifies over 350 occupational categories, including "baby chick seller, frozen dessert handler, private school recruiter, outdoor guide, cider retailer, industrial homemaker, second-hand bedding wholesaler, and wrestling match ticket taker."[12] Members of a particular profession are given authority to regulate that occupation and to decide who may practice it. Under the guise of state authority, those already in a profession seek to limit the entry of new practitioners.

Judges, too, receive the attention of interest groups who challenge laws they oppose in court. For example, the National Association for the Advancement of Colored People (NAACP) may contest a law in court, hoping it will be declared unconstitutional.

Finally, interest groups circulate and campaign for initiative laws and constitutional amendments if the state constitution provides for these processes. If all else fails, they can engage in protest rallies or demonstrations to publicize their grievances.

REGULATION OF LOBBYING

Lobbying is not a closely regulated activity, perhaps because the right to "petition the government for a redress of grievances" is protected by the First Amendment to the U.S. Constitution. In all states, lobbyists must register with some public authority, usually the secretary of state or the clerk of the House or Senate. In most states they must file monthly or quarterly reports with this same authority. These reports vary greatly in the detail that is required; they are not even necessary in six states. Noncompliance is usually punished as a misdemeanor, but New Mexico can revoke the registration of guilty lobbyists and prohibit them from lobbying. In extreme cases, Oklahoma may banish them from legislative halls.

The tenor of state lobbying legislation resembles the plea of the young St. Augustine before his conversion: "Lord, give me chastity—but not yet." Lobbyists have what legislators need: information, expertise in the diverse areas of legislation, advice on parliamentary strategy, campaign contributions. Hence, there *is* state regulation of lobbying, but it is not too restrictive.

An interesting topic of scholarly inquiry would be to rank state lobbyist-regulation laws in terms of their restrictiveness, and then see whether the ranking is related to political culture. Based on Elazar's theory, it is reasonable to assume that moralistic states would have the most restrictive laws and individualistic states the least, with traditionalistic states in between but leaning in the individualistic direction. California, which Elazar correctly considers primarily moralistic, has a strict law that requires lobbyists to register, report all lobbying expenses, and spend only ten dollars *per month* "wining and dining" a particular state or local official. However, since there are no limits on campaign contributions, and since competitive Assembly races cost well over $200,000 and competitive Senate contests considerably more than $400,000, California has a robust interest group system.

SOME CONCLUDING THOUGHTS ON INTEREST GROUPS

The influence of lobbyists is probably limited when it comes to highly visible issues such as busing of schoolchildren, nuclear power, welfare benefits, law and order, and capital punishment. But on less visible or more technical issues, especially those concerning interests closely regulated by the state, lobbyists can be highly influential. Visible issues prompt "interference" from the public, political parties, or the media. But narrow, more specialized matters concerning railroads or liquor interests or schoolteacher salaries can be subjected to intense lobbying. While the public is not watching, a highly advantageous "private" arrangement can be worked out concerning subsidies, tax rates, or regulation. That these matters are not highly visible does not mean they are unimportant. On the contrary, "private" settlements can cost the taxpayer or consumer considerably.

Despite the manifest self-interestedness of special interest groups, they do perform a representative function in state government. Representation in American politics is generally thought of as being territorial: representatives are selected from specific districts. But interest groups provide functional representation, especially on social or economic issues that cut across territorial boundaries. Moreover, some groups do not lobby for their own narrow economic self-interest, but for what they perceive to be a broader public interest. Consumer groups and clean-air advocates might be considered in this light. Even the much-discussed Moral Majority may be included here. Many of the issues that interest its members are dealt with by state and local government. The control of pornography, the teaching of sex education in public schools, and the teaching of creationism versus evolution might be good examples. Moral Majority leader Jerry Falwell is able to raise a great deal of money for political action, and he can have his followers register to vote and support conservative candidates. Furthermore, fundamentalist Protestants are especially adept at using the direct-democracy tactics described in the following section.

DIRECT DEMOCRACY

The direct-democracy devices of initiative, referendum, and recall frequently play an important role in the political process of the states that permit them. The initiative and referendum are especially used by interest groups to further their aims. By means of the first two processes, average citizens rule (decide public issues) *directly,* rather than through representatives. The *initiative* is voters making laws, the *referendum* is voters repealing laws, and the *recall* is voters removing public officials before the end of their term of office.

In 1978, California voters touched off a nationwide tax revolt by passing Proposition 13, the Jarvis-Gann Amendment. But this measure is an example of only one of many issues that voters face each year. Other recent ballot measures have included proposals to: legalize casino gambling or pari-mutuel betting (Florida, Arkansas, Colorado), impose deposits on beverage containers (Alaska, Nebraska), restrict construction of nuclear power plants (Montana), ban the use of tax money for abortions for poor women (Oregon), approve the Equal Rights Amendment, or ERA (Nevada), restore or expand the death penalty (California, Oregon), allow the state to set maximum charges for health services (North Dakota), establish a right-to-work law (Missouri), restrict busing (Washington), permit unmanned bank-teller machines (Texas), and reinstitute a hunting season on mourning doves (South Dakota).

It is clear that some of the most explosive issues in American politics can be presented for consideration by the voters. Almost half of the states have direct democracy at the state level—whether to have it is a matter of state discretion. Those states that do allow direct-democracy processes are generally western or Plains states in which the Progressive movement was strong early in this century.

The theory of direct democracy (described later in the chapter) dovetails nicely with a moralistic political culture: both are concerned with ideological issues, both see politics as a means to promote the public welfare, and both seek to encourage widespread public participation in politics.

Initiative

The initiative is a means voters can use to enact laws and amendments to the state constitution. The procedure begins with petitions, which are circulated in an attempt to get the required number of signatures within the time allowed by state law. If the proper number of valid signatures has been obtained, the question goes on the ballot. Signature requirements vary, but usually range from 3 percent to 15 percent of the votes cast for governor at the last general election. The most common requirement is 8 percent or 10 percent, with a higher percentage usually needed for amendments to the state constitution than for statutes. Some states provide for an indirect initiative, through which voters can force the legislature to vote on a measure if they have gathered the required number of signatures. The legislature may pass the statute, amend it significantly, or reject it. If the legislature chooses either of the latter two, the statute's sponsors can require that the original measure go on the ballot. In the six states having both a direct and indirect initiative, the direct initiative is almost always used. Initiative provisions are summarized in Table 4-3.

How have intiative proposals fared at the ballot box? Over one third are approved, with the passage rate slightly higher for initiative statutes than for constitutional amendments. See Table 4-4. States vary widely in their tendency to approve or reject initiatives: North Dakota approves 46 percent, but California only 29 percent.

The periods of greatest use of the initiative were 1910–19, when the process first came into general use; the Depression decade of 1930–39; *and the 1970s and 1980s.* Numerous reasons have been advanced for the recent increase. Since Vietnam and Watergate, the public has had less confidence in politicians, political parties, government, bureaucracy, business, labor, and established institutions generally.[13] The rise of single-interest groups has enabled the intense activists who compose them to bypass the state legislature and go directly to the voters. If they lobby the legislature, they may have to compromise on some of their claims, but if they use the initiative, they may be able to get all of what they want. Moreover, there is a snowball effect, in which successful initiatives inspire sponsors in other states. California's Proposition 13 led to imitators in states as diverse as Idaho and Massachusetts.

Many states limit the subject matter of initiatives. For example, Alaska forbids initiatives involving revenues, the courts, or local laws. Nevada requires that any initiative to spend money provide a source of revenue to cover the expenditure. Table 4-5 describes the subject matter of initiatives passed in all states between 1950 and 1978. Almost one of every four deals with reforming the structure of state government. The modernization of state government has been furthered by initiatives providing for civil service, merit selection of judges, and, a streamlined administrative structure. Long before the tax revolt of the 1970s, questions regarding

TABLE 4-3   Initiative Provisions

State	Initiative Constitutional Amendments	Initiative Statutes	Indirect Initiative	Initiative Used in Local Government Only
Alaska		X		
Arizona	X	X		
Arkansas	X	X		
California	X	X		
Colorado	X	X		
Florida	X	X		
Georgia				X
Idaho		X		
Illinois[a]	X			
Kentucky				X
Louisiana				X
Maine			X	
Massachusetts[b]	X		X	
Michigan	X	X	X	
Minnesota				X
Missouri	X	X		
Montana	X	X		
Nebraska	X	X		
Nevada[c]	X	X	X	
New Jersey				X
North Dakota	X	X		
Ohio	X	X	X	
Oklahoma	X	X		
Oregon	X	X		
Pennsylvania				X
South Carolina				X
South Dakota	X	X	X	
Texas				X
Utah		X	X	
Vermont				X
Virginia				X
Washington		X	X	
West Virginia				X
Wyoming		X		

[a] Only the article in the Illinois Constitution dealing with the legislature may be amended by the voters, and such changes require a majority of the total number voting in that election or three fifths of those voting on the amendment.

[b] Amendments to the Massachusetts Constitution must twice be passed by the legislature before being submitted to the electorate.

[c] Nevada constitutional amendments must be approved by a majority vote in two consecutive general elections.

TABLE 4-4 Statutory and Constitutional Initiatives Proposed and Approved by Voters for All States, 1898–1979

State[a]	Statutes			Constitutional Amendments			Total Initiatives		
	Number Proposed	Number Approved	Percentage Approved	Number Proposed	Number Approved	Percentage Approved	Number Proposed	Number Approved	Percentage Approved
Oregon	126	43	34%	101	28	28%	227	71	31%
California	67	19	28	93	27	29	160	46	29
North Dakota	135	55	41	30	18	60	141	65	46
Colorado	50	22	44	75	21	28	125	43	34
Arizona	66	22	33	46	19	41	112	41	36
Washington	74	35	47	—	—	—	74	35	47
Oklahoma	28	7	25	44	11	25	72	18	25
Arkansas	23	11	48	45	24	53	68	35	51
Missouri	15	5	33	34	7	21	49	12	24
Ohio	8	2	25	38	9	24	46	11	24
Michigan	5	4	80	36	14	39	41	18	44
Montana	33	21	64	3	1	33	36	22	61
Massachusetts	28	13	46	2	2	100	30	15	50
Nebraska	14	1	7	15	7	47	29	8	27
South Dakota	23	3	13	2	0	0	25	3	12
Nevada	13	7	54	5	3	67	18	10	56
Maine	16	5	31	—	—	—	16	5	31
Idaho	11	6	55	—	—	—	11	6	55
Alaska	10	5	50	—	—	—	10	5	50
Utah	8	2	25	0	0	0	8	2	25
Florida	0	0	0	2	1	50	2	1	50
Illinois	1	1	100	1	1	100	2	2	100
Wyoming	0	0	0	0	0	0	0	0	0
Total	754	289	38%	572	193	34%	1,326	482	36%

SOURCE: David Magleby, *Direct Legislation* (Baltimore: Johns Hopkins University Press, 1984), p. 71.

[a] States are listed in order of total use.

TABLE 4-5   Number of Initiatives by Subject Matter, All States, 1950–78

Subject	Constitutional Amendments	Statutes
State Government Organization and Administration (a)	62	44
State and Local Taxes and Tax Limits (b)	39	30
Legislative Apportionment, Membership, and Compensation	26	6
Liquor Control, Gambling, and other Social-Moral Issues (c)	22	34
Local Government Organization and Powers	11	7
School District Organization and Finances	11	12
Right-to-Work and Other Labor Issues	7	25
The Environment, Conservation, and Natural Resources (d)	6	36
Discrimination and Minorities (e)	6	2
Campaign Disclosures and Sunshine Provisions	3	7
Consumerism and Regulation (f)	4	14
Social Assistance and Welfare Benefits	3	5
Death Penalty	1	4
Miscellaneous Issues (g)	15	22
Total	216	248

SOURCE: *The Popular Interest versus the Public Interest* (Albany: New York State Senate Research Service, 1979), Table 5.

(a) Includes the civil service, the courts, reorganization of state government, officials' salaries.
(b) Includes earmarking of revenues, tax reductions or exemptions, tax limitations, expenditure ceilings, shifting of tax burdens.
(c) Includes removal of state curbs on pari-mutuel betting, greyhound racing, casino gambling, lotteries, bingo; also relaxation of liquor controls, sale of liquor by the drink, increase in drinking age; also drugs, obscenity, gun control.
(d) Includes siting of nuclear power plants and plant safety standards, designation of scenic rivers, air pollution abatement, bottle bills.
(e) Includes school busing, the ERA, employment of homosexuals, fair housing legislation.
(f) Includes public-utility rate making.
(g) Includes daylight savings time, fluoridation.

who should pay how much tax and for what purposes were fought out in initiative campaigns. Finally, highly emotional and ideological social and moral issues are resolved through the initiative process: gambling, liquor regulation, censorship of obscenity, gun control, the death penalty, school busing, the ERA, employment of homosexuals, and the safety of nuclear power plants.

Referendum

The petition referendum, or simply the referendum, is the electorate's means of stopping a recently enacted law from going into effect. Except for urgency measures, which deal with crises and go into effect immediately, laws passed by the legislature may not go into effect immediately: there is a waiting period, which is frequently ninety days. During this period, opponents of the statute circulate referendum petitions, trying to obtain the required number of signatures. This number is usually 2 percent to 15 percent of the votes cast in the last gubernatorial election. About one third of the states use 5 percent, and another one third require 10 percent. If the requisite number of valid signatures is gathered, the law is suspended until the next statewide election, when voters may approve or reject the statute.

The states offering a referendum on state legislation are Alaska, Arizona, Arkansas, California, Colorado, Delaware, Idaho, Kentucky, Maine, Maryland, Massachusetts, Michigan, Missouri, Montana, Nebraska, Nevada, New Mexico, North Dakota, Ohio, Oklahoma, Oregon, South Dakota, Utah, Washington, and Wyoming. An additional seven states have the referendum at the local level only.

Referenda on state legislation are far less frequent than statewide initiatives. The likely reason is that the time allowed for circulating

---

READING 4-1 USE OF THE REFERENDUM IN SAN JOSE, CALIFORNIA

After a fierce campaign, voters here overwhelmingly rejected two "gay rights" ordinances that sought to ban employment and housing discrimination against homosexuals.

"Our whole theme was, 'Don't Let it Spread,'" Dean Wycoff, executive director of Moral Majority, a group opposing the ordinances, said. . . . "We don't want the cancer of homosexuality spreading from San Francisco down to Santa Clara County."

Wycoff's organization, along with others, had collected enough signatures to force a referendum on ordinances passed last year by the San Jose City Council and the Santa Clara County Board of Supervisors.

During the campaign, religious leaders fought the ordinances on moral grounds, pointing to nearby San Francisco, where a large population of homosexuals is much in evidence and exercises substantial political power.

Televised advertisements showed a girl crying in a park, surrounded by homosexuals and lesbians. Widely distributed brochures contained photos of homosexuals embracing, partly nude or dressed in drag. Public "demands" by homosexual activists—including "gay quotas" for colleges—were circulated as evidence of gay militancy.

Supporters of the ordinances accused opponents of lies and distortions, contending the issue was civil rights, not morals. In the last few days before the election, scores of posters opposing the ordinances disappeared almost as fast as they were put up.

Voters rejected the county ordinance 244,095 to 103,479. The city ordinance was defeated 109,238 to 35,957.

SOURCE: "San Jose Area Voters Reject Two Gay Rights Ordinances," *Los Angeles Times*, June 5, 1980, p. I-21.

referendum petitions is usually less than the time allowed for circulating initiative petitions. However, a group that does not move quickly enough to qualify a referendum before the targeted law goes into effect *might* try to strike down the law by means of an initiative that overrules the law. In addition to the *petition* (or *protest*) *referendum,* there are the *compulsory referendum,* by which certain matters such as bond issues or constitutional amendments passed by the legislature must receive the final approval of the voters, and the *optional referendum,* by which the legislature may, if it wishes, refer laws to the voters for their approval.

Theoretical Issues Associated with the Initiative and Referendum

The merits and demerits of direct democracy have been debated for the last ninety years, and they came up again when Illinois and Florida adopted the initiative and referendum in the 1970s. Moreover, some reformers suggest that the federal government adopt these processes. The advocates of direct democracy are squarely in the Progressive, moralistic tradition, which holds that the people are wise and commonsensical and have a right to control their own government, and that government must be recaptured from the "special interests." Since representative institutions do not accurately reflect public opinion from time to time, there must be a "gun behind the door" to enable average citizens to express their will. Arguing on behalf of the initiative, one Illinois reform leader noted that wealthy special interests pay lobbyists to secure legislation for them. They can also employ professional legislative lobbyists to block popular bills and to sneak through special-interest legislation in the frantic atmosphere that dominates the end of the legislative session. The initiative, on the other hand, is the poor man or woman's way to lobby.

In addition, an unresponsive state legislature can be prodded into action by the threat of an initiative, and the referendum can be used to strike down special-interest legislation. Moreover, proponents of direct democracy promote it as a means to increase voter turnout and decrease public apathy. Finally, direct-democracy advocates point out that if voters are informed and responsible enough to select a president, a decision that may affect the vital security and welfare of the nation, they clearly are sophisticated enough to vote on ballot propositions.

Opponents of direct democracy argue that it is undesirable in theory and will produce in practice exactly the opposite of what its friends intend. According to this school of thought, representative democracy and not direct democracy is the true American tradition favored by the American Founders. We elect a governor and a state legislature to make decisions on our behalf—and that is what they should do. On a more practical level, opponents note that many initiative measures are poorly drafted because they have been drawn up by zealots, and that propositions clutter an already long ballot. After voting on federal, state, county, and special-district officials, the electorate must then decide on a host of ballot propositions. Furthermore, direct democracy has been labeled a *minority* and not a *majority* device. It takes a large number of signatures to put an initiative on the ballot; in many states, only a wealthy group employing paid petition circulators can qualify an initiative or referendum for the ballot. Then, a campaign-management firm must be hired to run the initiative campaign and to produce the prohibitively expensive television and radio commercials needed to win it. Wealthy groups can therefore further their economic interests by means of the initiative. In addition, single-issue groups can promote their social-moral beliefs in divisive campaigns that reduce complex issues to slogans.

Direct democracy may be biased not only in favor of wealthier groups, but also in favor of upper-status voters. David Magleby has conclusively demonstrated that people with some of the following characteristics are *less* likely to vote on ballot propositions than in candidate elections: low-income, less educated, blue-collar, female, nonwhite, over sixty-five.[14] Such evidence challenges the claim that direct democracy expresses public opinion more accurately than representative democracy. In addition, a study of state initiative use between 1960 and 1978 shows that when the southern states are removed from the analysis, states that allow the initiative do not have a consistently higher voter turnout than states without it.[15]

Recall

The recall is a means by which voters may remove from office elected state or local officials from the governor to local school-board member before the end of their term. Six states exempt at least some judges from the recall on the basis that judges are entrusted with the duty of protecting minority rights and should be somewhat shielded from majoritarian pressures. Montana voters, on the other hand, can recall *all* public officials, whether elected officers or appointed judges and administrators. Since members of the U.S. House of Representatives and U.S. senators are federal officials, they cannot be recalled.

The theory supporting recall is that the public should not have to endure two more years, four more years, or whatever, of an official who is incompetent or whose decisions do not reflect public opinion. Critics of the recall argue that vocal or wealthy interests may threaten public officials (especially local ones) with a recall and thereby gain excessive access to officials or unwarranted influence over them. It is sometimes argued that because of the possibility of a recall, elected officials may be afraid to make controversial or difficult decisions, even when such decisions are necessary. For example, lawmakers may be afraid to raise taxes.

Those states providing for recall of both state and local officers are

---

READING 4-2   THE RECALL IN MICHIGAN

State Sen. David Serotkin conceded Wednesday night that he had lost his attempt to fend off recall because he had supported a state income tax increase. He was the second Democratic state senator to be recalled in eight days.

With 52% of the vote counted, there were 13,953 votes for recall and 6,991 against.

The recall of Philip Mastin of Pontiac on Nov. 22 and of Serotkin was engineered by anti-tax activists angered by the legislators' support of Gov. James J. Blanchard's push to boost the state flat-rate income tax to deal with a projected $900-million budget deficit. The tax rate was increased to 6.35% from 4.6% and will drop to 6.1% in January.

SOURCE: "Second State Senator Recalled in Michigan Tax-hike Backlash," *Los Angeles Times*, December 1, 1983, p. I-14.

Alaska, Arizona, California, Colorado, Idaho, Kansas, Louisiana, Michigan, Montana, Nevada, North Dakota, Oregon, Washington, and Wisconsin.[16] An additional fifteen states have recall of local officials only. The process, like other direct-democracy devices, begins with a petition. The signature requirements are 10 percent to 40 percent of the votes cast in the last general election for governor. Two thirds of the states require 25 percent. Collection of the proper number of valid signatures forces a special election, in which a majority vote is sufficient for recall. Although North Dakota once recalled its governor, the process is not a realistic threat at the *state* level because of the large number of signatures that must be gathered.

SUMMARY

Direct democracy is government "of the people, by the people" in its purest form. The initiative, referendum, and recall are processes by which an outraged citizenry can take the governmental machinery into its own hands. Whether the hazards of these devices are real or imagined depends on whether American citizens are informed, public-spirited, and above all vigilant.

Americans are also group-minded. We have seen in this chapter that interest groups promote a wide variety of interests and viewpoints; however, not all groups have equal access to decision makers. Since the self-seeking of interest groups sometimes leads to influence peddling or corruption, almost all states regulate lobbying. But the regulations vary according to the political culture in which they are drafted.

NOTES

1.   L. Harmon Zeigler, "Interest Groups in the States," in *Politics in the American States*, 4th ed., eds. Virginia Gray, Herbert Jacob, and Kenneth N. Vines (Boston: Little, Brown, 1983), pp. 111–14.

2.   L. Harmon Zeigler and Hendrick van Dalen, "Interest Groups in State Politics," in *Politics in the American States*, 3rd ed., ed. Herbert Jacob and Kenneth N. Vines (Boston: Little, Brown, 1976), pp. 95–109.

3.   Ibid., p. 102.

4.   Raymond A. Bauer, Ithiel deSola Pool, and Lewis Anthony Dexter, *American Business and Public Policy: The Politics of Foreign Trade*, 2nd ed. (Chicago: Aldine-Atherton, 1972), p. 266.

5.   Zeigler, "Interest Groups in the States," p. 99.

6.   George Berkley and Douglas Fox, *80,000 Governments* (Boston: Allyn & Bacon, 1978), p. 67.

7.   John Kingdon, *Candidates for Office* (New York: Random House, 1966), p. 72.

8.   Zeigler, "Interest Groups in the States," p. 99.

9.   Samuel Patterson, "The Role of the Lobbyist," *Journal of Politics*, 25 (February 1963), 83–84.

10.   Quoted in Harmon Zeigler and Michael Baer, *Lobbying: Interaction and Influence in American State Legislatures* (Belmont, Calif.: Wadsworth, 1969), pp. 77–78.

11.   Keith Hamm, Charles Wiggins, and Charles G. Bell, "Interest Group Involvement, Conflict, and Success in State Legislatures" (paper presented at the annual meeting of the American Political Science Association, Chicago, 1983).

12.   "Regulatory Reform in the States," *Regulation*, September-October 1982, p. 11.

13.   David D. Schmidt, "Referenda and Initiatives: Hot New Campaign Areas," *Campaigns and Elections*, 3 (Winter 1983), 74–80; Texas Advisory Commission on Intergovernmental Relations, *Initiative and Referendum* (Austin: Texas ACIR, 1979), p. 7; David Magleby, *Direct Legislation* (Baltimore: Johns Hopkins, 1984), pp. 14–16.

14.   Magleby, *Direct Legislation*, pp. 100–121.

15.   David Everson, "The Effects of Initiatives on Voter Turnout," *Western Political Quarterly*, 34 (September 1981), 415–25. Additional information on the use of the initiative can be found in Russell Maddox and Robert Fuquay, *State and Local Government*, 3rd ed. (New York: D. Van Nostrand, 1975), pp. 280–87; and Michael J. Ross, *California: Its Government and Politics*, 2nd ed. (Monterey, Calif.: Brooks/Cole, 1984), chap. 5.

16.   Wisconsin, which gave the nation the La Follette Progressives, has only the recall, not the initiative or referendum.

chapter 5

Executives
and Administrators

THE GOVERNOR

The central figure in the executive branch, indeed in all of state government, is the governor. The governor is really the primary, driving force in state government. Both supporters and opponents look to the governor to lead, to chart a course for the state—and if this leadership is not forthcoming, state government usually just marks time or stagnates. Fortunately, most of the men and women who have captured the governorship sought the post because they had goals they wished to accomplish. But when a governor proves to be unable to lead, there seldom is anyone who can fill the resulting vacuum: legislatures consist of two contending chambers, and even unicameral Nebraska has warring factions; the courts can act only through cases brought to them, and they must depend upon others to enforce their decisions.

In recent years, many notable governors have made a national name for themselves: Abraham Ribicoff of Connecticut, Adlai Stevenson of Illinois, William Milliken of Michigan, Nelson Rockefeller of New York, Terry Sanford of North Carolina, William Scranton of Pennsylvania, and of course Jimmy Carter of Georgia and Ronald Reagan of California.

What are the characteristics of governors, whether famous or not? Most are married Caucasian males between forty and fifty, lawyers, and Democrats. Governors and those who serve as gubernatorial time schedulers report that governors spend the bulk of their time managing state government. Other time-consuming duties are working with the legislature, meeting the general public, and attending to ceremonial duties.[1] Governors must also work with the media and with local governments and the federal government, must engage in political activities, and must recruit and appoint various officeholders. Governors note that working

78

TABLE 5-1   Formal Powers of the Governor

State	Index*	State	Index
Kentucky, Massachusetts	24	Alabama, Arizona, Colorado,	17
Michigan	23	Georgia, North Dakota,	
California, South Dakota	22	Utah, West Virginia,	
Maryland, Minnesota,	21	Wisconsin	
Montana, New Jersey		Idaho, Louisiana, Oregon,	16
Hawaii, Kansas, Pennsylvania,	20	Washington	
Virginia, Wyoming		Florida, New Mexico, North	15
Alaska, Illinois, Missouri, New	19	Carolina, Oklahoma	
York, Tennessee		Arkansas, New Hampshire	14
Connecticut, Delaware, Iowa,	18	Indiana, Maine	13
Ohio, Nebraska		Mississippi, Nevada, South	12
		Carolina, Texas, Vermont	
		Rhode Island	11

SOURCE: Adapted from David R. Morgan, "Gubernatorial Power and State Policy" (paper presented at the annual meeting of the Midwest Political Science Association, Chicago, 1979), Table 1. Morgan expands and updates a similar table by Joseph A. Schlesinger, "The Politics of the Executive," in *Politics in the American States,* 2nd ed., ed. Herbert Jacob and Kenneth N. Vines (Boston: Little, Brown, 1971), Table 10.

* The higher the index, the greater the governor's power.

with the legislature and performing ceremonial activities are particularly difficult aspects of their job, as are the interference with family life and the invasions of privacy that the position entails.[2]

Governors and reformers of state government have long contended that the state's "chief" executive is not given power equal to his or her responsibilities. There is an old adage that "the governor is not given the power to govern, but merely the power to struggle to govern." Whether or not the governor is successful in this struggle, the voters will still hold him or her responsible for the performance of the executive branch.

The amount of power actually given the governor varies from state to state. Table 5-1 represents one attempt to rank governors in terms of their formal powers. The formal powers evaluated were: how long governors may stay in office, whether they must share with others responsibility for drawing up the budget, the extent of their power to appoint persons to various offices, the types of gubernatorial vetoes allowed, and the amount of gubernatorial authority to reorganize the executive branch. David Morgan has found that there is no consistent relationship between amount of formal gubernatorial power and such state characteristics as population size, manufacturing base, urbanization, and whether the state is northern or southern.[3]

It is frequently said that the governor performs several roles—for example, chief of state, chief executive, federal systems officer, legislative leader, and party leader. Looking at gubernatorial activity in terms of roles can help us categorize and clarify what functions governors perform, but it can also be highly misleading. Governors engage in a rather wide variety of activities in a typical day, as Reading 5-1 indicates. By categorizing these activities in terms of roles, we can see what part the governor plays in the total context of state government. But the role approach seems to imply that the governor consciously decides "This morning I will be chief of state, but this afternoon I'll be federal systems officer." As it looks to the governor, his or her daily activity consists of resolving conflicts between department heads or legislators or interest group leaders; trying to take care of some pressing problem on the morning's calendar of activities ("putting out fires"); fending off political opponents; polishing up his or her media image; or simply trying to wade through all of the paperwork. The role approach also imples that the governor can play only one role at a time. But as we shall see, acting as chief of state can easily be confounded with being the legislative leader. With these qualifications, we will use the concept of gubernatorial roles to better understand what governors do.

READING 5-1   A DAY IN THE LIFE OF A GOVERNOR

8:00–9:00 A.M.

Scheduled office time; no staff or calls allowed. The Governor instituted this practice after realizing that if he wanted to work alone for as much as an hour, he would have to demand it.

Reads newspaper stories on state government; dictates short congratulatory notes to juvenile delinquency director for fine press coverage on opening of new facility, and to editorial staff of major newspaper for editorial commending his support of the facility. Writes note to health director on press story about beating of retarded child in state facility.

Notes local controversy about highway location in southern part of state; makes mental note to discuss it with highway commissioner. Notes editorial and news comment that next legislative session is likely to be a rough one. Notes speculation that he is about to appoint Jones as new bank commissioner; tells press secretary to get speculation killed; he hasn't decided, but knows it won't be Jones.

Starts working on screened morning mail (a small part of mail actually received). Mayor of large city wants to be moved up on sewer project priority list; refers mayor's letter to the department. Official of smaller city complains that mass transportation money is unfairly going to larger cities; refers letter to department. National party chairman requests Governor's cooperation in upcoming congressional campaign financing; Governor writes a reminder to discuss with political advisor. Major contributor comments that branch banking law changes being considered by the staff would seriously threaten savings and loan institutions; Governor dictates letter indicating he is aware of problems and is concerned.

Reviews telegrams from environmental groups requesting that he reverse his decision to support Corps of Engineers water supply project; other telegrams from local mayor and county leaders and builders ask him to reaffirm support of project. Decides to stay with earlier decision.

9:00 A.M.

Receives delegation of legislators and mayor of suburban community seeking superhighway. Highway department briefing materials say that the road shouldn't be built at all; and if it is, it couldn't be started for 10 years, unless, of course, the Governor wants to propose new gasoline taxes to fund commitments to other areas. Governor tells delegation he is working on the problem and is sympathetic, but has other pressures for use of funds.

Asks friendly legislator to stay after the meeting, and finds out that the county chairman is wavering from support of his candidate for state senate and is unhappy with the way state party headquarters is run.

10:00 A.M.

Kicks off National Cancer Week campaign with pictures and awards plus handshaking with county chairmen. One person catches him at end of meeting and asks that he solve problem of son who is in trouble with the Army. Governor pleads inability to handle problem, but offers to try. Calls federal relations aide aside to explain, and asks if aide can work something out to get friendly Congressman to check on the case.

10:30 A.M.

Checks secretary for phone calls: has calls from two cabinet offiers, one board chairman, his wife, two legislators, one local business leader, plus three aides who "must" see him.

Starts to return phone calls, but gets interrupted by press secretary who says major local issue is developing over announced layoff of 20 employees in state TB hospital; department says it's true; press secretary recommends saying Governor is looking into it and to tell the department to hold off. Governor tells press secretary to hold off comment until he has talked to department.

Now makes calls, postponing 11 A.M. meeting with transportation secretary and budget director on additional matching money for highway construction until 11:30 A.M., and 11:30 meeting with insurance commissioner until noon.

Mental health director advises that he is having some success with local mental health directors in meetings Governor had asked him to hold. Notes in passing (obviously real reason for call) that he is having some trouble with Governor's political advisor on staffing the department and is convinced that the professionalism of the department must remain inviolate.

Arts board chairman says he's getting lots of pressure from legislators for local interest arts projects and has decided to emphasize these projects almost solely in this year's fund allocation. Reports considerable sentiment in the business community that administration spending is getting out of hand and warns against proposing any tax increases.

Wife reminds him to do something about getting some state agency to support a statewide program to put art and music in state institutions for mentally retarded. Governor calls budget director and asks for prospects of doing it. Budget director believes the art board has no new statewide projects this year—concentrating on local concerns instead. Does Governor want it changed? Governor is not sure, and budget director offers a memo later in the week explaining the choices; Governor decides to wait for the memo.

Expecting the first of the legislators on the telephone, Governor gets his legislative aide instead—his secretary explaining that he had asked that Governor talk to him before the legislator. Legislative aide says legislator is extremely upset because Governor's budget bureau and perhaps higher education coordinating council are apparently not going to approve a community college for which locals have already raised money. Legislative aide feels it is absolutely essential that the project be approved before the fall election and asks the Governor to pry the issue out of whatever agency it is in.

Legislator says just what legislative aide said he would. Governor agrees to look into it and call him back.

The other legislator whose call Governor returns is concerned about a rumor that Governor is firing employees in TB hospital and planning to close it; says he understands problem but hopes that Governor will understand his, and that he'll have to issue a press release this afternoon criticizing lack of concern with TB patients and local community if Governor goes through with it. The local business leader is also concerned about the TB issue.

12:00 noon

Secretary says transportation secretary, budget director, and transportation aide are waiting; also insurance commissioner. Meeting at 12:15 P.M. with major newspaper reporter pending, and more phone calls.

Governor has brief meeting on transportation funding. Budget director argues for passing up federal money for new highway construction on grounds of Governor's austerity program. Transportation secretary notes that funds are 80 percent federal and argues for a go-ahead. Governor says he'll read both memoranda and decide after checking with executive assistant.

Governor is scheduled to leave at 1 P.M. for a ribbon-cutting highway opening about an hour away. Asks secretary to see if he can scrub highway opening and to hold calls, and says he will see the reporter after press secretary has a minute to brief him. Press secretary says press is all over him on TB thing—what has the Governor decided? Governor asks secretary to get health director on phone, finds he is addressing public health association lunch right now—does the Governor want to interrupt? No, have him call just as soon as he is through speaking.

Reporter comes in to begin interview on whether Governor is taking position in key party leadership fight over mayoral nomination in eastern part of the state; Governor sets ground rules as background and begins to expound on his preferences.

Secretary buzzes on intercom and reports that top aides (all of whom are now waiting to see him) advise OK to cancel highway opening, highway commissioner will handle but Governor should call mayor and apologize because there may be a big crowd which the mayor gathered. Governor tells her to call mayor on his behalf and explain situation, and that he will call the mayor himself later in the day.

Interview concluded, secretary brings in lunch that he was originally scheduled to have during trip to ribbon cutting.

1:15 P.M.

Health director on the phone reminds Governor that there are no more TB patients to be cared for, that most of the people in TB sanitorium are alcoholics who can be readily cared for elsewhere, that firings are part of his budget plan, and that he has no funds to continue employees. Governor finds employees were offered jobs elsewhere, but many of them don't want to leave the community. Director says he can keep the facility open as long as the Governor provides the money. Governor asks press secretary to tell press of meeting on subject at 2 P.M.

Asks secretary to tell legislator to please hold off the press conference criticizing the TB closing for another day. She says she has had three calls from union leaders and a couple of legislative calls protesting the closing and that his political advisor wants to talk about them as well as other things. Governor sets up meeting for 2 P.M. with health director, budget director, press secretary and political advisor.

Secretary provides messages from other calls: . . . Three different people with candidates other than Jones called to express hope that the press story on Jones was not true. One wanted to talk to Governor before an appointment is made so he could tell him some confidential information about Jones . . . Jones called, said he didn't know he was being considered, but would be happy to talk about the job . . . Chairman of the commission on higher education said please make no commitment on the community college matter without talking to him. Budget director called with the same message . . . Federal relations aide called, wants a decision this afternoon on what to ask Senator Smith to do on strip-mine control amendments affecting state regulation. Senate votes tomorrow, and the Senator wants to go with Governor's position. Memo in in-box (which has been resting untouched on desk since 10 A.M.).

1:45 P.M.

Governor tries to call federal relations aide while reading memorandum. Can't reach, he is on the way back from Washington. Governor asks secretary to find out whether he has talked to head of state environmental protection agency on subject . . . no one knows, he'll call in about an hour.

Governor tells secretary to tell insurance commissioner he is sorry to keep him waiting and for him to get lunch and check back about 3 P.M. Secretary says aides are still waiting, some of their business is pretty urgent, plus remember the 4 P.M. meeting on office space, and that he has an engagement this evening.

2:12 P.M.

Meeting with health director and others (now including legislative personnel and legal advisors) on TB matter. Political and legislative advisors say they don't care how we got where we are, it is imperative that the state not be laying off employees right before election, and with key labor negotiations going on in other departments. Personnel advisor tends to agree, but notes that employees had some prior knowledge of likely layoffs. Budget director and health director are adamant on merits of closing the facility; health director says he will keep it open if budget is increased; budget director says no chance, the legislature cut the overall health budget last year. Legal advisor proposes compromise to keep the facility open until after election, funds to come from health budget, but administration would have to seek some supplemental appropriation to reimburse health budget. Health director is dubious, budget director opposed, personnel advisor says that where he comes from, if you are going to bite a bullet you do it all at once, not in stages. Meeting drags on. Obvious that these layoffs are just the beginning if Governor stays with health director's plan.

Meeting continues while Governor takes call from federal relations aide. Yes, he has talked to the environmental protection agency, and the position he recommends on strip mining is concurred in by them. Governor returns to TB meeting. Finds potential solution is to have mental health department take over part of facility instead of closing it. Unknown if mental health director will agree; health director is on phone to him now.

Governor leaves TB meeting with legal advisor to discuss status of suit by welfare rights organization to require higher welfare payments.

3:20 P.M.

Returns to TB meeting, which now includes mental health director. Mental health director says he can't make a final decision now, needs to review the facility and prospects for transferring some patients and doctors from another of his facilities. Press secretary proposes to tell media the administration is looking into new possibility and layoffs are deferred. All agree, except budget director, who argues for closing, and political advisor, who urges a solution that will hold for a few months, not a few weeks. Governor accepts the solution anyhow. Instructs press secretary to inform media and legislative advisor to inform local legislators.

3:35 P.M.

Secretary advises that insurance commissioner is back, other advisors are waiting, and Governor hasn't done anything about in-box. Plus more messages: . . . Neighboring Governor called and wants to discuss developing a common regional position on safety rules for zinc mining. Governor has secretary call federal relations aide to get in touch with neighboring Governor's staff to see what can be worked out . . . Press secretary calls with information that P.M. papers are breaking a story that a legislative leader of the Governor's party is suspected of selling real estate to the highway department, using inside information on new highway location . . . Highway commissioner is back from ribbon cutting and needs to talk . . . President of largest state university would like to chat briefly about prospects of a new law school . . . Speaker of the house wants to talk, important and personal . . . Secretary has arranged the scheduling meeting at 5 P.M., after the office space meeting.

Insurance commissioner is still waiting, has staff with him and two hours worth of visual aids. Governor calls the commissioner in alone—commissioner is prepared to talk about the new insurance consumer protection program he was asked to prepare; meeting was rescheduled twice already. Governor tells him he's sorry about the scheduling problem, asks him to leave the written material and promises to try to read it tonight and to make apologies to his staff.

Calls political advisor in. Asks about speaker's call; finds that speaker wants to be reassured that Governor would not back rival for speakership even if party wins handily in fall election. Political advisor says leave him hanging for awhile; call tomorrow and say that Governor doesn't control the membership but appreciates his support in the past, etc.

Political advisor discusses bank commissioner appointment and recommends someone other than Jones; Governor agrees and asks him to prepare press release. Political advisor stops at door to remind him that he had agreed to spend more time away from the office and with the people; says he must schedule more local events like the ribbon cutting today and then keep to the schedule; asks if mayor who arranged it has been called yet.

4:30 P.M.

Governor calls the mayor and has a 15-minute conversation in which the mayor says pretty much what the political advisor did. Agrees to check a bridge situation within city limits and instructs secretary to check the point with the highway commissioner.

4:45 P.M.

Governor begins the 4 P.M. office space meeting, knowing he still has the scheduling meeting and a couple of calls to go and that he should be receiving guests at the mansion at 6:30. The meeting requires his presence because the public works department, which allocates office space, is at loggerheads with the agencies. The agencies want more space—whether they have to lease it, get private companies to build it, or whatever—while public works wants to hold them off and build a new office building which would require the Governor's approval. The meeting is incredibly dull, with charts and graphs about office space, so at 5 P.M., the Governor leaves, indicating he has another meeting and leaving two or three agency heads, budget director and one aide with instructions to work out a recommendation for him that they can agree on.

5:00 P.M.

Handles more messages. Has secretary get the facts on the law school from budget bureau and commissioner of higher education before calling president of university back tomorrow. Reminds secretary to call the speaker tomorrow. Calls the highway commissioner to find out what the mayor has already told him.

Has secretary tell aide who is waiting to talk about a project for cooperation between university students and law enforcement department to wait until tomorrow. Has consumer protection advisor do likewise.

Reviews brief remarks prepared for dinner session with group of business leaders. Remembers that one of the leaders is board chairman of the community college that all the fuss was about earlier in the day. Asks an aide to quickly collect the views of the higher education commissioner and the budget director and give him a briefing before he leaves the office.

5:30 P.M.

Governor enters scheduling meeting. His secretary asks if he wants the aide left in the office space meeting or brought into the meeting; he answers "both." The scheduling meeting is no different from the last one, not likely to be different from the next.

The political advisor wants Governor to make fund-raising appearances at five geographically diverse places in the next week, appear at supermarkets with two legislative candidates, and attend two rallies for legislative candidates. In addition, advisor suggests strongly that Governor drop in at the Chinese-American society dinner next Saturday night and appear at a teacher's convention the following day.

Secretary says wife wants to hold Saturday all day at home and prefers to spend that evening with friends. Wife does not want to travel on Sunday, secretary says, reminding Governor that one of his children is making his debut as a high school football player on Friday. Governor's scheduler ticks off the remaining demands for time the following week:

- One state trade association meeting (already accepted) and two more which request his presence and will schedule for a major address if he can make it;
- One statewide labor meeting;
- Three requests for local political functions, beyond the ones the political advisor knows the Governor had;
- A request from the federal relations aide to visit the congressional delegation in Washington next week and deliver testimony for the National Governors' Association before a Senate subcommittee;
- A request from two key agency directors to accompany them to Washington to resolve problems with federal agencies;
- A request from the press aide for a news conference announcing the new bank commissioner, a backgrounder with a representative of a national magazine, and at least one additional general-purpose news conference during the week;
- Six cabinet officers and three board or commission chairmen wanting to discuss one subject or another; and
- Three county chairmen, four legislators, five major contributors, six local delegations seeking highways or other state construction, and the usual flow of private citizens wanting to see their Governor.

In addition, the schedulers report back on various events the Governor requests be scheduled, which have not been scheduled yet, including a visit to a mental hospital for inspection and employee relations, a meeting with educational advisors on potential for improving the state aid formula, a meeting with the planning director and several cabinet officers on land-use planning, and the remainder of the meetings on the consumer protection program similar to that with the insurance commissioner today.

Secretary reports Governor should take one complete day off just to concentrate on the paperwork in the in-box.

The scheduling meeting goes on to 6 P.M., at which time the governor expresses preferences, delegates the exact schedule to the group, and receives a delegation from the office space meeting seeking to resolve a couple of questions. Indicating that he has to shower and change to be ready at the mansion by 6:30, Governor asks them either to write it up or talk to him in the morning (not remembering that tomorrow's schedule is worse than today's).

His secretary shouts out a couple of other phone calls; he says "tomorrow" and leaves office accompanied by aide trying to brief him on the community college situation, matching him pace for pace as he walks out. The community college situation is complicated indeed, so Governor decides not to decide yet and to finesse the question if it comes up in the evening.

After a quick shower and change accompanied by as much recitation of family affairs as time permits, Governor finds himself in the receiving line not quite promptly at 6:40, facing the ordeal of trying to remember 40 people whom he knows he should know. Cocktail conversation centers on bank regulation issues, exhortations to avoid tax increases, discussion of the business climate, costs of workers' compensation, and some general discussion of national politics. After dinner Governor talks briefly about some of his major programs and the need for good business climate in the state and retires to family quarters about 9:45 P.M.

In these moments of potential relaxation, Governor retrieves in-box correspondence from his briefcase. First, the "information only" items consisting of magazine articles, FYI memos from the staff, and the like; these he scans briefly, primarily to see if there is any action he need take. A memo from the welfare secretary which indicates negotiations may break down with hospitals over Medicaid reimbursement rates is sent to his political advisor with a question, "Can we handle this if negotiations fail?"

Now the "action" items. Some 20 letters to sign prepared by staff; 16 are OK, two require rewrite instructions to someone, and two more the Governor rewrites himself. Now it is 10:15 P.M., and his definite cutoff time for relaxation and talking to his family, even though he has five or six complicated problems, including the community college issue, left hanging.

SOURCE: Center for Policy Research, National Governors Association, *Governing the American States: A Handbook for New Governors* (Washington, D.C.: National Governors Association, 1978), pp. 10–20.

Chief of State

In his role as chief of state, the governor acts as a symbol for the state. This symbolism entails a great deal of ceremonial activity, such as "receiving foreign dignitaries, receiving petitions, announcing national dill pickle week, crowning the queen of the gooseberry festival, shooting film extolling the virtues of his state or its products, presiding over the opening of the state fair or the graduation of the state police academy, and having his picture taken with the state's oldest veteran."[4] It has been noted that governors complain that ceremonial duties are very time-consuming, but they are also a way to build political goodwill for oneself, to acknowledge ("stroke") various powerful interest groups, and perhaps to intimidate present or potential opponents.

Chief Executive

The governor is frequently described as chief executive, but how much actual control he or she has over the executive branch is a matter of some dispute. When Glenn Abney and Thomas Lauth surveyed 778 state department heads they concluded that "it is quite likely that the administrative machinery of many state governments remains under the control of administrators rather than the governor."[5] When asked to name the actor with the most influence on their departmental programs and objectives, only 38 percent of the administrators chose the governor. Probably one unintended consequence of state government reform has been to increase the power of bureaucrats in making public policy.

The executive, or administrative, branch of government is responsible for carrying out the laws—that is, doing the day-to-day work of government. This part of state government is so important that it will be considered separately at the end of this chapter.

At least in theory, administrators are under the direction of the governor; it significantly enhances the governor's influence if he or she has appointed the state's workers (as in a patronage state such as Pennsylvania) rather than having to direct workers whose positions are protected by the civil service (as in a merit state such as Wisconsin). In every state, there are some officials that governors always get to appoint: their personal staff, heads of most departments, and members of some boards and commissions. It is ironic that Wisconsin, which initially fought patronage, has recently extended political control over the civil service bureaucracy by increasing the number of top-level agency political appointees. The appointive power of governors is greatest in the area of public safety (such as disaster preparedness and the state police) and lowest in purchasing and pre-auditing. Another significant area of appointive control is budgeting and planning.[6]

On the other hand, governors may find it very difficult to remove someone they have appointed to serve on a state commission or to head a department, for these people are usually afforded the due-process protections of notice and hearing. Getting rid of one's unsatisfactory appointees may thus be a drawn-out affair fraught with political embarrassment for the governor. It might be better to wait out the appointee's term. Fortunately, such instances are few; more difficult is waiting for the terms of *previous* governors' appointees to expire.

Reading 5-1, "A Day in the Life of a Governor," demonstrates clearly the time pressures that plague governors. This case study also shows how a reliable personal staff can help a governor manage his or her time. Most members of gubernatorial staffs are relatively young (under forty), have worked in the governor's election campaign, are generalists rather than specialists, and are engaged primarily in the creation, projection, and protection of the governor's public image.[7] There are several principal staff positions. A *policy secretary* converts the governor's general campaign speeches into concrete legislation by developing policy proposals with state agencies and by working with the legislature on behalf of the governor's legislative program. A *budget director* draws up the state budget. An *administrative secretary* handles appointments to boards and commissions and acts as a liaison with political party officials. A *legal secretary* advises the governor on the constitutionality of bills and the use of reprieves, commutations, and pardons. An *intergovernmental relations officer* works with federal agencies and the federal government. A *press secretary* (sometimes known uncomplimentarily as a "flack") keeps up a steady flow of press releases and stories, all intended to remind the media and hence the public of what a fine job this governor is doing. Finally, a *staff director* or *chief of staff* supervises all these staffers and their assistants.[8]

There is some controversy regarding what role the chief of staff should play. "Democratic governors tend to organize their staffs in a diffused, horizontal pattern and Republican governors follow the classical pyramidal, hierarchically arranged model" with the chief of staff in charge.[9] The Democratic approach, in which authority is delegated by the governor in a generous and somewhat overlapping fashion, is said to provide the governor with varied sources of information and to increase his or her range of options among different courses of action. The hierarchy model with the chief of staff at the top is faulted for allowing the latter to act as a "gatekeeper" who insulates the governor from the public and from information he or she may need to make wise decisions. Proponents of a strong chief of staff respond that many states have well over one hundred departments or agencies that are supposed to report to the governor. If someone did not act as a screening agent, the governor would be overwhelmed. Some research indicates that strong gatekeepers do not seal the governor off from the public, but rather "clear some of the detail work that comes to a governor's desk, thereby allowing the governor to get out from behind that desk to hear from and to communicate with his or her constituents; . . . the gatekeeper role may, paradoxically, contribute to a more open gubernatorial administration."[10] Whichever staff arrangement is preferred, it should be clear that those persons who are clustered around the governor are powerful people who have the capacity to affect significantly the workings of state government.

In sixteen states, the governor can reorganize the administrative branch as long as his actions are not blocked by one or more chambers of the state legislature. The purpose of executive-branch reorganization is to rationalize administrative structure and to make the plethora of departments, boards, agencies, and commissions more responsive to gubernatorial control. However, interest groups may feel that a fragmented and disorganized executive branch increases their influence, and they will fight the governor's reorganization. Because reorganization may take more of the governor's time and political capital than it yields in administrative efficiency, this power is seldom used.

Probably the most significant action of a state's chief executive is drawing up the budget. Most of the important decisions of state government are reflected in programs that require the spending of money—for example, financing education or welfare or transportation. Of course, states can also make significant decisions (which are often high in ideological content) that do *not* require the spending of money—for example, legalizing homosexual activity between consenting adults in private. But the key point is that money talks, and it is the governor who speaks with a very loud voice because it is he or she who draws up the budget. The governor's political priorities are expressed in dollar signs for all to see. As we will note when we discuss the governor's role as legislative leader, the state legislature usually does not make drastic changes in the governor's budget. Hence, what the governor favors will usually receive at least sufficient funding, and what he or she considers unimportant may be severely shortchanged. In all but two states, formulation of the budget document is controlled by the governor; this is one of the most significant reforms of state government, and one that has come about largely in the last twenty years. However, earmarked taxes and statutory formulas governing how state money shall be spent restrict the ability of governors to change dramatically state spending priorities.

Two powers that governors have possessed since colonial times are military powers and clemency powers. The governor is commander in chief of the state's militia, the national guard. In an emergency such as a riot or civil disorder, tornado, hurricane, flood, earthquake, or drought, the governor can order out the militia to maintain order and to provide essential services. The troops receive specific direction from a trained military officer appointed by the governor, but the decision to send them into action rests with the governor.

The governor's clemency powers involve reprieves, commutations, pardons, and parole for persons convicted of a serious crime. A *reprieve* is a postponement in the imposition of a sentence. For example, a prisoner who is sentenced to die in the state penitentiary may receive a sixty-day reprieve that will allow his or her lawyers to file additional legal motions. A *commutation* is a reduction in a prisoner's sentence—for example, from death to life imprisonment. A *pardon* frees a person from further punishment for a crime, and a *parole* allows a prisoner who has served part of a sentence to be released subject to various restrictions.

In thirty-one states, the governor has complete clemency powers, and in seven others he or she has final authority after a preliminary review by a special board; two states give the governor principal control over clemency, and the remaining ten grant all clemency power to special boards.[11] Regardless of the extent of their clemency power, governors are usually quite cautious in acting as a "thirteenth juror" by granting mercy to someone who has been convicted of a serious crime. When they do exercise their clemency powers, they do so perhaps because they believe the convicted person is innocent, the sentence was too severe for the crime committed, mitigating circumstances surrounded the crime, or the convicted person is in poor health and would not survive a term in prison.

When requested to do so by the governor of another state, a governor has a moral duty to *extradite* (return) a fugitive from that state. However, the U.S. Supreme Court has ruled that no governor can be *forced* to return a prisoner; hence it is a "moral duty." Occasionally, governors refuse to extradite a prisoner.[12]

An important duty of the governor in his or her role as executive or administrator is to coordinate state policies. This is a duty that no one else in state government is as advantageously situated to perform. The need for such coordination is obvious: bills introduced in the state legislature are the product of a multiplicity of sources; numerous legislative committees and political actors shape important legislation; different state and local agencies carry out the laws that are enacted. The result is ample opportunities for

> undirected and uncoordinated implementation of public policy . . . [A] side from the office and person of the governor, there is no one in a position to provide constant and authoritative review and coordination of policy—the kind of review and coordination needed to minimize program duplication and overlap, . . . to see to it that certain vital problems are not forgotten or ignored, and to make sure that one set of state policies does not counteract others. . . . [He or she] is in a position to maintain some amount of overall perspective on state government activities.[13]

The governor receives some assistance in furthering this overall perspective because he or she can appoint some sympathetic department heads and some members of regulatory commissions.

Federal Systems Officer

As we saw in Chapter 2, states have become heavily dependent on federal grants and are competing fiercely with one another for a larger slice of the federal-aid pie. Governors and their staffs must work with the state's congressional delegation, and the governor must personally lobby for funds in Washington, D.C. About half of the states maintain offices in the nation's capital in order to secure grant money and to guarantee that federal programs are enacted and administered in a way that furthers the state's interest. Some grant programs designate the governor as the program planner and channel money for the program through his or her office. Furthermore, governors must work with the governors of neighboring states to solve regional problems, such as air or water pollution, and with local officials to administer state programs.

Legislative Leader

Every governor has a legislative program, a number of bills he or she believes the legislature must pass in order to solve the state's problems. The typical governor is usually quite successful in getting this program through the legislature, but success depends on a number of factors: the governor's popularity with the public, as reflected in public opinion polls or as gauged by competent observers such as legislators; whether the governor's party controls none, one, or both of the legislative chambers— and whether party members feel that they must support a governor of their own party; how well the governor can work with his or her party's legislative leadership and how competent these persons are; and finally, whether the governor has chosen popular issues on which to stake his or her prestige.

A governor whose party has a legislative majority in a two-party state is in a particularly advantageous position. Fellow partisans in the legislature

> are usually sympathetic to the governor and his program, and some of them are likely to be intensely loyal. The party is organized, sometimes under skillful leadership, and it is most likely to vote with the highest degree of cohesion on issues that are of greatest importance to the governor. The members have a stake in the governor's success, and some of them believe that their fate at the polls is tied to his.[14]

Under such conditions, a governor is likely to exercise overwhelming policy leadership, especially if he or she can work effectively with party leaders.

The governor of a one-party state benefits from the absence of an effective opposition party, but this situation has some peculiar disadvantages. The lack of an opposition party may mean that the governor has no dependable legislative majority and must assemble a personal following in order to pass his or her legislative program. On the other hand, governors may handpick their legislative leaders (especially in southern states), which strengthens their hand.

A more common situation is *divided control* of state government: the governor and at least one chamber of the legislature are of different parties. This occurs about half of the time and is especially common in states in which Democrats and Republicans are politically competitive.[15] A number of factors account for divided control. The minority party in a state dominated by the other party may field a candidate who can capture the governorship, but may be able to take only a few seats in the legislature. Incumbent governors may lose their legislative majority in the midterm election because their administration has become unpopular or because national political trends no longer favor them. Or there may be gerrymandering of legislative seats. When control is divided, the governor must make nonpartisan appeals, distribute patronage to both parties, and be prepared to compromise in order to achieve his or her legislative goals.

Two prominent observers have written that the varying amounts of patronage available in different states are a major reason governors vary in legislative influence:

> The governor can offer a wide variety of services and favors to the legislator's district. State funds are available to build new roads and bridges, to improve the old ones, and to build or improve a variety of other facilities, such as parks, hospitals, and community colleges. These projects are important to legislators because their constituents are usually far more interested in a new road or project for the district than in any aspect of the legislator's voting record. Highways are a particularly valuable form of patronage. . . .
>
> Another form of patronage is the awarding of state contracts, whether for highway work, the supply of state liquor stores, the purchase of textbooks, the insurance of state buildings, or the bonding of state employees. Most contracts for these purposes must be let through competitive bidding, but in most states, some types of contracts are exempt from these regulations. . . . Legislators associated with legal, insurance, and other firms sometimes do business with the state. Because the state legislator (unlike the congressman) is a part-time representative with a full-time, long-term interest in some other profession or occupation, he is more receptive than the congressman to patronage offers that benefit him personally.[16]

Jobs, roads, and contracts can help the governor win legislative victories in any kind of state, but they may be particularly helpful in one-party areas such as the South, where the governor must assemble a personal following to secure passage of his or her legislative program. In states that are more rural or are poorer, government "pork" can have great political appeal.

In addition to securing the passage of legislation they favor, governors also attempt to defeat bills they oppose by using the veto or the threat of a veto. All governors except the governor of North Carolina have a veto, and they use it on about 5 percent of all bills. Veto use varies from state to state: over one quarter of all bills are vetoed in New York, but none in Vermont or Wyoming.[17] Veto use is higher in states with divided control or in one-party states in which the governor and legislature belong to different factions of the same party.

Legislators are especially concerned about vetoes of *pork-barrel* bills, pet bills that benefit their particular district or constituents. The possibility of such a gubernatorial veto is a powerful inducement for legislators to support the governor's measures, as Reading 5-2 clearly demonstrates.

Approximately 6 percent of governors' vetoes are overridden by the legislature, especially in situations of divided control. Governors are almost always successful in sustaining their vetoes because they need the assistance of only one third or two fifths of the legislators to do so, or because they have used their veto on that myriad of bills the legislature passes at the very end of the session. The tendency of state legislatures to pass a large number of bills, often the most important ones, at the very end of the session also increases the potency of the *threat* of a veto. With adjournment only a few hours away and with half a dozen major bills still to be voted upon, harried legislators may need only the threat of a veto to kill a bill or to make major changes in it. In addition, governors in fifteen states have a *pocket veto*, which they can employ after the legislature has adjourned.

Two special forms of the veto are the item veto and the amendatory veto. The *item veto*, found in forty-three states, allows the governor to

---

READING 5-2 THE GOVERNOR'S THREAT OF A VETO IN KENTUCKY

When the 5 percent sales tax bill left the House for the Senate yesterday, unscathed after being subjected to a multitude of amendments and two days of fervent oratory, it marked a victory for Republican Gov. Louie B. Nunn and GOP representation in the lower chamber.

But it couldn't have been done without the Democrats.

During the five hours of oratory yesterday, Rep. Norbert Blume, D-Louisville, explained how 57 Democrats can match votes with 43 Republicans and lose:

"Last night, many an arm was twisted."

One that was twisted is fastened to Rep. William Cox, Democratic freshman from Madisonville. He drew applause from both parties when he took time to explain on the floor how the power of the governor's office is traditionally used in Kentucky to capture votes on key issues in the legislature.

Tuesday, Cox supported the food-medicine-clothing amendment to the sales tax bill. Yesterday, in a vote to reconsider the amendment, he opposed it. He explained why:

"Today, each of us must vote for what we think are the best interests of our people," Cox said. "Yesterday I let my emotion and dedication to my Democratic colleagues override my sense of responsibility to my district."

Cox represents Hopkins County. He told the House that buried among the thick pages of appropriations in Nunn's $2.47 billion budget bill are projects for Hopkins County that total some $1 million.

Included are $500,000 for an area vocational school, $330,000 for a community college, $75,000 for airport improvements, plus money for tuberculosis and mental hospitals in Hopkins County.

Although Cox did not say it, all legislators know that the governor holds the power of "line-item veto" over the budget that will cross his desk. He can approve the whole document by signing it, but he can also veto any simple appropriation with a short pen stroke.

"When you receive much, much must be given," Cox said. "While I know enactment of a 5 percent sales tax will impose a considerable burden on some of my constituents, I know they are the ones who will benefit most from this budget. . . ."

SOURCE: "Legislators Explain Nunn's Fiscal Arm-Twisting," *Louisville* (Ky.) *Courier-Journal*, March 7, 1968, p. B-4. Reprinted by permission.

reduce or eliminate appropriations in spending bills. Hence, the governor may choose among various appropriations; he or she cannot be presented with a spending bill on a take-it-or-leave-it basis, as can the president. The governor of Massachusetts may use the item veto even on nonfiscal matters in appropriations bills—a truly significant grant of power.

The *amendatory veto*, found in Illinois, Montana, New Jersey, and Massachusetts, can be a powerful tool for changing the substance of legislation. If the governor dislikes certain parts of an otherwise acceptable bill, he or she need not sign it or veto it in its entirety, but may return the bill to the legislature with specific recommendations for change. These recommendations may be accepted or overridden by the legislature. More often than not they are accepted. Somewhat related to the amendatory veto is the power of legislatures in thirty-three states to recall a bill before the governor gets a chance to veto it. Changes can then be made in the bill to satisfy the governor's objections to it. This procedure saves time and effort for all involved, and reduces the number of vetoes made per session.

A final facet of the governor's role as legislative leader is his or her power to call special sessions of the legislature. This power is particularly important in those states in which the legislature meets for only a limited amount of time each year, but it is used even in California, which has a full-time legislature. The governor can call a special session to run concurrently with a regular session. The purpose of calling a special session is to force the legislature to face some issue the governor wants it to deal with: the legislature may consider only those matters mentioned in the governor's call. The governor thus turns the political spotlight on the legislature and forces it to take the heat if it fails to pass the legislation he or she desires.

Party Leader

The final gubernatorial role is that of party leader. As we have seen, this role can greatly help a governor get his or her legislative program passed in a two-party state in which he or she has a legislative majority. The position of party leader must be earned—it is not inherited. A governor may have to share the title of "The State's Number One Democrat" or "Number One Republican" with a high-ranking United States senator or a popular mayor or even a former governor who still has political aspirations. Many governors are not leaders of the entire political party, but only their faction of the party. This is especially the case if the incumbent governor had to engage in a bruising primary battle to get the party's nomination.

Interestingly, interviews with former governors reveal that governors do not place a great deal of importance on being a party leader. The role helps them to deal with fellow partisans in the legislature, or to obtain sympathetic treatment of the state's problems when the president is a member of the governor's party, or even to secure renomination. But governors report that they pay little attention to party ideology and seldom consult with party leaders in formulating the administration's policies.[18]

As the leader of his or her political party, the governor is called upon to distribute patronage, the political "loaves and fishes," to the party faithful. The amount of patronage available varies from state to state: dispensing political jobs is a very potent political weapon in Indiana or Illinois but is relatively insignificant in strong civil service states such as Wisconsin and California. Even if a state has a civil service system on paper, there are ways of getting around it. For example, many "temporary" employees may work for decades, or large numbers of workers may be put in an exempt category. Under the widely used *rule-of-three*, the appointing authority may select from the three highest-ranking applicants. Even if the loyal party member scores only third, he or she will always be selected.

One interesting kind of patronage carries very little monetary reward for the recipient but may provide substantial psychological satisfaction. This is the governor's appointments to boards or commissions such as the state's Arts Council, a higher education governing board, or a mental health board. Such positions may pay only travel expenses or carry a modest per-diem allotment. But wealthy individuals avidly seek them because to hold such a post means that one is a "concerned" person who wants to improve the state, or that one can pursue an interest (the arts, education, mental health), or that one can wield governmental power without having to undergo the grubby rigors of an election campaign. Many of these positions go to important campaign contributors and are the state-level counterpart of federal ambassadorships.

Patronage can be an effective tool in building and maintaining a strong party organization. Those who work for the party at election time can be rewarded with state jobs that will tide them over until the next election. The city of Chicago and the state of Illinois demonstrate this. The governor can also keep a legislator "voting right" by threatening to fire the legislator's supporter who holds a patronage job, or by threatening to cancel a valued contract.

Patronage has recently been somewhat circumscribed by the U.S. Supreme Court. The Court has ruled that before an employee of the opposing party may be fired to make way for an employee of one's own party, the hiring authority must "demonstrate that party affiliation is an appropriate requirement for the effective performance of the public office involved."[19] Employees fired for being members of the opposite party may sue to retain their jobs; courts will have to determine case by case the appropriateness of such terminations.

Further restricting the use of patronage is the increasing complexity of state government. A position to be filled may require a specific technical skill, and loyal party members possessing that skill may be hard to find. The governor or a party leader now says "We need a seismic engineer who happens to be a Democrat" rather than, as formerly, "We need a good Democrat who may know something about seismic engineering." The difference may be subtle but it is nonetheless significant.

Finally, there is always the problem of disappointing the unsuccessful office seekers. It has long been said that for every position filled, the governor creates "one ingrate and nine enemies." Even though the governor may have an appointments secretary or a political (patronage) adviser to rely upon for assistance, the duty of dispensing the goodies may be very time-consuming and may appear to the governor as more of a curse than a blessing.

GUBERNATORIAL ELECTIONS

The election of a governor is the premier state political event. It is then that the most important state issues are likely to be debated, and possibly a new course for the state charted. About three fourths of the states have moved their gubernatorial elections away from the years in which a president is selected. Unless there is an election for U.S. senator, this move concentrates the voter's attention on state issues—and removes presidential coattails. New Jersey, Virginia, Louisiana, Mississippi, and Kentucky have isolated gubernatorial elections entirely by staging them in odd-numbered years.

Gubernatorial candidates are most likely to come from the state legislature, with the lieutenant governorship also being an excellent springboard to the state's highest office. The positions of attorney general, secretary of state, and, recently, member of the U.S. House of Representatives are also excellent stepping-stones.

If an incumbent governor is seeking reelection, he or she has some formidable assets: high name identification; usually superior access to campaign funding; and the disposition of voters, especially members of the governor's party, to stick with experience. But incumbency is a two-edged sword. One observer of Illinois politics has written:

> The governor faces such severe problems, in Illinois and in most of the states, that he speedily wears out his political appeal. The whole state is his constituency and in a state as complex as Illinois it becomes impossible for all interests to be pleased. Rising costs of state government have tended to involve the governor in controversies which lessen the chances of his re-election.[20]

The governor has a record to defend against an opponent who may not carry this burden and who has the luxury of laying every state problem, controversy, or scandal on the governor's doorstep. Furthermore, the voters may believe that the governor has more control over state government than he or she really has, and they may wonder why he or she has not done more about taxes, inflation, busing, or crime. Despite all of these drawbacks, only about one third of incumbent governors seeking reelection since 1940 have been defeated, and their vulnerability is decreasing.[21]

Increased taxes may loom as a particularly troublesome issue for governors seeking reelection, for they are caught in a difficult five-way crossfire: (1) the public wants improved state services, which are increasingly expensive in inflationary times; (2) taxes are a salient issue to the public, which wants tax relief; (3) almost all state constitutions require a balanced budget; (4) the Reagan administration is reducing federal aid to the states; (5) cutting state services will harm the needy and will allow the governor's opponents to charge him or her with being callous. Governors who choose to seek a tax increase are advised to do so at the very beginning of their term—and to hope that the voters' memories are short! Some scant solace comes from the finding that from 1948 to 1964, governors who sought increased taxes generally did not suffer significantly at the polls.[22] But some did, and that may be enough warning.

After governors leave the statehouse, whether voluntarily or involuntarily, they usually hold no other office. It is this fact that has caused some commentators to call the governorship a political dead end. But about 46 percent do gain some other office—for example, United States senator, member of the President's cabinet (especially western governors as secretary of the interior), or even the presidency itself, as in the case of two former Georgia and California chief executives.[23] Jimmy Carter and Ronald Reagan were able to break a long monopoly that U.S. senators had held on the White House.

Should a governor leave the statehouse in midterm because of death or resignation (for example, to allow his or her successor to appoint him or her to the U.S. Senate), the line of succession usually begins with the lieutenant governor, but occasionally with the president of the senate or even the secretary of state. In 1977–78, Arizona had a startling series of "revolving-door" governors: the incumbent resigned to become U.S. ambassador to Argentina and was succeeded by the person who had been secretary of state for thirty years. This man unfortunately died in office after six months and was succeeded by the attorney general, who later won the governorship in his own right.

THE GOVERNORSHIP IN PERSPECTIVE

The American governorship, indeed nearly all of state government, has changed dramatically since midcentury. New responsibilities have been thrust upon the state, more competent people are being elected to state office, and, perhaps most important, state decision makers are coming to look at themselves in a new light, as men and women who can solve state problems and meet the needs of their people. Larry Sabato has captured this change in the title of his book on the governorship, *Goodbye to Good-Time Charlie: The American Governor Transformed*. The governor and state legislators are far less likely these days to be people who meet in Tallahassee or Pierre or Santa Fe for a few months in order to carouse with each other and with lobbyists, pass a few laws, and generally have a good time away from their more important regular occupations.

Governors are necessarily becoming men and women of genuine ability, and they are also receiving the tools to do an effective job. The formal powers of governors (ranked in Table 5-1), such as tenure potential, budgetary powers, appointive power, veto power, and reorganization authority, have all been strengthened in recent years. Probably foremost among these is *tenure potential*—the length of a governor's term and the number of consecutive terms he or she may serve. States have recently moved away from the highly restrictive two-year term or the four-year term with a one-term limit. See Table 5-2. Longer tenure is important

TABLE 5-2 Gubernatorial Tenure

Four-Year Term with Unlimited Reeligibility (18 States)	Four-Year Term with a Limit of Two Consecutive Terms (24 States)	Single Four-Year Term (4 States)	Two-Year Term with Unlimited Reeligibility (4 States)
Arizona	Alabama	Kentucky	Arkansas
California	Alaska	Mississippi	New Hampshire
Colorado	Delaware	New Mexico	Rhode Island
Connecticut	Florida	Virginia	Vermont
Idaho	Georgia		
Illinois	Hawaii		
Iowa	Indiana		
Massachusetts	Kansas		
Michigan	Louisiana		
Minnesota	Maine		
Montana	Maryland		
New York	Missouri		
North Dakota	Nebraska		
Texas	Nevada		
Utah	New Jersey		
Washington	North Carolina		
Wisconsin	Ohio		
Wyoming	Oklahoma		
	Oregon		
	Pennsylvania		
	South Carolina		
	South Dakota		
	Tennessee		
	West Virginia		

SOURCE: *Book of the States, 1984–85* (Lexington, Ky.: Council of State Governments, 1984), p. 49.

because to have a significant impact on state policy—for example, through budgetary decisions—a governor needs time to plan and to see these decisions through. Furthermore, longevity strengthens the governor's informal powers, such as patronage and superior access to the media (and hence superior access to public opinion). If the governor can be in power for eight or more years, rather than a mere four years, opponents are less likely to take a political cheap shot at him or her. Moreover, it is illogical to deprive the public of the services of a governor who is performing well, simply because he or she has served eight years.

Other ways in which the governorship has changed are increased gubernatorial salaries, greater funding for staff support, and increased financial assistance for the governor-elect during the crucial transition period between administrations. Coleman Ransone cites other particularly significant changes.[24] For one, most states are now either strongly Democratic or overwhelmingly Democratic (see Table 3-1). This shift of political power has led to widespread instances of divided government. Finally, Ransone argues that the governor is becoming less of a policy maker and more of an administrator. However, as we have seen, governors have great difficulty controlling the executive branch of government.

Beyond any formal or informal powers are the characteristics of the man or woman who holds the governor's chair. Is this person *willing* to use whatever powers are given? Is this person *capable* of using those powers? Joseph Kallenbach has described the qualities of a great governor: the ability to judge people and to delegate duties to them; the ability to make hard decisions and to assume the responsibility for them; political sensitivity and timing; a zest for political combat; the ability to inspire confidence and loyalty; a sense of proportion and perspective; the ability to withstand unfair criticism.[25] Kallenbach's composite is useful, but it also approaches a political version of the Beatitudes.

OTHER ELECTED EXECUTIVES

The governor is only one of many elected executives: others are the attorney general, treasurer, department heads, and members of important boards and commissions such as the Public Utilities Commission. The decision to have these people elected, rather than appointed by the governor, was made during the era of Andrew Jackson and was viewed as a way to increase the power of the voters and to insure that those elected would be responsive to the public. Today, that long-ballot reform is viewed as restricting the ability of the governor to lead the executive branch: these separately elected officials may be members of a different party, may be members of a different faction within the governor's party,

TABLE 5-3 Separately Elected State Officials: 1965 and 1984

Office	1965	1984	Change 1965–1984
Lieutenant Governor	38	42	+4
Board of Education	9	12	+3
Attorney General	42	43	+1
Controller	9	10	+1
Governor	50	50	0
Agriculture	13	12	−1
Land Commissioner	7	5	−2
Treasurer	40	38	−2
Insurance	10	8	−2
Labor	6	4	−2
Secretary of State	39	36	−3
Mines	4	1	−3
Public Utilities Commission	14	11	−3
Auditor	29	25	−4
Superintendent of Education	22	17	−5

SOURCE: *Book of the States, 1984–85* (Lexington, Ky.: Council of State Governments, 1984), p. 45.

or may be sharply at odds with the governor over state policies (see Table 5-3).

It has already been noted that many of these offices are excellent stepping-stones to the governorship. Furthermore, separate election may actually *reduce* responsiveness to the public. Voters may know very little about the agriculture commissioner or the insurance commissioner and may care even less. But the affected interest groups are vitally concerned and support and fund the election of a particular candidate. Ironically, there may be limits on how long the governor can stay in office, but there usually are no limits on how long the other executives can stay in office—and many of them stay twenty or thirty years (see Table 5-2).

Lieutenant Governor

Forty-two states have lieutenant governors. In thirty-eight of these states that person becomes governor if the incumbent dies or resigns; in two thirds of them he or she can preside over the state senate. Meager as they are, such are the duties of the lieutenant governor.

Since the governor usually remains in good health and since the senate's presiding officer may vote only in the unlikely event of a tie, the typical lieutenant governor is clearly underemployed, particularly if he or she is a competent person. In 1981, the lieutenant governor of Illinois resigned his post saying, "Any half-way intelligent person could learn the job in a week." The lieutenant governor may or may not receive additional duties from the governor, depending upon whether the governor has confidence in him or her. Such confidence may not be forthcoming, because in just twenty-two states do the governor and lieutenant governor run as a ticket, like the president and vice-president, and in only nine states do governors have substantial control over who shall be their running mate. Thus, the governor's "second in command" may be a member of a different party or a different party faction. We have already indicated that being lieutenant governor is an important stepping-stone to the governorship. It is therefore easy to see why governors may be reluctant to increase the political visibility of lieutenant governors by delegating them significant powers. But the public is unaware of the lieutenant governor's lack of duties and believes that the number-two position is a good preparation for the number-one position. Therein lies the lure of a post with few powers.

The lone important responsibility of the lieutenant governor is mired in constitutional controversy. In ten states he or she has the legislative power of appointing some standing senate committees and assigning senate bills to committee. An additional nine states allow the assignment of bills only. Many constitutional scholars question the propriety of an elected executive officer intruding in the operation of a constitutionally co-equal branch of government. Moreover, there have been cases in which a lieutenant governor belonging to the minority party has had to preside over the state senate.

Attorney General

Unlike the previous position, the post of attorney general is a powerful one. The "AG" or a member of his or her staff represents the state in all court cases. Furthermore, the attorney general advises state officers and state departments on the legality of actions they might be considering. Such opinions are legally binding unless reversed by a court—and most of these opinions are never reviewed by a court. The attorney general's office sometimes acts as a bill-drafting agency for the legislature in some smaller states. In addition, the attorney general may become involved in prosecuting a criminal case, but this is almost always left to the local state's attorney or district attorney.

Attorneys general have recently taken on an important duty in the areas of consumer and environmental protection: protecting the public from shoddy merchandise, slick business practices, unscrupulous nursing home operators, polluting industries, and hazardous-waste dumpers. In addition to investigating these dangers and seeking indictments, they have also suggested remedial legislation to the state legislature. Consumer protection and environmental protection provide a valuable public service—and an excellent "good guy" image for those AGs who wish to run for governor!

Secretary of State

The secretary of state has custody of various public records and documents. For example, the official (correct) copy of a law is the one in the secretary of state's office. The secretary of state may also manage the state archives, issue drivers' licenses, register lobbyists, issue corporations their certificates of incorporation, receive initiative and referendum petitions, and publish election returns. The latter two duties reflect the fact that the secretary of state is usually the state's chief election officer, and as such, the person who supervises elections.

Auditor

The auditor acts as an accountant who conducts a postaudit to make sure that public money has been spent legally and faithfully. This person is an elected executive officer in half of the states, but he or she should really be a nonpartisan employee of the legislature, because it is that body that has the power of the purse and has determined the purposes of public expenditures.

Treasurer

The treasurer is also an elected official who should be appointed, in this case by the governor. The treasurer's duties are to invest and pay out state funds. The functions of this office are largely technical and nonpolitical. That this person and also the secretary of state and the auditor are elected as partisan candidates is another reflection of the Jacksonian long-ballot tradition. The voters have little information on which to select candidates for these low-visibility offices, except their partisan affiliations. It is probably wiser to have these officials appointed, as at the federal level, with the appointing authority bearing responsibility in any cases of poor performance.

Superintendent of Public Instruction

The superintendent heads the state department of education, which provides technical assistance such as information on teaching aids to local school districts. This department also establishes graduation requirements, curriculum standards, teacher certification requirements, building guidelines, and so on, for local schools. The stimulus for local districts to follow the leadership of the state department is the latter's power to dispense the state education money upon which local schools are so dependent.

Miscellaneous Officials

Alaska, Hawaii, Iowa, and Nebraska have an ombudsman who is either elected or appointed to investigate citizen complaints about harsh, abusive, or unfair actions by state officials and employees. This person not only discloses abuses, but helps the public with government problems. Various other elected officials are the secretary of agriculture, insurance commissioners, land commissioners, board of education members, and public utility commissioners.

It is clear that state voters have no shortage of electoral choices. There may also be no shortage of jostling among these various officials as each tries to move up the ladder to the ultimate rung of governor. To move up, one needs vital name identification among the voters and/or the support of party leaders. These objectives can be achieved by engaging in running partisan battles with other executives or by provoking highly publicized disputes with the governor. In any case, normal political ambition added to the separate election of various officers means that the executive branch, from the governor down to the most obscure commissioner, may perpetually be a house divided against itself.

STATE ADMINISTRATION

Administrators do the day-to-day work of running state government whether as state-capital office workers or freeway repair crews or state park rangers or prison guards or as any of thousands of other state workers. Referred to variously as civil servants, bureaucrats, or the fourth branch of government, these men and women have the duty of administering (carrying out) state laws. Average citizens have far more contact with state administrators than with state legislators, judges, or governors. Some commentators argue that administrators have the greatest practical effect on people's lives!

Administrators work for the numerous departments, bureaus, boards, agencies, and commissions constituting the administrative branch of state government. However, students of public administration are not impressed by this bureaucratic sprawl: they argue that having well over one hundred administrative units in a state reduces democratic control and promotes inefficiency, waste, and duplication.

The present fragmentation of state administration came about partly by accident and partly by design. There is a natural drive for agency autonomy: agency heads believe that their department cannot be consolidated with any other because their department's duties and services are unique; integration will result in decreased services to its clients. The Jacksonian long-ballot tradition also holds sway, and the voters are reluctant to give up voting for separate department heads. There is a long-standing misconception that establishing an independent board in areas such as education or public utilities or liquor regulation will keep these areas "out of politics." Interest groups feel that they can dominate an agency more easily if it is separate. For example, sportsmen do not want the Fish and Game Agency to be part of a larger Natural Resources

Department. Not only do interest groups want "their" agency to be separate, they want agency funds to be separate from the state's general funds. If hunting and fishing license fees are earmarked for an autonomous Fish and Game Agency, nearly complete control is assured.

The professions, federal categorical grant-in-aid programs, and legislative distrust of the governor have also helped fragment state administration. Professionals such as doctors, engineers, librarians, teachers, and social workers "have organized bodies of knowledge generally available only to members; group standards of training and performance; codes of ethical conduct; and particularly close group ties and associations. Such [professions are] necessarily set apart by the possession of a special lore and [their] members have a strong group consciousness that leads them to insist on being distinct from the common herd."[26] Similarly, an agency whose activities are technical or complex or obscured by an arcane vocabulary may be nearly incomprehensible to a lay person. Federal categorical grant-in-aid programs have built up particularly strong vertical links among federal, state, and local program specialists in welfare, hospitals, education, and many other fields. These specialists usually bear a greater loyalty to each other than to elected generalists such as governors or legislators. Some activities are believed to need special insulation from political pressures—for example, "regulatory activities, particularly those that involve determination upon the basis of evidence presented through a formal hearing process," and programs in which objectivity is especially necessary, such as property tax assessment or alcoholic beverage control.[27] Finally, legislative distrust of the governor may cause legislators to increase administrative fragmentation by placing an agency beyond the governor's control.

Several viewpoints are reflected in this account of state administrative fragmentation. Underlying most of these positions, some of which may be self-serving, is the belief that public policy should not be left to politicians. Furthermore, the decisions to create a separate agency here or an autonomous bureau there were made individually over long periods and were often a response to new problems or needs. Altogether, they add up to an unrationalized, patchwork state administrative structure. However, state governments have made great strides in reducing administrative fragmentation: twenty-two states underwent comprehensive reorganizations in the period 1965–79 alone.[28]

The Reorganization Movement

The movement to reorganize the state executive branch in order to rationalize it and bring it under greater gubernatorial control has been proceeding for over seventy years. This movement is guided by a set of principles of organization that have remained remarkably constant over the years.[29] First, authority and responsibility must be concentrated in the governor, with clear lines of authority running from the governor down to the lowest levels of state government. Second, departments must be integrated or grouped according to function so duplication can be eliminated. The number of departments should be limited because the governor's span of control is limited: there are only a small number of people he or she can effectively supervise. Third, boards having little administrative discretion should be replaced by single administrators appointed by the governor. Fourth, adequate staff assistance for the governor should be provided so that he or she can adequately supervise subordinates. Fifth, there should be a controller appointed by the governor to do a pre-audit and an auditor appointed by the legislature to do a post-audit.

In addition to attempting to implement the foregoing principles, state reorganizations take place for many other reasons.[30] State government might be reorganized to strengthen or weaken the governor's power vis-à-vis the legislature, or to increase or decrease the influence of a particular interest group. State leaders may urge reform of state government because they wish to emulate federal innovations (the Hoover Commission of the 1940s) or other states' innovations ("Little Hoover" commissions). Opinion leaders might feel that their state lags behind other states and must modernize.

A key question to ask about reorganization efforts is what effect they have on the spending patterns of states. T. R. Carr has found that "reorganizing the state executive branch of government has no demonstrable impact on policy priorities." He also cautions that reformers' claims of increased democratic accountability through heightened gubernatorial control and increased gubernatorial efficiency have yet to be empirically tested.[31]

The Bureaucrats

Who are the men and women who work for state and local governments, and what services do they provide? Table 5-4 gives an answer. Most subnational employees are in the field of education and they work for local school districts. There are also large numbers of workers providing health services, police protection, and road construction and repair. Local employees far outnumber not only state employees but also federal civilian employees (at 2,875,000).

Deil Wright has studied the characteristics of those people who direct state agencies. They are almost always white males, have a median age of forty-eight, were raised in a small city but soon moved to a larger one, have earned at least a B.A. degree, and have partisan preferences strikingly similar to the general public's.[32] About one third have recently served in private enterprise, one third came up through the ranks of their agency, and one fifth transferred from another state agency. This group of top-level administrators is clearly more professional than senior administrators

TABLE 5-4 **State and Local Employment in 1983**
(in thousands, full-time and part-time)

Function	Total	State	Local
Education	6792	1666	5125
Teachers only	3808	495	3313
Highways	527	243	284
Health and Hospitals	1399	670	730
Welfare	397	176	221
Police	671	76	595
Fire Protection	310	NA	310
Sanitation and Sewerage	216	1	215
Parks and Recreation	249	29	220
Natural Resources	196	159	37
Other	2402	795	1607
Total	13,159	3,816	9,344

SOURCE: *Statistical Abstract of the United States, 1985*
(Washington, D.C.: U.S. Department of Commerce, 1984),
p. 292.

of twenty-five years ago in terms of education, career patterns, and ties to professional organizations.

Wright and F. Ted Hebert have identified four types of agency heads: aggrandizers, advocates, apathetics, and altruists.[33] *Aggrandizers* favor the expansion of their own agency's programs, activities, and expenditures within a context of overall expansion of state programs and activities. These agency heads come closest to the stereotype of the empire-building bureaucrat. *Advocates* favor expansion of their own agency and a lid on overall state activities: they want a larger piece of a static state pie. Their position is probably a response to tax revolt movements such as the one leading to California's Proposition 13. *Apathetics* oppose expansion both of their own agency and of overall state activity. Their motto is: hold on to what you've got. Finally, *altruists* wish to expand other state programs but not their own. They are altruistic because they are responding more to some conception of the public interest than to their own interest. The percentages of agency heads falling into each category are as follows: aggrandizers, 46 percent; advocates, 32 percent, apathetics, 21 percent; and altruists, 1 percent. Elected administrators are more likely to be apathetics or altruists.

Agency heads seem to get about what they ask from the governor and the legislature.[34] Those asking for a substantial budgetary increase will get their request trimmed, but on the other hand, no agency gets a large increase without asking. Agency heads who ask for no increase will not be cut, nor will they get an increase. See Chapter 10 for further discussion of budgetary strategies.

Collective Bargaining

Thirty-eight percent of state government employees and 52 percent of local government workers are members of labor unions. Teachers, police, and state hospital workers are most likely to be unionized. States with large union membership probably have collective bargaining laws. The existence of such laws, in turn, further encourages unionization. States with a high percentage of their public work force unionized are New York, Rhode Island, Connecticut, Massachusetts, and Hawaii. In fact, state and local governments are more heavily unionized than the private sector. A particularly important and militant union is the American Federation of State, County, and Municipal Employees (AFSCME). In the background of all labor-management bargaining is the threat to strike. Public employee membership increased dramatically in the 1970s and 1980s, and so did the number of strikes and work stoppages (see Table 5-5).

Ten states (Alaska, California, Hawaii, Minnesota, Montana, Ohio, Oregon, Pennsylvania, Vermont, and Wisconsin) have legalized the right to strike for some public employees. With the exception of police and fire fighters, public employees may strike after completing an *impasse procedure* without an agreement. Even though they do not have a legal right to strike, police officers may suddenly be hit in large numbers by a "blue flu." Opponents of public employee strikes argue that the services provided by government are monopolies. They distinguish between public and private strikes: "If Ford workers go on strike, you can buy a Chrysler or General Motors car." Proponents, on the other hand, contend that without this ultimate weapon, public employees have no leverage over employers (see Reading 5-3).

TABLE 5-5   Public Sector Strikes, 1958–78

Year	Union Membership	Number of Strikes
1958	1,035,000	15
1960	1,070,000	36
1962	1,225,000	28
1964	1,453,000	41
1966	1,717,000	142
1968	3,857,000	254
1970	4,080,000	412
1972	4,520,000	375
1974	5,345,000	384
1976	5,852,000	378
1978	6,019,000	481

SOURCE: Myron Lieberman, *Public-Sector Bargaining* (Lexington, Mass.: Lexington Books, D.C. Heath & Company, 1980), p. 35. Reprinted by permission of the publisher. Copyright © 1980, D.C. Heath & Company.

READING 5-3 TRASH PILES UP, HEALTH PERILED IN HAWAII STRIKE

As the Pan American 747 approached Honolulu International Airport, a flight attendant switched on the intercom and suggested that passengers use the restrooms on the airplane before they landed.

"There's a labor problem and the lavatory facilities at the airport won't be very good," she said.

It was an understatement, as the passengers would soon see for themselves. The airport lavatories not only were not "very good," they were dirty, odorous and poorly supplied. The terminal building itself was littered with discarded food wrappers, newspapers, soft drink containers and assorted debris.

A strike by a public employee union composed of trash collectors, custodians, janitors and other blue collar workers has Hawaii awash in a sea of garbage and there apparently is no end to the strike in sight.

So far, Gov. George R. Ariyoshi has resisted pressure to call out the National Guard for clean-up efforts but told a statewide audience in a television address last week that he was "prepared to do that if it becomes necessary to maintain order."

Ariyoshi described the situation as a "very troubled time in our state" and said the strike has "caused extreme inconvenience to the citizens of Hawaii and, in some cases, a genuine health threat. . . .

"It has caused litter to despoil our airports and create a negative image of our state in the eyes of tens of thousands of visitors who have passed through them in the past two weeks."

Schools have been closed. The airport, indeed, is a mess. Garbage and trash are strewn along roadsides and piled high on public beaches. Plastic garbage bags, stuffed full, line the corridors of the state Capitol, Honolulu City Hall and other public buildings. Trash bins in the parks have long since overflowed.

A broken pipe is spewing raw sewage into a stream not far from downtown Honolulu, but striking union workers won't repair it and officials have not succeeded in getting a private contractor to cross picket lines.

And strikers, despite threats of contempt citations, have ignored a court order directing them to provide "minimal essential services" to protect the "public health and safety."

To be sure, potential health problems now are the chief worry of state and local officials, a situation that was not helped this week when a heavy rain caused garbage bags left at curbsides to split open, spilling their contents.

"The garbage is breeding maggots, flies and rats," state Health Director George Yuen said. "It's gradually becoming a serious problem. This coming week we're going to reach a point where something needs to be done and I really don't know what we can do."

SOURCE: William Endicott, *Los Angeles Times*, November 15, 1979, p. l-1. Copyright 1979, Los Angeles Times. Reprinted by permission.

Mediation, fact-finding, and arbitration are becoming increasingly important impasse procedures. Through *mediation*, a neutral third party who cannot force an agreement tries to settle the disagreement by working out a compromise. *Fact-finding* comes into play if mediation fails. A neutral fact finder holds quasi-judicial hearings, and makes recommendations to the parties involved. Under *arbitration*, a third party makes a binding decision, frequently by splitting the difference between the two parties.[35] But in a variation called *final arbitration*, the arbitrator selects the final offer of one of the parties. This arrangement prevents the arbitrator from splitting the difference between the parties, and it further encourages the parties to make reasonable proposals so that the arbitrator will not select the final offer of the other side.

Public employers generally oppose arbitration because they feel employees can get a better settlement from it than they might without it. Furthermore, since the arbitrator usually does not live in the city in which the labor dispute has taken place, he or she does not have to live with the settlement. That is, he or she can be very generous with the public's money because his or her taxes will not go up!

Public-sector bargaining has recently been criticized as a process in which the public interest goes unrepresented. Critics point out that public employee unions have often contributed heavily to the campaign coffers of public officials—who then sit down with employee unions to negotiate salaries. The relationship is said to be a form of "political incest." The proposed solution is submitting public-sector labor agreements to a vote of the public. Opponents of such referenda point to the mechanical problems involved: in jurisdictions that bargain with several unions, the referendum would be a year-round process.[36] Instead, they favor coordinating negotiating schedules more closely with election schedules as a means of opening up what may be a closed process.

But public officials who depend on the campaign contributions and/or votes of public-employee unions may "give away the store" on more than salary issues. Generous pension or retirement benefits may be negotiated that do not result in current tax increases but later cause serious long-term obligations. Today's elected officials may have safely moved on by the time expensive pension costs are felt by the public.

Productivity

Interest in increased public-employee productivity is important. Such improvements can do one of three things: "(1) increase service levels while holding costs constant, or (2) decrease costs for current service performance levels, or (3) increase performance levels while simultaneously reducing costs."[37] Since the Reagan administration is reducing aid to state and local governments, public managers will have to "do more with less." However, Grover Starling notes various barriers to productivity. For example, "government management systems generally penalize bad performance more than they reward good performance. Thus, there is more incentive to avoid egregious failure than to achieve success."[38] Moreover, government has other perverse disincentives to productivity. Each department receives a budget allocation for the fiscal year; the public manager who wishes to rise in the bureaucracy should get a bigger budget each year. Returning money to the public treasury at the end of the fiscal year is usually not rewarded. Other writers claim that "whatever the pluses of collective bargaining might be, one minus is a very substantial cost in terms of lower productivity."[39] Union contracts are said to inhibit productivity through *featherbedding*—keeping on more employees than are really necessary to do the work. Some public jurisdictions engage in *productivity bargaining* with employees, whereby increases in productivity are passed on to workers in the form of higher salaries.

SUMMARY

In this chapter, we have considered the executive branch: the governor and the roles he or she might play; other elected executives, such as the attorney general and secretary of state; and state employees, who do the day-to-day work of running state government. A theme that has permeated this chapter is competition, if not conflict. All three actors (governors, other elected executives, bureaucrats) seek to further their own interests, often at the expense of one of the other actors. Such conflict is seen as beneficial when it occurs *between* branches—then it is known as the process of checks and balances. But conflict *within* the same branch may seriously reduce government efficiency, if not democratic accountability.

NOTES

1. Thad Beyle, "The Governor as Chief Legislator," *State Government*, 51 (Winter 1978), Table 1.

2. Thad Beyle, "Governors' Views on Being Governor" (paper presented at the annual meeting of the Midwest Political Science Association, Chicago, 1979), p. 3.

3. David R. Morgan, "Gubernatorial Power and State Policy" (paper presented at the annual meeting of the Midwest Political Science Association, Chicago, 1979), Table 2.

4. Center for Policy Research, *Governing the American States* (Washington, D.C.: National Governors Association, 1978).

5. Glenn Abney and Thomas Lauth, "The Governor as Administrator," *Public Administration Review*, 43 (January-February 1983), 40.

6. Thad Beyle and Robert Dalton, "Appointment Power: Does it Belong to the Governor?" *State Government*, 54 (1981), 4–5.

7. Donald Sprengel, *Gubernatorial Staffs* (Iowa City: University of Iowa Institute of Public Affairs, 1969), pp. 6–18.

8. Coleman Ransone, Jr., *The Office of Governor in the United States* (University: Uni-

versity of Alabama Press, 1956), p. 318. The titles of these various positions differ from state to state; smaller states may combine some of these posts.

9.   Sprengel, *Gubernatorial Staffs*, pp. 37–38.

10.   Charles H. Williams, "The 'Gatekeeper' Function on the Governor's Staff," *Western Political Quarterly*, 33 (March 1980), 92–93.

11.   Larry Sabato, "Gubernatorial Clemency: A Time of Trial?" *State Government*, 53 (Winter 1980), 43.

12.   See *Kentucky* v. *Dennison*, 24 Howard 66 (1861). The correct legal term for this process is *rendition*.

13.   John Straayer, *American State and Local Government*, 2nd ed. (Columbus, Ohio: Chas. E. Merrill 1977), pp. 110–11.

14.   Malcolm Jewell, *The State Legislature*, 2nd ed. (New York: Random House, 1969), p. 81.

15.   Robert C. Clark and Charles Wiggins, "The Persistence of Divided Party Control of State Governments," *Polity*, 8 (Spring 1976), Table 1. See also Jewell, *The State Legislature*, pp. 16–17, 80–82.

16.   Malcolm Jewell and Samuel Patterson, *The Legislative Process in the United States*, 3rd ed. (New York: Random House, 1977), pp. 271–72.

17.   Charles Wiggins, "Executive Vetoes and Legislative Overrides in the American States," *Journal of Politics*, 42 (November 1980), Table 1. Interestingly, a study of vetoes in 1947 also found that 5 percent of all bills were vetoed: Frank Prescott, "The Executive Veto in the American States," *Western Political Quarterly*, 3 (March 1950), 98–112. However, Ransone notes that between 1945 and 1975 the percentage of vetoed bills remained the same while the percentage of successful veto overrides rose from about 1 percent to about 6 percent: Coleman Ransone, Jr., *The American Governorship* (Wesport, Conn.: Greenwood Press, 1982), p. 140.

18.   Lynn Muchmore and Thad Beyle, "The Governor as Party Leader," *State Government*, 53 (Summer 1980), 121–24.

19.   *Branti* v. *Finkel*, 445 U.S. 507 (1980). See also *Elrod* v. *Burns*, 427 U.S. 347 (1976).

20.   David Kenney, *Basic Illinois Government*, rev. ed. (Carbondale: Southern Illinois University Press, 1974), p. 237.

21.   J. Stephen Turett, "The Vulnerability of American Governors, 1900–1969," *Midwest Journal of Political Science*, 15 (February 1971), 118–22. Turett finds that vulnerability is not correlated with urbanization, industrialization, crime, unemployment, tax burden, educational effort, or expenditure effort.

22.   Gerald Pomper and Susan Lederman, *Elections in America*, 2nd ed. (New York: Longman, 1980), pp. 114–15.

23.   Larry Sabato, *Goodbye to Good-Time Charlie: The American Governor Transformed*, 2nd ed. (Washington, D.C.: CQ Press, 1983), p. 46. Solomon notes that three former governors served on the Michigan Supreme Court in the 1970s: Samuel Solomon, "Governors: 1970–1980," *National Civic Review*, 70 (March 1981), 148. Defeated governors and governors barred by the state constitution from seeking a second or third consecutive term may later be elected to the governorship.

24.   Ransone, *The American Governorship*, pp. 15–16, 162–63.

25.   Joseph Kallenbach, *The American Chief Executive* (New York: Harper & Row, Pub., 1966), pp. 257–67.

26.   York Willbern, "Administrative Organization," in *The 50 States and Their Local Governments*, ed. James Fesler (New York: Knopf, 1967), p. 348. My discussion of administrative fragmentation relies on pp. 346–52 of Wilbern's article.

27.   Ibid., pp. 350–51.

28.   *The Question of State Government Capability* (Washington, D.C.: Advisory Commission on Intergovernmental Relations, 1985), p. 144.

29.   A. E. Buck, *The Reorganization of State Governments in the United States* (New York: Columbia University Press, 1938), pp. 14–28, provides the classic statement of these principles.

30. James Garnett, *Reorganizing State Government: The Executive Branch* (Boulder, Colo.: Westview Press, 1980), pp. 13–21.

31. T. R. Carr, "State Government Reorganization: The Impact of Executive Branch Reorganization on Public Policy" (paper presented at the annual meeting of the Midwest Political Science Association, Cincinnati, 1981), p. 21.

32. Deil Wright et al., "State Administrators: Their Changing Characteristics," *State Government*, 50 (Summer 1977), 152–55; F. Ted Hebert and Deil Wright, "State Administrators: How Representative? How Professional?" *State Government*, 55 (1982), 22–28.

33. Deil Wright and F. Ted Hebert, "Bureaucratic Expansion, Organizational Autonomy, and Institutional Influence in American State Governments" (paper presented at the annual meeting of the Midwest Political Science Association, Chicago, 1980), pp. 7–19.

34. Ira Sharkansky, "Agency Requests, Gubernatorial Support and Budget Success in State Legislatures," *American Political Science Review*, 62 (December 1968), 1225.

35. Robert Pursley and Neil Snortland, *Managing Government Organizations* (North Scituate, Mass.: Duxbury Press, 1980), pp. 344–47. Under *voluntary arbitration*, the two parties seek arbitration on their own; under *compulsory arbitration*, they are required by law to seek arbitration if they cannot agree.

36. Myron Lieberman, *Public-Sector Bargaining* (Lexington, Mass.: Heath, Lexington Books, 1980), pp. 3–16. See also pp. 35, 76.

37. James Jarrett, "Productivity," in *Book of the States, 1980–81* (Lexington, Ky.: Council of State Governments, 1980), p. 237.

38. Grover Starling, *Managing the Public Sector*, rev. ed. (Homewood, Ill.: Dorsey, 1982), p. 350.

39. Pursley and Snortland, *Managing Government Organizations*, p. 474.

chapter 6

State Legislative Politics

To many Americans, *state government* means the state legislature. The activities of the legislature are sometimes carefully reported, at least by the large-city daily newspapers. Almost all of the major issues of state government are thrashed out in the legislature: it is an important arena for political conflict. It is also true, unfortunately, that many of the headline-catching scandals involving purported "deals," "bribes," or "payoffs" have a tendency to involve the legislature. However, state legislatures have come a long way from the day when "it was hard to swing a dead cat around a state capitol rotunda without slapping in the back of the neck either a knave or fool, or both."[1] In fact, one authority on state legislatures wrote in 1983 that they "have progressed more in the past 20 years than any other American political institution."[2] The changes undergone by state legislatures will be an important theme of this chapter.

POWERS OF STATE LEGISLATURES

State constitutions vest significant powers in legislatures. The principal powers of the Missouri General Assembly, for example, are noted in Reading 6-1.

Although the state legislature is frequently called upon to decide weighty and monumental issues, the vast majority of its business is somewhat technical and rather mundane. For example, the legislature must decide

> the effect on highways of an increase in the truck weight limit, how much paregoric may safely be dispensed without a prescription, the size of a standard prune crate, the limit on balloon payments to second mortgages,

---

READING 6-1 POWERS OF THE LEGISLATURE

The police power, or the power to pass any law promoting the public health, safety, morals, and welfare. Example: set minimum wages, prohibit child labor, prohibit gambling, require vaccination. By its very definition, the police power is so broad as to include a large segment of the state's powers. Some of the items that follow are examples of the police power or can be used to give expression to it.

Define crimes and their punishment, and administer penal and correctional institutions.
Establish and maintain hospitals and health programs.
Provide for education.
Grant licenses for practicing the professions.
Regulate marriage and divorce.
Regulate the taking of fish, game, and other natural resources of the state.
Encourage and regulate agriculture.
Regulate the conditions of labor, and safeguard the interests of laborers.
Incorporate business firms, banks, and public utilities, and regulate their activities.
Enact laws for counties, cities, towns, villages, and other subdivisions of the state.
Regulate elections.
Regulate the courts.
Maintain the militia.

In addition, some special functions are assigned to the legislature by either the federal or state constitution:

Make appropriations according to law.
Draw up new boundaries for congressional districts and judicial circuits.
Submit to the people proposed amendments to the state constitution.
Act on proposed federal constitutional amendments.
Act as an agency of impeachment.

SOURCE: Robert F. Karsch, *The Government of Missouri,* 14th ed. (Columbia, Mo.: Lucas Brothers Publishers, 1978), p. 84.

---

the effect on sanitation of fishing in reservoirs, the closing date of squirrel season, the relation of attorney to physician in private adoptions, the impact of oil severance taxes on petroleum production, salaries of beginning teachers versus experienced ones. . . .[3]

In a normal day the legislature will be called upon to

create a medical-vision advisory panel in the division of motor vehicles, change the required minimum age for amusement-ride operators from sixteen to eighteen, designate the horse as the state animal, direct the council of the arts to conduct a competition for a state song, authorize the department of environmental protection to prepare standards for marine toilets, permit municipalities to regulate the construction of public mausoleums, and on and on.[4]

Most matters coming before the state legislature do not concern large numbers of people directly and crucially, but these matters may be of critical importance to smaller groups of people (truckers, pharmacists, prune growers, amusement-ride owners, and so forth).[5] The legislative atmosphere is frequently permeated by some special group seeking help or favors or preferential treatment. Because the interests of the broader public may not be at stake, or can be quietly ignored, legislators often feel free to "help out friends" or to grant special favors. It is a very short step to the corrupt practices and secret deals rumored in many state capitols.

CHARACTERISTICS OF STATE LEGISLATURES

Size

With one exception, all state legislatures are *bicameral*, or two-chamber bodies. Nebraska has a *unicameral*, or one-house, legislature. The upper house in every state legislature (and the lone chamber in Nebraska) is called the Senate. The lower chamber is usually called the House of Representatives, but four states prefer to call it the Assembly, and a few southern and border states use House of Delegates. The senate is always smaller than the lower house, frequently much smaller. Houses range in membership from 40 in Alaska and Nevada to 203 in Pennsylvania and 400 in New Hampshire. The large size of the typical house of representatives has long concerned reformers. Though it is acknowledged that a chamber should be large enough to represent the diverse needs, concerns, and interests of the state's people, too large a membership is unwieldy and ineffective. An experienced observer of the large New Hampshire house has noted that "about 15 members really determine things; the others more or less follow."[6]

Limitations on Time

The frequency and length of state legislative sessions are restricted. This restriction is a legacy of the late-nineteenth-century fear of pervasive legislative venality: it was believed that "no person's life, liberty, or property is safe while the legislature is in session." It also reflects a preference for the part-time "citizen-legislator." Many state legislatures still meet according to a schedule that allowed nineteenth-century farmer-legislators to do a little lawmaking between planting and harvesting.

Forty-three legislatures now meet annually, up from only four as recently as 1942. However, almost three fourths of the states limit how long the legislature may be in session, with the restrictions in New Mexico, Utah, and Virginia particularly stringent. On the other hand, nearly three fifths of the legislatures may call themselves into special session.

Limitations on time have been described by some reformers as crippling. These limitations are often used as justifications for other weaknesses of some legislatures: "modest salaries, the negligible staff assistance, the inadequate facilities."[7] On the other hand, a survey of over 1100 legislators found only 38 percent highly favorable toward the idea of a year-round legislature.[8] The key point to remember is that the amount of work a legislature has to do should determine how long it stays in session, not an unjustified limitation established many years earlier.

Terms and Salaries

In three fourths of the states, senators serve four-year terms; the remaining states have two-year terms. House members have terms of two years in all but four states.

Salaries of legislators vary greatly, from as low as $5 per day in Rhode Island and $30 a day in Wyoming to over $50,000 per two-year session of the full-time legislatures of New York and California. Salaries are set by the constitution in some states: legislators in Rhode Island last got a raise in 1900, and lawmakers in New Hampshire have been paid $200 per session since 1889. Some states augment the salaries of legislators with per-day living expenses while the legislature is in session, insurance policies, travel and telephone allowances, and pensions. Legislative leaders may receive substantial additional compensation. Unusual benefits afforded legislators include: free ski passes in Colorado, one hundred free trees for distribution by each Indiana lawmaker in his or her district, and immunity from speeding tickets for legislators on state business in Wyoming.

Turnover

Membership turnover in state legislatures is quite high, far higher than in the U.S. Congress. For the period 1971–76, turnover per session was 32 percent in senates and 37 percent in houses. However, turnover varies greatly from state to state, from chamber to chamber, and from decade to decade. For the years 1931–76, the lowest senate turnover was in California (20 percent) and the highest in Alabama (83 percent). For the lower chambers in those years, the New York Assembly averaged 25 percent, the Alabama house 68 percent. In general, turnover is decreasing, and is usually lowest in urban, industrial states.[9]

Turnover has serious consequences. The many new members must learn the ropes—and the session is short. There may be a shortage of specialists with the expertise to master some of the technical issues coming before the legislature. But knowledge is power, and there are forces outside the legislature, such as the executive branch and interest groups, that will assist the legislature in lawmaking. The price, however, is legislative independence.

That most house members must run every two years accounts for a great deal of turnover in that chamber, but longer sessions and increasing compensation decrease turnover, especially in senates. Staggering the terms of senators also depresses turnover.[10] It has generally been thought that turnover is voluntary: legislators simply decline to serve another term because of low salaries, because a few members have disproportionate power, or because being a state legislator often lacks prestige. However, a study of the 1976 and 1978 elections in fifteen states found 82 percent of the incumbents seeking reelection, and 29 percent having to face a primary challenger.[11]

Occupations of Legislators

The occupations of state legislators are shown in Table 6-1. As the table indicates, many legislators hold positions that they can leave in the hands of a business partner for the few months the legislature is in session. Lawyers, business owners or self-employed persons, farmers, realtors, or insurance salespersons would be good examples. Those who would be unable to serve easily in a nonprofessional, part-time legislature are those who work for employers who will not let them off two or three months each year to be in the capital.

Rules of the Game, Norms, and Role Orientations

Whatever their occupations, legislators tend to share a common set of values. These values have been described as the rules of the legislative game:

1. Honor obligations: Don't violate your word; keep your promises to other members.
2. Respect other members' legislative rights: When a bill concerns only the affairs of a single district, support it if the legislator from that district favors the bill. Don't railroad bills.
3. Avoid personal attacks.
4. Be courteous.
5. Don't speak too much on the floor.
6. Don't conceal the real purpose of bills or amendments.
7. Don't be a publicity hound.[12]

These rules perform valuable functions. They promote cohesion and solidarity in the chamber (especially numbers 2, 3, and 7), make behavior more predictable (1 and 6), expedite legislative business (5), and channel and restrain conflict while promoting compromise. The importance of the

TABLE 6-1   Occupations of Legislators

Lawyers	20%
Owners of businesses, self-employed	15
Farmers and food producers	11
Education	10
Professionals (doctors, nurses, dentists, engineers, architects, etc.)	7
Executives, managers	6
Real estate, construction	6
Insurance	5
Other business jobs	5
Government employees	4
Communications, arts	3
Homemakers, students	3
Labor unions and non-profit organizations	1
Information not available	4

SOURCE: *U.S. News & World Report*, December 17, 1979, p. 74. Copyright 1979, U.S. News & World Report, Inc.

rules is underscored by the sanctions for their violation: obstruction of the offending member's bills, denial of political rewards such as patronage and choice committee assignments, distrust manifested by cross-examination on the floor, and ultimately ostracism.

Very similar to these rules of the game are *norms*, which have been defined as "widely held expectations of what members must do, should do, or ought to do in particular circumstances, the violation of which leads to some kind of sanction or punishment."[13] Norms can be highly formalized and written as standing orders or rulings of the chair; they can be traditional and unwritten, such as the seniority system, or they can be informal, such as reciprocity and logrolling. An important norm is "If you want to get along, go along." Some of the unfortunate by-products of this norm are described in Reading 6-2.

Closely associated with norms and the rules of the game are legislators' *role orientations*. These are a legislator's expectations of what he or she should do as a legislator. They also include the expectations of other legislators, the governor, party leaders, and so on, concerning what the legislator should do. Political science has produced a voluminous literature describing legislators' role orientations toward their constituency, political party, interest groups, executive officials, and others. We will be concerned here with *purposive role orientation*—legislators' expectations of what a legislator's job should be.

Five purposive role orientations have been identified by Wahlke and his fellow researchers: ritualist, tribune, inventor, broker, and opportunist.[14] The *ritualist* is the most common role orientation. The legislator of this type is concerned with the strategies, tactics, and rituals of legislative procedure. For this person, the mechanics of the process have become an

**READING 6-2   FORMER MEMBER OF THE CALIFORNIA ASSEMBLY SAYS
"JOINING THE SYSTEM" COST HIM HIS FAMILY
AND HIS IDEALS**

When Paul Priolo, a Santa Monica camera store retailer, was persuaded to seek an Assembly seat 15 years ago, he knew the decision would have a tremendous impact on the rest of his life.

It did. And he rues the day he made that decision.

"If I had it to do over again? I wouldn't do it," he said quietly, shaking his head as he stared at the dark brown carpet in his wood-paneled Capitol office. "I wouldn't go into politics. No. Never."

An outspoken cynic, the retiring West Valley–Malibu assemblyman admits that during his tenure in office he learned to compromise his ideals, bowed to the pressures of lobbyists and became an expert "political animal." In exchange, he felt frustration, insecurity, and eventually, the loss of his dearest possession, his family, shattered by divorce.

Now, with a new wife, Priolo is determined to put his life back together. He's getting out of politics.

"I'm so damn happy now that I've made that choice," Priolo said jubilantly. "I feel fantastic!"

Priolo said when he was first elected in 1966, his supporters told him, "You're going to Sacramento and we don't expect you to beat that system up there. But we don't want you to join it."

Despite the warning, Priolo said, "I think I joined the system. I came up here and found that, for whatever reason, to be an effective legislator or to get along with people up here . . . I don't know, but I think I found myself as a part of the system.

Now, Priolo says he has "gone full circle" to return to the attitudes he held prior to his election in 1966. "I don't like what goes on in Sacramento," he said. "I have reflected on the system and I'm very unhappy with it. . . ."

"The corporations and special interest groups run government," he said. "The big money interests are neither Republican nor Democratic. They have no philosophy except showing a dividend to their investors. If you can provide a service to the people in the private sector, they don't care where your political philosophies lie. They don't have the courage of their convictions."

Priolo said he is disgusted by the ability of a relatively few groups active in Sacramento to guide legislation. "The unions pull strings," he said. "I don't mean to sound so holier than thou about it. There have been times that people yanked my strings. I found myself casting votes that I wasn't happy with. . . ."

The constant battle to win reelection is another issue that draws Priolo's criticism. "Legislators are interested in their reelection more than anything else," Priolo said. "That's their primary interest. And the way to get reelected is to not make waves, to go along with the pressure groups, the special interest people, the people who take the time to see what's going on in Sacramento. And because of that, I don't think the Legislature has the capacity to cut the cost of government. . . ."

end in itself and the legislative procedure described later in this chapter can take on a life of its own. It is easy to see how one can become bound up in an orientation somewhat akin to "the process is the message." The second most common orientation is one rooted deep in legislative theory— the *tribune*. This legislator sees himself or herself as reflecting, advocating, and defending popular interests, needs, and demands. The third most common role, but one that may become increasingly important as states struggle with fiscal stringency, is that of *inventor*. This person believes that he or she has been sent to the state capital to discover solutions to the state's problems. Wahlke and his associates gathered their interview data from legislators in the late 1950s, before most state legislatures became professionalized. Now that more competent and activist people are being attracted to legislatures, the number of inventors may increase. The least common orientation is *broker*. Considering the intensity of the interest-group struggle described in Chapter 4, it is not surprising that few legislators would want to attempt to arbitrate, compromise, or reconcile the demands of powerful interest groups. A final role, and one that legislators are reluctant to acknowledge, is the *opportunist*. This person is not really interested in being a legislator, and is in the legislature for some other purpose.

Party Composition

Party conflict frequently pervades many state capitols: some state legislatures are evenly balanced between Democrats and Republicans, and disagreement may be quite bitter. In other states, one party overwhelmingly controls the legislature. In this case, factions within the dominant party may struggle for control. Figure 6-1 shows that the Democratic party has dominated state legislatures for the last quarter of a century, and Table 6-2 shows the party lineup by state for a recent legislative session. We noted in Chapter 3 the important role played by gerrymandering, the process by which the party controlling the legislature draws district lines in a manner intended to preserve control of the chambers and to win even more seats. The gerrymander helps perpetuate a party's control of the chamber even if public opinion has started to turn against the party. However inventive parties may be in creating noncompetitive districts, though, all districts must conform to the *one-person-one-vote* criterion required by the United States Supreme Court.

Apportionment

Originally, the Supreme Court was reluctant to prescribe standards for legislative districts. In the case of *Colegrove* v. *Green*, 328 U.S. 549 (1946), the Court described legislative apportionment as a political matter and not a judicial matter. The nation's highest court felt that this subject must be dealt with by the political branches of government, not the judicial

FIGURE 6-1 Control of State Legislatures, 1961–85

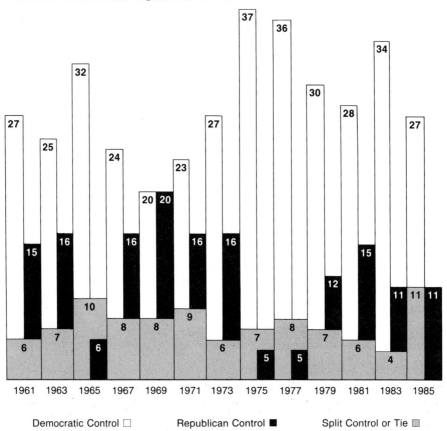

Democratic Control □   Republican Control ■   Split Control or Tie ▨

SOURCE: *State Legislatures*, January 1985, p. 13. Published by The National Conference of State Legislatures.

Note: Until 1972 there were two non-partisan legislatures, Minnesota and Nebraska. Since then only Nebraska has had a non-partisan legislature.

branch: it was a "political thicket" that courts should not enter. But sixteen years later the Court changed its mind, in *Baker* v. *Carr*, 369 U.S. 186 (1962). Tennessee had not reapportioned state legislative districts since 1901, despite substantial population growth and population mobility within the state. Some legislative districts had nineteen times as many people as other districts. Wide variations in district populations such as those found in Tennessee were common in almost all state legislatures. In *Baker* v. *Carr*, the Supreme Court ruled that legislative apportionment is a "justiciable constitutional cause of action" under the equal protection clause of the Fourteenth Amendment of the U.S. Constitution. This meant that in the future, courts would take jurisdiction over suits challenging unequal-population legislative districts.

Such suits were not long in coming. In the landmark case of *Reynolds v. Sims*, 377 U.S. 533 (1964), Chief Justice Earl Warren held that both houses of a state legislature must be apportioned on a population basis. "To the extent that a citizen's right to vote is debased [by living in a legislative district more populous than other districts], he is that much less a citizen," said Warren. The principle that must be followed is one-person-one-vote. The lower houses of state legislatures had generally been apportioned roughly according to population, but state senates often gave equal representation to counties, regardless of size. In this way, state senators were somewhat analogous to the U.S. Senate, which gives equal representation to each state. The federal analogy was decisively rejected by the court.

TABLE 6-2 Party Control of State Legislatures, 1985–86 Session

State	Lower House Dem.	Rep.	Upper House Dem.	Rep.	State	Lower House Dem.	Rep.	Upper House Dem.	Rep.
Alabama	88	12	28	4	Montana	50	50	28	22
Alaska	21	17	9	11	Nebraska*				
Arizona	22	38	12	18	Nevada	17	25	13	8
Arkansas	90	10	31	4	New Hampshire	103	297	6	18
California	47	33	25	15	New Jersey	44	36	23	17
Colorado	18	47	11	24	New Mexico	43	27	21	21
Connecticut	64	87	12	24	New York	94	56	26	35
Delaware	19	22	13	8	North Carolina	83	37	38	12
Florida	78	42	32	8	North Dakota	41	64	24	29
Georgia	154	26	47	9	Ohio	59	40	15	18
Hawaii	40	11	21	4	Oklahoma	69	32	34	14
Idaho	17	67	14	28	Oregon	34	26	18	12
Illinois	67	51	31	28	Pennsylvania	103	100	23	27
Indiana	39	61	20	30	Rhode Island	78	22	39	11
Iowa	60	40	29	21	South Carolina	97	27	37	9
Kansas	49	76	16	24	South Dakota	13	57	10	25
Kentucky	74	26	28	10	Tennessee	62	37	23	10
Louisiana	90	14	38	1	Texas	97	53	25	6
Maine	84	67	24	11	Utah	16	59	6	23
Maryland	124	17	41	6	Vermont	72	78	18	12
Massachusetts	126	34	32	8	Virginia	65	34	32	8
Michigan	58	52	18	20	Washington	52	39	26	22
Minnesota	64	70	42	25	West Virginia	76	24	29	5
Mississippi	115	5	49	3	Wisconsin	52	47	19	14
Missouri	108	55	22	12	Wyoming	18	46	11	19

SOURCE: *State Government News*, December 1984, p. 5.

* Legislators in Nebraska are elected without party designation.

Having stated the principle in *Reynolds* v. *Sims*, the Supreme Court in later cases provided standards for giving effect to the principle. In drawing *congressional* districts, state legislatures must make a "good-faith effort to achieve precise mathematical equality."[15] But in drawing their own district lines, state legislatures are allowed some departure from precise mathematical equality if the districting plan promotes a rational state policy of respecting the integrity of city and county boundaries. For example, a plan to reapportion the Virginia House of Delegates was approved even though some districts varied over 16 percent from mathematical equality.[16]

Respecting the integrity of city and county boundaries has definite benefits: the residents of these subdivisions of the state "have certain common interests and needs, and their local governments must often seek the assistance of their state legislators in sponsoring and supporting legislation to deal with specific local problems."[17] Such local legislation takes up a great deal of the legislature's time and is very important to cities and counties. Furthermore, if state legislators are elected from districts that are unrelated to familiar city and county boundaries, they will very likely be less visible and identifiable to the voters, possibly unknown to them. This can seriously damage the representative character of state legislatures. As a final touch, the U.S. Supreme Court applied the one-person-one-vote rule to general-purpose units of local government, in *Avery* v. *Midland County*, 390 U.S. 474 (1968).

What have been the effects of the Supreme Court's reapportionment decisions? Many observers initially thought that the decisions would be a great boon to financially strapped large cities. With equitable apportionment plans, political power would now shift from the formerly overrepresented rural areas to urban areas. And the money would really start to flow, or so it was thought. More recent analyses have found the effects to be "subtle, selective, limited."[18] Overall state spending has increased, and a greater percentage has gone to metropolitan areas rather than to rural areas, especially in the fields of education, health, and welfare. State spending for highways, long favored by rural legislators, has commanded a smaller percentage. Firearms control and voting-rights legislation, measures supported largely by urban representatives, have been enacted. Ironically, the main beneficiaries of the one-person-one-vote decisions may be the rapidly growing suburbs, rather than central cities. The partisan implications of the decisions are less clear: there are fewer rural legislators (who are frequently Republicans) and more central-city representatives (who are usually Democrats), but if Republicans can capture suburban seats, GOP net losses can be kept to a minimum. Samuel Patterson notes increased party competition for legislative seats and a greater degree of party voting as a bloc within the legislatures as a result of the reapportionment decisions.[19]

About 42 percent of house members and 18 percent of the state senators are elected in multimember rather than single-member districts. Some multimember districts are quite large, providing a big field of candidates in primary elections, but greatly increasing voter confusion. A multimember district benefits the political party having a majority in the district because that party can win all five seats in a five-seat district with slightly over 50 percent of the vote, if we assume straight-ticket voting (voting for all of the party's candidates). Were this multimember district split into five single-member districts with the minority party concentrated in a few areas, the minority party might win one or two seats. The effect of multimember districts is to deprive the minority party of its "fair share" of the seats: in some respects, multimember districts have the same effects as the gerrymander. Years ago, some southern states also used multimember districts to prevent black areas from sending blacks to the state legislature.

Leadership

Because so many state legislatures are in session for only a few brief months, and because numerous members are inexperienced, legislature leadership is particularly crucial. Leadership in the house is provided by the Speaker. This person is usually the second most important person in state government, ranking behind only the governor. Long-term, powerful Speakers often do run for governor.

In many respects, the Speaker is the key variable in the effectiveness and independence of the house and of the whole legislature. If the house is to devise a well-prepared response to state problems and to make good use of its limited time, the Speaker and those he or she appoints to chair key committees must firmly guide the legislature. But such an arrangement can easily become a boss-ruled oligarchy of "old hands." If the legislature is to be the constitutional equal of the governor, the Speaker must be able to stand up to the governor. Yet in many states, a governor whose party controls the lower house plays a behind-the-scenes role in selecting the Speaker. Like the governor, powerful interest groups are always in session and always want the legislature to do their bidding. To keep interest groups in their place, the Speaker must be able to "take the heat." But it is also well known that many Speakers are too closely associated with one or two special interests. Such is the paradox of state legislative leadership.

The Speaker is not only an institutional leader but a party leader. In the latter role, the Speaker is "the principal leader and grand strategist of the majority party in the lower house . . . the guardian of party fortunes and policies."[20] What kind of party record Speakers can fashion in the current session and what kind of party image they can present to the voters for the next election may well determine the electoral fortunes of their party, the amount of their power, and any hopes they may have for higher office.

The Speaker's role as institutional leader is intertwined with his or her role as party leader. For one thing, the Speaker usually appoints the members of all committees. To aid their constituents or to further their policy goals, legislators from farm areas may want to be on the Agriculture Committee or teachers may want to be on the Education Committee. Speakers not only place those who share their views on favored committees but also often appoint the chairpersons of committees. Friends and supporters of the Speaker can be rewarded, and others put in his or her debt. In addition to seniority, there are "other factors weighed by the House leader in making appointments, [including] party loyalty, expertise, political expediency, district location, and personal relationships."[21]

The Speaker refers bills to committees. This is frequently not a routine matter. By sending a bill to favorable committee A, the Speaker gives it a legislative boost; by sending it to hostile committee B, he or she consigns it to extinction. However, the Speaker does not assign bills in a totally arbitrary fashion. Bills often deal with two or more separate subjects, and committee jurisdiction may overlap. Therefore, the Speaker must use his or her discretion, and can also thereby influence legislative results.

As the presiding officer, the Speaker recognizes those who wish to speak and rules on points of order—for example, ruling a motion out of order. The Speaker also decides when to put a question to a vote. Knowledge of parliamentary tactics and judicious use of procedure can spell life or death for many bills. Furthermore, the Speaker

> has it within his power to assist a member with a "pet" bill or to sandbag it; he can ease the way for new members or ignore them; he can advance the legislative careers of members or throw up roadblocks before them. All these prerogatives contribute to a network of influence. And, finally, if the Speaker has the strong support of the governor, if he meets with him regularly and is privy to administration plans and secrets, new measures of power and influence come his way.[22]

How long a person serves as Speaker varies from state to state. At one extreme are states such as North Dakota and Arkansas, which select a new Speaker every two years. Usually, however, a Speaker serves one or two terms, but a particularly strong or skillful individual may secure three or more. In a few states—for example, Mississippi and South Carolina—one person has had an extraordinarily long tenure (six or more terms) as Speaker. How much longevity Speakers can amass is also affected by factors largely beyond their control: if their party loses a majority in the chamber, they are nearly certain to lose their leadership post. Two scholars assess the impact of shorter tenure in this manner: it "does not guarantee weak leadership, but it is symptomatic of less independent authority for a leader."[23]

There may be forces at work that encourage longer speakerships. State constitutions have been amended to allow the governor to serve longer, thereby reducing the opportunities for Speakers to move up to the governorship. More important, state legislatures are becoming more professional (higher salaries, longer sessions, better staffing, and so on,). Because the institution they lead is more effective and commands more respect, Speakers are prompted to serve longer.

The politics of leadership selection also varies from state to state. In states in which one party overwhelmingly controls the lower chamber (see Table 6-2), the party caucus of the majority party selects its nominee, who then easily defeats the nominee of the minority party. In other states there may be bipartisan selection of the Speaker. This can be the case if the party balance in the house is very close, or if party discipline is weak, or if there are warring factions (regional, ideological, personal) in the majority party. "The leader chosen is normally a member of the majority party, but he is dependent on a bipartisan coalition for election, and he may allocate committee chairmanships and other prizes to members of both parties."[24] The promise of receiving a choice committee chairmanship is probably the key negotiating point in the politics of selecting the Speaker in every state. Other bargaining chips are better office space, patronage, promises of support on pet bills, and extra money in the state budget for one's district. Additional factors include the location of the aspirant's district, his or her political ideology, endorsement by powerful interest groups, and the candidate's interpersonal skills.

The lieutenant governor is usually the presiding officer of the Senate. If the lieutenant governor does not usually preside or is given few powers, the elected senate leadership consists of the president pro tempore or the senate majority leader. Much of what has been said about the House Speaker can also apply to these latter two individuals.

LEGISLATIVE PROCEDURES

In this section we outline the stages through which a bill progresses on its way to becoming a law. (Some states vary this process in minor details.) After briefly listing the different stages, we will describe each in greater detail.

1. The bill is introduced.
2. The bill is given its first reading (by number, title, and author only) and is then referred to committee.
3. A committee acts on the bill.
4. The bill is given a second reading on the chamber floor; amendments from the floor may be considered.
5. A third and final reading is made. The chamber votes its approval or rejection.
6. If approved, the bill is sent to the other chamber, where steps 1 to 5 are repeated.

7. A conference committee resolves differences in the versions of the bill passed by the two chambers.
8. The bill goes to the governor for signing.

Introduction

The sources of bills are many and varied. The subject matter of a bill may have been something its author was thinking about for some time, or it may have been suggested by a constituent. As we saw in Chapter 4, interest groups suggest many bills. The governor plays a large part in setting the legislature's agenda; he or she is an important source of legislation, as are the agencies and departments of state government. Local governments are regulated by the state; not surprisingly, they or their statewide organizations have many proposals for new legislation. Committee staff members, interim committees of the legislature, and legislative councils (to be described later in the chapter) also have many recommendations.

Whatever the source of a bill, only a member of the legislature can introduce it.[25] Members introduce a bill simply by giving a signed copy of it to the clerk or secretary of the chamber. The number of bill introductions in state legislatures is rising dramatically. Over forty state legislatures allow the filing of bills prior to the start of the session. In fact, a few states permit newly elected members to file bills even before they are sworn into office.

First Reading and Referral

Most state constitutions require that each bill receive three readings. The first reading is perfunctory only. After the bill is read, the Speaker or lieutenant governor refers it to committee.

Committee Consideration

Because of the large number of bills introduced each session, legislatures must divide themselves into committees (see Table 6-3). When a bill is referred to committee, the committee studies it and holds hearings at which interested parties—for example, the bill's author, representatives of the governor, and especially lobbyists—may give their views. This committee stage is a crucial one because many bills do not emerge from committee. Although the chamber may vote to discharge a bill from committee, this procedure is rarely employed. In a survey of over 1100 state legislators, more than 38 percent rated committee meetings as the place where the most significant decisions of the legislature are made.[26]

Committee performance is affected by a number of factors.[27] Although a large number of committees leads to disjointed policymaking, the proliferation of committees is encouraged because committee chair-

TABLE 6-3   Committees of the Illinois Legislature

House	Senate
Agriculture	Agriculture, Conservation, and Energy
Appropriations	Appropriations
Cities and Villages	Assignment of Bills
Counties and Townships	Education: Elementary and Secondary
Elections	Education: Higher
Elementary and Secondary Education	Elections and Reapportionment
Environment, Energy, and Natural	Executive
Resources	Executive Appointments and
Executive	Administration
Financial Institutions	Finance and Credit Regulations
Higher Education	Insurance and Licensed Activities
Human Resources	Judiciary
Insurance	Labor and Commerce
Judiciary	Local Government
Labor and Commerce	Pensions, Personnel, and Veterans Affairs
Motor Vehicles	Public Health, Welfare, and Corrections
Personnel and Pensions	Revenue
Public Utilities	Transportation
Revenue	
State Government Organization	
Transportation	
Veterans Affairs, Registration, and	
Regulation	

manships are favors bartered in leadership contests, because members like to list many committee affiliations when running for reelection, and because interest groups want separate committees in their areas of concern. Some committees handle far more bills than other committees; in fact, many state legislatures have the most important bills of the session sent to committees that have been carefully "packed" by the leadership. The revenue and taxation committees usually are properly staffed, but other committees may not have this important resource (which will be discussed later in the chapter). If seniority is not the basis for committee assignments and committee chairmanships, turnover and lack of expertise and independence will result. Finally, if political parties or factions are influential in committee deliberations, the committees perform poorly.

The weaknesses of state legislative committees are in many respects the weaknesses of the whole legislature. The shortness of legislative sessions, coupled with the fact that a great deal of important legislation is introduced late in the session, means that committees often have scant time for careful review. Relatively high turnover in state legislatures means consequent turnover on committees and lack of specialization and expertise.[28] Pervasive interest-group influence is reflected on committees: bankers are appointed to the Banking Committee, tavern owners are selected for the Alcoholic Beverage Control Committee, insurance agents predominate on the Insurance Committee, and so on. Although this kind of selection may alleviate the problem of expertise, it is fraught with conflict of interest. Most state legislators spend more time as bankers or tavern owners or insurance agents than as lawmakers, yet they are called upon to regulate the very occupation they practice. Surely this practice protects various special interests; whether it promotes the public interest is another matter.

Second Reading and Floor Amendment

Assuming that the committee has reported a bill out, any amendments that the committee has made and any amendments proposed on the floor must be voted on. Not all amendments are intended to strengthen a bill. Opponents may try to add sections that will make the bill less likely to pass on the final vote.

Third Reading and Final Vote

If a bill can make it through committee and through the amending process, its chances of passage are excellent. Based on studies in six states, Rosenthal concludes that fewer than 1 percent of all bills were defeated on the final vote in their chamber of origin.[29] Since the vast majority of bills are noncontroversial, the key factors in passage are the popularity or prestige of the sponsor, his or her skill in guiding the bill through the legislature (for example, securing important co-sponsors, such as party leaders or the chair and members of the committee to which the bill is referred), and how well the sponsor explains the bill on the floor.[30]

The key factors influencing legislators' final votes on more controversial bills are: their personal attitudes, cue taking, interest groups, political parties, and the governor.[31] (Interest groups were discussed in Chapter 4, political parties in Chapter 3, and governors in Chapter 5.) Legislators' personal attitudes include whether they consider themselves representatives of the state as a whole or of only one district within the state, whether they follow the wishes of their constituents or their own conscience, and their ideology. Moreover, legislators are particularly inclined to take *decision cues* from watching other legislators, especially personal friends in the legislature and legislators who are specialists in the subject matter of the bill under consideration. (The subject-matter specialist may be particularly important in state legislatures because so many members are part-timers or amateurs who have limited information on the rather large number of issues that come up for a vote.) The legislator who is cross-pressured by considerations such as "Should I vote according to my political ideology, which on this issue is in conflict with my district's opinion?" is especially inclined toward cue taking. The person sought for a decision cue is usually a member of one's own party or region of the state. In addition, the alignment of major interest groups for or against the bill provides a powerful cue.

Probably the best predictor of how a legislator will vote is his or her party affiliation. There are three types of issues that are very likely to stimulate cohesion among party members in state legislatures.[32] The first of these are issues involving the prestige and fundamental programs of the administration—for example, the governor's appointments, and appropriations and revenue measures. The chief executive is the leader of his or her political party. This role rallies fellow partisans to support him or her—and members of the other party to dig in their heels in opposition. Another type of polarizing issue is any issue that involves the special interests of the state or legislative parties. In this case, the political party itself acts somewhat like a pressure group. Votes to elect the Speaker or to organize the house, votes on patronage matters or gerrymandering or election laws are party-line votes. A final type of issue encouraging party alignments is a social or economic issue on which liberals and conservatives and major interest groups representing their point of view are likely to have taken conflicting stands. Labor-management issues are a good example.

Party voting and party cohesion may also result from the differing types of constituencies represented by Democrats and Republicans. Democrats tend to represent districts that are more urban and densely populated, have lower assessed valuation of housing, and contain more racial or ethnic minorities than the districts of Republicans. Party voting is most common in northern, urban, industrial states with strong electoral competition between the parties and least common in rural, sparsely populated states. When district interests and party philosophy coincide, as do many urban-versus-rural issues, it is easy for legislators to vote with the party.

Party voting, therefore, seems to stem from a number of factors: the symbolic and material powers of the governor, habitual patterns of friendship, alliance, and interdependence, "common ideologies, bargaining arrangements in which members of each party support the projects of fellow partisans while opposing those of the opposition, [and most important, the] coincidence of constituency interests and party program."[33]

Frank Sorauf has shown why there is greater party cohesion in about half of the electorally competitive states than in the Congress of the United States.[34] First, in the states there are fewer centers of power, such as stronger committees based on seniority, to compete with parties. Second, there is more patronage for deserving legislators at the state than the federal level. State party organizations, moreover, are stronger than national party organizations and can sometimes deny renominations to mavericks. Finally, state parties are more homogeneous than the national parties.

Second-Chamber Action

A bill now follows substantially the same course of action in the other chamber. If the second chamber makes no changes in the bill, it is sent to the governor for his or her consideration. Should the second chamber amend the bill (a strong possibility), it is sent to the chamber of origin with a request that the original chamber accept the changes that have been made. If the chamber of origin refuses to accept the changes that have been made in its bill, a conference committee must be called.

Conference Committee

The presiding officers of the two chambers each appoint three or more members of their respective chamber to serve on the conference committee established for this bill. Conference committees have a great deal of leeway in working out an agreement between the chambers; they often may deal with matters *beyond* those in dispute between the chambers. When a majority of each delegation has approved the conference committee's work, the delegations present the conference committee's bill to their respective chambers on a take-it-or-leave-it basis. If the two chambers accept the bill exactly as presented to them by their conferees, the bill goes to the governor for his or her consideration. Should one or both of the chambers refuse to accept the conference committee's actions, a new conference committee must be appointed.

Conference committees often work on the most important bills of the session at the very end of the session. In such a situation, conference committees have even greater powers than usual. Conference committees may also be particularly important in situations of divided control, for the different parties will bargain hard for their chamber's version of the bill.

Reception of Bill by Governor

If the governor signs the bill, it usually takes effect after a brief waiting period. Governors normally have about two weeks in which to sign or veto the bill; if they do nothing, the bill becomes law without their signature. As we have seen, governors veto few bills and are almost always successful in sustaining these vetoes.

> There are several reasons why the governor in most states can nearly always make his veto stick. His political power is usually great enough so that he can maintain the support of the one-third or two-fifths majority to uphold a veto. Moreover, a large proportion of bills are passed in the closing days of a session, and on these the governor can exercise his veto after the legislature has adjourned.[35]

END-OF-SESSION RUSH, MONEY BILLS

Legislatures find it exceedingly difficult to adhere to a schedule and to meet deadlines faithfully, a not uncommon human failing. Almost all states have deadlines for the introduction of bills, but a legislator can almost always receive a waiver. There may also be deadlines for final committee action or for conference committee action. The failure to meet deadlines results in a mad end-of-the-session logjam of bills. As the minutes tick away and the end of the session nears, legislators resort to odd tactics: they unplug the clock or cover it with a towel. In Colorado, an employee of the legislature once broke his leg when the chair he was standing on to unplug the clock suddenly tipped over. Keefe and Ogul write that "as many as 50 percent of all bills passed during a session receive final approval in the last week."[36] Another key aspect of the end-of-the-session rush is that the most important bills of the session are frequently considered then. Earlier in the session, the legislature spent valuable time on less important matters. The recent lengthening of sessions has done little to alter this situation.

In defense of the legislature, two observers note, backlogs "reflect the *politics* of the legislative process. Many reformers decry these backlogs as an affront to good government, but if they understood that backlogs give the leadership another opportunity to exercise its traditionally powerful role, the reformers might be more successful in their efforts to suggest alternatives."[37] Legislative leaders frequently hold members' pet bills hostage in order to insure the members' votes on key bills—for example, the budget. Another reason bills pile up at the end of the session is that bills called early in the session undergo more careful scrutiny. No legislator wants his or her bill nitpicked to death. Moreover, someone sponsoring blatantly special-interest legislation may find it easier to sneak it through in the end-of-session confusion. Also, the astute legislator-politician who can delay consideration of his or her pet legislation until late in the session can meanwhile do favors for other members, engage in vote trading, and generally acquire political IOUs that may be redeemed near the end of the session.

Usually the most important bill of the session is the budget bill (or bills). So as not to relinquish control over crucial decisions on state spending, legislatures are increasingly turning to computers in an attempt to exert independence from the executive in fiscal matters. Michigan and New York are good examples, with the latter using its computer capability to forecast state revenues. Legislatures are steadily moving from cursory review of the budget to the making of informed policy choices. A related matter is the disposition of funds coming from the federal government. If this substantial amount of money is not appropriated through the budget, executive agencies can spend it according to their own priorities.

Three fourths of the legislatures make specific appropriations of federal funds. Without effective scrutiny, executive agencies could use these funds to begin or continue programs that the legislature has disapproved.

SUPPORT SERVICES

The importance of adequate professional staffing in providing independence from the executive branch and from interest groups has been stressed throughout this chapter. Table 6-4 shows the number of professional staff members working for different state legislatures. The benefits of additional committee staff can be seen in

> changes in the amount of information available to legislators; changes for the better in the technical characteristics of legislation [fewer unclear sections of bills passed last session must be corrected this session]; a decline in the trend toward the sweeping delegation of increasing amounts of authority to the executive branch; an increase in the ability of the legislature to oversee executive agency activities; the legislature's resumption of an initiatory stand on several policy areas. . . .[38]

Greater staff can help members by analyzing the growing number of bills introduced each session, as information from Illinois indicates:

> The reason staff people are there is simple. Somebody has to read everything. Even the most conscientious legislator can't read all of the bills. This past session the Legislative Reference Bureau drafted nearly 5,000 documents for the legislature—that's about 15–20 million words. Of these, 3,200 bills were introduced, or about 10–12 million words. These bills, plus amendments, produced a stack nearly four feet tall—thousands of pages, all in legalese.[39]

In fact, a case can be made that some state legislatures have gone too far in the direction of additional staff assistance. Adding staff clearly slows down the legislative process, but whether this is a drawback depends on one's point of view. Rosenthal argues that

> hiring staff has increased the legislator's workload. A good staffer is motivated and wants to distinguish himself (and more and more, herself) to get ahead. He seeks out problems, devises legislative solutions, and confronts legislators (whether leaders, committee chairmen, or rank-and-file members) with agendas for action. How can they resist? The result is more bills introduced, more laws enacted, more work for everyone.[40]

Legislative councils, which consist of legislators and a permanent research staff, have greatly assisted legislators in making informed choices and in making better use of their time. Found in forty-three states,

TABLE 6-4 Number of Professional Staff Members Serving State Legislatures

States	Number of Staff
Delaware, North Dakota, Vermont, Wyoming	1–25
Idaho, Maine, Nevada, New Hampshire, New Mexico, North Carolina, South Dakota, Utah	26–50
Iowa, Kentucky, Mississippi, Missouri, Montana, Oklahoma, Rhode Island, South Carolina, West Virginia	51–75
Alaska, Hawaii, Indiana, Kansas, Nebraska	76–100
Oregon, Alabama, Colorado, Connecticut, Tennessee, Arizona, Georgia, Virginia, Arkansas, Maryland, Washington	101–200
Louisiana, Ohio, Massachusetts, Minnesota, Wisconsin, Illinois, New Jersey	201–300
	301–400
Texas, Pennsylvania	401–500
Michigan	501–600
Florida	601–700
New York, California	701–800

SOURCE: Lucinda S. Simon, *A Legislator's Guide to Staffing Patterns* (Denver, Col.: National Conference of State Legislatures, 1979), p. 43.

legislative councils usually operate between sessions, conducting research on state problems and developing a general legislative program for consideration by the succeeding session. Because of the large number of new members each session and the shortness of most legislative sessions, it is imperative that legislators not waste valuable time early in the session trying to organize a legislative program. Legislators not named to the legislative council may be jealous of its power or feel it is trying to usurp their powers. Legislative council members therefore stress that their role is only advisory and that any bills they draw up are recommendations for consideration by the regular committees of the legislature. Legislative councils do *not* draw up specific programs intended to compete with the governor's program, but they do lessen reliance on the administration or interest groups for information. According to a political scientist who served for thirty years as research director of the Kansas Legislative Council, the "teaming together of the practical legislator with his inquiries and the technical [research] staff with their training is the fundamental achievement which has made the legislative council movement a success."[41]

CHANGE AND REFORM

A number of changes intended to strengthen the position of state legislatures have been proposed or adopted.

Oversight of the Bureaucracy

One of these is increased legislative oversight of the bureaucracy. With the possible exception of the heavily staffed California legislature, hardly any state legislature engages in sustained review of administrative activity. Administrators have substantial discretion in the making of decisions that affect people's lives, and they have the power to issue rules and regulations that have the force of law. Yet administrators serve for long periods, usually under civil service protection, without ever having to face the voters in an election. These facts raise a serious question of democratic accountability. If the legislature passes laws and then proceeds to ignore how *and if* they are carried out by administrators, it can hardly be considered a very effective body.

The intent of legislative oversight is to determine if the laws passed by the state legislature are being administered faithfully and efficiently and are meeting their objectives; to guarantee that there has been no arbitrary abuse of administrative discretion; and to monitor the spending of public money. The state legislature achieves these objectives by means of committee hearings and investigations, the budget process, the state auditor, the establishment of agencies and departments and the specification of their objectives (unless they are provided for in the state constitution), the approval or rejection of the governor's nominees to high administrative positions, and legislators' responses to requests for assistance made by constituents. Legislators will look closely at bureaucratic activity if substantial new expenditures or new authorizations in controversial areas are requested; if a crisis was not adequately handled by administrators; if the governor is a member of a different political party or faction; if their constituents are receiving poor service from a state agency, and if they lack confidence in administrators.[42]

Despite all of these incentives to oversee the bureaucracy, state legislators really do not perform this task, for several reasons. They sometimes lack the staff to do it, this kind of time-consuming activity usually has no political payoff, and as part-time citizen-legislators they may not be able to figure out the often byzantine workings of bureaucracy. Moreover, there is a political *danger* in legislative oversight. If an ineffective or wasteful program is ended, the interest groups benefiting from it will protest vigorously. On the other hand, the tens of thousands of taxpayers who are each saved a small amount of money will be unaware that they have benefited.

One area that might merit greater legislative concern is the rules and regulations issued by administrators. As we have seen, such rules and regulations have the force of law, and "in most states today, the body of law created by the rule-making process matches or exceeds the statutory law of those states."[43] If this is true, provisions in state constitutions granting "full legislative power" to the legislature have a hollow ring. In Florida, it was discovered that provisions dropped from a bill during its consideration by the legislature were resurrected by administrators carrying out the law. In New York, parts of a bill vetoed by the governor found their way into state law by means of administrative regulations.[44]

Over thirty states have provisions for legislative review of regulations, either by the regular committees of the legislature or by a joint committee composed of members of both chambers. In some states all rules may be reviewed, in others only proposed rules, and in still others only existing rules. In two thirds of the states, the legislative review is advisory only and agencies cannot be forced to withdraw a rule. Of course, the legislature always has the power to repeal the statute under which the regulation was issued. Usually the whole legislature must affirm what its reviewing committee has done.

Objections have been raised to the practice of legislative review of rules and regulations: it supposedly violates the separation-of-powers concept because it allows the legislature to intrude into executive-branch responsibilities; some states permit only a committee and not the whole legislature to veto rules; the review process entails too heavy a workload for legislators working in brief sessions; and the process enhances the influence of interest groups (especially business) over state government. The legal status of state legislative review of administrative regulations is clouded by a U.S. Supreme Court ruling that may or may not apply to the states, *Immigration and Naturalization Service* v. *Chadha*, 462 U.S. 919 (1983). The Court held that a similar procedure of Congress violated the separation-of-powers doctrine at the federal level.

A recent proposal for increasing bureaucratic responsiveness is to establish *sunset laws*. The theory behind sunset legislation is that state programs and agencies should not be considered permanent, that they should be periodically reviewed from scratch, with wasteful or inefficient programs simply fading into the sunset. Sunset shifts the burden of proof from those who feel an agency is doing a poor job to the agency itself, which would have to justify its existence. This process has attracted broad support, and has been adopted in thirty-three states. Conservatives favor sunset because it reflects their "reduce the size of government" philosophy, while liberals see it as a way for government to get its house in order in preparation for taking on important new responsibilities in an age of fiscal stringency. Critics of sunset legislation argue that the process usually covers only regulatory boards or occupational licensing agencies and not the major departments of state government. It is also argued that sunset is not cost-effective. Colorado spent about $200,000 to eliminate four boards whose total budget was $11,000. The more agencies reviewed, the less thorough is each evaluation. In Alabama, one hundred hours were spent to review two hundred agencies, or thirty minutes per agency.

Finally, political reality confirms that all programs have some constituency; special interests will fight repeal of favored programs even if shown that they do not work.

As legislators bring state bureaucracies under closer scrutiny, it bears remembering that these individuals, whatever their faults, are at least elected by the people and thus answerable to them. If administrators use their expertise, especially in technical areas, to withhold information from nonspecialist legislators, the democratic process is short-circuited.

Unicameralism

Since Nebraska adopted its unicameral legislature in 1934, there has been a persistent minority urging unicameralism for other states. For example, the National Municipal League endorses this reform in its Model State Constitution (see Chapter 1). The proponents of unicameralism argue that a single chamber, with its larger prestige, will attract better-qualified legislators; that one chamber is more efficient than two, because there is no need for double consideration of bills or for conference committees; that a single chamber is more economical (a desire for fewer salaries for members and staff prompted Nebraska to adopt its Depression-era reform); that there can be no rivalry, friction, or jealousy developing between two separate sets of legislative leaders; and especially, that a single chamber minimizes buck passing and makes it easier for the media and the public to pinpoint responsibility for legislative action and inaction. The supporters of bicameralism respond that a second chamber can serve as a check on the first, perhaps preventing the passage of hasty or careless or defective legislation. More important, two chambers allow the possibility of dominance by two different interests or parties, as is frequently the case in New York.[45]

A Reform Program

Throughout this chapter, various reforms for strengthening state legislatures have been mentioned. These suggestions are generally part of the reform program of the Citizens Conference on State Legislatures, which operated in the 1960s and early 1970s. The Citizens Conference evaluated state legislatures on the following bases:

1. *Functionality:* Does the legislature have enough time to do an adequate job? Is there sufficient staff to research issues? Are physical facilities (committee hearing rooms, individual offices for legislators, electronic voting machines) adequate? Is the legislature too large? Are orderly and decorous procedures followed?

2. *Accountability to the public:* Are single-member districts used instead of multimember districts? Are legislative rules and procedures clear enough for the public to understand? Do committees meet in open sessions? Are legislators (and their families and business partners) required to disclose their income?

3. *Availability of information:* Are there so many committees that coherent policies cannot be adopted? Are committee meetings announced sufficiently in advance that interested parties can testify? Do interim committees supply information to the legislature? Does the legislature employ adequate professional, legal, and fiscal staff?

4. *Independence:* Can the legislature call itself into session? Does the legislature properly oversee the bureaucracy? Are there effective conflict-of-interest laws and lobbyist-regulation laws?

5. *Representativeness:* Are legislative salaries so low that people of modest means cannot afford to serve in the legislature?[46]

As this and preceding chapters have attempted to show, state legislatures have made great strides toward reform. It is clear that the reforms advocated by the Citizens Conference are procedural and structural. That is, they are intended to help the legislature perform its constitutional duties. We might inquire whether these changes affect the kinds of public policies enacted by legislatures thus reformed. The answer is rather mixed. One study found no difference in levels of expenditures between reformed and unreformed legislatures; another study discovered no relationship between the Citizens Conference criteria and educational and welfare expenditures, revenue raised, the scope of state government, or state innovation.[47] On the other hand, a different researcher found assumption of new state responsibilities, progressivity of the tax structure, welfare liberalism, per capita expenditures to be related to some of the criteria.[48] Reformed legislatures are said by another writer to engage in increased *nonexpenditure* activity for urban areas (on open-space programs, a state air-pollution agency, metro-area planning commissions, and so forth).[49] Another investigator noted that the Indiana General Assembly did not enact more progressive or urban-oriented legislation after creating annual sessions, higher salaries and more staff, committee hearing rooms and open committee meetings, and procedural deadlines.[50] Perhaps we should not assume that reform *will* make a difference just because it ought to make a difference. Yet the suggested reforms are worthwhile in themselves and should not be discounted.

SUMMARY

In this chapter, we have considered state legislatures: their powers, characteristics, procedures, and support services. Change and reform make state legislatures of the late 1980s far different from those of the late 1960s. One agent for change is the increased difficulty of getting elected to a state legislature. Those men and women who *do* get elected want to feel that they are accomplishing something in the state capital: "I put a lot into getting here, so now I want to get something done."

NOTES

1. Charles Adrian and Charles Press, *American Politics Reappraised* (New York: Mc-Graw-Hill, 1974), p. 189.

2. Alan Rosenthal, "Contradictions of Legislative Life," *State Legislatures*, August-September 1983, p. 31.

3. John C. Wahlke et al., *The Legislative System* (New York: John Wiley, 1962), p. 214.

4. Alan Rosenthal and Rod Forth, "The Assembly Line: Law Production in the American States," *Legislative Studies Quarterly*, 3 (May 1978), 269.

5. Charles R. Adrian, *State and Local Governments*, 4th ed. (New York: McGraw-Hill, 1976), p. 289.

6. Quoted in Citizens Conference on State Legislatures and John Burns, *The Sometime Governments* (New York: Bantam, 1971), p. 67. For a similar view voiced two centuries ago, see Alexander Hamilton, James Madison, and John Jay, *The Federalist Papers* (New York: Mentor Books, 1961; first written in 1788), p. 360.

7. Citizens Conference and Burns, *The Sometime Governments*, p. 56.

8. Eric M. Uslaner and Ronald E. Weber, *Patterns of Decision Making in State Legislatures* (New York: Praeger, 1977), pp. 14–17. Assessing the stringency of limitations on session length is complicated by the fact that in many states, such limitations are expressed in legislative days rather than in calendar days. A single legislative day may extend over several calendar days.

9. Kwang Shin and John S. Jackson II, "Membership Turnover in U.S. State Legislatures: 1931–1976," *Legislative Studies Quarterly*, 4 (February 1979), 95–104.

10. Ibid. See also Alan Rosenthal, "Turnover in State Legislatures," *American Journal of Political Science*, 18 (August 1974), 612–13.

11. Craig Grau, "Competition in State Legislative Primaries," *Legislative Studies Quarterly*, 6 (February 1981), 47–48.

12. Wahlke et al., *The Legislative System*, pp. 144–61. The rules mentioned are a partial list.

13. Malcolm Jewell and Samuel Patterson, *The Legislative Process in the United States*, 3rd ed. (New York: Random House, 1977), p. 328.

14. Wahlke et al., *The Legislative System*, pp. 245–66.

15. *Kirkpatrick v. Preisler*, 394 U.S. 528 (1969).

16. *Mahan v. Howell*, 410 U.S. 315 (1973).

17. Malcolm E. Jewell, "Commentary," in *Reapportionment in the 1970s*, ed. Nelson Polsby (Berkeley: University of California Press, 1971), p. 47.

18. Yong Hyo Cho and H. George Fredrickson, "The Effects of Reapportionment: Subtle, Selective, Limited," *National Civic Review*, 63 (July 1974), 357–62.

19. Samuel Patterson, "American State Legislatures and Public Policy," in *Politics in the American States: A Comparative Analysis*, 3rd ed., ed. Herbert Jacob and Kenneth N. Vines (Boston: Little, Brown, 1976), p. 155. See also p. 152.

20. William J. Keefe and Morris S. Ogul, *The American Legislative Process*, 6th ed. (Englewood Cliffs, N.J.: Prentice-Hall, 1985), pp. 239–40.

21. Abdo I. Baaklini and Charles S. Dawson, *The Politics of Legislation in New York State* (Albany: Comparative Development Studies Center, State University of New York at Albany, and the New York State Assembly, 1979), p. 21.

22. Keefe and Ogul, *The American Legislative Process*, p. 240.

23. Malcolm E. Jewell and Samuel C. Patterson, *The Legislative Process in the United States*, 3rd ed. (New York: Random House, 1977), p. 136. See also "Survey on Selection of State Legislative Leaders," *Comparative State Politics Newsletter*, May 1980, p. 11.

24. "Survey on Selection of State Legislative Leaders," p. 13. See also Alan Rosenthal, *Legislative Life* (New York: Harper & Row, Pub., 1981), pp. 159–60.

25. In Massachusetts, citizens have a *right of free petition*, which means that if a citizen wants a bill introduced, his or her representative *must* introduce it. In fact, the right of free

petition "requires that each bill be acted upon by a committee, including a public hearing and a final committee report": Edwin Andrus Gere and Peter Chisholm, "The Massachusetts General Court: A Closeup View," in *The Massachusetts General Court*, ed. Edwin Andrus Gere (Washington, D.C.: American Political Science Association, 1972), p. 17. Furthermore, these bills must be reported out of the committee and sent to the floor. See also Harmon Zeigler and Michael A. Baer, *Lobbying* (Belmont, Calif.: Wadsworth, 1969), p. 163.

26.   Uslaner and Weber, *Patterns*, pp. 41–42.

27.   Alan Rosenthal, *Legislative Performance in the States: Explorations of Committee Behavior* (New York: Free Press, 1974), chap. 2.

28.   Malcolm E. Jewell, *The State Legislature*, 2nd ed. (New York: Random House, 1969), pp. 52, 56–57. One study argues that committee turnover is *not* related to the quality of committee performance: James R. Oxendale, Jr., "The Impact of Membership Turnover on Internal Structures of State Legislative Lower Chambers" (paper presented at the annual meeting of the American Political Science Association, Washington, D.C., 1979).

29.   Rosenthal, *Legislative Life*, pp. 79–80.

30.   Samuel Gove, Richard W. Carlson, and Richard J. Carlson, *The Illinois Legislature* (Urbana: University of Illinois Press, 1976), chap. 7.

31.   James S. Lee, "Toward an Understanding of State Legislative Decision-Making," in *Dimensions of State and Urban Policy Making,* ed. Richard Leach and Timothy O'Rourke (New York: Macmillan, 1975), pp. 156–75.

32.   Jewell and Patterson, *The Legislative Process*, p. 394.

33.   Julius Turner and Edward V. Schneier, Jr., *Party and Constituency*, rev. ed. (Baltimore: Johns Hopkins, 1970), pp. 234, 236. Another scholar places great stress on the effectiveness of socialization into the legislative party, partisan recruitment, and a common stake in party prestige in producing a community of interest and hence party voting: Judson L. James, *American Political Parties* (New York: Pegasus, 1969), p. 151.

34.   Frank S. Sorauf, *Party Politics in America*, 5th ed. (Boston: Little, Brown, 1984), pp. 353–56.

35.   Jewell, *The State Legislature*, p. 67.

36.   Keefe and Ogul, *The American Legislative Process*, p. 206. Harvey Tucker studied thirty-seven state legislatures in the early 1980s and found that 38 percent of all bills were passed in the final 10 percent of each session. Scheduling deadlines (e.g., for bill introductions, committee reports, and floor action in the chamber of origin) was the most effective way to prevent logjams: Harvey Tucker, "Legislative Logjams," *Western Political Quarterly*, 38 (September 1985), 437–44.

37.   Baaklini and Dawson, *The Politics of Legislation*, p. 35 (emphasis in original).

38.   Alan P. Balutis, "Legislative Staffing: Does It Make a Difference?" in *Legislative Reform and Public Policy*, ed. Susan Welch and John G. Peters (New York: Praeger, 1977), p. 136.

39.   Patrick O'Grady, "What's It Like to Work for the General Assembly?" *Illinois Issues*, November 1981, p. 27. An additional benefit of having *personal* staffers is that they can help the member respond to constituents' requests—for example, for aid in securing unemployment compensation or welfare.

40.   Rosenthal, "Contradictions," p. 32.

41.   Frederic H. Guild, *Legislative Councils after Thirty Years* (Carbondale: Southern Illinois University Public Affairs Research Bureau, 1964), p. 22. However, Pound writes that in the last two decades, "legislative councils have been gradually disbanded in favor of more decentralized and specialized staff arrangements": William T. Pound, "The State Legislatures," in *Book of the States: 1984–85* (Lexington, Ky.: Council of State Governments, 1984), p. 81.

42.   On oversight in general see, John F. Bibby, "Oversight: Congress' Neglected Function" (paper presented at the annual meeting of the Western Political Science Association, Denver, 1974), p. 7.

43.   National Conference of State Legislatures, quoted in "How Two States Monitor the Cost of New Regulations," *State Legislatures*, November-December 1978, p. 21.

44. Keith Hamm and Roby Robertson, "Factors Influencing the Adoption of New Methods of Legislative Oversight in the U.S. States," *Legislative Studies Quarterly*, 6 (February 1981), 135.

45. These arguments for and against unicameralism have been taken from George S. Blair, *American Legislatures* (New York: Harper & Row, Pub., 1967), pp. 143–44.

46. Citizens Conference and Burns, *The Sometime Governments*.

47. Leonard Ritt, "State Legislative Reform: Does It Matter?" *American Politics Quarterly*, 1 (October 1973), 499–510; Albert K. Karnig and Lee Sigelman, "State Legislative Reform and Public Policy: Another Look," *Western Political Quarterly*, 28 (September 1975), 548–52.

48. Lance T. Le Loup, "The Policy Consequences of State Legislative Reform," *Georgia Political Science Association Journal*, Fall 1977, pp. 23–40.

49. Michael Le May, "Expenditure and Nonexpenditure Measures of State Urban Policy Output," *American Politics Quarterly*, 1 (October 1973), 511–28.

50. James L. McDowell, "Legislative Reform in Indiana: The Promises and the Products," in *Legislative Reform and Public Policy*, ed. Welch and Peters, pp. 157–72.

chapter 7

State Judiciary

State courts play a vital role in the American system of government because the vast majority of legal disputes are settled in state rather than federal courts. State legislatures have the police power, which as we have seen, is the power to pass laws promoting the health, safety, welfare, and morals of the people. Therefore, the issues coming before state courts span a broad spectrum: crimes, auto accident cases, domestic relations, business regulation, wills, and many other matters. Moreover, most political issues eventually become legal questions, so "all American officials live in the shadow of the courthouse."[1] The power of the state judiciary is pervasive and it merits close attention.

STRUCTURE OF THE STATE COURTS

Court organization varies markedly from state to state. But however a state may structure its courts, one fact stands out: most civil and criminal cases never go to trial. Nine out of every ten cases are settled out of court.[2] Civil cases are negotiated by the attorneys for the two parties, who agree upon a monetary settlement. By avoiding having to go into court, lawyers can handle more cases and thus increase their incomes. Criminal cases are settled by *plea bargaining*, in which the accused person pleads guilty to an offense less severe than the one with which he or she has been charged. Prosecutors favor this arrangement because it increases their record of convictions, and defense attorneys are often able to save their client from a long prison sentence. Judges encourage both of these processes as a way of relieving crowded court calendars.

An overview of state court organization is presented in Table 7-1.

143

TABLE 7-1 State Court Organization

Trial Courts of Limited Jurisdiction

Illinois and Iowa have no courts of limited jurisdiction, twelve states have one, eight states have two, seven states have three, nine states have four, and twelve states have five or more. These courts are usually called justice-of-the-peace courts, municipal courts, county courts, probate courts, courts of common pleas, or magistrate courts.

Trial Courts of General Jurisdiction

Forty-two states have one of these courts, five states have two, and three states have three or four. They are usually called circuit courts, district courts, or superior courts.

Intermediate Appellate Courts

Thirty-seven states have intermediate appellate courts, and three of these have separate courts for civil appeals and for criminal appeals. The most typical name is court of appeal.

Court of Last Resort

All states have a court of last resort, which is normally called the supreme court, but occasionally the supreme judicial court.

Trial Courts of Limited Jurisdiction

At the bottom of many state court systems are justices of the peace. These rural officials are usually elected, and do not need legal training to hold their post. Justices of the peace try minor criminal cases (*misdemeanors*), preside over civil suits for small amounts of money, and perform marriages. Their salary is derived from fees collected from the losing party. Because justices of the peace can send a person to county jail but may have had no legal training whatsoever, bar associations have tried strenuously to eliminate their positions. The urban counterpart of the justice-of-the-peace court is the magistrate court or municipal court. Each of these courts is often thought of as local, but they are in fact state courts. In some states, trial courts of limited jurisdiction have mushroomed, each having a very specialized function: small claims, juvenile matters, probate (wills), or traffic.

Trial Courts of General Jurisdiction

The really important state trials take place in trial courts of general jurisdiction, because it is here that felonies are tried and large civil suits are litigated. If it wishes, the party that lost in a court of limited jurisdiction can have its case heard *de novo* in a court of general jurisdiction. This means that everything done in the lower court is thrown out, and the case begins anew.

One authority on the American legal system has argued that "repeat players," who use the trial courts frequently, will win more often than one-time users.[3] Collection agencies and real estate management firms have developed the legal expertise to use the court system to their own advantage. Moreover, these and other repeat players are much more likely than individuals to appeal an adverse decision. Since most trial-court cases are not appealed, the decision of the trial court of general jurisdiction is likely to be final.

Intermediate Appellate Courts

Intermediate appellate courts, in those states that have them, reduce the workload of the court of last resort. As we have seen, most trial-court cases are not appealed. Moreover, an intermediate appellate court may choose not to take an appeal, and if it does take an appeal, its decision is final.

Appellate courts conduct hearings rather than trials. The purpose of the hearing is to determine if proper legal procedures were followed at the trial-court level. For instance, did the judge apply the law correctly? Were the jurors unbiased? The facts of the case—who was guilty or who was at fault—were supposedly determined by the trial court; hence there is no interrogation of witnesses or introduction of evidence. Attorneys present short, oral summaries of their cases, answer questions from the justices, and then submit written arguments called *briefs*. Sometimes the lawyers do not appear at all, but only forward their written arguments to be read by the judges. Since intermediate appellate courts are intended to provide a final resolution for routine cases, only controversial issues or novel questions of law may be appealed from these courts to the state supreme court.

Court of Last Resort

At the top of the state court system is the supreme court, a position of power and prestige to which all attorneys aspire. The state's highest court is clearly an important policy maker within the state, and the supreme courts of New York, California, and numerous other states have decided cases in ways that influenced how the U.S. Supreme Court dealt with the same issue.

There are six types of state supreme court policy making.[4] Through *innovative policy making*, the supreme court overturns an existing state policy or fills a gap in state policy by imposing an alternative policy. In this most dramatic manifestation of its power, the court may strike down social legislation such as antisodomy or antimarijuana statutes, or economic legislation such as fair-trade laws. By means of *agenda-setting policy making*, the court overturns a long-standing policy but does not provide an alternative. For example, supreme courts have invalidated school finance programs and land-use ordinances. On the other hand, state legislatures have been aided by *complementary policy making*, where the court nullifies a policy the legislature was afraid to tackle—for example, the requirement of an extraordinary majority of voters to approve city bonds. By *elaborative policy making*, the state supreme court extends U.S. Supreme Court rulings in areas such as defendants' rights or the right to privacy. Conversely, *restrictive policy making* seeks to limit or evade decisions of the federal high court. For example, some of the liberal decisions of the U.S. Supreme Court under Chief Justice Earl Warren were given a very narrow interpretation by state supreme courts. Finally, state supreme courts engage in *institutional policy making* when they seek to protect the independence or integrity of the court system, as when they require adequate funding for the judiciary.

When writing decisions or granting interviews to scholars, supreme court justices usually deny that they play a policy-making or lawmaking role. When justices of four state supreme courts were interviewed, less than one in four would acknowledge that they play a lawmaking role.[5] Most prefer to say that they merely apply the state constitution, interpret the law as written by the legislature, correct errors in lower-court decisions, or provide guidance for lower courts to follow in future cases. As we shall see in our discussion of how judges are selected for office, all selection procedures are to some extent political and almost all judges have a background in political activity. Men and women do not discard long-cherished beliefs regarding good public policy when they assume the position of judge. Judges may view themselves not as actually making policy, but rather as defending the state and federal constitutions, protecting individual rights, or promoting justice. The long-standing American image of the judge as neutral interpreter of the law also helps to preserve the power of state judges.

The policy-making role of appellate justices becomes apparent in cases when they cannot agree upon a single written opinion and a minority issues one or more dissenting opinions. The dissents usually castigate the majority for policy making or point out that state law or the state constitution is ambiguous or equivocal and can be interpreted from different points of view. Rates of dissent vary from state to state; the supreme courts in Michigan, New York, and Pennsylvania have almost as many minority opinions as the U.S. Supreme Court.[6] States with close competition between the Democratic and Republican parties and/or states with urban versus rural divisions tend to have more conflict in the state supreme court. Lawyers who supported different interests may continue their struggle after becoming judges. Also, supreme courts with larger numbers of judges have more dissent because there are more people who can look at judicial issues differently. States with intermediate appellate courts have a higher rate of dissent in the court of last resort because intermediate appellate courts have screened out the routine and noncontroversial cases.

Democratic judges are much more likely than Republican judges to favor: the administrative agency in business-regulation cases, the claimant in unemployment-compensation cases, the employee in employee-injury cases, the defense in criminal cases, the finding of a violation of the defendant's constitutional rights in a criminal case, the government in tax cases, the tenant in landlord-tenant cases, the consumer in sales-of-goods cases, and the injured party in motor-vehicle accident cases.[7] The first three tendencies are particularly strong, and all nine are in conformance with the postures generally taken by Democratic and Republican governors and state legislators.

COURT REFORM

The Model State Constitution noted in Chapter 1 describes the reformers' ideal court system: unified organization, centralized administration, and selection of judges by the Missouri Plan. The goal is to centralize judicial power in the state supreme court in a manner similar to the reformers' ideal of centralizing executive branch power in the governor. Components of a reformed court system would include:

1. A *consolidated court structure*, with the elimination of overlapping and conflicting jurisdictions for trial courts
2. *Centralized management* of the court system, with responsibility vested in the chief justice of the supreme court and a state court administrator chosen by him or her
3. *Centralized rule making* by the supreme court, not subject to a veto by the state legislature
4. *Unitary budgeting* for all of the state's courts, prepared by the court administrator without review by the governor
5. *State financing* for the entire judicial system, with all fees and fines collected at the local level paid into the state treasury[8]

(Other reforms, such as the Missouri Plan for selecting judges and judicial disciplinary commissions, will be considered later in the chapter.)

A consolidated structure simplifies the court system by eliminating all trial courts except one of limited jurisdiction and one of general jurisdiction. Reformers would prefer the Kansas system shown in Table 7-2. Centralized management allows the chief justice to temporarily reassign judges from one court to another in order to equalize work loads and reduce backlogs. Because the state supreme court has greater expertise in judicial procedure and evidence, it and not the state legislature should make rules for the courts. By means of unitary budgeting, the indepen-

TABLE 7-2 Two Different Court Systems

	Kansas	Tennessee
Trial Court of Limited Jurisdiction	Municipal courts	County courts General sessions courts Municipal courts Juvenile courts Domestic relations courts Trial justice courts Probate courts
Trial Court of General Jurisdiction	District courts	Circuit courts Criminal courts Law-equity courts
Intermediate Appellate Court	Court of Appeals	Court of Appeals Court of Criminal Appeals
Court of Last Resort	Supreme Court	Supreme Court

dence of lower state courts can be reduced. State financing achieves the same objective and also guarantees that since court services no longer depend on local revenues, there will be a uniform level of court services throughout the state.

The current reform movement grew from the Progressive movement of the early twentieth century, the National Municipal League, the teachings of legal scholar Roscoe Pound, and the urgings of prominent jurists such as former New Jersey Supreme Court chief justice Arthur Vanderbilt. It now includes the American Bar Association and its state affiliates, the League of Women Voters, and high-status lawyers. Those who might oppose reform are trial lawyers and general-practice lawyers, some of whom are comfortable with the court system as it exists; court employees whose jobs might be eliminated in a consolidated system; and the Democratic party, which now controls most urban court systems.

SELECTION AND REMOVAL

There are five different methods for selecting judges: partisan election, nonpartisan election, gubernatorial appointment, legislative appointment, and gubernatorial appointment followed by a retention election (Missouri Plan). An important point to remember is that whatever system a state may formally employ, many judges initially reached the bench as interim appointments by the governor to fill the unexpired part of the term of a judge who resigned or retired. In most states judges commonly retire or resign shortly before the end of their term, creating a vacancy for the governor to fill. Many states use a combination of methods for selecting judges, as shown in Table 7-3.

TABLE 7-3 Methods of Selecting State Judges

Partisan Election [a]	Nonpartisan Election	Gubernatorial Appointment	Legislative Appointment	Gubernatorial Appointment and Retention Election
Alabama (all) [a]	California (trial)	Arizona (all app, most trial)	Connecticut (all)	Alaska (all)
Arkansas (all)	Florida (trial)	Delaware (all)	Rhode Island (app)	California (app)
Georgia (all app, some trial)	Idaho (all)	Georgia (some trial)	South Carolina (all)	Colorado (all)
Illinois [b] (all)	Kansas (trial)	Hawaii (all)	Virginia (all)	Florida (app)
Indiana (some trial)	Kentucky (all)	Indiana (all app, some trial)		Iowa (all)
Mississippi (all)	Louisiana (all)	Maine (all)		Kansas (app)
Missouri (some trial)	Michigan [b] (all)	Maryland (all)		Missouri (all app, some trial)
New Mexico (all)	Minnesota (all)	Massachusetts (all)		Nebraska (all)
New York (some trial)	Montana (all)	New Hampshire (all)		Oklahoma (some app)
North Carolina (all)	Nevada (all)	New Jersey (all)		South Dakota (app)
Tennessee (some app, all trial)	North Dakota (all)	New York (all app, some trial)		Tennessee (some app)
Texas (all)	Ohio [b] (all)	Rhode Island (some trial)		Wyoming (all)
West Virginia (all)	Oklahoma (some app, some trial)	Vermont (all)		
	Oregon (all)			
	Pennsylvania [b] (all)			
	South Dakota (trial)			
	Utah (all)			
	Washington (all)			
	Wisconsin (all)			

SOURCE: *Book of the States, 1984–85* (Lexington, Ky.: Council of State Governments, 1984), pp. 154–55.

[a] *All* means all judges selected by this means; *app* means only appellate judges selected by this means; *trial* means only trial judges selected by this means.

[b] Nomination in a partisan primary followed by nonpartisan election or retention election.

There is no "nonpolitical" method for selecting judges: all systems are to some extent based on political considerations, and none is without at least some drawbacks. Some procedures maximize the influence of political parties and others maximize the influence of state bar associations. A continuum ranging from maximum political-party influence and minimum bar-association influence at one end to minimum political-party influence and maximum bar-association influence at the other end would show the five systems placed as follows: partisan election, legislative appointment, gubernatorial appointment, nonpartisan election, and gubernatorial appointment followed by a retention election (Missouri Plan).

Proponents of *partisan elections* argue that courts are political institutions: almost all political questions eventually end up as legal questions, almost all judges have histories of partisan activity, and Democratic judges decide cases differently from Republican judges. Why not elect judges on an outright political basis and stop engaging in charades? they ask. Law cannot be separate from politics: an openly partisan legislature wrote the laws, and it is naive to assume that these laws will be interpreted and applied in a nonpartisan manner. Opponents of partisan elections respond that judges should be "above" politics and should not be indebted to any political party. Voters participating in partisan elections will select judges on the basis of party affiliations, and thus less-qualified persons and party hacks will be selected. Moreover, judicial races are unseemly and undignified, and will decrease public respect for the courts. Opponents of partisan elections point to examples like the following from Illinois.

Nonpartisan elections remove party labels from the ballot but cannot prevent political parties from working behind the scenes for preferred candidates. Removing party designations is intended to force voters to focus on the qualifications of the candidates, but instead it may cause fewer voters to cast ballots in judgeship races. It also increases the importance of incumbent status, ethnicity of candidate surname, newspaper endorsements, and bar association ratings of judges. As a practical matter, voters know very little about the qualifications of judicial candidates, even in important races that are extensively publicized.[9] Furthermore, the election of judges raises the troublesome issue of campaign finance. Judicial campaigns are likely to be financed by lawyers who will later conduct business before the winner. Those who financed the loser must appear in the same courtroom.

Gubernatorial appointment (with senate confirmation) allows the state's chief executive to select the most qualified person, but it can also be used as a tool to reward former supporters, such as campaign contributors or legislators who voted for the governor's bills. Judicial appointments can also be used to further the governor's reelection strategy by allowing him or her to appeal to interest groups, ethnic groups, liberal or conservative activists, different regions of the state, and other factions. Requirements in some states that the governor select at least a few judges from the

---

READING 7-1   JUDGESHIP RACE "EMBARRASSING"

Early in the campaign, the Supreme Court race shed any pretense of being a traditional low-key election and instead degenerated into a bitter battle that has failed to illuminate the issues.

"Embarrassing" is the word being uttered most often by local lawyers and judges in assessing the campaign.

For many, the acrimonious race has become the most potent argument yet in favor of removing the judiciary from partisan politics and adopting some sort of merit selection system.

At stake is the key seventh seat on the court, which will determine whether the Republicans or Democrats hold the majority. The outcome could be significant because the court is expected to review the politically sensitive legislative redistricting due to be worked out next year.

So far Republican Robert Sklodowski has accused his opponent of being immoral, soft on crime, naive, ignorant of criminal law, too liberal, too old, possibly senile, and having less legal knowledge than a first-year law student.

Democrat Seymour Simon, on the other hand, has charged that Sklodowski twists and distorts facts, misleads the public, engages in slander, borders on being hysterical, makes foolish and ridiculous assertions, and doesn't understand how reviewing courts work.

SOURCE: Lee Strobel, "Judgeship Race 'Embarrassing,'" *Chicago Tribune*, November 2, 1980, pp. I-16. Copyright © November 2, 1980 Chicago Tribune Company. All rights reserved. Used with permission.

---

opposing party leads to the selection of atypical jurists such as liberal Republicans or conservative Democrats—in other words, those who will do the least amount of damage from the governor's standpoint.

Legislative appointment, on the other hand, nearly guarantees the selection of a judge affiliated with the party that controls the legislature. Not incidentally, legislative appointment results in the choice of a rather large number of legislators or former legislators as judges.

The selection system most preferred by the reformers mentioned earlier is *gubernatorial appointment followed by a retention election*, usually known as the *Missouri Plan*. In the heated debates over which selection system to adopt, this procedure is usually referred to as the *merit system*. Its supporters thereby intend to imply that only the Missouri Plan selects judges on the basis of merit. The popularity of this procedure is shown by the fact that all states that have recently reformed their selection procedures have chosen it.

The Missouri Plan in pure form must contain all the following elements. (As noted in Table 7-3, twelve states have selected some, *but not necessarily all*, of these elements.) A judicial nominating commission consisting of judges, lawyers chosen by the bar association, and nonlawyers picked by the governor presents the chief executive with a list of names. The judges and lawyers are on the panel to assess the judicial abilities of candidates (hence, it is "merit" selection), and the nonlawyers represent the interests of the public and the political interests of the governor. The chief executive must select one of the names on the list, or ask for a new list of names. The person selected then runs in a retention election in which the voters are asked this question: "Shall _____ be retained in office as Judge of _____ Court? Vote Yes or No." Since Missouri Plan judges never face an opponent, they are said to "run on their record." But voters in these elections probably know less about the candidates than voters in nonpartisan judicial elections featuring opposing candidates. In the period 1934 to 1979, only thirty-three judges were defeated in retention elections in the twenty states that used this type of election for at least part of the period.[10]

A key feature of the Missouri Plan is the judicial nominating commission. Although bar association influence is maximized under this selection system, there are potential cleavages among the lawyers on the commission—for example, between plaintiffs' and defendants' attorneys in personal injury cases. At least two other groups of lawyers compete for seats on the nominating commissions: those who graduated from prestige law schools and who work for large firms representing important economic interests, such as banks or insurance companies or real estate companies, versus graduates of night law schools who practice by themselves and represent individuals or small businesses.[11] Judges on the nominating commissions are particularly influential because they work hard to insure the nomination of compatible colleagues and because nonlawyer members of the commission will defer to their expertise. Despite assertions that the Missouri Plan is a significant improvement over systems of outright gubernatorial appointment, governors in both systems operate in much the same manner. That is, they view "selection under the Plan almost entirely from a personal or a political standpoint [and use] their appointments to reward friends or past political supporters."[12]

Because state judges must periodically go before the voters, they are probably more accountable to the public than federal judges, who never face the electorate. This is true even though few state judges are defeated for reelection. The question remains, though: Do the different selection systems produce judges who decide cases differently? Despite the claims of the advocates of one or another of the selection methods, "formal judicial recruitment processes have little impact upon the kinds of decisions that courts make."[13] In fact, as one specialist on state courts concludes, "court reform usually fails to produce important improvements or significant changes in court behavior. . . . The political appeal of reform is inviting and reassuring and holds out the prospect of improved justice, but the promise probably is more illusion than reality."[14]

There are six formal processes for removing unfit state judges: recall (see Chapter 4), impeachment, concurrent resolution by the legislature, legislative address, reelection defeat, and action by a judicial disciplinary commission. (Only impeachment is available at the federal level.) The first four processes are very rarely used; the last two are more common. Judicial disciplinary commissions, found in every state, hear complaints of improper behavior by judges, investigate the charges, and make a recommendation to the state supreme court. Commission members consist of judges appointed by the supreme court, lawyers appointed by the bar association, and nonlawyers appointed by the governor. The supreme court can reprimand, suspend, or remove a judge for "willful misconduct in office, willful or persistent failure to perform judicial duties, habitual intemperance, or conduct prejudicial to the administration of justice that brings the judicial office into disrepute."[15] Disabled or senile judges may also be involuntarily retired. On-bench activities that have led to discipline include "rudeness, racist or sexist language, show of favoritism, abuse of power, failure to perform duties, and alteration of court records." An example of the last-named offense would be ticket fixing. Off-bench behavior might include "criminal conduct as well as impropriety in business and social dealings."[16] According to the introduction to the American Bar Association's *Standards Relating to Judicial Discipline and Disability Retirement*, disciplinary commissions are primarily intended not "to punish judges, but to protect the public, preserve the integrity of the judicial process, maintain public confidence in the judiciary, and create a greater awareness of proper judicial behavior on the part of judges themselves."[17] The six removal processes, along with the judges' own standards of proper conduct, serve the democratic ideal of government that is responsive to the governed.

JURIES

Grand Juries

Courts are assisted by two kinds of juries, grand juries and trial juries. Usually consisting of twenty-three people who hold office for one year, the grand jury decides whether to bring to trial people charged with crimes. The public prosecutor or district attorney presents evidence to the grand jury that he or she hopes will establish a probability of guilt and cause the jury to return a true bill of indictment, or simply an *indictment*. The public prosecutor dominates grand jury proceedings because the person being accused may not have an attorney present. Hence grand juries almost always return indictments. Nonetheless, in almost all states, including the twenty that have grand juries, the normal method of accusation is for the public prosecutor to file with the court an affidavit known as an *information*. This procedure is quicker, and the public prosecutor does not have to reveal any of his or her evidence. The grand jury may be reserved for cases that have a potential political benefit for the prosecutor—for example, those involving organized crime.

Although the indictment function of grand juries is becoming less important, their *investigatory* function remains. This function consists of investigating local government, either for possible reform or to uncover wrongdoing. Should the grand jury discover possible crimes, it may accuse on its own by means of a *presentment*.

Trial Juries

The vast majority of trial court cases are decided by a judge only, in what is known as a *bench trial*. However, in a minority of cases (especially criminal cases), the defendant insists upon a jury trial. The duty of the jury is to decide the facts of the case: who was at fault or who was guilty. About 80 percent of the time, bench trials and jury trials would reach the same verdict.[18] When the verdicts diverge, the jury is more likely to favor a plaintiff suing a wealthy defendant and is much more likely to acquit a defendant in a criminal case.

The requirement of a unanimous verdict to convict in criminal cases has traditionally been thought to be a protection for criminal defendants. However, the U.S. Supreme Court has ruled that six-member juries are constitutional (*Williams* v. *Florida*, 399 U.S. 78 [1970]) and that ten out of twelve votes for conviction in a noncapital case is also constitutional (*Apodaca* v. *Oregon*, 406 U.S. 404 [1972]). On the other hand, a jury of only five in a serious criminal case violates the U.S. Constitution (*Ballew* v. *Georgia*, 435 U.S. 223 [1978]), and conviction in a serious criminal case by a non-unanimous six-member jury is similarly unconstitutional (*Burch* v. *Louisiana*, 441 U.S. 130 [1979]). Having fewer jurors has various consequences. It speeds up trials, since it reduces the lengthy process of selecting jurors. But it also means that the jury is less likely to represent the community, is less deliberative, and is less accessible to different points of view.

OTHER JUDICIAL ISSUES

Crowded court calendars and congestion are a continuing problem in American state courts. Also, attorneys frequently seek delay as a strategy for encouraging out-of-court settlements. Ten states have sought to relieve overcrowded dockets by taking certain legal matters out of the normal court process by establishing neighborhood justice centers and panels for negotiation, mediation, and arbitration.

In an attempt to improve the public's knowledge of the judicial system, twenty-seven states allow televised criminal trials. The U.S. Supreme Court has ruled that televising trials does not deny the defendant a fair trial as long as the judge has the right to prohibit cameras in certain circumstances (*Chandler* v. *Florida,* 449 U.S. 560 [1981]). Moreover, most states "require either that the consent of the defendant be obtained before the television cameras may operate or that the cameras be cut off when the defendant, his lawyer, a juror, or a witness objects to the television coverage."[19] Despite the popularity of televised trials in many states, some observers fear that cameras in the courtroom may inhibit certain kinds of witnesses or that elected judges may alter their courtroom procedures as election day nears.

"While the judicial system goes to great expense to protect the rights of defendants by providing legal counsel, personal protection, housing and food, up until recently little has been done to insure—or even to recognize—the rights of victims."[20] Therefore, thirty-nine states have established victim-compensation programs that pay for medical expenses not reimbursed by insurance, for lost wages, and for burial expenses. These programs are viewed as a form of humanitarian aid and are financed from general revenues or from penalties assessed convicted persons. No payments are made for property loss or property damage, however. To qualify for compensation, minimum losses of $100 to $250 are necessary; maximum awards have also been established. Ironically, most citizens are unaware of these programs and do not apply for the benefits.

Some states ensure that victims be aware of their opportunities to participate in the proceedings against the accused. Indiana requires that prosecuting attorneys inform felony victims that they may appear and make suggestions about any proposed plea bargain; other states require that victims be given notice that they can participate in sentencing or parole hearings.[21]

SUMMARY

As we have seen, states differ in the extent to which they approach the simplified, unified, and centralized judicial model favored by court reformers. Much more difficult to assess, however, is the extent to which state courts approach the ideal of equal justice for all persons, regardless of their station in life. The latter is an elusive goal, sometimes achieved but always formidable.

NOTES

1. York Willbern, "Administrative Organization," in *The 50 States and Their Local Governments,* ed. James Fesler (New York: Knopf, 1967), p. 356.

2. Henry R. Glick and Kenneth N. Vines, *State Court Systems* (Englewood Cliffs, N.J.: Prentice-Hall, 1973), pp. 70–71.

3. Herbert Jacob, "Courts," in *Politics in the American States*, 4th ed., ed. Virginia Gray, Herbert Jacob, and Kenneth N. Vines (Boston: Little, Brown, 1983), p. 23.

4. Mary Cornelia Porter and G. Alan Tarr, "Introduction," in *State Supreme Courts*, ed. Porter and Tarr (Westport, Conn.: Greenwood Press, 1982), pp. xvi–xviii.

5. Henry R. Glick, *Supreme Courts in State Politics* (New York: Basic Books, 1971), pp. 34, 41; see also John Wold, "Political Orientations, Social Backgrounds, and Role Perceptions of State Supreme Court Judges," *Western Political Quarterly*, 27 (June 1974), 241.

6. Glick and Vines, *State Court Systems*, pp. 80–82.

7. Stuart Nagel, "Political Party Affiliation and Judges' Decisions," *American Political Science Review*, 55 (December 1961), 843–50. However, David Adamany has found that "Republican justices made records as favorable to the worker as their Democratic counterparts": "The Party Variable in Judges' Voting," *American Political Science Review*, 63 (March 1969), 64.

8. G. Alan Tarr, "Court Unification and Court Performance," *Judicature*, 64 (March 1981), 358–63.

9. Charles A. Johnson et al., "The Salience of Judicial Candidates and Elections," *Social Science Quarterly*, 59 (September 1978), 371–78.

10. Susan Carbon, "Judicial Retention Elections: Are They Serving Their Intended Purpose?" *Judicature*, 64 (November 1980), 211–12. Not all of the states using retention elections are classified as Missouri Plan states.

11. Richard A. Watson and Rondal Downing, *The Politics of the Bench and the Bar: Judicial Selection under the Missouri Nonpartisan Court Plan* (New York: John Wiley, 1969), chap. 10.

12. Ibid., pp. 338–39. See also Robert Karsch, *The Government of Missouri*, 14th ed. (Columbia, Mo.: Lucas Brothers Publishers, 1978), p. 194.

13. Burton Atkins and Henry Glick, "Formal Judicial Recruitment and State Supreme Court Decisions," *American Politics Quarterly*, 2 (October 1974), 447. See also Victor E. Flango and Craig Ducat, "What Difference Does Method of Selection Make?" *Justice System Journal*, 5 (Fall 1979), 25–44.

14. Henry Glick, "The Politics of State-Court Reform," in *The Politics of Judicial Reform*, ed. Philip Dubois (Lexington, Mass.: Heath, Lexington Books, 1982), pp. 29, 31.

15. Irene Tesitor and Dwight Sinks, *Judicial Conduct Organizations*, 2nd ed. (Chicago: American Judicature Society, 1980), p. 4.

16. Jolanta J. Perlstein and Nathan Goldman, "Judicial Disciplinary Commissions," in *The Analysis of Judicial Reform*, ed. Philip Dubois (Lexington, Mass.: Heath, Lexington Books, 1982), pp. 95–96.

17. Quoted in Tesitor and Sinks, *Judicial Conduct Organizations*, p. 3.

18. "We, the Jury, Find the . . . ," *Time*, September 28, 1981, p. 47.

19. "Television in the Courtroom," *Editorial Research Reports*, January 16, 1981, p. 23.

20. Mindy Gaynes, "New Roads to Justice: Compensating the Victim," *State Legislatures*, November-December 1981, p. 12. For further information, see William Hoelzel, "A Survey of 27 Victim Compensation Programs," *Judicature*, 63 (May 1980), 485–96.

21. John R. Anderson and Paul L. Woodard, "Victim and Witness Assistance," *Judicature*, 68 (January 1985), 230.

chapter 8

Structures
and Policy Makers

In this chapter, we will study the characteristics of the eighty-two thousand local governments spread across America: cities, towns and townships, counties, special districts, and school districts. These units of government have an amazing variety of relationships with one another and with the state governments from which they receive their powers. The frustrations of big-city mayors and the importance of local bureaucracies will also be emphasized. The following chapter provides a picture of local political parties and interest groups, and confronts the issue of whether a behind-the-scenes power elite secretly rules American cities. Also in that chapter, we consider metropolitan reform and local government finance to see what light they can shed on the fiscal crises of American cities.

CENSUS DATA

America is an urbanized nation—a fact that is hardly surprising. What needs to be remembered is that we are also a nation of small cities. Table 8-1 shows that more people live in cities of 2,500 to 25,000 than in cities of over 250,000. In fact, if we take 2,500 people to 100,000 people as the criterion of small-to-medium-size cities, then about 60 percent of all Americans living in cities reside in such places. Although concentrating on the problems of big cities, this chapter and the next one will give due notice to smaller cities as well.

The problems facing large cities are indeed severe. These include high levels of crime—in fact, a disproportionately larger share of crime than the population of these cities justifies. The risk of becoming a victim of a violent crime in cities of 250,000 or more is over twice (221 percent) as great as in the nation generally.[1] To make matters worse, the most

TABLE 8-1   Cities Classified According to Population

	Cities		Population	
Population Group	Number	Percent	Number	Percent of Total Population
2,500 to 5,000	2,665	34	9,377	4.1
5,000 to 10,000	2,181	28	15,361	6.8
10,000 to 25,000	1,765	22	27,656	12.2
25,000 to 50,000	675	8	23,457	10.4
50,000 to 100,000	290	3	19,798	8.7
100,000 to 250,000	117	1	17,048	7.5
250,000 to 500,000	34	.004	12,189	5.4
500,000 to 1,000,000	16	.002	10,872	4.8
1,000,000 or more	6	.0007	17,530	7.7

SOURCE: *Statistical Abstract of the United States, 1982–1983* (Washington, D.C.: Bureau of the Census, 1982), Table 23.

likely victims of crime are the large concentrations of poor people living in slum neighborhoods. City housekeeping services are declining in quality: streets are dirtier, mass-transit facilities are less reliable, abandoned housing is more common, hospital and school buildings are deteriorating. Finally, the tax base is eroding as middle- and upper-class families move to the suburbs. Moving too are employers, who used to pay income taxes and property taxes, and stores, which used to generate sales tax revenue. Each of these also provided jobs. Big cities face the vicious crossfire of a decreasing tax base (those who pay for city services are the ones most likely to leave) and an increasing need for services (those who consume services form a higher percentage of the people remaining).[2] Such problems are concentrated in the Frostbelt areas of the Midwest and the Northeast, but they are also a nationwide phenomenon.

The country's thirty largest cities, as reflected in the 1980 census, are presented in Table 8-2. A comparison of cities gaining population with those losing it clearly shows the movement to the Sunbelt mentioned in Chapter 1. The fastest-growing city in the country is San Jose, California; other Sunbelt cities showing large increases are Phoenix, El Paso, Houston, and San Diego. Conversely, some Frostbelt cities are experiencing huge losses in population—for example, St. Louis (which lost over one out of every four of its people), Cleveland, Detroit, Pittsburgh, and Washington, D.C. However, it is also true that a city's growth rate is strongly affected by how successful it is in annexing surrounding areas.

It was noted earlier that large cities are losing population to their suburbs. Perhaps the decreases in residents shown in Table 8-2 are merely a reflection of this trend. The Census Bureau's concept of a standard metropolitan area can help us confirm this. A *standard metropolitan area* contains one or more counties with at least one city of more than 50,000 people. Nearby urban areas that are integrated economically and socially with the central city are included. The last census counted 288 standard metropolitan areas, and these are depicted in Figure 8-1; the thirty most populous are shown in Table 8-3. Note that some cross county lines, and the Detroit and San Diego ones actually cross into Canada and Mexico, respectively. Metropolitan areas showing huge increases in population are Phoenix, Houston, and Tampa–St. Petersburg. On the other hand, those with losses are all in the Frostbelt: New York, Cleveland, Pittsburgh, Philadelphia, Milwaukee, and St. Louis. The latter suffered severe losses in the central city, but only negligible reductions in the metropolitan area.

TABLE 8-2   The Thirty Most Populous Cities

Rank	City	1970 Population	1980 Population	Percent Change since 1970	
1	New York City	7,896,000	7,072,000	Down	10.4
2	Chicago	3,369,000	3,005,000	Down	10.8
3	Los Angeles	2,812,000	2,967,000	Up	5.5
4	Philadelphia	1,949,000	1,688,000	Down	13.4
5	Houston	1,234,000	1,595,000	Up	29.3
6	Detroit	1,514,000	1,203,000	Down	20.5
7	Dallas	844,000	904,000	Up	7.1
8	San Diego	697,000	876,000	Up	25.5
9	Phoenix	584,000	790,000	Up	35.2
10	Baltimore	905,000	787,000	Down	13.1
11	San Antonio	654,000	786,000	Up	20.1
12	Indianapolis	737,000	701,000	Down	4.9
13	San Francisco	716,000	679,000	Down	5.1
14	Memphis	624,000	646,000	Up	3.6
15	Washington, D.C.	757,000	638,000	Down	15.6
16	Milwaukee	717,000	636,000	Down	11.3
17	San Jose	460,000	629,000	Up	36.9
18	Cleveland	751,000	574,000	Down	23.6
19	Columbus	540,000	565,000	Up	4.6
20	Boston	641,000	563,000	Down	12.2
21	New Orleans	593,000	558,000	Down	6.1
22	Jacksonville	504,000	541,000	Up	7.3
23	Seattle	531,000	494,000	Down	7.0
24	Denver	515,000	492,000	Down	4.3
25	Nashville-Davidson	462,000	456,000	Down	1.3
26	St. Louis	622,000	453,000	Down	27.2
27	Kansas City, Mo.	507,000	448,000	Down	11.2
28	El Paso	322,000	425,000	Up	32.0
29	Atlanta	495,000	425,000	Down	14.1
30	Pittsburgh	520,000	424,000	Down	18.5

SOURCE: *Statistical Abstract of the United States, 1982–1983* (Washington, D.C.: Bureau of the Census, 1982), Table 26.

FIGURE 8-1

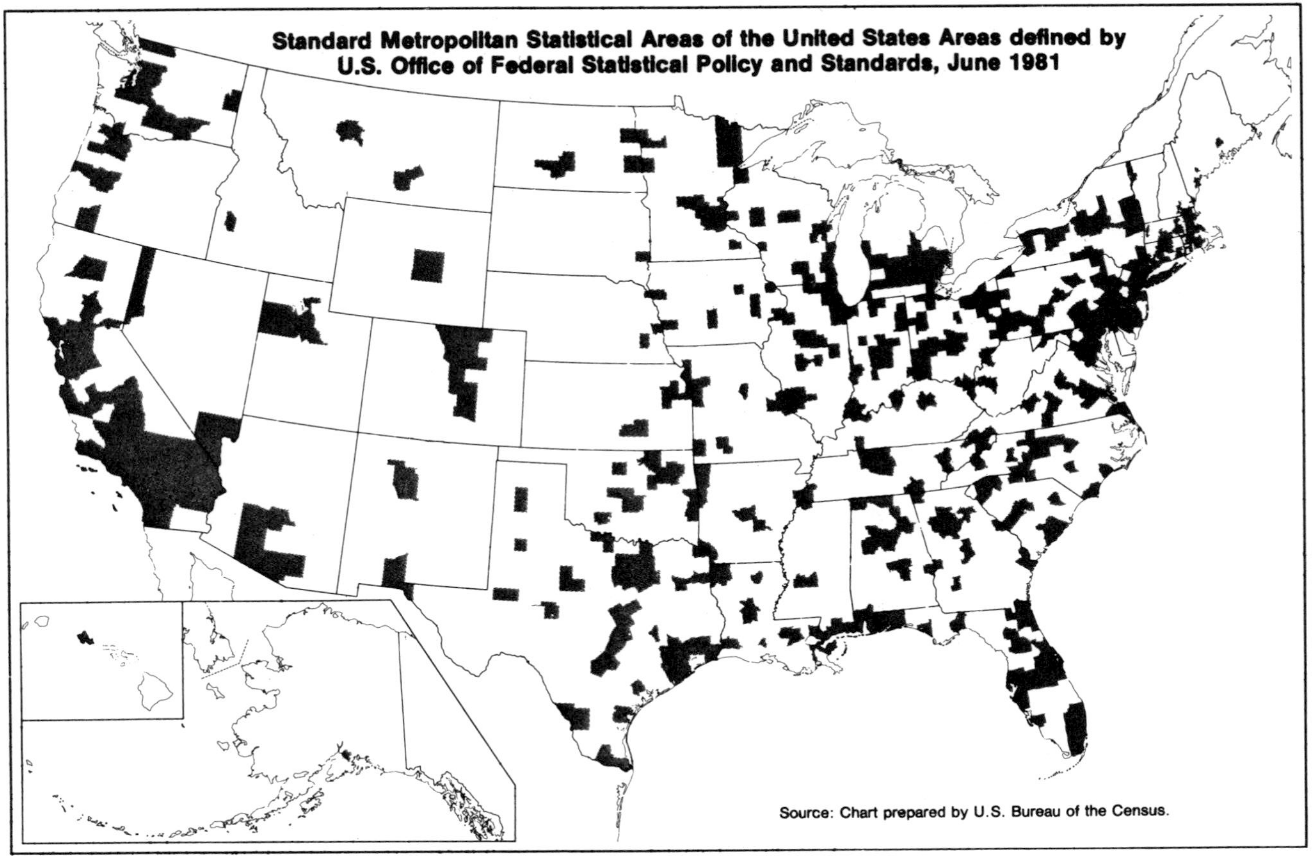

Standard Metropolitan Statistical Areas of the United States Areas defined by
U.S. Office of Federal Statistical Policy and Standards, June 1981

Source: Chart prepared by U.S. Bureau of the Census.

SOURCE: *Statistical Abstract of the United States, 1982–83* (Washington, D.C.: Bureau of the Census, 1982). p. 894.

The political results of this population movement are twofold: votes in the U.S. House of Representatives and the electoral college are shifting to different regions, and seats in state legislatures are gravitating from central cities to suburbs. Not only is suburbanization increasing, but the population density of central cities *and* suburbs is decreasing as people move to nonmetropolitan areas. There is also an interesting demographic contrast between certain metropolitan areas. Northern, northeastern, and larger ones have poor central cities with many aged and black people, but affluent suburbs. Southern, western, newer, and smaller metropolitan areas tend to be just the opposite.[3]

TABLE 8-3   The Thirty Most Populous Standard Metropolitan Areas

Rank	Standard Metropolitan Area	1970 Population	1980 Population	Percent Change since 1970	
1	New York	9,974,000	9,120,000	Down	8.6
2	Los Angeles/Long Beach	7,042,000	7,478,000	Up	6.2
3	Chicago	6,977,000	7,104,000	Up	1.8
4	Philadelphia	4,824,000	4,717,000	Down	2.2
5	Detroit	4,435,000	4,353,000	Down	1.8
6	San Francisco/Oakland	3,109,000	3,251,000	Up	4.5
7	Washington	2,910,000	3,061,000	Up	5.2
8	Dallas/Fort Worth	2,378,000	2,975,000	Up	25.1
9	Houston	1,999,000	2,905,000	Up	45.3
10	Boston	2,899,000	2,763,000	Down	4.7
11	Nassau/Suffolk	2,556,000	2,606,000	Up	2.0
12	St. Louis	2,411,000	2,356,000	Down	2.3
13	Pittsburgh	2,401,000	2,264,000	Down	5.7
14	Baltimore	2,071,000	2,174,000	Up	5.0
15	Minneapolis/St. Paul	1,965,000	2,114,000	Up	7.5
16	Atlanta	1,596,000	2,030,000	Up	27.2
17	Newark	2,057,000	1,966,000	Down	4.4
18	Anaheim/Santa Ana/ Garden Grove	1,421,000	1,933,000	Up	36.0
19	Cleveland	2,064,000	1,899,000	Down	8.0
20	San Diego	1,358,000	1,862,000	Up	37.1
21	Miami	1,268,000	1,626,000	Up	28.2
22	Denver/Boulder	1,240,000	1,621,000	Up	30.8
23	Seattle/Everett	1,425,000	1,607,000	Up	12.8
24	Tampa/St. Petersburg	1,089,000	1,569,000	Up	44.1
25	Riverside/San Bernardino/ Ontario	1,139,000	1,558,000	Up	36.8
26	Phoenix	971,000	1,509,000	Up	55.4
27	Cincinnati	1,387,000	1,401,000	Up	1.0
28	Milwaukee	1,404,000	1,397,000	Down	.5
29	Kansas City, Mo.	1,274,000	1,327,000	Up	4.2
30	San Jose	1,065,000	1,295,000	Up	21.6

SOURCE: *Statistical Abstract of the United States, 1982–1983* (Washington, D.C.: Bureau of the Census, 1982), Table 20.

TABLE 8-4   The Ten "Best" Places to Live

1. Pittsburgh
2. Boston
3. Raleigh-Durham
4. San Francisco
5. Philadelphia and nearby parts of New Jersey
6. Nassau-Suffolk counties
7. St. Louis
8. Louisville
9. Norwalk, Connecticut
10. Seattle-Everett

SOURCE: "Worst Place in U.S.? No Way, Yuba City Residents Say," *Sacramento Bee*, February 28, 1985, p. A-1.

(Few people can ever be satisfied in these disputes. The author holds out for his hometown of San Diego.)

Statistics always provide great cannon fodder for the perennial dispute over which is the "best" place to live. Richard Boyer and David Savageau have entered the fray by rating 329 places in terms of climate, crime, housing costs, education, health care, recreational opportunities, the arts, transportation, and prosperity.[4] Their choices for the top ten are listed in Table 8-4.

STATE RELATIONS WITH LOCAL GOVERNMENTS

Dillon's Rule

The legal relationship between local governments and the state government is entirely different from the relationship between state governments and the federal government. The powers of both the state governments and the federal government are said to be guaranteed by the United States Constitution; on the other hand, local governments receive their powers from the state. Dillon's Rule, after Iowa Supreme Court Justice John F. Dillon, describes the latter relationship:

> It is a general and undisputed proposition of law that a [local government] possesses and can exercise the following powers, and no others: First, those granted in express words; second, those necessarily or fairly implied in or Wincident to the powers expressly granted; third, those essential to the accomplishment of the declared objects and purpose of the [local government]—not simply convenient but indispensable. Any fair, reasonable, substantial doubt concerning the existence of power is resolved by the courts against the [local government], and the power is denied.[5]

In other words, unless a local government can show that it has been given a particular power by its local charter or a state law or the state constitution, courts will interpret the local government's authority narrowly and the disputed power will be denied.

Within the limits of Dillon's Rule, there are different factors that affect the amount of discretion local governments possess:

1. A state's traditional beliefs concerning the proper distribution of power tend to perpetuate existing practices.
2. The amount of time that the state legislature may meet affects its opportunities to control local governments. However, it is not necessarily true that a legislature having more time will automatically meddle in local affairs.
3. The length and specificity of the state constitution and especially how easily it may be amended determine whether the constitution or state law restricts local discretion.
4. The number of local governments influences state attempts to control them.
5. Powerful associations of local officials and public employee unions such as police and fire fighters can prevail on state legislatures to require local governments to take actions benefiting their members.[6]

Allowing substantial discretion to local governments has the advantage of speedier solutions to local problems, because those persons closest to the issue have the most intimate knowledge of it. Moreover, if issues are resolved locally, the state legislature is freed from a time-consuming task and can spend its limited time on matters of statewide concern.[7]

Means of State Control

Since the state is the source of local governments' powers, it may grant or withhold various powers—for example, the power to levy a sales tax or income tax. Six states limit local expenditures, thirty-four limit property tax rates, twenty-one place limits on property tax levies, and there are debt limits in nearly all states.[8] The last of these requirements has led to numerous evasions, which are described in the next chapter. Conservatives favor fiscal limitations as a way to control the size of government, to force elected officials to be more prudent in their spending decisions, and to assist local officials in resisting the salary demands of public-employee unions. Liberals, on the other hand, say that such limitations are simplistic solutions to complex problems, show mistrust of representative government, and discriminate against poor people.[9] Another form of state control is exercised through boards or departments in the administrative branch of state government. These agencies must frequently grant clearance before local governments can establish new policies or change present ones.

State mandates are a form of control especially resented by local officials. A *mandate* is defined as "any responsibility, action, procedure, or limitation that is imposed by one sphere of government on another by superior constitutional, legislative, executive, or judicial authority as a direct order or as a condition of aid."[10] The most common mandates are solid waste disposal standards, special education programs, and workers' compensation. Public-employee unions, especially police and fire fighters, have persuaded state legislators to impose compulsory binding arbitration on local wage disputes. Some states even set local library hours.[11] Mandates usually result from a determination by the state legislature (or the courts) that a matter is of sufficient statewide importance that local officers should not be allowed to decide the issue, or that statewide uniformity in the provision of a service is desirable. Mandates can be viewed in various conflicting lights: as attempts by the state government to save itself money by having a lower level of government provide a service, as the result of interest groups unsuccessful at the local level doing an "end run" to the state capital, or as a worthwhile decentralization of power to the local level.[12]

The Advisory Commission on Intergovernmental Relations has identified five types of mandates: rules-of-the-game, spillover, interlocal-equity, loss-of-tax-base, and personnel.[13] The forms of local government that can be established or the designation of local officers and their responsibilities, as well as procedures for local elections, are *rules-of-the-game* mandates. *Spillover* mandates prescribe new programs or expand existing ones in the areas of education, health, welfare, and the environment. Local governments are prevented from injuring each other in land use, tax assessment, and environmental standards through the use of *interlocal-equity* mandates. The state removes various items from the local tax base by *loss-of-tax-base*, or *tax-exemption*, mandates. Finally, *personnel* mandates set local public employment standards, wage levels, and pension provisions.

Few states reimburse local governments for the costs imposed on them. Illinois reimburses spillover, tax-exemption, and personnel mandates. If the Illinois legislature fails to pass a reimbursement appropriation, local governments are relieved of having to implement the mandate.[14] Before committee hearings on a mandates bill can be held, an estimate of the costs to be imposed must be prepared. The reimbursement process has not worked well in California, because the legislature regularly includes in mandates bills disclaimers alleging that no costs are involved or that the mandate will actually save local governments money.

State Aid to Local Governments

State aid is a vital source of local government revenue, as Table 8-5 shows. As we shall see in Chapter 10, about one third of the typical state budget is not spent by the state but is given to local governments. Some states, such as New York and Wisconsin, spend almost half their money for this purpose, while New Hampshire and South Dakota allot less than one fifth. The money goes primarily for education, but also for welfare, general support, and highways. State grants-in-aid are almost always formula grants rather than project grants. Unlike the federal grants

TABLE 8-5 State Aid to Local Governments as a Percentage of General Revenue from the Latter's Own Sources

	Cities	Counties	School Districts
1955	19.4%	59.9%	69.0%
1983	30.3%	53.2%	111.1%

SOURCE: *Significant Features of Fiscal Federalism, 1984 Edition* (Washington, D.C.: Advisory Commission on Intergovernmental Relations, 1985), Table 42.

discussed in Chapter 2, few state grants have matching ratios. Almost all states also have state revenue sharing for local governments.[15]

Joseph Zimmerman, a noted authority on state and local relations, has proposed what he calls a *partnership* model for reforming state-local relations:

> Constitutional prohibition of special state legislation or provision for a local veto of special legislation, unless requested by the governing body of the concerned local units.
>
> Constitutional devolution of all powers capable of devolution upon general purpose governments, subject to preemption by general law.
>
> Constitutional authorization for classified legislation, provided there are no more than three classes of local governments and at least three political subdivisions in each class.
>
> Recodification of state laws clearly identifying powers totally or partially preempted by the state legislature.
>
> Partial or total state reimbursement of added costs associated with state mandates.
>
> Removal of debt, levy, and tax limits on local governments.
>
> Creation of a state boundary commission.
>
> State-established minimum levels of service provisions in the most important functional areas.[16]

This model clearly favors greater autonomy at the substate level.

A few of the model's provisions deserve particular mention. *Special legislation* consists of laws passed by the state legislature that are intended to apply to only one city. Special legislation can be disguised as *classified legislation* (cities classified according to population size) if the legislature classifies cities according to population size but draws the population classifications so narrowly that only one city fits into a particular classification. The Indiana legislature has done this with the city of Indianapolis, and the Pennsylvania legislature has similarly singled out Philadelphia. By requiring *no more than* three population classes and by requiring that *at least* three cities or counties be in each classification, the legislature is inhibited from discriminating against particular cities or counties. A state boundary commission would have the power to abolish special districts (described later in the chapter). The controversy over whether special districts are in fact a problem is reserved for the next chapter.

CITY CHARTERS

As Dillon's Rule indicates, local governments receive their powers from the state constitution, the state legislature, or their own charters. Unless a charter is drawn up by a city's residents (a home-rule charter), it must be passed by the state legislature. The three types of charters granted by the legislature are special-act charters, general-act charters, and optional charters.

In the case of a *special-act charter*, the legislature passes an act granting a specific city a charter that prescribes the city's governmental structure and its power. Every time the city seeks to increase its powers or feels unsure whether it has the authority to undertake a proposed course of action, it must seek authorization from the state legislature. The opportunity for the state to meddle in local affairs is obvious, especially if the city mayor and the majority of the legislature's members are of different political parties. In practice, special-act charters lead to logrolling among legislative delegations from the largest cities ("You vote for my city's bill, and I'll vote for your city's bill"). They also consume a great deal of the legislature's limited time. By means of *general-act* (or *classified*) charters the legislature classifies cities according to population size and provides each classification with a standard charter. Under *optional* charters, cities have the option of choosing from different kinds of charters presented by the legislature. The city can select the size of the city council, whether election is by wards or at-large, and whether to have (1) a mayor and a city council or (2) a city council and a city manager or (3) a city commission only. Each of these different forms of city government will be described in the next section.

The final type of charter is the *home-rule charter*, which is drawn up by local residents. Home-rule charters attempt to stand Dillon's Rule on its head by allowing the city to do anything that the state has not specifically forbidden it to do. Unfortunately, state legislatures blunt the effects of home-rule charters by declaring various matters to be matters of statewide concern, and hence beyond local control. In most states, the largest cities are home-rule cities.

FORMS OF CITY GOVERNMENT

The three forms of city government are mayor-council, council-manager, and commission. As Table 8-6 indicates, the most populous cities (those with over 500,000 people) and the least populous (those with less than

TABLE 8-6 City Population and Form of City Government

Population Group	Number of Cities	Mayor Council	Manager	Commission
2,500 to 5,000	6,147	3,683	2,287	177
5,000 to 10,000	4,051	2,074	1,840	137
10,000 to 25,000	2,444	1,099	1,243	102
25,000 to 50,000	1,035	400	587	48
50,000 to 100,000	441	176	248	17
100,000 to 250,000	170	75	87	8
250,000 to 500,000	57	35	20	2
500,000 to 1,000,000	23	18	5	0
1,000,000 or more	6	6	0	0

SOURCE: *The Municipal Year Book, 1983* (Washington, D.C.: International City Management Association, 1983), p. xvi.

5,000) are quite likely to have a mayor and a city council. Medium-size cities, especially those in the 25,000-to-100,000 range, are likely to have a council and an appointed city manager. Commission cities, by far the least numerous of the three forms, are usually medium-to-small municipalities.

Mayor–Council Cities

Clearly the most common form, the mayor and council predominate in very large and very small cities. Large cities usually have the *strong* mayor-council type of government. By *strong* we refer to the amount of power given to the mayor by state law or the city's charter, and not to his or her personality or amount of political party support. The mayor has a four-year term, prepares the city budget, has the veto power, and can appoint and remove important administrators such as the police chief. In contrast, small cities are likely to have the *weak* mayor-council type. Here the mayor serves a two-year term and is, in fact, a member of the council, which has designated him or her to have the title of mayor. The position is largely ceremonial because the mayor has no veto or appointment and removal power. Although possessing little formal authority, many mayors in weak mayor-council cities are nonetheless influential because of their strong personality, negotiating skills, or long history of election victories.

Council–Manager Cities

Council-manager government was an important reform introduced by the Progressives of the early twentieth century, who were great believers in expertise and efficiency in government. The Progressives disliked the idea of having a mayor whose only claim to executive power rested on superior vote-getting ability; instead, they wanted someone to fulfill the executive function who was academically trained for the job and who would manage the city like an efficient business corporation. The title *manager* has somewhat nonpolitical connotations, and the Progressives hoped that "evil" politics could be banished from city government, or at least relegated to city-council decision making.

In addition to being medium-size, council-manager cities are usually socially homogeneous, white-collar, growing rapidly, and located in the West or South (rather than the East), and possess weak political parties. Since the city council is a part-time body that meets only once a week or once every two weeks, the manager has the duty of running the city from day to day. He or she appoints and dismisses department heads, prepares the agenda for council meetings, proposes policies for council approval, and has the important duty of drawing up the city budget for council adoption.

Since the manager is hired by the council and can be fired by it, the political situation within the city council may set the limits of the manager's effectiveness.[17] If the council has two factions of relatively equal strength, the manager can play one faction against the other. However, if one of the factions gains a council majority, the manager may be looking for a new job. On the other hand, two equally strong council factions can lead to a stalemate in which the manager keeps a low profile and does nothing controversial. If there is no stalemate but considerable conflict and no stable majority, the manager must put together an *ad hoc* majority for each issue. In such a situation, the manager is likely to be cautious—and soon unemployed. Perhaps more common are councils with a stable majority that trusts the manager, or councils with little or no conflict. If the city is prosperous and homogeneous, the latter is especially likely and leads to an influential manager.

It is well to remember that council members are part-time amateurs in governmental affairs and that the manager is a full-time trained professional. The manager and his or her staff have a "near-monopoly of technical competence," which means that in policy making, the manager has the initiative and the council reacts to his or her leadership.[18] Because the manager runs the city on a daily basis, he or she has far more information than any council member, even those with long service on the council. The manager can "limit the range of possible policies that the council considers and reduce the council essentially to the role of saying yes or no to his own policy recommendations."[19] This is less likely to be the case on controversial issues or with councils having factions and conflict. On less visible issues, the manager may not inform the council of important alternatives to his or her recommendations or may not present the inherent disadvantages to policy proposals he or she favors.

Differences in time perspectives may sometimes lead to contention between the manager and the council. Managers take a long-term perspective on the city's problems since they are trained professionals who look at problems somewhat like city planners. Council members, on the other hand, take a short-run view in which they respond primarily to influential community groups or to reelection pressures.

Before we consider the final form of city government, a word of caution is in order. How cities operate *in practice* may be more important than the pure forms of government described here. San Francisco is usually described as a strong mayor-council city, but like many other municipalities, it has a powerful appointed chief administrative officer (CAO). San Francisco is really a combination of the mayor-council and council-manager forms. Forms can be deceiving: if one were to read the San Diego City Charter, one would see described a council-manager city. In fact, San Diego is a strong mayor-council city because the mayor dominates the manager and the council by using the council's committee structure. It is usually easier to change day-to-day operating procedures than it is to change the city charter. Sometimes forms can mask reality.

Commission Cities

Commission government was once the rage among Progressive reformers, but has fallen on hard times. Portland and Tulsa are the largest cities to have this form; as Table 8-6 indicates, not many cities in the 50,000-to-250,000 range have a commission government either. Commission cities do not have a separately elected mayor or a manager, but only a commission (city council) of three or five members with legislative, executive, and administrative responsibilities. (However, one member may be designated *mayor* and empowered to preside at meetings and perform ceremonial duties.) Commission cities are an example of the fusion of powers rather than the separation of powers found in other forms of city government or at the state and national levels. Each commissioner is not only a legislator who writes the city's laws, but an administrator of a city department. This arrangement leads to noninterference in one another's department. Since there can be only three to five city departments, there is often an odd grouping of unrelated functions in each department.

COUNTIES

The nation's three thousand counties provide the traditional services of election administration, record keeping, property tax collection, construction and maintenance of roads, administration of the courthouse and jail, operation of hospitals and recreational facilities, police protection in unincorporated areas, welfare, and education. Once thought to be principally a rural form of government, the county, especially if it is populous, now provides such urban-oriented services as parking, mass transit, airports, noise pollution control, building codes, and stadia.[20] Ironically, almost two thirds of the American people live in counties of over 100,000 people, but nearly two thirds of all counties have less than 25,000 people.[21]

A leading authority on counties has classified six different kinds of counties.[22] *Metropolitan core counties,* such as Cook County, Illinois, contain most of the nation's largest cities. *Metropolitan fringe counties* completely or partially surround metropolitan core counties. The fringe counties may be densely populated or may contain small cities or farm areas, but they are usually growing rapidly and becoming wealthier. *Single-county metropolitan areas* do not receive the large numbers of commuters that core counties do, but the county seat serves as a shopping and trade center for a wide area. Spokane County, Washington, is a good example. *Urbanized nonmetropolitan counties* have a county seat of 20,000 to 40,000 people that is a growing commercial center serving a surrounding farm area. *Less urbanized counties* have 2,500 to 20,000 people and one city that supports the weekly shopping needs of the area's people. *Thinly populated counties* have no urban area with more than 2,500 people. Petroleum County, Montana, has a population density of less than one-half person per square mile.

The form of county government with which we are probably most acquainted is the *commission form* (or plural-executive form). More than three fourths of all counties utilize this form, and nearly half of all Americans live in commission counties.[23] In this type of county, a county board has both legislative power and such administrative responsibilities as directing road work, reviewing license applications, and appointing some employees. There are also numerous elected executives, such as the county clerk, auditor, recorder, treasurer, assessor, prosecuting attorney, sheriff, and coroner. These various officials may refuse to cooperate, especially if they are members of different political parties. Having these numerous officials elected rather than appointed by the county board is thought to be more democratic in the Jacksonian tradition, but voters often have little idea what they do. These officers are reelected to term after term, frequently running unopposed. Voters feel comfortable voting for familiar names, even if the officials are doing a mediocre job. It is important to note that this most common form of county government has no chief executive officer to unify county administration. However, one board member may be particularly powerful, or the county clerk may be an experienced, full-time official, or strong political parties can help to unify administration.

The *council-administrator form* is similar to the council-manager form of city government. Nearly one of every five counties is of this type, and together they contain almost one of every three Americans. Here the county board is able to utilize the skills of a professionally trained administrator and is freed from administrative responsibilities so that it can concentrate on developing county policy.

Finally, 5 percent of all counties (with 20 percent of the American people) have a *council and an elected executive.* The county executive is the chief administrator, who prepares the county budget, has a legislative program, and is armed with a veto. In a diverse, urban county, an elected executive may be required to provide the necessary strong political leadership and visibility. Such an officer is able to represent the county's interest at the state and federal levels, and can provide a clear system of checks and balances between the executive and legislative branches. On the other hand, this arrangement concentrates enormous power in a single person through control of appointments and the budget, and thus may increase conflict between the executive/administrative branch and the legislative branch on difficult issues.[24] Moreover, the office may come to be viewed as a stepping-stone to the governorship, as has happened in the state of Washington.

Counties are changing, although hundreds of them are still dominated by a patronage-dispensing "county courthouse gang." New services provided by counties include job training, drug control programs, food stamps, energy conservation, and consumer protection. There are more county charters, county home rule, and county managers. Intergovernmental linkages (such as councils of government, described later in this chapter) are increasing. Counties are less dependent on the property tax and more dependent on state and federal aid.

SPECIAL DISTRICTS

Special districts, or special-purpose local governments, are distinguishable from cities and counties, which are general-purpose local governments, in that special districts usually provide only one service. Special districts are created because cities and counties are unable or unwilling to provide a service desired by citizens or interest groups. Also, if cities or counties have reached their state-imposed debt limit and residents still want more government services, special districts can be created because each such district will have its own debt limit. Table 8-7 shows that special districts

TABLE 8-7 Number of Local Governments

	1982 Total	*1977 Number without any FTE Employees*
Counties	3,041	N/A
Municipalities	19,083	4,420
Towns/Townships	16,748	7,267
Special Districts	28,733	9,204
School Districts	15,032	N/A
Total	82,637	20,891

SOURCE: *The Municipal Year Book, 1983* (Washington, D.C.: International City Management Association, 1983), p. xiv.

are the most numerous form of government in the United States. In fact, over half of all American governments are special districts.

Special districts can provide almost any public service. The most common is education, followed by fire protection, soil conservation, urban water supply, housing and community development, and drainage. The number of school districts is decreasing, but the number of nonschool special districts is increasing. Although the most numerous American government, special districts are clearly the least well known: district trustees are either not elected because a city council or county board serves *ex officio* as trustees, or voter turnout in special district elections is exceedingly low.

Another problem with special districts is that many of them are "paper" governments without any full-time-equivalent (FTE) employees. Table 8-7 indicates that over one third of all nonschool special districts fit this category. Towns or townships are even more likely to be phantom governments. New England towns are really city governments, but in midwestern states such as Illinois and Indiana, townships are usually units of rural government providing few services. Unlike special districts, townships receive federal revenue-sharing funds; in fact, many townships remain in existence only because they receive this money.[25] Although it is accurate to say that the United States has eighty-two thousand governments, over one fourth of them exist on paper only.

REGIONAL AGENCIES

Many problems facing local governments, such as pollution, transportation, and housing, spill over city and county boundaries. Since such problems have a regional dimension, regional agencies have been created to deal with them. These units are usually called *regional planning councils* or *councils of governments* (COGs) and do not provide services directly to the public. Their membership consists of representatives of the region's governments, who hire a staff to develop a comprehensive regional plan for air quality, water quality, and other regional concerns.

In the past, regional organizations depended on federal funding and served as clearinghouses for reviewing and commenting upon whether local governments' applications for federal grants-in-aid conformed with the regional plan. However, President Reagan has reduced federal funding for these organizations and has signed Executive Order 12372, which is intended to decrease federal interference in this review process and to encourage state and local officials to create their own review and coordination procedures. Various reform proposals for governing the sprawling metropolitan area will be considered in the next chapter.

MAYORS, ADMINISTRATORS, AND LEGISLATORS

By becoming mayor of a large American city, one is almost guaranteed of being frustrated. Mayors may be given limited formal authority by the city charter or by the state.[26] But many important policy-making boards or commissions are independent of mayoral control. The city bureaucracy is characterized by inertia. The mayor does not have sufficient staff support to deal with problems before they reach the crisis stage, or to insure that administrators are following his or her wishes. There is not enough money to solve problems, and hence the mayor is reduced to crisis management, to simply putting out fires. Moreover, the mayor is caught between two contending political forces. On one side are the poor and the socially concerned wealthy white liberals. On the other side are working-class whites who feel that the city is not doing anything for them. Big-city mayors soon come to believe that there is no way of winning in their job—it is only a question of how fast they will lose.

Some opportunities for influence are enhanced by friendly newspapers and television stations and by a political party that can be mobilized. Making good appointments to head city departments helps the mayor to get a handle on the bureaucracy. Skill in raising new money from the state legislature or the city council or the voters helps to relieve the financial crunch. So does the ability to get grants from the federal government.

City workers are the service-providing arm of city government, and an important interest group as well. How these people are selected for their positions is of vital importance: patronage cities are more susceptible to mayoral influence than are civil-service ones. In fact, city employees in merit systems play an important role in selecting their employers, through campaign contributions and vote power. Salaries, benefits, and pensions are the largest items in city budgets; mayors, city council members, and school board members are usually favorable to the wage demands of the public employee unions that have helped put them in office. If city workers cannot achieve their objectives through politics, they may threaten to strike. This threat is particularly effective if it is coming from "a large city department performing services that are indispensable to the safety and health of the entire general public (e.g., fire, police, sanitation) or whose disruption, although not critical, is seriously inconveniencing to large numbers (e.g., schools, public transit, welfare)."[27] Moreover, as the vulnerability of large cities to crippling strikes becomes more and more apparent, leaders of employee unions are encouraged to hold out for greater and greater concessions by acting on the principle that "you get more by being impossible."

The typical mayor may get more cooperation from the city council than from the city bureaucracy. The mayor's budget is usually not dramatically altered by the council, which normally responds favorably to most initiatives of mayors and city managers. However, conflict between mayor and council is more likely if they belong to different political parties, or to different factions of the same party, or if the mayor's popularity appears to be slipping.

When the National League of Cities asked 512 members of city councils to select the most difficult functions for their council to perform, some interesting answers emerged:

1. Zoning and land-use decisions
2. Budgeting and finance
3. Developing new city programs
4. Evaluating city services
5. Establishing growth policies
6. Handling citizen complaints
7. Establishing administrative policy
8. Enacting legislation[28]

Land-use and fiscal matters were the most difficult, far outdistancing the enactment of legislation. The importance of the first two issues will be stressed in the next chapter.

When council members were asked what irritated them the most about their job, the pressures of time and paperwork led the list.

1. Excessive time spent away from family
2. Long hours required for "part-time" job
3. Inefficient use of elected officials' time
4. Too much paper to wade through to make decisions
5. Too many meetings to attend
6. Excessive time spent away from private business
7. Expensive election-campaign spending
8. Low public salary
9. Lack of staff assistance
10. Late-night calls from constituents[29]

Perhaps members of city councils would look on their job pressures more favorably if they received more adequate financial compensation or more public recognition. As for late-night calls from constituents, only a telephone answering machine can solve that.

SUMMARY

This chapter has emphasized the variety of the nation's eighty-two thousand local governments. Cities, towns, townships, counties, special districts, and regional agencies crisscross the landscape. An important feature of each of these units is its dependence on the state government for its authority to act. Such is the nature of Dillon's Rule. Important issues to be considered in the next chapter are: In whose interests are policies made? How is local government financed? How has the legacy of reform affected local government?

NOTES

1. Demetrios Caraley, *City Governments and Urban Problems* (Englewood Cliffs, N.J.: Prentice-Hall, 1977), p. 16. It should be noted that crime is also an underpublicized rural problem.

2. Caraley, *City Governments*, chap. 1, has an excellent overview of these problems.

3. Jay Goodman, *The Dynamics of Urban Government and Politics*, 2nd ed. (New York: Macmillan, 1980), p. 39. See also Carl Abbott, *The New Urban America* (Chapel Hill: University of North Carolina Press, 1981); and Richard Bernard and Bradley R. Rice, eds., *Sunbelt Cities* (Austin: University of Texas Press, 1983).

4. Richard Boyer and David Savageau, *Places Rated Almanac*, 2nd ed. (Skokie, Ill.: Rand McNally, 1985).

5. John F. Dillon, *Commentaries on the Law of Municipal Corporations*, 5th ed. (Boston: Little, Brown, 1911), Section 237.

6. *Measuring Local Discretionary Authority* (Washington, D.C.: Advisory Commission on Intergovernmental Relations, 1981), pp. 12–13.

7. Ibid., p. 18.

8. *Significant Features of Fiscal Federalism, 1984 edition* (Washington, D.C.: Advisory Commission on Intergovernmental Relations, 1985), Table 93.

9. Joseph F. Zimmerman, *State-Local Relations* (New York: Praeger, 1983), p. 53.

10. Max Neiman and Catherine Lovell, "Mandating as a Policy Issue," *Policy Studies Journal*, 9 (Spring 1981), 669.

11. *State Mandating of Local Expenditures* (Washington, D.C.: Advisory Commission on Intergovernmental Relations, 1978), pp. 2–3.

12. Ibid., p. 16.

13. Ibid., pp. 5–6.

14. Patrick O'Grady, "A Description of the State Mandates Review Process," *Illinois Municipal Review*, February 1981, p. 18.

15. George Break, *Financing Government in a Federal System* (Washington, D.C.: Brookings Institution, 1980), p. 181.

16. Zimmerman, *State-Local Relations*, p. 161.

17. Edward Banfield and James Q. Wilson, *City Politics* (Cambridge, Mass.: Harvard University Press, 1965), pp. 177–80.

18. Ronald Loveridge, *City Managers in Legislative Politics* (Indianapolis: Bobbs-Merrill, 1971), p. 100.

19. Caraley, *City Governments*, pp. 233–34. See also Loveridge, *City Managers*, pp. 130–31.

20. Herbert S. Duncombe, *Modern County Government* (Washington, D.C.: National Association of Counties, 1977), p. 132. See also pp. 29–32.

21. Ibid., p. 4.

22. Ibid., pp. 8–12.

23. Ibid., pp. 40–50.

24. "The Board of Supervisors" (issue paper prepared for the San Diego County Charter Review Panel, September 1984).

25.   However, Congress has voted to allow the revenue sharing program to expire in late 1987.

26.   Caraley, *City Governments*, pp. 215–23; Jeffrey Pressman, "The Preconditions of Mayoral Leadership," *American Political Science Review,* 66 (June 1972), 512–13.

27.   Caraley, *City Governments*, p. 258.

28.   Adapted from Raymond Bancroft, *America's Mayors and Councilmen* (Washington, D.C.: National League of Cities, 1974), p. 59.

29.   Adapted from Raymond Bancroft, *America's Mayors and Councilmen* (Washington, D.C.: National League of Cities, 1974), p. 60.

chapter 9

Money, Power, and Control

In the last chapter, we studied the structure of local governments and how they receive their powers. Now we can discuss some of the controversies swirling around local governments: how these governments should be financed; whether the governmental structure of metropolitan areas should be reformed; how extensive city planning and zoning should be; and whether a secret "power elite" runs American cities. Before considering these controversies, though, we must trace some of their historical underpinnings.

THE POLITICAL MACHINE

Today's local politics has its roots in the urban political machine that flourished in most large American cities in the late nineteenth and early twentieth centuries. The basis of the machine's power was the waves of immigrants who flooded the country in the years following the Civil War. Between 1861 and 1900, the immigrants came primarily from northern and western Europe, and secondarily from southern and eastern Europe; from 1901 to 1930, the proportions were reversed. With the exception of the Irish, the immigrants generally did not speak English. In addition to being unskilled, the new Americans had been raised in rural, peasant societies with strong traditions of hierarchy, religion, and family ties. These people were thrust into the life of "modern" American cities for which they were totally unprepared. At the same time, those cities had a crying need for facilities such as roads, bridges, docks, buildings, sewers, schools, and transit systems.[1] The situation was ready-made for the urban political boss who could get things done.

The ethnic immigrants voted for the boss and his political machine, enabling it to control city government. In return, the newcomers received jobs, favors, and recognition. City governments then, and to a great extent now, spread authority among many boards and commissions having a large number of elected officials. But the machine centralized in the boss the power the city charter had dispersed. Since the armies of elected officials and party workers received their marching orders from a single source, the machine was able to manipulate city contracts, utility franchises, taxes, and business regulations. This gave the boss leverage over the city's business community.

What the immigrants needed was jobs—and the machine could supply patronage positions in city "street departments, in police, fire, and sanitation departments, and sometimes in private industry."[2] In addition to jobs, the ethnics got "friendship and help from the organization, and in a language they could understand."[3] They went to "Boss" Jim Pendergast of Kansas City

> when they were in trouble and needed someone to soften the stern hand of justice. Many of them got fuel and other supplies from his precinct captains when they were down and out. Others ate his turkey and trimmings at the free Christmas dinners.[4]

In true American fashion, politics was also the way the ethnic immigrants could move up the socioeconomic ladder. In the words of one boss, "I had no education to speak of, a good many roads were closed to our people, and politics seemed the easiest way out."[5] It was also a way out of the dreadful slums and sweatshops.

In sum, the machine provided a rudimentary form of welfare, served as an employment agency, and gave the immigrants a chance to improve their station in life. But beyond all these benefits, the machine helped to assimilate the waves and waves of foreigners into American life. To appreciate this accomplishment, one need only note the separatist movements in Canada and Spain. The machine's role as melting pot was also greatly aided by the public school system.

Although the political machine was usually ethnically based, Democratic, and located in large northeastern cities, there were some important exceptions, as Lineberry and Sharkansky have noted. Some cities with large ethnic concentrations, such as Milwaukee, did not develop machines. There were Republican machines in some Pennsylvania and New York cities. Two of the most powerful machines, those in Kansas City and Memphis, were not located in old cities of the northeast. Finally, there were rural machines and statewide machines such as the Byrd organization in Virginia and the Long organization in Louisiana.[6]

In any event, one thing is certain: the machine was corrupt, even for that period in American life. Graft was a way of life for the boss, and many bosses amassed huge sums of money. The key was control of government offices, and hence the power to award construction contracts, lucrative public utility franchises (for trolleys, water, electricity, and so on), and favorable utility rates. Those people who received patronage jobs from the machine kicked back part of their salary to the machine, as did businessmen who signed contracts with the city. City government under the boss "looked the other way" when it came to illegal gambling or prostitution.

DEMISE OF THE NINETEENTH-CENTURY MACHINE

The obvious corruption of the political machine served as an effective rallying cry for a reform movement to "clean up" city government. The National Municipal League was the urban counterpart of the Progressive movement, which was seeking to reform state (and national) government. The struggle between immigrant and reformer involved not only different views about corruption, but also a struggle between classes, ethnic groups, religions, and world views. For the Progressive reformer, politics was the "arena for the realization of moral principles of broad application and even—as in the case of temperance and vice crusades—for the correction of private habits."[7] He and (after the passage of women's suffrage) she stressed good citizenship, civic responsibility, and "good government" characterized by efficiency. The Progressive was also a nativist who wanted to preserve a pure Anglo-Saxon, Protestant society. Many worked to curb immigration after 1921. The immigrant, on the other hand, had a peasant background and little experience in active political participation. He "looked to politics not for the realization of high principles but for concrete and personal gains, and he sought these gains through personal relationships" with the political boss. In short, "the immigrant wanted humanity, not efficiency."[8] The struggle was deadly serious because the winner would rule American cities.

The National Municipal League had a comprehensive program for reforming city government: civil service employment, auditing of city accounts, competitive bidding for contracts, the city manager or the commission form of government, and home rule. For local politics, the Progressives suggested nonpartisan elections, the short ballot, nomination by primary rather than by party caucus, and the initiative, referendum, and recall. *At-large* (citywide) elections would cause candidates to put the interests of the whole city above special or ward interests; *off-year* municipal elections, which were not keyed to state or national elections, would focus attention on local issues. The Progressive program was clearly intended to weaken political parties and hence destroy the machine. Civil service, auditing of accounts, and competitive bidding would dry up sources of money for the machine. Nonpartisan elections, off-year elections, and the initiative, referendum, and recall would decrease the saliency of political parties. The short ballot and primaries would mean fewer political offices for the boss to fill and less of a voice for him in naming political candidates.

The reform program was spectacularly successful: the only remaining urban machine is in Chicago, and it is now but a pale shadow of its former self. But the Progressives were aided by certain other trends. After the Depression, social-welfare services came to be provided by government. The ward heeler's emergency sack of coal and Christmas turkey were replaced by the more dependable and bureaucratized Aid to Families with Dependent Children, unemployment compensation, and Social Security. The immigrants could not stay poor forever; as they rose the economic ladder, they depended less on the boss. Besides, there were fewer and fewer immigrants because of restrictive immigration laws. As the ethnics became more educated, they relied more on newspapers or the radio for advice on how to vote. The voice of the boss was now one of many.

THE LEGACY OF MUNICIPAL REFORM

Political scientists Edward Banfield and James Q. Wilson have described the struggle between reformer and immigrant as a conflict between a "public-regarding ethos" and a "private-regarding ethos."[9] The Progressives favored efficiency, impartiality, honesty, and planning. These would be achieved by all of the reforms mentioned previously, plus city planning. Immigrants who held the private-regarding ethos identified with their own ward or neighborhood rather than the city as a whole, and they looked to politicians for material benefits. This ethos favored the mayor-council form of government, partisan ballots, and ward election from small wards; it was opposed to civil service and city planning.

How does the structure of city government reflect these two views? Manager cities tend to have nonpartisan ballots and at-large elections, but not civil service.[10] Nationwide, mayor-council cities may or may not have partisan elections and ward elections, but the northeastern part of the country does favor the mayor-council form and partisan elections. The west prefers city managers and nonpartisan elections. Only in the Midwest do mayor-council cities have a much higher ethnic population than manager cities. Cities with large ethnic populations do not consistently lack civil service coverage, nor do they consistently spend less on city planning. In sort, the wave of structural reform that swept over American cities in the early twentieth century was quite uneven, and it was more successful in certain regions of the country than in others.[11]

Robert Lineberry and Edmund Fowler have written that the Progressives believed there is a public interest for the whole city that must transcend any partial interests. Hence, the reformers sought to reduce the impact of what they perceived as "artificial" cleavages based on party, social status, religion, or ethnicity.[12] The tax and expenditure policies of reformed cities are far less responsive to socioeconomic cleavages in their population than the policies of unreformed cities. Nonpartisan elections reduce turnout among the working class, the less educated, and Democrats by removing the cue of party from the ballot. Party workers are also less likely to try to get out the vote in such elections. Nonpartisan elections also increase the influence of the media: according to one newspaper writer, "you can't tell the players without a scorecard, and we sell the scorecards."[13] In strong mayor-council cities, on the other hand, turnout is increased by election of the mayor. Moreover, turnout is higher in older, eastern cities in which the population is less educated, highly ethnic, and not mobile.

It is ironic that reform sometimes leads to unintended consequences and even to "new reform" or "re-reform." The Progressives favored at-large election of all council members rather than election by district because they believed that those elected at large would put the interests of the whole city above district interests. However, as the years passed and black people began voting and running for office in greater numbers, at-large election came to have the effect of decreasing the number of blacks on city councils. Hence, there is a new reform movement to go back to the election of council members from smaller districts.[14]

To give another example, we noted earlier that the tax and expenditure policies of reformed cities are not particularly responsive to socioeconomic cleavages. But it does not necessarily follow that these policies are less costly. Adoption of the Progressive reform program has led to more expensive urban government. Reform requires employing professional administrators, many of whom are also innovative and activist: they are constantly looking for bold new programs to institute. These professionals are dedicated to improving the quality of urban life—and that costs money. Furthermore, there is some empirical evidence that "reformed institutions tend to decrease responsiveness to public opinion and enhance responsiveness to group demands."[15] We now consider urban interest groups.

URBAN INTEREST GROUPS

It could be argued that interest groups are more influential at the local level than at the state or national level: decision makers, interest group leaders, and interest group members are nearer to one another at the local level. What is done by mayors, council members, or county commissioners can hardly escape the notice of interested groups.

Large cities have an impressive array of interest groups.[16] Municipal labor unions are concerned about public employee pay and benefits. Their campaign contributions and votes can be quite influential. Trade associations, business interests, realtors, and developers are perhaps the most powerful urban interest groups. They favor economic growth, which may bring them into conflict with environmentalists opposed to new freeways, airports, or skyscrapers. When business interests join with their normal adversaries, labor unions, in a pro-growth coalition, they constitute a formidable force. Neighborhood interests such as homeowners' organizations want high-quality public services for their neighborhood. They are also concerned with preserving property values. There are also ethnic interests, such as the NAACP and the Italian-American Civil Rights League; "good government" groups, such as the League of Women Voters and taxpayers' associations; and interests oriented toward a particular problem—for example, a parks association or a historic sites preservation group.

Urban interest groups use the techniques described in Chapter 4, including campaign contributions. Although giving money to politicians for election expenses is an important avenue of access for interest groups, incumbent officeholders also "shake the money tree." Reading 9-1 describes former Chicago mayor Jane Byrne engaging in what amounts to legal extortion. Such practices are common in all large cities.

Mayors and council members in fifty-one cities were asked which interest groups have their preferences acted upon favorably by city government. The results are presented in Table 9-1. Perhaps the most

TABLE 9-1   Responsiveness Scores of Urban Interest Groups*

Type of Organization	Average Responsiveness
1. Private sector unions	3.68
2. Neighborhood associations	3.56
3. Business organizations	3.36
4. Church or religious organizations	3.33
5. Clients of city services (e.g., parents of school children, welfare recipients)	3.30
6. Campaign organizations	3.21
7. Civic and charitable groups (e.g., League of Women Voters)	3.21
8. Civil rights, black, and ethnic groups	3.20
9. Environmentalists	3.17
10. Public employee unions	3.11

SOURCE: Paul Schumaker and Russel Getter, "Structural Sources of Unequal Responsiveness to Group Demands in American Cities," *Western Political Quarterly*, 36 (March 1983), 15.

* "In your judgement, how often has the city government responded favorably to the requests or policy preferences of each of the groups which you have listed?
1. Almost never
2. Less than half of the time
3. About half of the time
4. More than half of the time
5. Almost all of the time

striking aspect of the table is the closeness of the average responsiveness scores to one another.

There is a long-standing dispute in political science over whether business-oriented elites run American cities. We now consider that controversy.

READING 9-1   POLITICAL FUND-RAISING SOMETIMES LOOKS LIKE A SHAKEDOWN

Those famous Indian maharajahs who collected their weight in gold and gems every year on their birthday had nothing on Jane Byrne.

Although few people thought Mayor Byrne could or would surpass the legendary Richard J. Daley in political savvy, the mayor already has relegated Daley and just about everyone else to the minor leagues when it comes to fund-raising bashes.

Last Monday, Her Honor raised $1.7 million when she entertained 13,000 persons at a McCormick Place dinner. Tack that onto the $1.4 million affair she threw in October, 1979, and the mayor's take after 18 months in office is more than $3 million before expenses.

Only presidential candidates raise that kind of loot, and even then it's not common. . . .

The mayor inherited from her predecessors the tradition of huge fund-raising dinners, but she is doing her best to perfect the fund-raising art. Many Democratic leaders are concerned that Mrs. Byrne believes practice makes perfect, because it is apparent she plans annual affairs rather than waiting to put the arm on her followers only in an election year.

One ranking Chicago Democrat said, "It's appalling that office-holders have dinners in years when they're not running for election. The party workers and other contributors can only take so much and we just went through a rough year."

Nevertheless, few people avoided the mayor's $100-a-plate affair. City Hall employees, policemen, labor unions, bankers, business executives, realtors, lawyers—always the lawyers—purchased the tickets that attest to the loyalty that was a part of doing business in Chicago before Jane Byrne was born.

One politically connected lawyer explained: "I buy tables because I'm paranoid and she's the mayor. A great number of lawyers do business with the city. So do contractors, suppliers, all kinds of people. They feel they have to buy tables.

"It's a small investment. Even those who aren't getting the business buy tables because hope springs eternal—maybe they'll get theirs in the future. Everyone wants the mayor to know how many tables they bought.

"I was sitting there looking out at that vast audience the other night and I said, 'With all the trouble and the criticism and problems this woman has, look at the crowd. Why?'

"The answer is, the system produces it. And the system is quid pro quo."

Lawyers aren't the only people who understand how the system works. That's why such business chiefs as Brooks McCormick of International Harvester and John Swearingen of Standard Oil Co. of Indiana were pleased to sit on the dais at the mayor's dinner. . . .

Banks buy tickets. John Perkins—president of Continental Illinois Bank and Trust Company of Chicago, considered the banker with the most influence in City Hall—made a brief appearance at the dinner but had to leave because of a travel commitment. . . .

All banking and financial institutions have a vested interest in City Hall.

The city invests its money in banks. The city's commitment to development means that someone will have to borrow money for projects, and the city's perspective on real estate transactions affects the banking industry, as it does the insurance and real estate industries.

But no private group is as anxious to ingratiate itself to City Hall as the labor unions. People like Edward Brabec of the plumbers union and Louis Peick of the Teamsters follow the pattern established by their predecessors and Daley to protect the jobs of their union members and their access to the mayor's office.

The laborers union raised a considerable amount for last Monday's dinner, assessing each worker $50 and buttonholing each supervisor for $100.

But that is deemed a minor tribute compared with the potential gains. "It helps to smooth relations," a labor boss said. "Our men are going to get a point higher than other city workers next year. We've got our foremen back on a monthly (salary) basis. You see, 'collective bargaining' is an ongoing process in this town. The dinner is a part of it."

Despite the almost guaranteed support of those seeking favors from the mayor's office, most of the contributions and the attendance continue to come from the political sector, and not necessarily with a smile.

One city supervisor complained, "I've never seen city workers hit like this before—the forestry workers, the asphalt crews—50 bucks a man, 100 for upper-level guys. A lot of it was done through the unions. The guys hadn't been squeezed like this before. It used to be the ward organizations would raise money to buy the tables. I've never seen them hit the workers direct like this before."

The ward organizations were not remiss. Several wards were big spenders. One committeeman, hoping the mayor will support his planned bid for higher office, purchased 20 tables.

Others are more realistic than ambitious. One South Side committeeman said: "Jobs. We need 'em and she's got 'em. That's why you buy tickets to the dinner."

Another said, "Let's face it. We want jobs. And if you want to do something in the party, it's better to have the mayor with you than against you."

But for the average person, it remains a puzzle why the mayor can command so much homage despite her reputation as a ruthless politician.

"Fear. That's why they came," said a powerful committeeman. "They may hate her guts, but as long as she's in that office with her hand on the spigot, they'll buy tables because she can turn it on and turn it off."

SOURCE: F. Richard Ciccone and David Axelrod, "As Fund Raiser, Byrne One in a Million," *Chicago Tribune*, December 7, 1980, Section 1, p. 16. Reprinted by courtesy of the *Chicago Tribune*.

COMMUNITY POWER THEORIES

Floyd Hunter used the reputational technique to study power in Atlanta: he asked local leaders to tell him who had power in general and who had power over certain specific decisions.[17] What emerged was a pyramidal structure of power with the highest elected official only fourth from the top. The real political power rested with those persons who had economic and social power—the owners and top managers of local industry. Even within this elite was a smaller group of people who were exceptionally powerful. Community elites see each other frequently in informal settings—for example, at dinner clubs. The key points of *elitist* or *power-structure theory* are that a behind-the-scenes, nonelected elite controls elected officials, that the business and financial leaders who have wealth and social position constitute the elite, that the elite rules American cities in its own interest, and that these power relationships continue over time: those who wielded real power in the past still do, and will continue to do so.

In opposition to elitist theory is *pluralist theory*, which "rejects the stratification thesis that *some* group necessarily dominates a community."[18] Pluralists argue that elitist theorists who ask "Who runs this community?" are asking something like the old chauvinist query "Have you stopped beating your wife?" They are assuming that someone runs the community, which is exactly what they should be proving. Elitists believe that

> power distributions are a more or less permanent aspect of social structure. Pluralists hold that power may be tied to issues, and issues can be fleeting or persistent, provoking coalitions among interested groups and citizens ranging in their duration from momentary to semipermanent.[19]

According to pluralists, such coalitions are *ad hoc*. That is, they form for a particular issue or decision, then break up.

Pluralists argue further that Hunter should have looked at actual cases to determine who won or lost. The reputational approach does not actually measure the exercise of power, but only the reputation for power. In Hunter's defense, it should be pointed out that if one is believed to be powerful, one does in fact have power.

The major pluralist work is Robert Dahl's study of New Haven. Dahl found that those people who are influential in one particular area (say, education) were not influential in other areas (such as urban renewal or political nominations).[20] Another pluralist argument is that economic and social elites, unlike political scientists, may not really be interested in politics. Nor do they always employ their economic and social resources skillfully and effectively. Finally, pluralists contend, it is unrealistic to consider local communities apart from state and national politics. The last chapter showed extensive state and even national involvement in local affairs.

Perhaps the best conclusion to draw from the elitist-pluralist debate is "It depends." Power elites are most likely to be found in small towns or in states dominated by a single industry.[21] Diverse cities—those with vigorous party competition, robust interest groups, and an inquisitive media—are unlikely to be dominated by a single power structure. Table 9-1 indicates that unions, businesses, civil rights groups, and environmentalists—groups that may normally be antagonists—each have a cut of the local political action.

A powerful challenge to elitists and pluralists is posed by Bachrach and Baratz, who note that a person or group can exercise power "by confining the scope of decision-making to relatively 'safe' issues. . . . To the extent that a person or group . . . creates or reinforces barriers to the public airing of policy conflicts, that person or group has power."[22] Such barriers can be created by influencing community values and political procedures and rituals. Ironically, those persons or groups who dominate may not be "conscious of [their domination] themselves, simply because their position of dominance has never seriously been challenged."[23] When issues are kept off the public agenda, they are reduced to the status of nondecisions.

FRACTIONALIZED GOVERNMENT IN URBAN AREAS

Whether or not a single elite controls urban government, there are clearly a large number of governments in urban areas. The Chicago standard metropolitan area has 1172 governments, Philadelphia has 852, Pittsburgh 698, and New York 538.[24] This proliferation of governments is said to reduce efficiency, accountability, and equity. There is no single metropolitan-wide government able to deal with metropolitan-wide problems, but instead many overlapping governments with different jurisdictions and duties. The problem of spillover effects is intensified: decisions made in one unit of local government affect other units in such areas as pollution control, transportation, police protection, and especially zoning. Different levels of government may provide duplicate services—for example, health services, police services, or property-tax assessments. Because many of the units of government are small, they cannot achieve economies of scale and reduce costs. These small units are charged with being unprofessional, too small in area, and lacking in tax base and legal powers. Since no officials are elected on an area-wide basis, which officer or unit of government will be held accountable if something goes wrong? Finally, those who want to reform this system of fractionalized government note that because there are differing amounts of wealth in the various communities in the metropolis, there are differing levels of governmental services. A single area-wide government would have the effect of redistributing or evening out differences in wealth.

However, fractionalized government may have its positive points as well.[25] Many of the communities in the fragmented metropolis are small, and their affairs are easier to manage. Because there are many local governments in the metropolis, there are many forums for airing public grievances, and thus more points of citizen access. More groups can take advantage of these access points to influence public policy. Groups that are in a minority in a larger unit of government (for example, the county) can be in a majority in smaller unit of government. Defenders of a multiplicity of local governments, who are usually called *public-choice theorists*, respond to the economies-of-scale argument by saying that such economies are really realized only in governments that emphasize capital-intensive services requiring expensive physical facilities, such as sewage treatment plants. The costs of these capital projects can be spread over many users. Local governments, on the other hand, are labor-intensive: high percentages of their budgets go for salaries, benefits, and pensions of workers such as police officers and teachers. Savings from economies of scale are said to be exhausted by governments serving 50,000 to 150,000 people.[26] Many units of government in a metropolis are already this size.

Ten proposals for dealing with fractionalized urban government are presented in Figure 9-1. These proposals range from moderate to drastic.

Through *interjurisdictional agreements*, local governments join together to solve a common problem. These cooperative endeavors are more effective than separate action, can save money, and do not disturb the legal status of the participating governments. Moreover, smaller units of government can band together to achieve economies of scale, as in joint

FIGURE 9-1   Ten Proposals Dealing with Fractionalized Urban Government

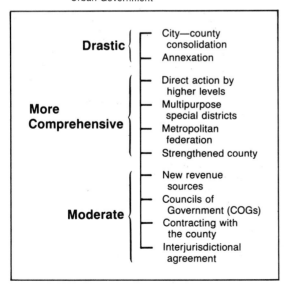

property-tax assessment and collection. Some examples of interjurisdictional agreements in the Chicago area include

> the City of Chicago/Suburban Cook County Water Supply Service, through which Chicago supplies water at its city limits to suburban cities willing to build the connections. The North Suburban Library System links the resources of the libraries of north and northwest suburban libraries. The Aurora-Naperville Boundary Agreement reduces unseemly competition between the two cities over the unincorporated area between them. The Evanston North Shore Health Department permits Winnetka, Glencoe, and an unincorporated part of New Trier Township to use the facilities of the Evanston Health Department. And there are a large number of mutual aid pacts for fire and rescue services.[27]

Agreements of this sort do not usually involve basic public services over which there might be ideological disagreement—for example, public education. Moreover, incremental arrangements such as these provide the benefits of consolidation without its liabilities.

Local governments can formally *contract with the county* to obtain fire protection, law enforcement, election administration, property tax assessment, libraries, and many other services. These contracts can save cities money, but poorer cities in the county may not be able to afford the services. Contracting with the county is sometimes called the Lakewood Plan, after the California city that pioneered the practice.

Other moderate proposals for dealing with fragmented government in metropolitan areas are the *councils of government* discussed in Chapter 8 and *new sources of revenue* for local governments. The latter would require action by the state legislature or in some states an amendment to the state constitution. New income sources might include a sales tax or income tax.

A more comprehensive change would be for a *strengthened county* to provide more county-wide services, such as health services, law enforcement, and solid-waste collection. *Metropolitan federation* is based on the federal analogy. Cities transfer matters of area-wide concern to a larger unit of government, which may or may not be the existing county, but maintain jurisdiction over purely local functions. The problem with metropolitan federations is how to agree upon the proper allocation of functions. Are water, sewers, and land-use planning area-wide? Are street maintenance and garbage collection purely local? Two other approaches, suggested by George Blair, are *multipurpose* (rather than single-function) *special districts* and *direct action by higher levels* of government.[28] Under the latter possibility, the state or even the federal government might take over welfare, streets, or health and hospitals.

A more drastic approach would be the central city's *annexation* of its suburbs. If the suburbs are already incorporated, they will resist this action. Requirements in many states that a majority vote be obtained in the area to be annexed and in the annexing city reduce the number of annexations. Perhaps the most far-reaching reform is *city-county consolidation*. Examples are Nashville and Davidson County, Indianapolis and Marion County, and Jacksonville (Florida) and Duval County. Successful consolidations are most likely to take place in the South, where counties have historically been important units of local government.

The practical politics of comprehensive reform proposals may be more important than their theoretical merits or demerits. Between 1947 and 1982 only seventeen out of seventy-nine such proposals were passed.[29] The forces favoring reform include downtown merchants who feel that reform will aid the deteriorating central business district. The Chamber of Commerce dislikes recent tax increases, inefficient government, and lack of growth—and hopes that reform will cure these. The Committee for Economic Development (CED), a group of civic-minded liberal business people, and the League of Women Voters carry on the Progressive tradition. Large daily newspapers dependent on advertising from the central business district also favor reform.

In opposition are big-city incumbent officeholders, especially if they are Democrats and suburban officials are Republicans. The latter also oppose restructuring, as do their constituents, who fear that federation or consolidation will lead to higher taxes. These fears are usually well founded. As the number of black voters in the central city increases, they too oppose reform, fearing a dilution of their political strength. Black leaders feel that it is better to have a majority in the central city than a minority in a larger reformed unit.

Voter turnout in reorganization elections is usually low, often less than 30 percent. However, higher turnout probably would not increase a reform proposal's chances of success. Since the issues in this type of election tend to be somewhat abstract or complex, voters are usually guided by the position taken by local political leaders whom they respect. If the public is dissatisfied with the status quo in local services or local government, reorganization proposals are more likely to pass.

THE SUBURBS

The flight of middle-class and upper-middle-class white people to the suburbs has been occurring since the 1950s. The exodus has been so pronounced that more Americans now live in suburbs than in central cities or nonmetropolitan areas. There has been a movement not only of people but also of businesses—for example, quality manufacturers and private nonresidential construction. Suburban shopping malls have shown significant increases in retail sales that once went to central-city merchants. Such sales are an important source of sales-tax revenue for local governments.[30]

There is some dispute about whether people are "pushed" to the suburbs by the characteristics of central cities, or "pulled" to the suburbs by their purported good features. Probably it is a combination of both. Whites may flee the central city's crime, high taxes, public employee strikes, pollution, congestion, noise, and large black population. One study concludes that it is more likely that people are "drawn to the suburbs rather than pushed to them."[31] The suburbs are said to feature less crime; less crowding; more open space (homes are built on individual lots); better public services, such as police or street repair or garbage collection, at lower cost; and more parks and playgrounds. But most important is superior schools. Better schools plus all the other amenities are said to produce the most promising environment for raising children.

Suburban government reflects many of the "good government" beliefs mentioned earlier, such as nonpartisanship, the council-manager form of government, and an emphasis on consensus. Suburban residents want a government that is small enough so that they can influence its policies, yet they want to be near enough to a large city so that they can take advantage of its facilities.[32] There are, however, some issues that can shatter the apparent calm of suburban politics. Land use and zoning (discussed in the next section), plus the regulation of growth, can fracture a community. Those already in the community may want to "raise the drawbridge" to ward off newcomers and preserve the suburb's small-town character. If the homogeneous character of the suburb begins to change because lower-status people are beginning to move in, conflict can be intense. If a federal or state judge orders a metropolitan busing plan in which central-city black schools and suburban white schools are merged to promote racial balance, the suburbs will be increased. There can also be bitter struggles over what books should be permitted in school libraries. Such battles pit self-styled "cosmopolitans" against "traditionalists." Critics of the suburbs point out that

> poverty is . . . concentrated in the [central] cities, and the political independence [of the suburbs] allows suburbanites to escape the financial burdens of supporting welfare programs, public hospitals, special school programs, increased police expenditures, and other services which cannot be . . . provided by poor residents.[33]

Moreover, it is sometimes said that suburban residents take advantage of the central city because they work there and thus increase its costs for street repair and police or fire protection, yet they pay their property taxes to a suburban government. Central-city mayors who call for a municipal income tax based on place of employment make this argument. On the other hand, two writers argue that census data reveal that "for every fringe area dweller who travels into the core municipality to work, two commute to places of employment in suburbia."[34]

Up to this point, suburbs have been described as "dormitories" of wealthy or middle-class people. But there are also working-class suburbs and even a few suburban slums. In addition, there are industrial suburbs (near interstates), suburbs consisting primarily of a shopping mall, recreational suburbs of lakes and parks, and suburbs that are a mixture of two or more of these. There may also be greater differences of opinion between suburbanites of different social status than between suburbanites as a whole and central-city residents as a whole.

In any event, there are some developments on the horizon that may slow the movement to the suburbs. The higher cost of homes in the suburbs and the possibility of finding cheaper housing in the large city may keep people in the city, especially first-time home buyers. Moreover, suburban property taxes are rising, thus reducing one of the "pull" features of the suburbs.

LAND USE AND ZONING

By means of their decisions regarding zoning and the use of land, suburbanites have often been able to keep racial minorities, poor people, and tenants of subsidized housing penned up in the central city.[35] *Exclusionary zoning* can ban the construction of apartments and the introduction of mobile homes. Large-lot zoning—for example, setting the minimum lot size at more than two acres—is used in wealthy communities such as Schaumberg, a suburb of Chicago. Another Chicago suburb's refusal to grant a request to rezone a parcel of property from single-family classification to multiple-family classification led to the famous U.S. Supreme Court case of *Arlington Heights* v. *Metropolitan Housing Corp.*, 429 U.S. 252 (1977). The Court ruled that those objecting to a zoning ordinance must prove a "racially discriminatory intent or purpose," rather than merely showing a "racially disporportionate impact."

The planning staff of a city or county draws up a long-range comprehensive plan for how the city or county shall be developed. Land is zoned for uses such as residential, commercial, industrial, and agricultural. Those wishing to construct a building most receive a building permit from the city or county. The zoning ordinance usually allows nonconforming use of land or buildings if such use existed prior to the adoption by the city council or county commission of the planning staff's comprehensive plan. Through *spot-zoning*, the plan can be changed to allow land to be used for a purpose other than the one for which it was zoned. *Variances* (exceptions to the comprehensive plan) are also allowed. The greater the number of nonconforming uses, spot-zonings, and variances, the less integrity the plan has.

The theoretical basis of planning and zoning is that the professional planners hired by the city or county have been academically trained to do their job and possess the expertise to discern the long-range interests of the city or county. Without professional planning, it is said, the future of the city or county will be determined by the self-interest of real estate developers, business people, and private citizens. Moreover, advocates of planning say that zoning laws can be viewed as a way of protecting private-property rights, not infringing upon them. For example, my house retains its value because no one can build a slaughterhouse next door.

Critics of the planning process point to the immense powers of planners and ask, "Who elected them?" The decisions made by planners regarding the uses of land can cost one person a great deal of money and benefit others. Moreover, the elected officials who enact the zoning ordinance usually follow the advice of their planning staff. Bryan D. Jones poses three other serious questions:

> First, who is to plan? Who is to say what form cities are to take? Different people have different values, and these values can imply vastly different urban forms. The power to plan and enforce the plan carries with it the power to coerce other citizens into conforming to the values of those who plan.
>
> The second question concerns the ability to plan successfully. Can urban planners foresee all possible developments that ought to be incorporated into a plan? . . .
>
> The final question involves limits on the use of government coercion. How much government coercion are we willing to use in a pluralistic, relatively open society in order to impose a plan?[36]

On a less philosophical level, zoning is said to discriminate against low-income people, regardless of race. Zoning decreases the supply of housing, which bids up its price. Large-lot zoning and the requirement for expensive design features ("snob zoning") exclude poor people. Since zoning increases the costs of building, these costs are passed on to the consumer. Moreover, large builders benefit at the expense of small builders: "Obtaining zoning approval may take months or years and that involves the expense of holding or optioning property. These conditions are eliminating small builders to the advantage of the large ones who are in a much better position to cope."[37]

LOCAL FINANCE

Expenditures

Expenditures for city governments are given in Table 9-2. The figures in Table 9-2 must be viewed with caution. First of all, cities of widely varying sizes have been grouped together. Cities of over one million people may spend proportionately more money than other cities on such functions as education, welfare, health, and hospitals. For example, the

TABLE 9-2 City Expenditures

Function	Percentage
Police protection	11.9
Education	10.9
Highways	8.3
Sewerage	7.8
Fire protection	6.6
Interest on general debt	5.6
Public welfare	5.3
Parks and recreation	4.8
Hospitals	4.8
Housing and urban renewal	4.8
Sanitation other than sewerage	3.6
General control	3.1
Financial administration	2.5
Health	1.5
All other functions	18.5

SOURCE: U.S. Bureau of the Census, *City Government Finances in 1982–83* (Washington, D.C.: Government Printing Office, 1984), p. vi.

position of education as the number-two expenditure results from the fact that New York City and some other northeastern cities finance education as part of the city budget, rather than through an independent school district. Moreover, some states have the state government or county governments provide some of the services listed in Table 9-2.

Because of need, demand, and resources, large cities spend more money per capita than small cities.[38] In terms of *need*, big cities have higher concentrations of poor people and the elderly. Also, greater population density results in greater expenditures per capita for police, fire protection, health, and sanitation. Cities with old housing stock must pay more for building inspections and fire services.

Because of greater *demand*, the residents of large cities may expect more services than small-town people. Big cities provide services usually not found in smaller cities: consumer protection, drug rehabilitation, family planning, day-care centers, and others. Moreover, bigger cities are more likely to have a unionized municipal work force, which leads to higher wages and benefits. The role of the American Federation of State, County, and Municipal Employees (AFSCME) is particularly important in this respect. As we have noted, local governments are labor-intensive enterprises, and it is politically expedient for many elected officials to attempt to conceal as many personnel expenses as possible. Rather than vote for a 10 percent salary increase for city employees and have your opponent in the next election charge you with being a stooge of city unions, it might be wiser to vote for a 6 percent raise and put the remaining

TABLE 9-3 County Expenditures

Function	Percentage
Public welfare	15.1
Education	14.6
Hospitals	11.7
Highways	8.9
General control	7.0
Health	5.9
Police protection	5.4
Interest on general debt	4.7
Corrections	4.0
Financial administration	2.9
General public buildings	1.8
All other	18.0

SOURCE: U.S. Bureau of the Census, *County Government Finances in 1982–83* (Washington, D.C.: Government Printing Office, 1984), p. vi.

4 percent in employee benefits, pension provisions, or early-retirement options, which are less visible.

Some cities have greater *resources* than other cities: they spend more because they have more. This increases the per-capita spending of many medium-size cities. Wealthier residents want their city to have well-financed amenities such as parks, libraries, and museums. Finally, cities receiving large amounts of state and/or federal aid are able to spend more on public services.

The expenditures of counties (Table 9-3) are subject to many of the caveats expressed earlier for city expenditures. County per-capita expenditures are highest in the South and West, lowest in New England. Urban counties spend a higher percentage on education, welfare, highways, and hospitals. Many county costs may be mandated by the state.

Revenues

As we noted in the previous chapter, local governments depend heavily on state and federal aid. Intergovernmental aid is particularly important for counties and for cities over one million in population. Buffalo, Detroit, and Pittsburgh are especially reliant on this money.[39] Sources of revenue for cities and counties are noted in Table 9-4.

The property tax is the most important source of income that cities and counties raise locally. However, it has become less important in recent years, partly as a result of tax-limitation movements such as Proposition 13 in California and Proposition 2½ in Massachusetts. Some problems with the property tax are that it is regressive, inefficiently administered, and more inconvenient to pay than other taxes. It is regressive because people of differing wealth pay it at the same rate; therefore, the tax places a heavier burden on poorer people. However, the regressivity of the property tax is softened by the *circuit breaker* in thirty-two states that have this form of state-financed property-tax relief; namely, if a person's property-tax payments are higher than a state-determined percentage of the person's income, the state refunds the excess or provides a state income tax credit, thus benefiting poorer people. The program also applies to renters.

Another defect of the property tax is that income-producing (business) property is taxed at the same rate as residential property. However, commercial and industrial property usually contributes much more to tax receipts than residential property because of its higher assessed valuation.

The person who must determine the value of real estate for tax purposes is an elected official known as the *assessor*. Property-tax administration is inefficient because it is very difficult to determine the exact value of real estate: assessments can vary widely. Furthermore, the assessor is an elected official who may not have been trained for the job and who is under tremendous political pressure to underassess property.

Moreover, some real property is exempted from taxation by state constitutions. Property owned by nonprofit or charitable organizations—churches, hospitals, retirement homes, colleges, libraries, museums—may be exempt. Land owned by the federal or state government is not taxed (but the federal government reimburses local governments through a payments-in-lieu-of-taxes program). The point to remember is that whenever any property is exempted, nonexempt property must bear a heavier burden.

Finally, property taxes are usually paid in two lump sums. Since the property tax is not withheld, as are income taxes, or paid in small amounts, as are sales taxes, it is a very inconvenient tax to pay.

TABLE 9-4   Revenue Sources of Cities and Counties

	Cities	Counties
State aid	20.2	32.2
Federal aid	11.0	5.7
Property tax	21.5	27.8
Income tax	5.4	1.0
Sales tax	11.5	5.6
Charges	11.0	20.2
Interest earnings	5.6	4.7
Other and unallocable	13.8	2.8

SOURCES: U.S. Bureau of the Census, *City Government Finances in 1982–83* (Washington, D.C.: Government Printing Office, 1984), p. 1; and U.S. Bureau of the Census *County Government Finances in 1982–83* (Washington, D.C.: Government Printing Office, 1984), p. 1.

The property tax is usually levied on *real property*, or real estate (land and buildings). However, some states have a tax on *personal property* such as automobiles, furniture, art objects, household appliances, clothes, jewelry, cash, and bonds. Needless to say, these items can be concealed from the assessor. In practice, the personal-property tax is levied only on automobiles, business machinery and store inventories, farm machinery, and livestock. The tax on business inventories has caused some stores to locate their warehouses in nearby states having no personal-property taxes, or to engage in "inventory sales" right before the day the inventory is to be assessed.

Despite all of these limitations, the property tax is retained by local governments, for two reasons: it produces large amounts of revenue, and local governments may not have any other alternatives. Because property *appreciates*, or increases in value, the tax base for the property tax constantly expands. This is fortunate because many states refuse to give their local governments an income tax or a sales tax.

Eleven states allow local governments to levy an income tax, but 87 percent of all local governments with this tax are in Pennsylvania alone. The local income tax, called a *payroll tax*, is a flat-rate tax on earned income or on both earned and unearned income.[40] Twenty-six states allow their local governments to have a sales tax, which is usually *piggybacked* on the state sales tax.[41] Cities or counties with a sales tax run the risk of large retail sales being made in nearby areas without such a tax.

As the property tax has decreased in importance, *user charges* have played a more prominent role in local government revenues. According to the *benefits-received principle* of taxation, if a person receives a government service such as visiting a city zoo or playing on a county tennis court, he or she should pay a fee sufficient to support provision of that service. Proponents of user charges argue that these fees are fair because no one is coerced into paying for a service that he or she does not receive, and that user charges promote conservation. If water or electricity are metered and paid for, conservation is promoted, especially if the unit price increases as consumption increases. Opponents of user charges note that they may cause poor people to be denied some government services and that there are some benefits that cannot be financed by user charges. Police and fire protection and air pollution control programs, for instance, benefit all residents, including those who do not pay for these services. They are what are known as *collective goods*: they could not be financed by user charges.

Debt

State and local governments go into debt to finance expensive construction projects or because tax revenues might not arrive before public bills must be paid. The latter situation, also familiar to almost all private citizens, is known as a *cash-flow problem*. When governments go into debt, they issue *bonds* (known also as *securities*), which are notes similar to an IOU. About 95 percent of state and local debt is long-term and is intended to pay for the building of schools, highways and sewers, or park acquisition. The major investors in municipal securities are households, fire and casualty insurance companies, and especially commercial banks seeking tax shelters (the earnings from these bonds are tax-exempt).[42] Because state and local government bonds are tax-exempt, the rate of interest on them is usually only 70 percent of the rate on taxable corporate bonds, which saves these governments a great deal of money.

Bonds can be either *term* or *serial*. In the former, all of the bonds in an issue mature on a set date—for example, thirty years. The issuing government is supposed to pay sufficient principal and interest into a *sinking fund* to retire the debt. Because elected officials sometimes did not pay enough money into sinking funds, serial bonds have become more numerous. Serial bonds mature at intervals—for example, twenty years, twenty-five years, or thirty years—and are considered to be more marketable.

Bonds are also categorized as full-faith-and-credit obligations and limited-liability obligations. Under *full-faith-and-credit obligations* (sometimes called *general-obligation bonds*), bondholders have a complete claim on the taxing authority of the issuer to repay the note. Municipal governments seldom default, despite the well-publicized cases of New York City, Cleveland, and Wayne County, Michigan.

Limited-liability obligations are guaranteed by a specific source of income. For example, *revenue bonds* are redeemed by the revenues or earnings generated by the facility being built, which might be a waterworks, sewer system, recreational facility, or parking garage. Limited-liability obligations are riskier investments than full-faith-and-credit obligations; hence they carry a higher interest rate. In 1983 the state of Washington Public Power Supply System (WPPSS or "Whoops") defaulted on $2.25 billion worth of bonds intended to pay for nuclear power plants. Revenue bonds financing a facility that requires mandatory public use (such as a water or sewer system) are more salable than bonds financing a facility that the public uses voluntarily (a recreational facility or a garage).[43] In any event, revenue bonds are not included as part of the debt limit that states impose on local governments, and their use has increased dramatically in recent years.

Two other types of limited-liability obligations that are put to interesting and sometimes controversial uses are industrial development bonds (IDBs) and tax increment financing (TIF). An *industrial development bond*

> is issued by a city to help a private corporation. Normally, the bond is issued so the company will build or expand a plant within the borders of the city issuing the bond.
>
> The main advantage to the city is a development tool to lure or retain

industry. The big advantage for the company is that the city's name on the bond lowers the borrowing cost.

Because the interest earned by the investor who buys an IDB is exempt from federal (and sometimes state) income taxes, he'll accept a lower interest rate.

No taxpayer money is involved in an IDB, because the company, not the city issuing the bond, is responsible for repaying it. The maximum size of an IDB bond issue permitted by federal law is $10 million.[44]

The rationale behind industrial development bonds is that the company benefiting from them will create jobs in the community. These bonds were not controversial in the 1940s and 1950s because few of them were issued, and most of them went to factories. Now, however, the biggest user is K-Mart Corporation. McDonald's Restaurants, Kroger Department Stores, Nabisco, and General Mills also use IDBs. Even a topless bar in Philadelphia got one.

Critics of IDBs point out that the recipients are hardly struggling corporations, and that so many IDBs are being issued that they are driving up state and local interest costs on other debt instruments. The U.S. Treasury Department estimates that it loses about $2 billion in revenue per year because IDBs are exempt from the federal income tax. Finally, some oppose this intermeshing of the public and private sectors, arguing that government should not be involved in assisting private business in this way. To curb the abuse of IDBs, Congress has capped the amount of these bonds that any state and its localities can issue in a single year.

Through *tax increment financing*, bonds are issued to improve blighted areas of the city. The enhanced value of the property so improved generates higher property taxes, which are used to pay off the bond. Cities in thirty-three states use this innovative method of encouraging communitites to undertake needed improvements.[45] TIF bonds, like revenue bonds, are not included in local debt limits.

Bond–Rating Services

The two most important private agencies that rate state and local full-faith-and-credit bonds are Moody's Investors Service and Standard & Poor's Corporation. In order to determine a city's credit risk, these two services consider such factors as the city's amount of existing debt, history of indebtedness, adequacy of tax base, increases in assessed property values, population growth, amount of unemployment, and pension commitments. Moody's and Standard & Poor's bond ratings are listed in Table 9-5. Bond ratings are a very serious business. The lower the rating, the higher the interest cost for the issuing government. Over the life of a twenty-five- or thirty-year bond issue, one grade difference can amount to many millions of dollars in borrowing costs.

In recent years, older Frostbelt cities "have gone through population losses, flight of industry, labor troubles, and often poor management."[46]

TABLE 9-5   Bond Ratings

	Moody's	Standard & Poor's
Prime or gilt edge	Aaa	AAA
High quality	Aa	AA
Upper-medium grade	A	A
Medium grade	Baa	BBB
Speculative	Ba	BB
Very speculative	B, Caa	B, CCC, CC
In default	Ca, C	D

Their bond ratings have gone down, making it very difficult for them to borrow money. These troubles, in addition to reductions in federal aid under the Reagan administration, have sharply reduced the construction or improvement of roads, transit systems, schools, hospitals, and other facilities. The Frostbelt cities in the worst condition are New York, Cleveland, and Detroit. Not far behind on the rocky road to ruin are Philadelphia, Boston, and Pittsburgh. In contrast, Sunbelt cities with high bond ratings are Houston, Dallas, Denver, and Phoenix.

THE URBAN FISCAL CRISIS

Since at least the early 1970s, the "urban crisis" has been a lively topic of national discussion. The causes of the crisis have been noted in various chapters of this book, but they merit repeating here. Middle-class families in large numbers have left the big cities of the Midwest and the Northeast for the suburbs of those cities or the Sunbelt. In addition to these taxpayers, businesses that generate jobs and revenue from property taxes, sales taxes, and income taxes have departed. Banks and other financial institutions are reluctant to invest money in these older central cities, which further accelerates their downward slide. Inflation has eroded municipal purchasing power, the Reagan administration has cut federal aid, state governments have imposed unfunded mandates, and the property tax has been pushed to its limits. In sum, the large cities of the Midwest and Northeast are caught in a nasty whiplash: income is down at the very time that the poorer residents who remain and unionized municipal employees are demanding that more money be spent.

Richard Nathan and James Fossett have used the age of a city's housing, the amount of its poverty, and its population change as an index of urban hardship. Their findings are presented in Table 9-6. It is perhaps some consolation that large cities nationwide are not equally affected, but this is small solace to the twelve Frostbelt cities in greatest difficulty.

TABLE 9-6   Urban Hardship*

Cities Ranked by Most Hardship	Cities Ranked by Least Hardship
1. Buffalo	1. San Jose
2. St. Louis	2. Honolulu
3. Cleveland	3. Phoenix
4. Newark	4. Jacksonville
5. Pittsburgh	5. Albuquerque
6. Rochester	6. Baton Rouge
7. Boston	7. Nashville
8. Detroit	8. Tucson
9. Philadelphia	9. Houston
10. Minneapolis	10. Austin
11. Chicago	11. Charlotte
12. Cincinnati	12. Dallas

SOURCE: Richard Nathan and James Fossett, "Urban Conditions: The Future of the Federal Role," Table 1. (Paper presented at a meeting of the National Tax Association, Philadelphia, 1978.)

* New York City was excluded because of lack of data.

In times of fiscal stringency, which may be long-term for Frostbelt cities, mayors almost universally reduce expenses in the following order:

1. Maintenance of buildings, streets, and equipment
2. Purchase of equipment
3. Operating expenses, purchase of materials and supplies
4. Salaries of nonadministrative personnel
5. Salaries of administrative personnel

Should better times return, increases will be made in the reverse order. These priorities explain why many large cities appear shabbier and more run-down than before, why city equipment such as buses and snowplows are frequently out of order, and why cities must now pay more for something they could have repaired for less if they had done it sooner.

TABLE 9-7   Metropolitan Areas with Highest Expected Increase in Employment for the Rest of This Century

1. Houston	6. Denver
2. Anaheim–Santa Ana	7. Phoenix
3. Los Angeles–Long Beach	8. Washington, D.C.
4. San Jose	9. San Diego
5. Dallas	10. Boston

SOURCE: *U.S. News & World Report*, March 18, 1985, p. 16. Copyright 1985, U.S. News & World Report, Inc.

The short-run future for Frostbelt cities may not be particularly bright. America seems to be becoming a "post-industrial society" that stresses service jobs or nonmanufacturing employment rather than the manufacture of heavy, tangible goods. Most new jobs are found in service industries or high-technology businesses such as electronic components, computers, telecommunications, and oil and gas extraction. Table 9-7 shows the ten metropolitan areas with the highest expected job growth for the rest of this century; eight are in the Sunbelt. A note of caution is sounded by conservative commentator Kevin Phillips: an overemphasis on our post-industrial future can be "an excuse, a philosophic escape hatch, for politicians anxious to avoid the grey, gritty reality of cities like Pittsburgh with declining heavy industry and high unemployment."[47]

SUMMARY

In this chapter, we have studied the nineteenth-century political machine, the reform program that ended that machine, and especially the legacy of that reform program. The problem of fractionalized government in urban areas is part of that legacy. The suburbs are often thought to be an essential part of any comprehensive solution to that problem. In addition, we have considered city and county finance, paying special attention to the fiscal problems of Frostbelt cities. In closing our discussion of local government, it is appropriate to again note that cities and counties have been delegated the police power (the power to pass laws promoting the public health, safety, welfare, and morals) by the state government. Prominent economist Walter Heller stresses the importance of this power: "In more or less humdrum services like sanitation, open space, recreation, police and fire protection, street maintenance and lighting lies much of the difference between a decent and a squalid environment, the difference between the snug or smug suburb and the grinding ghetto. Much of the 'quality of life' is intimately dependent on these services."[48]

NOTES

1. Jay S. Goodman, *The Dynamics of Urban Government and Politics*, 2nd ed. (New York: Macmillan, 1980), p. 122.

2. Dennis R. Judd, *The Politics of American Cities*, 2nd ed. (Boston: Little, Brown, 1984), p. 57. See also pp. 52–53.

3. Goodman, *Dynamics*, p. 124.

4. William Reddig, *Tom's Town, Kansas City and the Pendergast Legend* (New York: Lippincott, 1947), p. 71. See also Lyle Dorsett, *The Pendergast Machine* (Lincoln: University of Nebraska Press, 1980).

5. The words are from a fictional Irish boss in Edwin O'Connor's novel *The Last Hurrah*, and are cited in Judd, *Politics*, p. 57. See also Goodman, *Dynamics*, p. 123. Robert Dahl describes politics as a rope dangling down the formidable slope of the socioeconomic

system. If the ethnic pulled himself up a bit with the help of the rope, he could often gain a toe hold in the system; the higher he climbed, the higher he could reach for another pull upward. (Robert Dahl, *Who Governs?* [New Haven: Yale University Press, 1961], p. 34)

6. Robert Lineberry and Ira Sharkansky, *Urban Politics and Public Policy,*, 3rd ed. (New York: Harper & Row, Pub., 1978), pp. 118–119.

7. Richard Hofstadter, *The Age of Reform* (New York: Random House, 1955), p. 182.

8. Ibid., pp. 183, 185. See also Alan P. Grimes, *The Puritan Ethic and Woman Suffrage* (New York: Oxford University Press, 1967).

9. Edward Banfield and James Q. Wilson, *City Politics* (Cambridge: Harvard University Press, 1965).

10. Raymond Wolfinger and John Osgood Field, "Political Ethos and the Structure of City Government," *American Political Science Review,* 60 (June 1966), 306–26.

11. Ibid., pp. 315, 320. See also Bradley R. Rice, *Progressive Cities* (Austin: University of Texas Press, 1977).

12. Robert Lineberry and Edmund Fowler, "Reformism and Public Policies in American Cities," *American Political Science Review,* 61 (September 1967), 708–16.

13. Quoted in Banfield and Wilson, *City Politics,* p. 157. See also Robert Alford and Eugene Lee, "Voting Turnout in American Cities," *American Political Science Review,* 62 (September 1968), 798–811.

14. "Reagan, Congress at Odds over Voting Right Changes," *Congressional Quarterly Weekly Report,* November 23, 1985, p. 2429.

15. Russel Getter and Paul Schumaker, "Contextual Bases of Responsiveness to Citizen Preferences and Group Demands," *Policy and Politics,* 6 (March 1978), 270. See also William H. Dutton and Alana Northrop, "Municipal Reform and the Changing Pattern of Urban Party Politics," *American Politics Quarterly,* 6 (October 1978), 439.

16. See Demetrios Caraley, *City Governments and Urban Problems)* (Englewood Cliffs, N.J.: Prentice-Hall, 1977), chap. 13.

17. Floyd Hunter, *Community Power Structure: A Study of Decision Makers* (Chapel Hill: University of North Carolina Press, 1953). See also Hunter, *Community Power Succession: Atlanta's Policy-Makers Revisited* (Chapel Hill: University of North Carolina Press, 1980).

18. Nelson Polsby, "How to Study Community Power," *Journal of Politics,* 22 (August 1960), 476.

19. Ibid., p. 478. See also Polsby, *Community Power and Political Theory,* 2nd, enl. ed. (New Haven: Yale University Press, 1980).

20. Dahl, *Who Governs?*

21. John Goldbach and Michael J. Ross, *Politics, Parties, and Power* (Pacific Palisades, Calif.: Palisades Publishers, 1980), p. 108.

22. Peter Bachrach and Morton Baratz, "Two Faces of Power," *American Political Science Review,* 56 (December 1962), 948, 949.

23. Ibid., p. 952.

24. John A. Williams, "Politics in Suburban Chicago," in *Illinois: Political Processes and Governmental Performance,* ed. Edgar G. Crane (Dubuque, Iowa: Kendall/Hunt, 1980), p. 251.

25. Thomas Dye, *Politics in States and Communities,* 5th ed. (Englewood Cliffs, N.J.: Prentice-Hall, 1985), pp. 347–50.

26. Vincent Ostrom, *Tne Intellectual Crisis in American Public Administration,* rev. ed. (University: University of Alabama Press, 1974), p. 119. See also Robert B. Hawkins, Jr., "Special Districts and Urban Services," in *The Delivery of Urban Services,* ed. Elinor Ostrom (Beverly Hills, Calif.: Sage Publications, Inc., 1976), pp. 176–77.

27. Williams, "Politics in Suburban Chicago," p. 254.

28. George S. Blair, *Government at the Grassroots,* 3rd ed. (Pacific Palisades, Calif.: Palisades Publishers, 1981), pp. 163–65.

29. The politics involved is described in John Bollens and Henry Schmandt, *The Metropolis,* 4th ed. (New York: Harper & Row, Pub., 1982), chap. 13.

30. White flight and suburban politics are described in Clarence Stone, Robert

Whelan, and William Murin, *Urban Policy and Politics*, 2nd ed. (Englewood Cliffs, N.J.: Prentice-Hall, 1986), pp. 124–31.

31. Harvey Marshall, "White Movement to the Suburbs: A Comparison of Explanations," *American Sociological Review*, 44 (December 1979), 991. See also Judd, *Politics*, pp. 163–76.

32. Robert C. Wood, *Suburbia: Its People and Their Politics* (Boston: Houghton Mifflin, 1958).

33. Judd, *Politics*, p. 175.

34. Bollens and Schmandt, *The Metropolis*, p. 84.

35. John Harrigan, *Political Change in the Metropolis*, 3rd ed. (Boston: Little, Brown, 1985), p. 261.

36. Bryan D. Jones, *Governing Urban America* (Boston: Little, Brown, 1983), p. 382. See also Jerome Rose, *Legal Foundations of Land Use Planning* (New Brunswick, N.J.: Rutgers University Center for Urban Policy Research, 1979), p. 147.

37. Bernard Siegan, *Other People's Property* (Lexington, Mass.: Heath, Lexington Books, 1976), pp. 40–41. See also John Gilmour, "Land Use and the Public Interest," *University of Virginia Newsletter*, 56 (May 1980), 35.

38. Caraley, *City Governments and Urban Problems*, chap. 19; Jones, *Governing Urban America*, pp. 290–95. See also Herbert S. Duncombe, *Modern County Government* (Washington, D.C.: National Association of Counties, 1977), pp. 219–23; and Oliver P. Williams et al., *Suburban Differences and Metropolitan Policies* (Philadelphia: University of Pennsylvania Press, 1965), chap. 8.

39. George Break, *Financing Government in a Federal System* (Washington, D.C.: Brookings Institution, 1980), p. 225. On the other hand, Deil Wright argues that the very largest cities are not "federal aid junkies": *Understanding Intergovernmental Relations*, 2nd ed. (Monterey, Calif.: Brooks/Cole, 1982), p. 436. However, Wright supplies no data in support of this claim.

40. Joseph F. Zimmerman, *State-Local Relations* (New York: Praeger, 1983), pp. 62–63. The New York City income tax is a graduated tax on earned and unearned income. The eleven states with local income taxes are Alabama, Delaware, Indiana, Iowa, Kentucky, Maryland, Michigan, Missouri, New York, Ohio, and Pennsylvania.

41. *Significant Features of Fiscal Federation, 1981–82* (Washington, D.C.: Advisory Commission on Intergovernmental Relations, 1983), pp. 49–53. Of the twenty-four states *without* a local sales tax, Delaware, Montana, New Hampshire, and Oregon do not have a state sales tax either.

42. John E. Petersen, "State and Local Government Debt Policy and Management," in *Essays in Public Finance and Financial Management*, ed. John E. Petersen and Catherine Lavigne Spain (Chatham, N.J.: Chatham House Publishers, 1980), p. 63. See also John Mikesell, *Fiscal Administration*, 2nd ed. (Homewood, Ill.: Dorsey, 1986), pp. 435–44.

43. Patrick Lucansky, "The Use of Revenue Bonds to Purchase or Construct Municipal Facilities," *Illinois Municipal Review*, 57 (June 1978), 8. Some revenue bonds are financed in part by special assessments on the users of the facility. Construction of sidewalks on a particular street may be funded by a special assessment on the residents of that street.

44. "What are IDBs?" *Chicago Tribune*, November 2, 1980, Section 5, p. 1. Industrial development bonds, which are sometimes called *industrial revenue bonds* (IRBs), are also issued by all but three state governments.

45. T. J. Kim, "Determining Potential Gains and Losses of TIF," Report 389 of the American Planning Association, Chicago, December 1984.

46. Neal Peirce and Jerry Hagstrom, "Federal Spending Cuts Could Worsen Older Cities' Ability to Borrow Money," *National Journal*, February 7, 1981, p. 216.

47. Kevin Phillips, "For Reagan to Succeed, He Must Roll up His Sleeves," *Los Angeles Times*, April 10, 1983, p. IX-1.

48. Walter Heller, quoted in Bruce Wallin, "General Revenue Sharing and Cities" (paper presented at the annual meeting of the Western Political Science Association, Sacramento, 1984), p. 51.

chapter 10

State Finance

State and local governments are big business: together they account for over one third of America's nondefense government spending and for 13 percent of the gross national product (GNP). Although state and local expenditures are increasing, federal spending is increasing faster, even if defense expenditures are excluded and federal aid to state and local governments is counted as spending by the latter.[1] The reasons for government growth are numerous. The public wants more high-quality government services (and at the same time lower taxes). As the nation becomes more affluent, its citizens feel that public services should be improved. With equality being increasingly stressed in recent years, "claimant" groups have dramatized their needs in such areas as welfare, old-age assistance, health care, housing, transportation, and education. With income inequalities lessening, observable differences in wealth are more acutely felt and feelings of relative deprivation increase. Added to these trends are the effects of inflation and population increases, as well as the fact that state and local employees are now paid better, partly as a result of pressure by the public employee unions mentioned in Chapter 5. Some analysts maintain that federal aid is the main reason that state expenditures have increased.[2]

PURPOSES OF STATE SPENDING

The state's biggest spending priority is education, which accounts for about one of every three dollars in the state budget. See Table 10-1. Much of this money is for colleges and universities, but almost half is state aid to local school districts. Welfare consists of aid to families with dependent children (AFDC) and assistance for the aged, blind, and disabled. County

TABLE 10-1   State Expenditures, 1982

Function	Percentage
Education	33.2
Welfare	17.7
Insurance Trusts*	10.9
Highways	8.0
Health and Hospitals	7.0
Prisons and Police	2.4
Natural Resources	1.6
General Control	1.2
Utilities	1.1
Financial Administration	1.1
Employment Security	.07
Liquor Stores	.07
Housing and Urban Renewal	.02
Miscellaneous	15.64

SOURCE: U.S. Bureau of the Census, *Statistical Abstract of the United States: 1985* (Washington, D.C.: Government Printing Office, 1984), p. 275.
* Includes employee retirement and unemployment compensation.

governments are usually the administering agents for welfare. States must also set aside money in trust funds for state employees' retirement and future claims for unemployment compensation. States maintain their own highway systems and provide generous amounts of money for city and county road building. Another expenditure of note is that for *natural resources*, by which the state seeks to conserve and develop vital resources such as forests, wildlife, and water. *General control* expenditures include the salaries of elected officials and the administrative expenses of the three branches of government. Some items that appear as expenditures may also generate revenue for the state. State liquor stores and the sale of utilities such as electricity and water fall in this category.

There are some interesting regional variations to state spending. Northern and western states spend about one fourth more money per capita than southern states. Moreover, northern and western states allot a greater proportion of their budgets for welfare, whereas southern states emphasize education and health services.[3] States also vary considerably in the percentage of their budget that is devoted to local governments. In the decade of 1976–86, some states assumed greatly increased responsibilities for funding elementary and secondary education, welfare, and courts. Among the fifty states, state aid to local governments as a percentage of the state budget averages about 36 percent. Some states, such as Wisconsin, New York, and California, exceed 45 percent; other states, such as South Dakota, Rhode Island, Vermont, and New Hampshire, spend less than 20 percent. State aid to local governments held up well in the 1980–83 recession: although spending for state-operated programs was reduced, aid to local governments was reduced less.[4]

Fiscal centralization is increasing, especially as states raise their proportion of total state-local taxes and as the proportion of local revenue derived from state aid rises. States that were initially less centralized are becoming more similar to states that have been centralized for a long time.[5] As we shall see later in the chapter, the reason for this trend is the superior revenue-raising capabilities of state sales and income taxes compared with local property taxes. A clear companion of fiscal centralization is diminution of local discretion: if the governor and the state legislature have incurred the political risks of taxing the voters to raise the money for state aid, they will surely tell local governments how the money should be spent. Such has been the case in California, where the state has stepped in to replace most of the local revenue lost after the passage of the property tax reduction measure, Proposition 13.

BUDGETING STRATEGY

A key point to remember about budgets is that they are *political* documents. Although budgets have the appearance of accounting ledgers with columns of numbers and a bottom line that balances, they are really expressions of deeply held political values and ideological preferences. Programs that pursue goals that governors or legislators care about, or that benefit politically powerful interest groups, will be generously funded. Those that do not, will not. Moreover, budgeting is an opportunity to "stick it to" one's political opponents (my pet programs and my political allies should receive the public money, while those people who never vote for me should foot the bill).

Important participants in the process of budgeting are the agency administrators who draw up the budgets in the first place. Their power, prestige, and perquisites are on the line because ranking in the bureaucratic pecking order is determined largely by the size of one's budget and the number of employees one has in the department.

Administrators follow approximately ten budgeting strategies vis-à-vis the governor's Budget Office and members of the legislature's appropriations committees:

1. Cultivate a powerful clientele. During the legislature's annual budgetary hearings, it is very advantageous to have representatives of significant interest groups and segments of the community tell what a marvelous job this program is doing and how it benefits the state (and them).
2. Always ask for an amount of money in excess of last year's appropriation. Administrators need to demonstrate that they are good politicians who are meeting the needs of the public and aggressively responding to current

problems. Administrators who ask for less money than they got last year may invite legislators' contempt and find that they get a lot less money.

3. Always give the governor's Budget Office and the legislature something to cut. They will assume that administrators pad budget requests; if bureaucrats ask only for the amount of money that they actually need, their programs will get shortchanged.

4. If the legislature reduces an administrator's budget, he or she should make cuts in the most politically *popular* programs. This is known as the Firemen First Principle. For example, the public appreciates fighting fires; so when your budget is reduced, lay off fire fighters first as a way of using the public to bring pressure on legislators to restore the funds.

5. Hide new programs in the base. The base is last year's appropriation; agencies usually get last year's amount of money plus an adjustment for inflation. New programs should be made to appear merely as continuations of existing programs. That way they will not invite the special scrutiny of budget officers or the legislature.

6. Begin new programs with a small amount of money. This is known as the *wedge*. Greater amounts of money can be added later, but it is important to get the program up and running with a clientele cultivated before possible opponents realize what has happened.

7. There is a saying in many state capitals: "Nothing is more permanent than a temporary program."

8. Try to convince the Budget Office that the program "pays for itself," that is generates revenue sufficient to cover its costs. A variant of this theme is "sometimes we need to spend money in order to save money." Guiding a budget through to enactment is not unlike selling used cars.

9. "We are in a crisis." The use of drama and a crisis mentality can shake loose an emergency appropriation that can last for years and years.

10. Always spend your appropriation. Having money left over at the end of the fiscal year does not indicate that you are a thrifty administrator; it means that you did not need all of last year's money.[6]

TYPES OF BUDGETS

There are four different types of budgets: line-item budgets, performance budgets, program budgets, and zero-base budgets. The *line-item budget* is likely to be found by itself or to be used as a complement to either the performance or the program budget. The virtue of this type of budget is its simplicity: items (such as typewriters or personnel positions) and their costs are listed, usually one to a line. The line-item budget is intended to help legislators control spending and prevent theft, but it cannot tell them whether the money is being used efficiently. Nor can it assist a governor or mayor in ranking priorities.

The limitations of line-item budgeting led to *performance budgets*, which show activities to be completed (for example, miles of street to be swept or gallons of waste water to be treated) and the amount of money needed for each.[7] See Table 10-2. Although this type of budget gives the legislature more usable information with which to make rational decisions,

TABLE 10-2 Performance Budget for a City

			Department	Number of Units	Total Cost
Function	01.	Provision of Streets and roads			
Program	.1	Street construction	Bureau of streets		$x
	.2	Street lighting	Bureau of streets		$x
	.3	Traffic control	Police department		$x
	.4	Street maintenance	Bureau of streets		$x
Performance	.41	Streets cleaned		y miles	$x
	.42	Resurfacing		y miles	$x
	.43	Inspections		Number	$x
	.44	Bridge reconstruction		Number	$x
	.45	Storm sewer repair		y miles	$x
Objects of expenditure		a. Personal services			$x
		b. Material and equipment			$x
		c. Other expenses			$x

SOURCE: Jesse Burkhead, *Government Budgeting* (New York: John Wiley, 1956), p. 149.

it assumes that all departments can develop valid performance measures. But for some departments, such as a police department, this is very difficult.

Program budgets, which were in vogue in the 1960s, are a form of planning-programming-budgeting system (PPBS). These budgets list expenditures in terms of objectives or goals (see Table 10-3). Because priorities can be ranked (police protection versus cultural activities versus environmental services), this type of budget can lead to a great deal of ideological conflict in the legislature. Such conflict is productive or counterproductive depending upon one's point of view. In any event, program budgets assume that objectives and goals are quantifiable and do not overlap—two assumptions that are hazardous at best.

The final type of budget is the *zero-base budget* (ZBB), which was much heralded in the 1970s, when then governor Jimmy Carter used it in Georgia. The main idea behind the ZBB is that each program should be evaluated from scratch; hence it is similar in intent to the sunset laws noted in Chapter 6. Like those first cousins, zero-base budgeting has not lived up to its promise, and for many of the same reasons. Program managers must prepare different budgets (*decision packages*) for performing their function at different levels of funding, starting with a base of zero. No self-respecting, power-maximizing administrator will prepare a convincing decision package at anything less than generous funding. Moreover, the various decision packages (at 0 percent of the base, 50 percent of the base, 75 percent, 100 percent, 110 percent, and so on) will bury the governor's Budget Office and the legislature in mounds of information. There is also this ultimate question: is ZBB politically realistic? If a program has enough political muscle behind it to get it rolling and keep it rolling, that program will not be killed off by a reformer's ideal of rational budgeting.

TABLE 10-3   Program Budget for a City

Function	Amount (dollars)	Percent of Total
Protection of people and property	$ 56,176.2	21.4%
Community cultural and recreation	13,227.0	5.0
Community development and welfare	24,893.1	9.5
Transportation and related services	27,237.3	10.4
Environmental services	26,435.7	10.1
Executive/legislative affairs of government	932.0	0.4
Administrative services	6,283.1	2.4
Total current expenditures	$155,184.4	59.2
Debt service	22,505.7	8.6
Capital outlay	84,334.2	32.2
Total expenditures	$262,024.3	100.0%

SOURCE: *Annual Report of the City of Indianapolis*, December 31, 1979.

Allen Schick, an authority on budgeting, argues that the term *zero-base* is somewhat misleading.[8] In reality, state budget makers do not evaluate every program from a base of zero. Schick describes zero-base budgeting as a *formal* process for "review of decrements below the budget base as well as increments above that base." Although state budget officials who responded to a survey by Schick found zero-base budgeting useful, they were unsure whether it has had a substantial effect on budget decisions. The growth rate of state expenditures is "much more sensitive to financial conditions and political attitudes than to budgetary procedures."[9] Mandatory expenditures such as entitlement programs and aid to local governments grow regardless of the budgetary method used. Moreover, ZBB does not necessarily lead to unproductive items being purged from the budget.[10]

Performance, program, and zero-base budgets have all been tried in various states, and some have met with limited success. But budget makers somehow continue to rely on line-item budgets.

GOALS OF A TAX SYSTEM

From the viewpoint of elected officials, state finances have a good-news-bad-news aspect: the spending of public money (on education, highways, parks, and so forth) gains votes, but having to raise the money from the public loses votes. To make matters worse, all state constitutions except Vermont's require that this pleasure and pain came in equal doses. States cannot constitutionally spend more than they receive in taxes or federal aid—a requirement that does not bind politicians at the federal level. From the standpoint of state voters, there probably is no such thing as a good tax, but some are clearly more objectionable than others. As Table 10-4 indicates, state taxes are not in as much disfavor as federal and local taxes.

Carefully drafted state tax systems should meet at least seven goals: simplicity, certainty, equity, economy (of administration), efficiency, adequacy and competitiveness.[11] These goals can also serve as criteria for evaluating the various state taxes. Taxes should be *simple enough* for people to understand. Otherwise, they will not pay the proper amount, either through error or through anger at an overly complex system that they feel exploits them. Federal income taxes (even the 1040 EZ form) and local property taxes (with mill rates, less-than-full-market-value appraisals, and property-tax multipliers) fail this criterion. State sales taxes and state income taxes (which are much simpler than their federal counterpart, and are sometimes levied at flat rates) fare much better on this criterion.

Individual taxpayers and businesses need to know in general how much they are going to have to pay. State governments also favor such *certainty* because they have plans for spending the money and cannot incur

TABLE 10-4   Public Ratings of the "Worst, Least Fair Tax"

	Percentages 1985	Percentages 1973
Federal income tax	38	30
Local property tax	24	31
State sales tax	15	20
State income tax	10	10
Don't know	12	11

SOURCE: *Changing Public Attitudes on Government and Taxes* (Washington, D.C.: Advisory Commision on Intergovernmental Relations, 1985), p. 1.

a deficit. Receipts from a particular tax should not fluctuate wildly from year to year. However, one specialist on state revenues writes that overall state finances "have ridden a roller coaster" since the end of World War II.[12] From the mid 1940s to the mid 1970s there was a boom. This was followed by the "unprecedented tax-cutting spree" fostered by California's Proposition 13; the fiscal stress and tax increases of the 1980–83 recession; and the current period, in which the states assume more prominent roles as the federal government reduces its responsibilities.

Equity carries the general meaning of fairness and is either horizontal or vertical. (It can also refer to the benefits-received principle noted in Chapter 9.) *Horizontal equity* means that people who have an equal ability to pay taxes actually pay nearly equal amounts. *Vertical equity* means that people who have differing capabilities of paying taxes pay different amounts of taxes. Few would disagree that those who have more should pay more, but should this idea be implemented by a proportional (flat-rate) tax or a progressive tax? Under a *proportional* income tax, those with higher incomes pay more in absolute dollars; under a *progressive* income tax, the tax rate expressed as a percentage rises as income level rises. The progressive income tax (unless accompanied by numerous deductions, exclusions, and loopholes) means that higher-income individuals will pay a greater amount of their income in taxes *and* that over the long run wealth will be redistributed from those who have more to those who have less. (Regressive taxes will be defined shortly.) Because of recent reforms in state and local taxes, to be noted later in the chapter, one expert on finances describes the state-local tax system as proportional.[13]

By means of *economy of administration*, states attempt to minimize the costs of collecting a tax. The sales tax is not expensive to administer, especially in those states that do not reimburse merchants for collecting it. Although the lottery is not a tax, economy of administration is one of its weaknesses.

Economists apply the terms *efficient* and *inefficient* to taxes according to their economic effects. For example, does a tax discourage businesses

from accumulating capital or hinder economic growth? If so, it is inefficient. Do a state's high cigarette or liquor taxes force its citizens to purchase
these commodities in nearby states? If so, they too are inefficient. If people
would rather have more leisure time than work extra hours and then have
to pay the higher tax associated with a progressive tax, the tax is not
efficient because government gets less money.

Adequacy means that as a state's economy grows, its taxes should
produce sufficient revenue. Adequacy is similar to *tax elasticity*, which
means that tax receipts should rise as taxable incomes rise. Progressive
income taxes are highly elastic, but the sales tax is not. Tax receipts from
highly elastic taxes also *fall* rapidly during periods of recession; inelastic
taxes are less sensitive to economic fluctuations.

Finally, a state's tax system must maintain the state's *competitiveness*
with neighboring states in attracting business. As we shall see in Chapter
12, taxes are not the main factor in business-siting decisions. But no state
should let its taxes get too far out of line with those of its regional
competitors, because economic growth is extremely important in paying
for increased state expenditures.

MAJOR REVENUE SOURCES

The major sources of state revenue are noted in Table 10-5, and the
prominent role played by federal aid is apparent. Although revenue from
the federal government exceeds any of the state's other revenue sources,
it has been declining in purchasing power since 1978, when it peaked in
the latter part of the Carter administration.

The importance of insurance trust revenue is often overlooked in
discussions of state revenue. As noted earlier, money must be paid into
this fund to meet retirement obligations for state employees and to pay
claims for unemployment compensation. These substantial sums of money
can be invested, and in which case they also earn interest.

Sales Tax

All states except Delaware, Montana, New Hampshire, Oregon, and
Alaska have general sales taxes. The rate runs from 3 percent to over 7
percent, with the median rate being 4 percent. In addition 26 states
piggyback a local sales tax on the state rate.

The sales tax is controversial because it is usually thought to be a
regressive tax—a tax that bears down most heavily on those least able to
pay. The poor person is said to pay a higher percentage of his or her
income in sales taxes than the wealthy person. However, this regressivity
is significantly moderated in the forty-four states that exempt prescription
drugs from the sales tax, in the thirty-one that exempt electricity and gas

purchases from utility companies, and in the twenty-eight that exempt food purchased in a grocery store. Such exemptions have led some authorities to judge the sales tax to be proportional rather than regressive.[14] Regressivity is further lessened in the nine states that credit all or part of a person's sales tax paid against his or her income tax liability or grant a rebate if there is no income tax liability.

The sales tax has many positive features, which make it a mainstay of state finance: it produces large amounts of revenue and is relatively reliable; it is convenient for the public to pay since it is paid in small amounts; opportunities for evasion are minimized; and it can be paid by nonresidents, especially in a state with many tourists, such as Florida. Hawaii, Washington, New Mexico, Iowa, South Dakota, and West Virginia apply the sales tax to a broad range of professional and personal services, such as investment counseling, interior decorating, bookkeeping, home and automobile repairs, barber and beauty shops, laundry and cleaning, and printing. An additional thirteen states tax these services, but to a lesser extent.

TABLE 10-5 Total State Revenues, 1982

	Percentage
Revenue from the federal government	20.6
Revenue from local governments	0.9
Insurance trust revenue	15.1
Sales tax	15.1
Individual income tax	13.6
Corporate income tax	4.2
Charges[a]	13.6
Motor fuels tax	3.1
Alcoholic beverages tax	0.8
Tobacco products tax	1.2
Other gross receipts taxes[b]	3.3
Property tax	0.9
Other taxes[c]	3.3
Motor vehicle licenses	1.6
Corporation licenses	0.5
Other licenses[d]	0.8
Liquor stores revenue	0.8
Utility revenue	0.6

SOURCE: U.S. Bureau of the Census, *Statistical Abstract of the United States: 1985* (Washington, D.C.: Government Printing Office, 1984), p. 275.

[a] Includes charges for college tuition, admission to state parks or state hospitals, etc.
[b] Includes tax on insurance premiums, public utility bills, etc.
[c] Includes severance tax, gift and inheritance taxes, etc.
[d] Includes licenses for alcoholic beverages dealers, motor vehicle operators, hunting and fishing etc.

Income Tax

The individual income tax is found in forty-three states, with rates ranging up to 16 percent of taxable income. Expressed as a percentage of the states' own sources of revenue apart from federal aid, the individual income tax has increased over 400 percent in the last quarter of a century—an important change in state finance and a reform that has significantly lessened the regressivity of state taxes in general. Only eight states have either a flat-rate tax or a very limited form of income tax; the income tax is progressive in the remaining thirty-five states, although not as progressive as the federal income tax. (See Table 10-6 for state taxes at different income levels.)

Two weighty reform issues relating to the income tax are the coordination of state and federal income taxes, and indexing of state income taxes. States have the choice of conforming their income taxes with the federal structure, and Nebraska, Rhode Island, and Vermont have done so. By means of *piggybacking*, these states make their income tax a percentage of the federal tax, a practice encouraged by the Internal Revenue Service, which will collect the tax at no charge to the state. Such coordination has certain advantages: it is more convenient for taxpayers; it saves the states some administrative expenses; and it increases state tax progressivity (if one favors that as a goal).

However, a key assumption of this book is that states should make their own choices and not be merely the wagging tail on the federal dog. If states want to tax income not reached by the federal tax, or in any way tailor their tax to their citizens' preferences, they should be encouraged to do so. The dangers of coupling state and federal income taxes can be shown by the 1981 Economic Recovery Tax Act (ERTA). Responding to President Reagan's theory of "supply-side economics," Congress substantially increased the allowable business depreciation on buildings, machinery, and vehicles. Although ERTA was subsequently amended by Congress, its original version would have reduced federal corporate tax collections by 40 percent and seriously affected state tax revenues.[15]

Three states conform completely, and eight states conform substantially with the federal tax structure, applying the state rate to the federal definition of taxable income. The IRS will act as the collecting agent for this procedure as well. Moderate conformity is the rule in the twenty-one states that base their tax on the individual's federal adjusted gross income (AGI) but apply their own personal exemptions, deductions, tax rates, and credits. Eight states practice low or no conformity.

Indexing (or *indexation*), adopted in ten states, protects workers from being knocked into a higher tax bracket when they receive a salary increase. Through indexation, income tax brackets are adjusted upward each year by an amount equal to the rate of inflation. As an aid to lower-income taxpayers, the standard deduction (called the *zero-bracket amount*)

TABLE 10-6 Total State Taxes for a Family of Four at Different Income Levels

At $15,000		At $25,000		At $50,000	
Minnesota	$1092	Minnesota	$2272	Minnesota	$4384
Hawaii	946	Hawaii	1903	Wisconsin	4080
Kentucky	852	Wisconsin	1828	Hawaii	3810
Michigan	833	North Carolina	1620	Oregon	3792
North Carolina	827	Utah	1571	Delaware	3713
Utah	821	Michigan	1553	Idaho	3356
Wisconsin	794	Delaware	1547	New York	3274
Iowa	744	New York	1542	Michigan	3253
South Carolina	708	South Carolina	1507	South Carolina	3177
Massachusetts	698	Oregon	1470	North Carolina	3041
Delaware	693	Idaho	1447	Iowa	2939
Maryland	689	Kentucky	1422	Massachusetts	2934
Virginia	686	Iowa	1392	Maine	2829
Indiana	685	Virginia	1340	Arkansas	2713
Arkansas	642	Arkansas	1300	Ohio	2696
Oregon	638	Massachusetts	1268	Utah	2568
Idaho	624	Georgia	1178	Virginia	2538
Pennsylvania	586	Montana	1171	Maryland	2507
Alabama	581	Indiana	1089	Montana	2464
New York	572	Colorado	1088	Kentucky	2458
West Virginia	524	Ohio	1068	Georgia	2454
Georgia	516	Missouri	1062	West Virginia	2437
Illinois	508	Maryland	1050	Oklahoma	2426
Missouri	504	Arizona	1050	California	2282
Ohio	499	Maine	1032	Vermont	2248
New Mexico	492	Alabama	1023	Rhode Island	2128
Colorado	486	West Virginia	1016	Missouri	2122
Arizona	477	Vermont	975	Mississippi	2101
Rhode Island	466	Rhode Island	954	Colorado	2080
Kansas	456	Kansas	922	Indiana	1986
Vermont	452	Pennsylvania	918	Nebraska	1938
New Jersey	437	California	913	Arizona	1885
Nebraska	424	Nebraska	875	Kansas	1804
Washington	423	Oklahoma	858	New Jersey	1682
Montana	409	Mississippi	808	Pennsylvania	1661
Maine	407	Illinois	808	Alabama	1570
California	403	New Jersey	730	New Mexico	1558
Mississippi	370	North Dakota	625	Illinois	1538
North Dakota	364	New Mexico	610	North Dakota	1225
South Dakota	360	Washington	576	Washington	782
Connecticut	336	South Dakota	474	Louisiana	740
Tennessee	323	Connecticut	467	Connecticut	656
Oklahoma	309	Tennessee	427	South Dakota	618
Nevada	299	Nevada	406	Tennessee	573
Wyoming	270	Louisiana	403	Nevada	548
Florida	259	Florida	361	Florida	507
Louisiana	182	Wyoming	353	Wyoming	459
Texas	179	Texas	247	Texas	346
New Hampshire	98	New Hampshire	118	New Hampshire	118
Alaska	73	Alaska	87	Alaska	87

SOURCE: Rochelle Stanfield, "State Taxes Are Up, But Don't Worry—Federal Taxes Are Down by Much More," *National Journal*, June 25, 1983, pp. 1322–24.

is sometimes also indexed. The Advisory Commission on Intergovernmental Relations gives indexation high marks as an instrument for promoting political accountability on the part of state politicians: if elected officials want more tax money from the public, they should go on record as voting for a tax increase and should not let inflation silently increase state tax coffers. During the fiscal woes of the early 1980s, some states with indexing laws suspending them.

State income taxes on corporations are found in forty-five states and generate about one quarter of all state income-tax revenues. A developing issue in this field is the use of the *unitary procedure* for computing state corporate income taxes. This procedure calculates the profits and losses of a company *and its subsidiaries* in order to determine the company's state tax. Some states apply the unitary tax procedure to domestic subsidiaries only, but others apply it to foreign subsidiaries as well. The purpose is to prevent a multi-state corporation from shifting its tax liabilities from a high-tax state to a low-tax one or to a foreign subsidiary. England, the Netherlands, and especially Japan are threatening not to operate businesses in states that tax overseas operations; at stake for these states is the possible loss of economic development, jobs, and tax revenue. However, as we shall see in Chapter 12, factors such as labor supply and markets may affect business location decisions as much as or more than tax policy.

Other Taxes

The *motor fuels tax* is levied on gasoline, diesel, and gasohol. The tax on gasoline ranges from very low in oil-producing states such as Texas and Oklahoma to over sixteen cents per gallon in other states; the national median is over eleven cents per gallon. Some states have made the motor fuels tax a percentage of the price of a gallon of fuel, perhaps assuming that the price will rise. In any event, the trend toward purchase of fuel-efficient cars has adversely affected motor fuels tax revenue. Although this is a regressive tax, it is not too controversial because receipts are usually *earmarked* (must be spent) for building and maintaining roads, a use the public generally thinks is fair. Out-of-state people also pay this tax, especially in a tourist state or one with a great deal of "through" traffic, such as Pennsylvania.

The *severance tax* is a tax on the extraction of depletable natural resources, such as oil, gas, coal, timber, or metals. Although thirty-eight states levy this tax, it is most prominent in Alaska and in the seven states that receive between 21 percent and 29 percent of their own sources of revenue from it: Louisiana, Texas, Oklahoma, New Mexico, Wyoming, Montana, and North Dakota. Over half of Alaska's revenues come from this single source. Since these eight states receive so much money from a single tax, they can reduce other taxes—for example, the corporate income tax, a drop in which may attract new business.

Because all of the energy-exporting states are located in the Sunbelt, the severance tax is a mechanism for redistributing wealth to this region from the Frostbelt. All the regional animosities noted in Chapter 2 are rekindled by this tax. Population, jobs, and political power are moving from the energy-importing states to the energy-exporting states. Frostbelt critics of the severance tax point out that the eight states previously mentioned are exporting their tax burden to consumers in other states. Spokespersons for these energy-rich states reply that the corporate income tax in any state is also viewed by business as a cost of doing business and is passed on to consumers in the form of higher prices. Said one Texan, "Just as Texas' severance taxes are paid in part by consumers in Michigan, taxes paid by automobile manufacturers to the city of Detroit are passed on to purchasers of cars and trucks in Dallas. Likewise, consumers of steel are indirectly paying taxes to Pittsburgh, and purchasers of securities on the New York Stock Exchange are paying taxes to New York—regardless of their state of residence. Florida exports its tourist taxes and Nevada exports its gambling taxes."[16]

The *alcoholic beverages tax* and the *tobacco products tax* are sometimes referred to as *sin taxes* because part of the original idea of taxing these items was to discourage their use. It is no longer seriously contended that raising the tax rate, especially the cigarette tax, will decrease consumption; the range of increases discussed by legislators is just too small to have a marked effect on consumption. However, a case could be made that these taxes should be raised and earmarked for treating the *public* costs of excessive use of the products. For example, excessive use of tobacco leads to cancer and emphysema (which entail public health care costs); excessive use of liquor results in alcoholism (public health costs), drunk driving (law enforcement costs), and loss of jobs (welfare and unemployment benefits costs). The cigarette tax is very low in tobacco-producing states such as North Carolina, Virginia, and Kentucky, but almost thirty cents per pack in some New England states; the national median price is over fifteen cents per pack. Cigarette bootlegging is a serious problem, and there is evidence that organized crime is smuggling truckloads of cigarettes from low-tax to high-tax states, counterfeiting tax stamps, altering tax-stamp meters, and engaging in bookkeeping fraud.

Almost all states have *inheritance taxes*, and nine states also have *gift taxes*. The former is a tax on the inheritance one receives from a deceased person; the latter is intended to prevent evasion of the inheritance tax by a donor who gives away his or her wealth while alive. Arguments for these taxes are that wealth is an indication of ability to pay taxes; that these taxes, like the progressive income tax, correct a bad distribution of wealth by redistributing it; and that the inheritance is unearned income for the heir.[17]

One problem with the administration of the inheritance tax in some states is said to be the plight of farmers whose land values have risen rapidly in recent years. On paper, these people are very wealthy, but their actual incomes may be fairly low. When the owner of a family farm dies, heirs receiving the land but little money may have to sell the farm in order to pay the taxes.

Lotteries

With hard-pressed states seeking new sources of revenue and voters becoming increasingly hostile to higher taxes, more and more states have turned to gambling as an alternative way to raise money. Twenty-one states, including such populous ones as New York, Pennsylvania, Illinois, Ohio, Michigan, New Jersey, California, and Massachusetts, run lotteries. In many states, as much as half of the adult population may try their luck at least once a year. From 1 percent to 2 percent of total state revenue comes from these games. The money usually goes to the state's general fund, but sometimes also to education, construction, or local transportation needs. The most popular type of game is the "instant winner," in which customers buy a card and scratch off part of the surface to see if they have won money. In other forms of legalized gambling, players choose a number for a drawing or buy a numbered ticket that may later be drawn. What lottery players may not realize is that the odds are heavily stacked against them. The chances of winning $1 million are 1 in 20 million; it is seven times more likely that one will be killed by lightning.

Lotteries have also proved controversial. Some people are morally opposed to gambling and find it especially objectionable that government should support it; others argue that it produces compulsive gamblers. The Pennsylvania lottery was once rigged by the game's television announcer. It is sometimes argued that legalized gambling removes the stigma from gambling and encourages people to try the illegal numbers rackets or illegal betting on horse races or sports contests. On the other hand, some observers claim that government-run gambling dries up lucrative profits that might otherwise to go organized crime.

Although a lottery is not a tax, it may be regressive in effect if low-income people are the principal bettors. A study of ticket purchasers in Arizona found that low-income people were least likely to participate. This finding runs counter to most common assumptions, however. For example, a study of the Michigan lottery found it to be twice as regressive as the state sales tax. The Arizona study also found that people who are unhappy with their life are very likely to play the lottery, perhaps hoping to "strike it rich" and change their circumstances.[18]

Finally, it is frequently suggested that a lottery is not an efficient way for states to raise money. Of the total revenue received, the state keeps only 40 percent to 45 percent; the rest is paid out in prizes, commissions for sales agents, and operating costs such as salaries for lottery workers.

ISSUES IN STATE FISCAL POLICY

Earmarked Funds

Rational budgetary policy is hampered in nearly every state by earmarked funds. Up to one half or more of all state revenues may be directed by state law or the state constitution to be spent for designated purposes. For example, the motor fuels tax might be spent only for highways, hunting and fishing licenses might be spent only by the Department of Fish and Game, or all sales tax revenues might be dedicated that is, directed by state law or constitution to be spent for designated purposes. Interest groups such as road builders or truckers or sportsmen or teachers' unions want "their" funds protected from encroachment. The result is that the governor and the legislature cannot balance needs with the funds on hand: a program benefiting from earmarked funds may be receiving more money than it needs, while another program is under-funded. If an elected official wishes to establish a new tax, his or her use of earmarking can co-opt powerful interest groups, such as senior citizens or teachers' unions. Many taxes would never have been instituted if at least part of the revenues had not been earmarked.

If there is not enough political support for instituting a new tax, an earmarked user charge may be established. This accounts in part for the prominent ranking of charges in Table 10-5. Lotteries are another alternative, because the needed money might not be raised any other way, because the lottery is a voluntary form of government finance, and because it yields "the most feathers for the least squawk." Still another voluntary financing measure consists of the increasingly popular income tax refund checkoffs that finance various worthy causes. Please see Reading 10-1. This approach to government finance may be getting out of hand, and, not surprisingly, California is leading the way. A recent income tax form in the Golden State allowed taxpayers to check off all or part of their refund for political parties, prevention of child abuse, a senior citizens' legislature, endangered wildlife and plants, and the U.S. Olympic Committee. Overuse of such checkoffs can encourage the governor and the legislature to avoid tough budgetary decisions by placing spending choices on the tax return.

Prudent Reserves

Another area in which rational planning and political realities clash is *prudent reserves*, or *rainy-day funds*. Bond rating services such as Moody's and Standard & Poor's favor banking 5 percent of the budget for unforeseen catastrophes such as floods, earthquakes, or tornadoes, or in case the state should lose some expensive lawsuits. However, such caution runs against the political grain: money spent aids one's reelection, money

---

READING 10-1   CHECKOFFS: GREENBACKS FOR TROUT

Colorado taxpayers are saving the greenback cutthroat trout, Oregonians are channeling new funds to local arts facilities, Idahoans will soon be helping Olympic athletes and Arkansans are renovating a football stadium.

But none of these efforts, all coming at a time of pinched state budgets, are being accomplished with tax money. Instead, they are the result of an increasingly common trend in states across the country to allow residents to divert part of their state income tax refunds to specific causes, most of which have traditionally been funded by tax revenues.

The approach has been adopted by at least 18 states since 1977, when Colorado wildlife officials dreamed up the tax refund diversion scheme. . . . By far the biggest beneficiary so far has been non-game wildlife. Seventeen states now allow for the dedication of tax refunds for such things as nature education and protection of endangered species.

SOURCE: *Los Angeles Times,* April 11, 1982, p. I-1.

---

sitting in a bank for an emergency that may never happen does not. However, state balanced-budget requirements necessitate the setting aside of at least some money.

Comparative Wealth of States

A final issue in state fiscal policy is the extremely touchy matter of whether some states are wealthier than others, and whether some states are overtaxing or undertaxing their residents. The usual method of gauging state wealth is the per-capita income of the state's residents. However, this measure does not account for all of the tax sources a state might tap. For example, we have seen that some states have vast energy resources (Alaska, Texas, Louisiana, Wyoming), others benefit from many tourists (Nevada, Hawaii), others are farm states with highly valued real estate (Illinois), and yet others have many business corporations (New York, New Jersey). None of these possible objects of taxation is directly accounted for if we use per-capita income, which is really "a better measure of the economic well-being of a state's residents than a government's ability to raise revenue."[19]

Hence, the Advisory Commission on Intergovernmental Relations has developed an index of *per-capita tax capacity*, which is the amount of revenue each state would have raised if it had applied to its tax base a national average set of tax rates. In Table 10-7, states with a tax capacity of more than 100 have high revenue potential, whereas those with less than 100 do not. The high-tax-capacity states are generally in the Southwest, the Rocky Mountains, or the Far West. States with the lowest tax capacity are in New England and the Southeast. On the other hand,

TABLE 10-7 State Tax Capacity

State	1982	1975	State	1982	1975
U.S. Average	100	100			
New England			Southeast		
Connecticut	117	110	Alabama	74	77
Maine	84	84	Arkansas	79	78
Massachusetts	101	98	Florida	104	102
New Hampshire	100	102	Georgia	84	86
Rhode Island	81	88	Kentucky	82	85
Vermont	89	94	Louisiana	113	97
Mideast			Mississippi	71	70
Delaware	115	124	North Carolina	82	85
Washington, D.C.	115	118	South Carolina	74	77
Maryland	100	101	Tennessee	77	84
New Jersey	106	109	Virginia	94	93
New York	92	98	West Virginia	92	89
Pennsylvania	89	98	Southwest		
Great Lakes			Arizona	96	92
Illinois	99	112	New Mexico	115	97
Indiana	89	98	Oklahoma	126	98
Michigan	93	101	Texas	130	111
Ohio	92	104	Rocky Mountain		
Wisconsin	87	98	Colorado	121	106
Plains			Idaho	86	89
Iowa	96	106	Montana	110	103
Kansas	106	109	Utah	86	86
Minnesota	99	97	Wyoming	201	154
Missouri	91	96	Far West		
Nebraska	97	106	California	116	110
North Dakota	115	101	Nevada	151	145
South Dakota	87	94	Oregon	99	100
			Washington	102	98
			Alaska	313	155
			Hawaii	117	109

SOURCE: *Significant Features of Fiscal Federalism, 1984 Edition* (Washington, D.C.: Advisory Commission on Intergovernmental Relations, 1985), p. 131.

rankings based on per-capita income generally show the Atlantic Northeast as being wealthier, but the Rocky Mountains and Southwest poorer.

Not only are differences in tax capacity large, they have gotten larger since 1975. But the tax-capacity measure does not answer the question of what use the state *has* made of its taxing potential. Hence, the ACIR has developed a *tax-effort measure*, which is the ratio of a state's actual tax collections to its tax capacity. As shown in Table 10-8, the national average is 100; Rhode Island, at 133, is 33 percent above the national average in exploiting its potential tax base; Nevada, at 63, is 37 percent below the national average. Generally speaking, states in the Northeast and the

TABLE 10-8   State Tax Effort

State	1982	State	1982
U.S. Average	100		
New England		Southeast	
Connecticut	99	Alabama	87
Maine	107	Arkansas	81
Massachusetts	119	Florida	72
New Hampshire	75	Georgia	96
Rhode Island	133	Kentucky	88
Vermont	102	Louisiana	82
Mideast		Mississippi	92
Delaware	84	North Carolina	94
District of Columbia	145	South Carolina	96
Maryland	106	Tennessee	86
New Jersey	113	Virginia	90
New York	170	West Virginia	86
Pennsylvania	106	Southwest	
Great Lakes		Arizona	92
Illinois	107	New Mexico	82
Indiana	88	Oklahoma	78
Michigan	120	Texas	66
Ohio	94	Rocky Mountain	
Wisconsin	128	Colorado	81
Plains		Idaho	85
Iowa	105	Montana	97
Kansas	88	Utah	97
Minnesota	111	Wyoming	105
Missouri	82	Far West	
Nebraska	93	California	99
North Dakota	83	Nevada	63
South Dakota	91	Oregon	95
		Washington	93
		Alaska	180
		Hawaii	105

SOURCE: *Significant Features of Fiscal Federalism, 1984 Edition* (Washington, D.C.: Advisory Commission on Intergovernmental Relations, 1985), p. 132.

Great Lakes region are taxing their residents very heavily, while those in the Southwest and the Rocky Mountains are not.

The ACIR's tax-capacity and tax-effort measures have raised some significant issues in fiscal federalism. Since most federal grant programs base their formulas on per-capita income rather than tax capacity, has the money been going to some states that really do not need as much money as they have been receiving? Should federal grants be based on tax capacity, with the states with *less* capacity receiving *more* money? On the other hand, the tax-capacity measure, which relies on twenty-six commonly used taxes, does not include charges. Considering the prominent role played by charges in Table 10-5, are states that rely heavily on this method of finance being misrepresented?

Moreover, the tax-effort measure leads to some interesting ideological questions. Conservatives would say that Rhode Island, New York, and Wisconsin are overtaxing their residents, but liberals would say that public services are being shortchanged in New Hampshire, North Dakota, Oklahoma, Texas, and Wyoming. One's answer depends not only on hard data, but on a well-thought-out view of the proper role for government. In any event, the public has spoken on this matter, and it is to their response that we now turn.

TAX REVOLT

In the late 1970s and early 1980s, the nation witnessed a tax revolt, beginning with the passage of California's Proposition 13 in 1978. Numerous explanations of the revolt have been offered:

1. It was an attempt to significantly trim a government perceived to be bloated.
2. Government was perceived as inefficient and wasteful; therefore the taxpayers were not getting their money's worth.
3. Those voting for tax-cut measures felt they were bearing an unfair portion of the tax load.
4. Members of the public were expressing concern over their individual finances and lack of economic progress.
5. The voters were losing faith in New Deal liberalism.
6. The public was losing confidence in government.
7. The voters were simply naive.

Although all of these factors explain some of the tax revolt phenomenon, and many of them overlap, probably the best explanation is that it was a symbolic issue. The voters were expressing diffuse, subjective, moralistic judgments rather than seeking to serve their immediate, tangible, economic interests.[20]

The tax revolt was manifested in various forms. The most controversial actions were votes by the people directly to cut taxes, such as Proposition 13 in California and Proposition 2½ in Massachusetts. Although the tax revolt was heralded as a political uprising, only four of fifteen such measures passed from 1978 through 1982—the heyday of the movement.

In addition to the tax revolt, voters approved various proposals to limit local government revenue sources by classifying property taxes and by requiring *full-disclosure procedures* (so-called truth-in-property-taxation plans). The latter require local governing bodies to announce in advance a vote to increase tax rates and to raise them only by a public vote in an open hearing. Furthermore, state legislatures indexed income taxes (as discussed earlier in the chapter) and voted to reduce various tax rates. These rates were frequently raised during the severe 1980–83 recession. In theory at least, perhaps the most far-reaching examples of the tax revolt were measures to limit state (and sometimes local) revenue and expenditure increases to increases in per-capita personal income (as was done in New Jersey and Tennessee) or to increases in the cost of living. In the 1978–82 period, the voters approved eight out of ten of these measures. These proposals were usually put on the ballot by conservative activists who believed that the public purse was not inexhaustible, and that if interest groups were not restrained, they would spend the state broke. Paul Gann, who had co-authored California's Proposition 13, qualified an initiative constitutional amendment to set a limit on total state and local government spending. His measure was an attempt to force interest groups to fight one another for a piece of the budgetary pie. Since the total spending pie could not be enlarged by elected officials wanting to satisfy all interest groups, claimants on the state treasury would have to engage in a "zero-sum game," in which one group could gain only at another group's expense.

These tax-and-spending limitations were only partially successful. Gann's constitutional amendment in California affects less than half of the state's general and special funds. In order to short-circuit the amendment's restrictions, the California legislature has directed money into accounts exempted by the amendment. The weakness of taxing-spending limitations is that they relate only to the state's general fund, which seldom handles "more than half of the moneys received and disbursed by a state government as a whole."[21] Outside the scope of such limitations are monies placed in funds to retire existing debts, state operations that sell water and electricity to the public, contributions to state employee retirement funds, federal aid, and earmarked taxes.

The ineffectiveness of current revenue and expenditure limitations is similar in certain respects to fiscal reform of the nineteenth century: the requirement of a balanced budget. All of the states except Vermont have a constitutional prohibition of deficits. Does this keep states and local governments from spending more money than they take in? Hardly. There are various strategies for making a budget appear to be balanced when it is not.[22] Governors or mayors can overestimate revenues for the upcoming fiscal year when they send their budget to the legislature. They can make overly optimistic assumptions about the economy, saying that a robust economy will lead to increased tax receipts. Since a state legislature or city council may not have the technical staff with which to determine for itself the amount of revenue various taxes are likely to generate under various economic assumptions, they may not be able to supply an independent check on the executive. Moreover, the governor or mayor can inflate estimates of anticipated federal aid. Spending items can be taken from the operating budget, which finances day-to-day state operations, and disguised in the capital budget, which funds construction projects and does not have to be balanced from year to year. The state or city can start crediting taxes that belong in the budget for the next fiscal year at the end of this year's budget. (This type of fiscal sleight of hand contributed to New York City's bankruptcy.) On the other hand, payment for purchases made at the end of this fiscal year can be delayed until next fiscal year. The cost of programs spanning several years can also be loaded onto future fiscal years.

Finally, the balanced-budget requirement, weak as it may be, usually applies only to the budget proposed by the executive or enacted by the legislature. It does not mean that the state or city must end the year with a surplus. For example, California carried over a massive $862 million debt from fiscal year 1983 into fiscal 1984. A significant advantage of tactics such as overestimating revenues or prematurely collecting taxes or carrying over deficits is that they spare today's elected officials the politically dangerous task of raising taxes. The piper will not have to be paid until after the next election—when today's politicians may be holding a different or higher office.[23]

The problem with fiscal reforms such as zero-based budgeting or revenue and spending limitations or balanced-budget requirements is that if they constrain elected officials too much, they will be evaded. On the other hand, if they do not constrain at all, they are worthless. If an elected official feels that more money should be spent either to further his or her ideological and policy goals or to aid in reelection, then the money will be spent somehow; constraining fiscal reforms will play only a minor inhibiting role.

SUMMARY

A leading book from the mid 1950s on public finance noted that a budget reflects "the relative distribution of economic and political power within the state."[24] That aphorism is still accurate today: budgets determine not only "who gets what" in public goods and services, but who will pay for them. It is ultimately political power and political ideology that specifically shape a budget. Political speeches and political posturing certainly have their place, but what governors and legislators are willing to spend money on is what they really believe in. And what they spend money on is public policies, the topic of the next two chapters.

NOTES

    1. Roy Bahl, *Financing State and Local Government in the 1980s* (New York: Oxford University Press, 1984), p. 12.

2. Aaron Wildavsky, "Why Government Grows: Cultural versus Economic and Political Theories" (paper presented at the annual meeting of the Western Political Science Association, Sacramento, 1984). The importance of relative deprivation was noted as long ago as the 1840s. See Alexis de Tocqueville, *Democracy in America*, ed. Phillips Bradley (New York: Random House, Vintage Books, 1945). See also Susan B. Hansen and Patrick Cooper, "State Revenue Elasticity and Expenditure Growth," *Policy Studies Journal*, 9 (Autumn 1980), 26–33.

3. Bahl, *Financing*, pp. 133–36.

4. Steven D. Gold, *State and Local Fiscal Relations in the Early 1980s* (Washington, D.C.: Urban Institute Press, 1983), pp. 2, 10, 13, 29.

5. Jeffrey Stonecash, "Fiscal Centralization in the American States: Increasing Similarity and Persisting Diversity," *Publius*, 13 (Fall 1983), 123–37.

6. Aaron Wildavsky, *The Politics of the Budgetary Process*, 4th ed. (Boston: Little, Brown, 1984).

7. John Mikesell, *Fiscal Administration*, 2nd ed. (Homewood, Ill.: Dorsey, 1986), chap. 4.

8. Allen Schick, "The Status of Zero-base Budgeting in the States," in *Readings in Public Administration*, ed. Felix Nigro and Lloyd Nigro (New York: Harper & Row, Pub., 1983), p. 289.

9. Ibid., pp. 293–94.

10. Ibid., p. 296.

11. According to the final report of the 1981 Pennsylvania Tax Commission, reprinted in Mikesell, *Fiscal Administration*, chap. 6.

12. Steven D. Gold, "Recent Developments in State Finances," *National Tax Journal*, 36 (March 1983), 1.

13. Bahl, *Financing*, p. 23.

14. Otto Eckstein, *Public Finance*, 4th ed. (Englewood Cliffs, N.J.: Prentice-Hall, 1979), p. 55; Mikesell, *Fiscal Administration*, p. 206.

15. Gold, "Recent Developments," p. 19. See also Robert Ebel, "Research and Policy Developments: Major Types of State and Local Taxes," in *Essays in Public Finance and Financial Management*, ed. John E. Petersen and Catherine L. Spain (Chatham, N.J.: Chatham House Publishers, 1980), pp. 12–13; and Donald Phares, *Who Pays State and Local Taxes?* (Cambridge, Mass.: Aelgeschlager, Gunn and Hain Publishers, 1980), pp. 121–23. The effect on *state* tax collections of *federal* tax reductions is difficult to gauge. Since sixteen states allow federal taxes paid to be deducted from state income taxes, lower federal taxes mean higher state revenues. On the other hand, the deductibility of federal income taxes reduces state tax progressivity.

16. Quoted in "Severance Taxes on Energy Seen Widening Gap Between Rich, Poorer Areas of Nation," *Congressional Quarterly Weekly Report*, February 20, 1982, p. 321. Another aspect of the dispute is that the severance tax can be viewed as a conservation tax, which encourages prudent use of finite resources. Although Montana is severely criticized for its high 30 percent severance tax on low-sulfur coal that is strip-mined and sent to the Midwest, Montana has already "experienced a bitter copper-mining bust, and half of severance tax revenues go into a trust fund designed to correct unforeseen environmental damage [from destructive strip mining and the influx of energy workers and their families] and to broaden the state's economic base." Ibid., p. 320.

17. Harold Groves and Robert Bish, *Financing Government*, 7th ed. (New York: Holt, Rinehart & Winston, 1973), pp. 277–79.

18. David Berman and Bruce Merrill, "The Arizona Lottery," *Comparative State Politics Newsletter*, 3 (April 1982) 22–23. See also Curt Suplee, "Lotto Baloney," *Harper's*, July 1983, p. 20; and H. R. Kaplan, "The Social and Economic Impact of State Lotteries," *Annals of the American Academy of Political and Social Sciences*, 474 (July 1984), 100.

19. Robert Lucke, "Rich States–Poor States: Inequalities in Our Federal System," *Intergovernmental Perspective*, Summer 1982, p. 22.

20. David Lowery and Lee Sigelman, "Understanding the Tax Revolt," *American Political Science Review*, 75 (December 1981), 972.

21.   J. Ward Wright, *Tax and Expenditure Limitation* (Lexington, Ky.: Council of State Governments, 1981), p. 18. See also David Magleby, "The Movement to Limit Government Spending in American States and Localities," *University of Virginia Newsletter,* 57 (November 1980), 11; and Steven Gold, "Is the Tax Revolt Dead?" *State Legislatures,* March 1984, p. 26.

22.   Mikesell, *Fiscal Administration,* pp. 103–107. It should always be remembered that state balanced-budget requirements do *not* include bonded indebtedness.

23.   The same point can be made regarding lavish spending on budgetary items, or generous public employee salary increases and pension contributions, or early-retirement options for police and fire fighters. Each can be a way of buying political support now and letting one's successors worry about paying the bill.

24.   Jesse Burkhead, *Government Budgeting* (New York: John Wiley, 1956), p. 59.

chapter 11

Policy Areas: Social Services

THE POLITICS-VERSUS-ECONOMICS DEBATE

States enact a large number of policies: they pay most of the cost of schools, welfare, and highways, and set many of the rules governing these programs; they write a state criminal code and pass laws governing family relations; they regulate commercial activity and attempt to protect the environment; and they establish many more policies, as we shall see. There has been a long-standing dispute in political science over how to explain variations in these policies: Why do some states spend more on education or welfare, while others spend less? Why do some states have strong consumer protection laws, but others do not?

The original explanation of such variations relied on the work of one of the great students of state politics, V. O. Key, Jr. It stressed such political factors as whether a state had high voter turnout, whether it had a one-party system or a system with two competitive parties, and how much party discipline there was in the legislature.[1] In a competitive, two-party state, each party would need the votes of the "have-not" elements of society in order to win, and would bid for their support with higher social welfare expenditures. Voter turnout would also thereby increase.

Despite the compelling logic of this argument, subsequent research showed that socioeconomic factors, especially per-capita income, had a greater effect on social welfare programs. The most prominent statement of this position has been presented by Thomas Dye.[2] Economically developed states have higher incomes, are more urbanized and industrialized, and have a more educated population; such states spend more on programs to aid the have-nots and tax themselves more heavily primarily because they have the economic resources to do so. In the more than two decades since this debate was joined, it has generated an immense number

228

of articles employing sophisticated statistical methodologies to argue one side or the other or to explore some facet of it.

The current state of opinion is probably that *neither* political factors *nor* socioeconomic factors best determine state policies, but that both provide an explanation, with one set of factors having greater explanatory power depending on the particular policy (welfare, education, highways, or whatever) one has in mind. Figure 11-1 has been developed by David R. Morgan, who notes that the social and economic environment is antecedent to the political system, but that both independently affect policy.[3] Socioeconomic factors can also influence policy outcomes through the intervening or mediating force of political factors. More specifically, the *level* of state-local taxing and spending is more responsive to socioeconomic characteristics, but the *distribution* of resources from "haves" to "have-nots" is determined more by political influences. Furthermore, political factors are more important in nonexpenditure policies than in taxing and spending policies, but a state that is urbanized, industrialized, and economically developed spends less on highways and the conservation of natural resources.

The politics-versus-economics debate has raised a large number of interesting issues concerning state public policies, only a few of which can be noted here. As we have seen, states differ in the percentage of total state and local spending that they bear. When only the state component of spending is considered, socioeconomic characteristics (especially per-capita income) are not strongly related to it; however, local spending is responsive to economic development. Moreover, states shouldering a higher percentage of state-local expenditures spend more overall.[4] The early politics-economics debate dealt with state expenditure policies, but more recent aspects of the discussion have extended to nonexpenditure policies on domestic violence, consumer legislation, energy conservation, state control of urban affairs, utility regulation, deinstitutionalization of the mentally retarded, and numerous other areas.[5] In addition, scholars

FIGURE 11-1   Relationship among Environment, Politics, and Policy

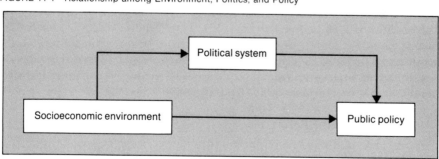

SOURCE: David R. Morgan, *Handbook of State Policy Indicators*, 4th ed. (Norman: University of Oklahoma Bureau of Government Research, 1982), p. 10.

have sought better empirical measures of state political characteristics—for example, state public opinion (see Chapter 1), interest group strength (Chapter 4), the power of the governor (Chapter 5), the professionalism of the legislature (Chapter 6), and the extent of divided control of state government (Chapter 5). Political factors are very important for those students of state government who assume that a state's socioeconomic character is generally given, and that therefore the only role for reform or liberal social change is to specify which political factors affect state policies the most. Finally, Ira Sharkansky, a prominent writer on the politics-versus-economic debate, has distinguished between spending levels and service levels. States do not necessarily provide higher levels of service simply by spending more money.[6]

LAW ENFORCEMENT

The first of ten policy areas we shall consider in this and the next chapter is law enforcement.

The crime rate, although unacceptably high, has been dropping in recent years. The causes of this fortuitous development are open to different interpretations. The Reagan administration credits more effective local law enforcement, citizen crime-watch programs, and longer jail sentences for convicted criminals; others point to the fact that there are now fewer persons in the most crime-prone age group (fourteen to twenty-four).

Whatever the reason for the decline, the reason the rate is still unacceptably high is that crime is not a very risky business. Of all serious offenses reported to the police, only 19.9 percent result in arrests. Only 17.1 percent result in charges being filed, only 5 percent result in the person so charged being found guilty, and a mere 2 percent result in incarceration.[7] Since the amount of actual crime is estimated to be two and one half times greater than the amount reported to police, a person's chances of going to jail for murder, forcible rape, robbery, aggravated assault, burglary, larceny, or auto theft *are less than one in fifty*. These data are well known to people "on the street" and lead to a telling conclusion: crime pays. For those persons seeking to avoid being victims of crime, the results are fear and deteriorating neighborhoods. The fear of crime breaks communities apart and forces people into self-protective isolation. Personal gun ownership is up, especially among women.

The Nature of Police Work

Unlike most people, police officers work in an extremely violent environment. They must be prepared for danger, especially the kind that is directed at them personally. Moreover, the police serve primarily a lower-class clientele:

> When the affluent face emergencies, they use private resources and facilities to cope. The poor call the police. Thus those who come to the police for help are not a random sample of the whole population. They are mostly the poor, the down and out, and the desperate.[8]

Another important aspect of police work is the large amount of discretion available to officers: "discretion *increases* as one moves down the hierarchy."[9] The officer on the beat must decide which laws to enforce, when, and how.

The nature of police work is said to attract, or at the very least to produce, people who are cynical, suspicious, unduly tough, and authoritarian. Working amidst weakness, vice, and hypocrisy, a fictional policeman in one of Joseph Wambaugh's novels says:

> We see them when nobody else sees them, when they're being born and dying and fornicating and drunk. We see people when they're taking anything of value from other people and when they're without shame or very much ashamed and we learn secrets that their husbands and wives don't even know, secrets that they even try to keep from themselves, and what the hell, when you learn these things about people who aren't institutionalized, people who're out here where you can see them function every day, well then, you really *know*.[10]

Not only do police officers see "the worst" people, they see "the best" people at their worst.

Suspiciousness is said to be an essential personality trait of police officers. "To be suspicious of situations or persons that appear out of the ordinary is the first step in a policeman's discretionary behavior. Suspicion keys the decision to investigate, which provides the basis for the arrest decision and the subsequent invocation of the criminal process."[11] Not only must officers be suspicious in their line of work, they must be tough. Veteran officers tell the newcomers, "You gotta be tough, kid, or you'll never last."[12]

Considerably more controversial than cynicism, suspiciousness, and toughness is authoritarianism. Considering the pleasant surroundings in which college professors work, it is easy for them to be tolerant, broad-minded, and liberal. The work environment of police officers, on the other hand, probably necessitates at least some authoritarianism in order to survive. But were these men and women that way *before* entering police work? "There is, in fact, no substantial evidence that police work attracts authoritarian personalities. Quite the contrary, police recruits generally appear to be psychologically sound and competent persons, little different from the larger population of which they are a part."[13]

Sentencing and Incarceration

Most people arrested for a serious crime were arrested previously—and probably will be arrested again. The frequency with which the same people pass through the criminal justice system is called the *recidivism* rate. The U.S. Bureau of Justice Statistics studied over five thousand inmates imprisoned on state charges and found that 84 percent were repeat offenders. About 46 percent of the repeaters who committed new crimes would still have been behind bars if they had served maximum sentences for the crimes for which they were originally convicted.[14]

Most crime is committed by a relatively small number of high-volume offenders who believe correctly that their chances of "doing time for the crime" are relatively slim. Remember that we pointed out earlier that the chances of going to jail for murder, forcible rape, robbery, aggravated assault, burglary, larceny, or auto theft are less than one in fifty. In an intensive study of imprisoned armed robbers by the Rand Corporation, "a majority of [the] habitual felons . . . said that nothing—not harsher treatment in prison, the possibility of a longer sentence, stricter parole supervision, nor the certainty of being caught—would have prevented their return to crime. Of the few who felt their course could have been changed, the certainty of being caught was cited as the most influential deterrent."[15] State legislators, on the other hand, have been attempting to stem the crime wave by increasing the length and severity of punishment without increasing the chances that it will ever be imposed. In fact, assuming that a felon is actually caught, he or she will probably *plea-bargain* (plead guilty to a lesser offense) in order to avoid a long prison term.

According to another study done by the Rand Corporation, seven variables can be used to predict high-rate offenders:

1. Incarceration for more than half of the two-year period preceding the more recent arrest
2. Prior conviction for the crime type that is being predicted
3. Juvenile conviction prior to age sixteen
4. Commitment to a state or federal juvenile facility
5. Heroin or barbiturate use in the two-year period preceding the current arrest
6. Heroin or barbiturate use as a juvenile
7. Employment for less than half of the two-year period preceding the current arrest[16]

Offenders scoring 0 or 1 on this scale are low-rate; those scoring 2 or 3, medium-rate; and those scoring 4 or more, high-rate. The scale predicted accurately for 82 percent of the offenders studied. One of the conclusions of the study is that if low-rate offenders were free, they would commit one burglary and one robbery per year, but if high-rate offenders were free, they would commit ninety-three burglaries and thirteen robberies per year. The Rand researcher "applied his scale to California and found that if all low-rate robbers received two-year prison terms (most now receive longer ones) and all high-rate robbers received seven-year terms (most now receive shorter ones), the number of robberies committed in the state would drop by an estimated 20 percent with no increase in the prison population."[17]

If this scale (known as *selective incapacitation*) were used as a guide in prison sentencing, low-rate offenders would spend less time in prison and high-rate offenders more time—a more rational allocation of existing prison cells. However, selective incapacitation has its critics. It is difficult to infer the characteristics of individuals from the characteristics of aggregates. Moreover, based solely on a prediction of what he or she would do in the future, one person could receive a harsher sentence than another person for the same illegal act. Finally, the originator of the selective incapacitation concept (John Greenwood) concedes that it would be most effective as a control technique for burglary and robbery, but not for crimes such as homicide, rape, or assault, which may involve people who know each other.

It has long been a cherished hope of liberals that a prison sentence will reform or rehabilitate a lawbreaker. However, no method has yet been devised that will significantly lessen recidivism.[18] In fact, from the description of prison conditions that follows, a case could be made that American prisons "de-habilitate" or are even "schools for crime." This is considered by some as another reason for giving low-volume offenders a shorter sentence. The most that can be said in favor of American penal institutions is that the violent criminals confined in them cannot prey on an innocent public.

The conditions in almost all prisons are deplorable. A judge has ruled the Colorado maximum security prison at Canon City ("Old Max") to be "unfit for human habitation" because of "insufficient living space with inadequate sanitation, ventilation, light, noise control, and fire safety; lack of protection from violence; massive and pervasive idleness because of lack of productive activity; inadequate medical care (both mental and physical)."[19] Another judge has ruled the entire Tennessee prison system unconstitutional and virtually assumed control of its operation. At the time of the grisly 1980 riot at the New Mexico State Penitentiary (see Reading 11-1), a lawsuit challenging overcrowded conditions was pending in federal court. South Carolina crowds 8000 inmates into prisons designed for 4600; in Texas, three inmates share a five-by-nine-foot cell, with one prisoner sleeping on the floor. These conditions are aggravated by heavy drug use and by racial tensions spurred by the racial and ethnic gangs that virtually run many prisons. The threat of violence, especially sexual assault, is constantly present:

Virtually every slightly built young man committed by the courts is sexually approached within a day or two after his admission to prison. Many of these young men are overwhelmed and repeatedly "raped" by gangs of inmate aggressors. Others are compelled by the terrible threat of gang rape to seek protection by entering into a "housekeeping" relationship with an individual tormentor. Only the toughest and more hardened young men—and those few so obviously frail that they are immediately locked up for their own protection—escape penetration of their bodies.[20]

Usually as a result of court orders, a dozen states have adopted *emergency-release laws* to deal with overcrowding. When the prison population reaches a certain level, less-dangerous prisoners near the end of their terms are released. Such a law has repeatedly been triggered in Michigan. These laws force governors and legislators to ask, "How many prison cells are we willing to build, and how are we going to pay for them?" Until recently, elected officials were eager to posture as crime fighters by lengthening prison terms and requiring judges to send more people to prison, but they were reluctant to spend money on corrections. This is one of the few exceptions to a rule of thumb noted in the last chapter that spending money gets you votes. Moreover, legislators cannot continue for long saying in one breath "Put more people in prison" but in the next breath "Don't build a prison in my district."

READING 11-1   THE NEW MEXICO PRISON RIOT

SANTA FE, N.M.—Grisly accounts of execution by blowtorch, decapitations, mutilations, torture and other atrocities perpetrated by crazed inmates on their fellow prisoners surfaced Monday in the aftermath of weekend rioting at the New Mexico State Penitentiary.

A day after state troopers and National Guardsmen regained control of the prison, officials said 39 inmates were known dead. With 15 unaccounted for, the eventual toll could surpass the 43 persons killed eight years ago at Attica prison in New York.

Along with the reports of almost unspeakable acts of brutality came an account of prisoners rescuing one hostage guard by dressing him in inmate clothing, giving him an iron pipe and escorting him from a burning cellblock.

Several of the dozen guards who were seized by the rioting prisoners early Saturday were not as lucky. They suffered beatings and stab wounds and were still in serious condition in Santa Fe hospitals. But no prison personnel were among the fatalities from the 36 hours of violence.

Gov. Bruce King said that at least seven prisoners died of drug overdoses after inmates broke into the hospital pharmacy, and that others were victims of smoke inhalation from the widespread fires that still smoldered on Monday.

But about half "definitely did die of violence of other prisoners," the governor said. And the tales of brutality and murder stunned even veteran law enforcement officers.

One inmate, wearing a mask to conceal his identity, told reporters that an inmate "execution squad" had roamed through the cellblock after inmates overpowered the handful of guards on duty during the early morning hours Saturday and seized control of the institution.

This inmate said initial targets of the execution squad were prisoners believed to be informants or "snitches." Authorities offered some substantiation for this inmate's assertions.

The state Corrections Commission chairman, Steven Richards, said a state trooper told him of watching from outside the prison fence as a group of inmates held down another prisoner and used "a cutting torch to burn his face. They just burned him up."

A guard said he was told that some prisoners were herded onto the stage of the institution's gymnasium and bound and beaten before the stage was set afire.

During the negotiations that ultimately ended the uprising, inmates "had taken three prisoners and maimed them, and set them outside as a sign they meant business," said Ernie Mills, a Santa Fe radio and television personality who was part of the state's three-man negotiating team.

Then, Mills said, "The prisoners shouted, 'We've got another for you.' That's when they brought out the guy with his head severed and stuck between his legs."

When authorities regained control of the institution, they quickly found other signs of atrocities. State troopers said several bodies were charred beyond recognition. "A couple had their heads bashed in," one trooper said, "and this one guy had a rope around his neck like he had been hanged."

Another inmate's eyes were gouged out, Lt. Reyes Montoya said.

SOURCE: Gaylord Shaw, "Execution Squad Atrocities in Riot Told; Toll Hits 39," *Los Angeles Times,* February 5, 1980, p. I-1. Copyright 1980, *Los Angeles Times.* Reprinted by permission.

The incarceration rate varies from state to state, partly as a reflection of the states' varying views of crime. As indicated in Table 11-1, southern and western states jail proportionately more people than the states in other regions.

In addition, the amount of time served for the same crime can be profoundly different from one state to another; in fact, "it often matters less what crime has been committed than the state in which the felon chose to commit it."[21] A study conducted by the *National Law Journal* of the actual time spent behind bars (rather than the judge's initial sentence) by over 70,000 paroled persons revealed that average time served ranged from a high of fifty-three months in Massachusetts to a low of thirteen months in South Dakota.

However, averages such as those shown in Table 11-2 are affected by extremely high or low scores. For example, the Massachusetts average is pulled up by the fact that it chooses to punish murder very severely. If we use the median (the point at which half of the scores are above, and half below), a different pattern emerges. Utah is then the toughest state, followed by South Carolina, West Virginia, Florida, North Carolina, and,

TABLE 11-1   Adults under Correctional Supervision, 1982*

New England	101	East South Central	101
Maine	58	Kentucky	123
New Hampshire	52	Tennessee	81
Vermont	113	Alabama	108
Massachusetts	77	Mississippi	98
Rhode Island	108	West South Central	187
Connecticut	170	Arkansas	69
Middle Atlantic	106	Louisiana	128
New York	106	Oklahoma	111
New Jersey	117	Texas	237
Pennsylvania	98	Mountain	107
East North Central	96	Montana	76
Ohio	84	Idaho	76
Indiana	93	Wyoming	73
Illinois	116	Colorado	97
Michigan	88	New Mexico	83
Wisconsin	91	Arizona	129
West North Central	88	Utah	120
Minnesota	90	Nevada	167
Iowa	73	Pacific	143
Missouri	100	Washington	194
North Dakota	39	Oregon	121
South Dakota	59	California	138
Nebraska	91	Alaska	110
Kansas	101	Hawaii	106
South Atlantic	163		
Delaware	165		
Maryland	235		
District of Columbia	356		
Virginia	91		
West Virginia	43		
North Carolina	162		
South Carolina	150		
Georgia	266		
Florida	132		

SOURCE: U.S. Bureau of the Census, *Statistical Abstract of the United States: 1985* (Washington, D.C.: Government Printing Office, 1984), p. 181.
* Rate per 10,000 adult residents.

surprisingly, Wisconsin, which is usually thought of as a relatively liberal state.

Differences in average time served can also be very striking because some states choose to single out certain crimes for special punishment. For example, robbers in South Carolina serve more time on average than prisoners in at least seven states who are convicted of willful homicide. West Virginia car thieves average longer terms than rapists in at least sixteen states. If one believes that retribution or "just deserts" is a more important goal of sentencing than incapacitation, perhaps Nevada and

Alaska should increase their average prison times for rape to that of Arkansas.

As a final note on time served, we might recall that when the Colorado judge ruled his state's maximum security prison unfit for human habitation, he cited among other defects "massive and pervasive idleness because of lack of productive activity." Many observers over many years have suggested that prisons teach felons useful employment skills as a way of combating recidivism. (As we have seen, though, imprisoned felons told Rand researchers that only the certainty of being caught could prevent their returning to crime.) States have traditionally had prison industries teaching such nontransferable skills as stamping automobile license plates and making traffic signs, tasks that save the state government money. Other state prison industries have included refinishing furniture, stuffing mattresses, and making soap. Needless to say, labor unions and private industry oppose any competition provided by convict labor. However, Connecticut and Indiana offer tax incentives to those who bring factories inside prisons to employ inmates. In Kansas, a privately owned "metal fabrication plant employs 40 inmates three miles from the prison," with transportation to and from the site provided by the prison.[22] A successful Arizona program is described in Reading 11-2.

The Criminal Justice System and Minority Groups

Since people of different races or ethnic groups frequently receive unequal treatment in such policy areas as housing and education, it would not be surprising if such unfairness were found in law enforcement as well. However, the evidence is somewhat mixed. Although more than three fourths of all white police officers studied made prejudiced statements about blacks, in actual encounters the police did not treat blacks uncivilly more often than they did whites.[23] In fact, both white and black officers were more likely to use unnecessary force against members of their *own* race. On the other hand, a Rand Corporation study of 190,000 offenders in three states found that police use weaker evidentiary standards to arrest blacks and Latinos than they use to arrest whites.[24] Moreover, the same report showed that blacks and Latinos were sentenced to prison more often, received longer terms, and were required to serve greater portions of their sentences in prison than whites convicted of similar crimes and having similar criminal records. The difference can be attributed to cultural bias on the part of judges and to the fact that whites are more likely to plea-bargain than blacks or Latinos, thus receiving less severe sentences. Paradoxically, the national survey of time served conducted by the *National Law Journal* found that Latinos serve less time on average for crimes against persons than whites, but blacks serve more.

While many commentators note that minority group members are frequently the *perpetrators* of crimes, they often fail to observe that

TABLE 11-2 Prison Time Served (in months)

	Assault	Burglary	Car Theft	Forcible Rape	Larceny Theft	Negligent Manslaughter	Robbery	Willful Homicide	All Felonies
Alabama	19	19	14	50	11	—	40	70	25
Alaska**	28	—	—	14	26	11	23	—	22
Arizona*	21	18	15	36	18	—	25	58	23
Arkansas**	17	26	—	119	22	16	20	41	26
California*[1]	34	24	21	47	21	35	35	76	30
Colorado*	21	16	—	34	18	22	27	79	20
Delaware	13	15	—	35	11	23	18	—	15
D.C.	21	30	35	70	18	57	39	70	31
Florida	27	22	22	68	18	39	39	52	28
Georgia	23	25	18	62	16	28	35	63	28
Idaho	14	21	13	42	23	23	33	45	22
Illinois[7]	20	15	13	46	13	21	21	40	18
Iowa**	34	20	22	—	17	—	30	38	21
Kansas	19	16	—	31	15	15	29	69	18
Kentucky	18	13	16	35	11	17	28	39	18
Louisiana*	22	19	—	45	17	—	27	42	25
Maine	16	16	—	28	16	31	28	74	20
Maryland	18	19	9	52	14	34	41	78	22
Massachusetts*[2]	30	30	18	30	18	—	18	180+	53
Michigan	28	22	16	—	18	46	33	99	24
Minnesota*	32	23	15	34	19	—	40	65	30
Missouri	19	9	11	96	11	8	31	72	18
Nebraska	25	23	28	37	22	30	37	128	25
Nevada	21	20	21	14	19	15	25	89	23
New Jersey	19	10	16	42	12	27	20	62	17
New York*[1]	22	20	16	30	17	33	24	84	22

North Carolina	23	33	17	109	19	38	43	87	35
North Dakota	21	15	—	28	14	—	19	—	16
Ohio	27	22	29	47	16	32	39	86	26
Pennsylvania	22	22	21	32	15	25	27	46	24
Puerto Rico**	26	29	21	18	30	87	27	82	40
South Carolina	30	28	16	73	25	20	46	58	33
South Dakota	15	13	—	59	15	—	23	31	13
Texas	26	19	17	55	17	16	39	60	25
Utah³	19	41	—	52	32	107	53	111	41
Virginia	23	24	57	49	15	16	38	67	29
West Virginia⁴	44	31	41	16	24	20	60	72	32
Wisconsin	23	22	16	32	15	18	29	96	26
Wyoming	24	20	18	46	24	30	21	54	23
National Average⁵	23	20	17	52	16	32	31	62	25
Federal Crimes⁶	34	35	21	—	19	—	48	—	27
Federal Territories	34	21	16	74	21	—	35	55	33

SOURCE: "Huge Disparities in Jail Time," *National Law Journal*, February 23, 1981, p. 28.

* 1977 LEAA data.

** 1976 LEAA data.

¹ Median figures only. State medians on time served are generally about one-third lower than average or mean time served.

² Approximate average only. State supplied range figures, such as 24–36 months. Figures represent midpoint of range.

³ State parole board supplied figures for forcible rape and willful homicide. Other state figures did not agree with Uniform Parole Reports data and show lower penalties in most categories. Utah's self-reporting for 1977 runs as follows: assault (19), burglary (23), forcible rape (52), larceny theft (22), willful homicide (111), robbery (53), negligent manslaughter (28), all felonies (31).

⁴ Combines 1976 and 1977 figures for forcible rape.

⁵ National averages include only those states within the Uniform Parole Reports data. States not included in figuring the national averages were Alaska, Arizona, Arkansas, California, Colorado, Connecticut, Hawaii, Indiana, Iowa, Louisiana, Massachusetts, Minnesota, Montana, Oklahoma, Oregon, Rhode Island, Vermont and Washington.

⁶ Federal crimes refer to prisoners released from Federal Bureau of Prisons in 1977.

⁷ Illinois parole officials dispute the Uniform Parole Reports statistics for their state for willful homicide. State Officials said that murderers in the state must serve 16 years or more for murder and that the overall average for willful homicide is far higher than reflected by the UPR data.

READING 11-2   ARIZONA PRISON JOBS TRAIN INMATES FOR FREEDOM

Little did the woman calling from Texas know she was speaking to a prisoner in Arizona.

But 23-year-old Marcea, who is serving seven years for armed robbery, was polite and efficient as she swiftly booked a reservation for the caller at a Best Western International motel.

It was the sort of transaction that occurs nearly 2,000 times a day here under one of the nation's most extraordinary prison industries programs. Thirty inmates of the Arizona Center for Women hold regular jobs with Best Western, booking $17 million a year in room sales and learning job skills that lead to steady employment when they go free.

The 30 women are among 1,100 Arizona inmates—including some who own and operate their own businesses behind bars—involved in what is widely regarded as one of the nation's most advanced prison-industry efforts.

"Provides a Reference"

"Eventually, I'm going to be released and this will provide a reference and recommendation for me," says Marcea, whose daughter, now 2, was 3 weeks old when her mother was sentenced. Thirty percent of Marcea's $4.50-an-hour wage goes to her daughter's support. "It helps me care for my daughter and makes me self-sufficient," she said. "I've saved $3,000 in 18 months. . . .

"This is what I want my life to be from now on."

As prison systems seek more and better jobs for the swelling ranks of inmates, Arizona's effort to provide inmates with "free world" work skills is attracting increasing attention nationwide.

"Arizona and Best Western are probably one of the most successful programs I know of," says James C. Johnson, president of the Correctional Industries Assn.

"Meaningful" Employment

Such opportunities are the result of a 1981 state law mandating "meaningful" employment for inmates.

"'Meaningful' was defined as using or acquiring skills that are marketable on release," said Tom Lescault, director of the state's prison industries umbrella, ARCOR Enterprises. In two years, Lescault has changed ARCOR from a traditional, money-losing prison industry effort run by corrections department officials into a profitable venture managed by former business people.

"The only way to make this work," Lescault said, "was to run it like a business and treat the inmate as an employee."

So even the ARCOR-managed license-plate manufacturing operation makes a profit.

The Arizona legislation also took another important step; it broke one of the most significant roadblocks to greater use of prison-made products, the prohibition on selling inmate-made goods to the public or hiring inmates out to private industry.

"We are one of the few states allowed to sell to the general public," Lescault added, citing the ARCOR mattresses on sale among other brands of mattresses at a nearby store. "In fact, we could conceivably open a retail store, if we wanted to. And we can go into joint ventures with the private sector (like Best Western)."

All told, ARCOR encompasses:

—Eleven industrial programs that manufacture such things as license plates, signs, mattresses, office furniture and rocking horses.

—Five joint ventures employing 97 inmates in private businesses, including Best Western; National Switchboard, a telephone response company; a doll-making company and manufacturing and assembly. Another 20 such ventures are under discussion.

—Four agricultural operations.

—And 150 inmates working in inmate-owned businesses, which pay rent for their prison space.

Land Set Aside

The state has set aside a 40-acre tract of land at each of two new prisons for use by private companies willing to utilize inmate labor.

"Our position," Lescault said, "is we should afford the offender the opportunity to be better upon leaving than when he arrived."

Some inmates earn minimum wage; Best Western pays salaries identical to those of its main reservations center here—$4.21 an hour to start. (One inmate has even been named "Employee of the Quarter.")

In some cases, the state is providing prisoners with more than skills; small but increasing numbers of inmates are simply being retained by their employers—and even promoted—upon their release from prison.

"Going Downtown"

"I'm going downtown with Best Western," said 45-year-old Cale Morgano, describing the trip from her prison quarters to Best Western's main reservation center. Morgano will finish a five-year term for attempted theft at the end of this month. She makes $902 a month, of which 30% goes to the state toward room and board. In addition, she pays income taxes—and she has saved $5,400 for her new start in life.

"I've got money to get a start, get an apartment. Ninety percent of the women in here hit the streets with $50 (from the state) in their pocket.

"I have a roommate hittin' the streets this week with $50. She's had eight years of dead time. She doesn't know how she's going to make it."

The Arizona approach has thus far won high marks from the industries employing inmates, and even some support from organized labor, which has traditionally opposed the wider use of inmate labor at the expense of non-inmates.

"Those jobs were unfilled prior to (the inmates), and we still have jobs open," said Lewis Levy, chairman of Central Management Corp., which uses 13 inmates at The National Switchboard here, one of the nation's five largest area code 800 telephone response companies. "And all of them are guaranteed jobs when they get out of prison. We've been so happy, we've promoted some."

Agents Work "On Call"

"It's so successful, and we're so proud," said Wendy Black, director of corporate communications for Best Western, which began using inmate labor in August, 1981. The company turned to inmates because of a chronic inability to hire reservations agents willing to work "on call" to meet peak hours, days and seasons.

The company installed reservations terminals and telephones at the Arizona Center for Women, itself an old Travelodge motel at 32nd Street and Van Buren.

A total of 134 inmates have been hired, 28 have continued working at Best Western after release, and 11 still work there. Two have been promoted out of reservations.

"They are among our best employees," Black said.

"I just want to keep advancing in the company," said Fran Baker, 54, who began with Best Western while doing four years on a drug sales charge. She has been promoted three times. "They like to promote within, and the only record they're interested in is your work record," she said.

SOURCE: Bill Curry, "Arizona Prison Jobs Train Inmates for Freedom," *Los Angeles Times,* April 21, 1985, p. I-5. Copyright 1985, *Los Angeles Times.* Reprinted by permission.

minorities are very likely to be the *victims* of crimes as well. For example, 10 percent of all black households experience at least one burglary each year, compared with 6 percent of white households. Homicide is the leading cause of death among black men aged twenty-five to forty-four, far exceeding disease and accidents; in fact, black males are six times more likely to be murdered than white males.[25]

Political Corruption, A Special Kind of Crime

Some states have a long history of corruption. Neil Peirce, a writer on state government who travels the country continuously, lists Maryland, Illinois, New Jersey, New York, Pennsylvania, Florida, and West Virginia as chronically corrupt. As particularly upright, he includes Minnesota, Michigan, Virginia, South Carolina, but especially Wisconsin, Vermont, and Utah.[26] Without doubting the propriety of applauding virtue, it is probably unwise to hold up any state as being exceptionally clean—a scandal might break out at any time. The presence or absence of corruption in a state is probably a result of a state's political culture (recall the three political cultures noted in Chapter 1). If corruption is accepted as "just part of politics," then it will certainly flourish. But one must certainly be struck by the fact that only an imaginary line separates scandal-ridden Illinois from honest Wisconsin, West Virginia from Virginia, and New York from Vermont.

The forms of corruption are multitudinous, but we can note some of the more common: ghosting, bid rigging, "honest graft," diversion, shoddy material, kickbacks, bribes, and influence peddling.[27] *Ghosting* occurs when a government employee pays for goods or services that were not delivered, or when a phantom person is placed on the public payroll. By *bid rigging*, different corporations seeking the same government contract agree in advance that one will submit an inflated bid and that all the others will submit even more inflated contracts. Later, each will get a turn to bilk the government. "Honest graft" is the misuse of inside information; it is described in the immortal words of George Washington Plunkitt: "I seen my opportunities and I took 'em." *Diversion* is the private use of public resources, such as office supplies, gasoline, or employee time (as when city street crews pave the mayor's driveway). Government suppliers sometimes furnish *shoddy material* and can make a handsome profit if not detected. *Kickbacks* recently came to light in an FBI investigation of county commissioners in nearly all of Oklahoma's seventy-seven counties. Involving more than 250 people, it was "the largest investigation of public corruption in terms of sheer numbers in the nation's history."[28] The going rate was a 10 percent kickback to county commissioners purchasing a load of gravel, or a road-grader blade, or other equipment. As an example of how two or more forms of graft can be creatively merged, a twenty-eight-year-old rock-crushing machine worth $5000 was bought for only $42,000, and a used $14,000 road grader was leased at a yearly rate of $27,000. *Bribes* need no explanation, but recent revelations indicate that some judges in the Illinois Cook County courts are breaking new ground in fixing cases through mail fraud, racketeering, and extortion.[29] *Influence peddling* involves misusing one's official position for private gain, as when legislators sell votes.

John G. Peters and Susan Welch have provided a conceptual framework for evaluating actions challenged as being corrupt: the public official involved, the donor's relation to the public official, the actual favor, and the payoff.[30] Did the public official have a political or a "nonpolitical" (judicial) position? Was the act performed in the official's public or private role? Was the donor a constituent? Did the official act as a donor and directly enrich himself or herself? Does the favor benefit the donor privately or the public at large? Was the favor part of the normal routine of the official's duties, or was it an extraordinary activity? Was the payoff large? an immediate benefit or a long-delayed one? money and services or electoral support? campaign contribution or personal gift? Peters and Welch queried 441 state senators on various possibly corrupt acts. The following were thought to be particularly corrupt:

> A legislator accepting a large campaign contribution in return for voting "the right way" on a bill
>
> The driveway of the mayor's home being paved by a city crew
>
> A public official using public funds for personal travel
>
> A state legislator who chairs the Public Roads Committee authorizing the purchase of land he or she had recently acquired

Perhaps surprisingly, the following was *not* viewed as corrupt: a public official using influence to get a friend or relative admitted to law school.

It is perhaps ironic that charges of corruption made during a campaign, even credible ones, may not hurt a candidate. Voters may believe that all politicians are corrupt or that an ideologically correct but corrupt politican is better than an honest but ideologically incorrect one. Hence, we have the perverse situation in which "corrupt candidates have even more incentive to take distinct issue positions than do non-corrupt candidates."[31] Whether or not a crooked ideologue can thereby "dodge a bullet," it remains abundantly true that the principal evil of corruption is that it undermines the democratic process. Corruption is in fact a form of special privilege.

WELFARE

As we saw in Table 10–1, welfare is the second largest item in state budgets. Who are the poor, and how many of them are there? Each year, the Census Bureau publishes an income level for a family of four; those families whose incomes are less than this amount are defined as poor. Although poverty is spread throughout the nation, it is heavily concentrated in the South. The overwhelming majority of poor people are white, but 30 percent are black (blacks constitute about 12 percent of the total population). About two fifths of all poor people are children. About half of all families below the poverty line are headed by a woman; since this situation is increasing, it is often described as the "feminization of poverty." Very few of the poor are able-bodied men without jobs. The 1980 census revealed that for the first time, cities have greater concentrations of poor people than rural areas.[32] Table 11-3 shows the percentage of poor people in each state.

A lively debate has raged in recent years over how poor people's income should be defined. Should it be considered as money income only, such as job pay, Social Security payments, unemployment compensation, Supplemental Security Income (SSI assures a minimum monthly income for aged, blind, and disabled people), and welfare (Aid to Families with Dependent Children)? Or should *in-kind benefits* that have cash value also be included? Examples of the latter are food stamps, Medicare or Medicaid, government-subsidized housing, school lunches, legal services, and home-heating assistance. In recent years, in-kind transfer programs have become much larger than money transfer programs. Which of these programs one wishes to include or exclude in the definition of income can radically affect how much poverty one finds. To count only money transfers clearly overestimates the amount of poverty, but neither is it reasonable to assume that in-kind transfers are just the same as cash. People cannot eat medical

TABLE 11-3   Percentage of Americans Below the Poverty Level, 1980

	Percentage		*Percentage*
Mississippi	23.9	California	11.4
Arkansas	19.0	Illinois	11.0
Alabama	18.9	Alaska	10.7
Louisiana	18.6	Nebraska	10.7
Kentucky	17.6	Oregon	10.7
New Mexico	17.6	Pennsylvania	10.5
South Dakota	16.9	Michigan	10.4
Georgia	16.6	Ohio	10.3
South Carolina	16.6	Rhode Island	10.3
Tennessee	16.5	Utah	10.3
West Virginia	15.0	Colorado	10.1
North Carolina	14.8	Iowa	10.1
Texas	14.7	Kansas	10.1
Florida	13.5	Hawaii	9.9
New York	13.4	Maryland	9.8
Oklahoma	13.4	Washington	9.8
Arizona	13.2	Indiana	9.7
Maine	13.0	Massachusetts	9.6
Idaho	12.6	Minnesota	9.5
North Dakota	12.6	New Jersey	9.5
Montana	12.3	Nevada	8.7
Missouri	12.2	Wisconsin	8.7
Vermont	12.1	New Hampshire	8.5
Delaware	11.9	Connecticut	8.0
Virginia	11.8	Wyoming	7.9

SOURCE: U.S. Bureau of the Census, *Statistical Abstract of the United States: 1985* (Washington, D.C., Government Printing Office, 1984), p. 457.

care, nor can they use food stamps to heat their home. Moreover, not all of the poor use all of the in-kind benefits available.

The Institute for Social Research at the University of Michigan has conducted a significant study of poverty: rather than looking at poor families in just a single year, it used a panel study to track five thousand families over a five-year period.[33] The research found that people move in and out of poverty fairly often. Hence, there is no "culture of poverty" that permanently traps large numbers of people; commentators had previously speculated that low aspirations or feelings of powerlessness or extreme present-orientedness doom many people to be poor. Although the number of "hard-core" poor (those poor throughout the five-year period) was relatively small, poverty is nonetheless a threat to many people. Losing one's job, getting a divorce (for women), or giving birth to more children can easily pull those now above the poverty line to a point below it.

A controversial proposal for reforming welfare is "workfare," supported by President Reagan. Specifics of the program vary from state to state, but the general idea is that able-bodied adults should work in order to receive welfare benefits. Women with small children would be exempt, as would elderly people. Since most poor people are children or mothers with small children, many of the poor would therefore be exempt. People would work three days per week and would search for regular employment during the other two days; typical tasks would include working for a nonprofit self-help agency, insulating or repairing homes of the elderly poor, acting as teachers' aides, doing food-service work, and planting trees.

Proponents of workfare argue that it teaches low-skill people with no previous work experience or training some rudimentary skills and job habits; that it gives people a chance to prove themselves so that they can later qualify for regular, paid employment; and that workfare workers perform a valuable public service. Opponents argue that the program is punitive, that it exploits helpless people, and that it costs more money than it saves. Labor unions oppose workfare on the same grounds that they oppose prisoner-made goods, claiming that it is slave labor and takes jobs away from union members.

However one views the workfare controversy, the problem of moving people off the welfare rolls and on to the work rolls is indeed a difficult one. Many of those on welfare have low skills; the value of welfare (AFDC) and food stamps exceeds what they could earn working full-time at the minimum wage, especially when the costs of commuting to work and/or paying for child care are deducted from earnings. Furthermore, one can get laid off work, and it takes a while to get back on welfare.

Americans have adopted two public means for dealing with economic insecurity: social insurance programs and public assistance programs. In a *social insurance program*, workers pay into a fund out of which they are later legally entitled to draw benefits. Social Security (a federal government program, which will not be discussed in this book) and unemployment compensation (covered in the next chapter) are social insurance, or *entitlement*, programs. A *public assistance program* is financed out of general revenues and is *means-tested* (it requires recipients to demonstrate financial need in order to receive aid). Two examples of public assistance are welfare (Aid to Families with Dependent Children) and General Assistance.

Aid to Families with Dependent Children provides money for poor children and their mothers. About half of the states also extend coverage to unemployed, resident males under the AFDC-Unemployed Parent program. AFDC and AFDC–UP have always led to more political disputes than the federally run Supplemental Security Income program (SSI) because the latter aids the aged, blind, and disabled—groups toward which almost all segments of the public are willing to extend sympathy. Such is not the case regarding the recipients of AFDC or AFDC–UP, who are frequently black, or unwed mothers, or illegitimate children, or able-bodied men. The federal government establishes a minimum AFDC payment level, which may be supplemented by the states. Hence, grant levels vary widely, as shown in Table 11-4, with the highest being over five times as large as the lowest. States also decide who is eligible for welfare. Administering the program is the responsibility of state and local welfare departments.

Robert Albritton has provided an empirical measure of each state's welfare effort in Table 11-5. The first column shows a state's welfare spending in terms of its resources. (However, recall the warning, noted in the last chapter, about using per-capita income as an indicator of tax capacity.) The priority given to welfare in state budgetary decisions is reflected in the second column. The relative state-by-state concentrations of welfare recipients are shown in the third column. Of particular importance is the fourth column, which ranks the grants welfare families are receiving compared with the median family income in each state. In the last column, the value of food stamps is added to the totals in the previous column. The conclusion of Albritton's sophisticated analysis is that states in the Northeast are the most generous with welfare grants, while Sunbelt states (with the exception of California) are the least

TABLE 11-4   Maximum Monthly AFDC Grant, 1980*

1. Alaska	$514	27. District of Columbia	286
2. Vermont	492	28. Idaho	282
3. New York	477	29. Oklahoma	282
4. Hawaii	468	30. Maine	280
5. California	463	31. Maryland	270
6. Michigan	462	32. Delaware	266
7. Rhode Island	453	33. Ohio	263
8. Wisconsin	444	34. Nevada	262
9. Washington	440	35. Montana	259
10. Minnesota	417	36. Virginia	258
11. Connecticut	406	37. Indiana	255
12. Massachusetts	379	38. Missouri	248
13. Iowa	360	39. New Mexico	220
14. New Jersey	360	40. West Virginia	206
15. Utah	348	41. Arizona	202
16. New Hampshire	346	42. Florida	195
17. Kansas	345	43. North Carolina	192
18. Oregon	339	44. Kentucky	188
19. Nebraska	335	45. Louisiana	173
20. North Dakota	334	46. Georgia	164
21. South Dakota	321	47. Arkansas	161
22. Pennsylvania	318	48. South Carolina	129
23. Wyoming	315	49. Tennessee	122
24. Colorado	311	50. Alabama	118
25. Illinois	302	51. Texas	116
26. United States Mean	299	52. Mississippi	96

SOURCE: *Intergovernmental Perspective*, Spring 1982, p. 14.

* For a one-parent family of three persons.

TABLE 11-5 State Scores and Ranks for Five Indicators of State Welfare Efforts, 1978
(ranked by state expenditure per $1,000 personal income)

	State Welfare Expenditure per $1,000 Personal Income		Welfare Expenditure as a Percentage of Total State General Expenditure		Number of AFDC Recipients per 1,000 Population		Adequacy of AFDC Grants		Adequacy of AFDC Grants with Food Stamps	
	Score	Rank	Score	Rank	Score	Rank	Score	Rank	Score	Rank
Rhode Island	$33.79	1	26.2%	4	52.7	12	18.1%	7	21.9	8
Massachusetts	33.35	2	29.1	1	63.0	5	18.4	5	22.2	6
California	31.45	3	29.0	2	61.6	7	17.2	11	20.3	21
Pennsylvania	30.37	4	28.7	3	52.7	11	17.8	8	22.0	7
New York	29.78	5	24.4	7	63.4	4	22.1	1	25.2	3
Maine	29.71	6	21.6	9	54.7	9	15.8	19	22.4	5
Hawaii	28.53	7	15.6	25	65.9	3	20.7	2	25.7	1
Vermont	27.21	8	17.2	18	40.2	24	20.4	3	25.3	2
Michigan	26.71	9	24.9	5	67.5	2	19.3	4	22.6	4
Wisconsin	26.42	10	21.1	10	40.4	23	18.4	6	21.6	10
Minnesota	22.68	11	17.1	19	32.0	31	16.8	12	20.3	20
Mississippi	21.75	12	15.4	26	70.2	1	5.8	50	17.3	37
Illinois	21.69	13	24.8	6	60.9	8	14.9	21	19.8	25
Oregon	21.44	14	19.0	13	48.6	16	15.3	20	18.7	27
Arkansas	20.92	15	17.4	17	40.1	25	11.0	36	20.9	14
Kentucky	19.94	16	15.4	27	47.1	17	11.1	35	18.6	31
Oklahoma	19.60	17	19.0	12	30.2	35	13.6	27	18.9	26
New Jersey	19.52	18	21.7	8	62.5	6	15.9	18	20.2	23
Utah	18.40	19	13.4	35	28.0	38	16.2	15	20.3	22
Washington	18.15	20	16.3	21	36.5	28	17.8	9	21.5	11
Louisiana	17.91	21	13.4	33	13.4	13	8.4	44	16.9	40
Connecticut	17.85	22	20.1	11	43.8	20	17.7	10	21.6	9

Maryland	17.14	23	15.9	22	49.6	14	10.1	41	15.1	48
Georgia	16.60	24	15.6	24	41.1	22	6.6	47	14.7	49
Alaska	16.53	25	6.3	49	31.6	33	14.4	23	20.2	24
Delaware	16.49	26	12.5	38	52.9	10	12.1	31	16.9	41
South Dakota	16.48	27	14.0	32	29.8	36	14.8	22	20.1	17
West Virginia	16.48	28	11.7	41	36.0	29	12.1	30	20.8	15
Tennessee	16.41	29	16.4	20	36.8	27	7.6	45	16.5	43
Iowa	16.06	30	15.0	29	31.7	32	16.8	13	21.0	13
Kansas	15.94	31	18.1	15	27.0	40	14.3	24	18.6	30
Alabama	15.89	32	12.8	36	46.8	18	7.3	46	16.6	42
Ohio	15.75	33	18.5	14	30.2	35	12.9	28	18.5	32
Colorado	15.15	34	15.7	23	28.8	37	12.2	29	17.1	38
South Carolina	15.10	35	12.6	37	49.1	15	5.8	49	15.2	47
Montana	14.53	36	10.3	43	22.6	44	14.0	25	20.6	16
North Carolina	14.34	37	12.0	40	34.3	30	10.4	39	18.3	33
Idaho	13.81	38	11.4	42	22.1	45	16.3	14	20.5	18
New Mexico	13.80	39	8.7	47	41.7	21	10.3	40	17.7	35
North Dakota	13.68	40	10.0	44	20.4	48	16.2	16	21.3	12
New Hampshire	13.57	41	15.1	28	24.4	42	13.9	26	18.7	28
Virginia	13.34	42	13.4	34	31.1	34	11.9	34	17.4	36
Nebraska	13.31	43	14.3	31	22.6	43	16.0	17	20.4	19
Texas	11.58	44	14.4	30	22.1	46	6.3	48	14.2	50
Indiana	10.39	45	12.4	39	27.4	39	11.0	37	16.0	45
Missouri	8.86	46	17.9	16	39.9	26	12.0	32	18.6	29
Nevada	8.67	47	8.9	46	14.0	50	10.5	38	16.2	44
Wyoming	7.93	48	6.4	48	14.0	49	11.9	33	17.1	39
Florida	7.41	49	9.0	45	26.7	41	9.9	42	18.3	34
Arizona	6.28	50	5.7	50	21.1	47	8.6	43	15.5	46

SOURCE: Robert B. Albritton, "Subsidies: Welfare and Transportation," in *Politics in the American States: A Comparative Analysis*, 4th ed., eds. Virginia Gray, Herbert Jacob, and Kenneth N. Vines, pp 392–93. Copyright © 1983 by Robert B. Albritton. Reprinted by permission of Little, Brown, and Company.

generous.[34] The large differences in AFDC payments from one state to another has led to speculation that poor families move from low-AFDC states to high ones. Roy Bahl, however, writes that the "consensus of research" is that such is not the case.[35]

Another type of public assistance program is General Assistance, which is completely state funded. Hence, it exhibits even wider interstate variation than AFDC. In the three fourths of the states with General Assistance programs, poor people who do not qualify for AFDC or SSI may receive assistance.

A frequently repeated assertion in discussions of poverty and welfare is that only 10 percent of poverty program money ever makes its way into the hands of the poor—the rest is ground up in bureaucratic expenses.[36] Whether this is in fact the case would be a fascinating subject of scholarly inquiry. If found to be true, solving the problem might prove to be more intractable, however.

HEALTH

The largest and fastest-growing segment of state welfare expenditures is Medicaid. All persons receiving AFDC and SSI, as well as those over sixty-five whose medical bills exceed Medicare limits, receive Medicaid. States can also choose to extend medical coverage to low-income persons who are not receiving welfare ("the medically indigent").

Medicaid is the fastest-rising large program in state budgets, but this cannot be attributable to increased patient load or broadened services. The rate of inflation in health-care costs greatly exceeds the overall rate of inflation.[37] The policy of *third-party payment* (the state paying for a patient's care) means that patients, doctors, and hospitals have little incentive to keep costs to a minimum (see Reading 11–3). The federal government shares costs with the states and provides a higher percentage to the poorer states. Although the national government pays a fixed percentage of each state's costs, it cannot control the total amount of money spent; therefore, President Reagan wants to cap federal contributions to Medicaid. He cites instances of fraud, ineligible recipients, and crooked medical personnel as reasons the state-run program needs less money. The states are required to provide eight basic services, but they may decide to add an additional seventeen others.

To lessen medical-cost inflation, Maryland established in 1971 a system of *prospective reimbursement.* The Maryland Health Services Cost Review Commission determines in advance what rates hospitals may charge, thus allowing them to predict the revenue they will receive for treating patients and to stay within the rate determined in advance. Other states have established *certificate-of-need programs* to control overbuilding and to reduce the number of empty hospital beds. Hospitals, nursing homes, and clinics are required to demonstrate genuine need for new construction or for the purchase of expensive equipment. Yet another device for controlling costs is the *health maintenance organization* (HMO), which provides comprehensive medical care for members on a prepaid basis. Those who have enrolled pay a fixed periodic premium regardless of how many of the HMO's services they use. Unlike the fee-for-service system, which comes into play *after* a person has become ill, HMOs stress preventive medicine. This not only serves the patient, it helps reduce costs for the organization. Moreover, by providing quality care and protection against astronomical medical bills, the HMO is able to attract new customers. The existence of HMOs in a region also serves to restrain the prices charged by local fee-for-service providers. One frequently alleged

---

READING 11-3 ENLIGHTENED REFORM MAY HOLD DOWN HEALTH COSTS

There are good reasons for much of the increase in [the cost of medical care]: for example, inflation and the development of programs to increase access to care for the aged and the poor. But the system by which we pay doctors and hospitals also contributes to the high costs of medical care.

Most physicians are paid on a fee-for-service basis, which rewards them for providing more and more services, regardless of their benefit to the patient. Hospitals are reimbursed for their costs, so they are rewarded by adding services and increasing the costs of care. The patient, or consumer, also has few incentives to curtail the costs of health care because in most cases these are paid by a third party—an insurance company or the government.

A comparison of the health care system to the general market for goods and services will clarify the issues involved. In a "free market," both consumer and producer have strong incentives to purchase and produce the desired product at the lowest possible price. The more a consumer has to pay for a given item, the less money is available for other purchases. Similarly, the higher the price a producer charges, the greater the risk that the consumer will shop elsewhere.

These forces contribute to an "efficiency" in the exchange of goods and services in our society and, at least in theory, assure that the price a consumer pays for a product reflects its true value to the purchaser.

The medical care market, however, differs from such a "free market." Most notably, we have intervened as a society to assure that no one should be denied needed medical care because of an inability to pay for it. In attempting to achieve that goal, we have created both private and public programs that subsidize the costs of care, especially hospital care. The best known of these programs are Blue Cross–Blue Shield and the government-funded programs, Medicare and Medicaid. In 1979, 92 percent of all hospital bills in the United States were paid for by such third party programs.

Despite their positive benefits, these programs have contributed to the dramatic increase in the cost of medical care. Since patients do not have to pay directly for services covered by insurance, there is no incentive for physicians to refrain from ordering costly services or for hospitals to be otherwise efficient in delivering those services. On the contrary, the desire to provide the best quality care possible is a strong incentive for physicians to order laboratory tests, X-rays, or special procedures, even if the benefit might be small. The threat of malpractice is also felt to result in physicians ordering additional tests and consultations. This practice has been called "defensive medicine."

Similarly, there is no incentive for patients to seek other than the best and most expensive medical care available. This is especially true when the third party program provides "first dollar" coverage—that is, it pays for the entire bill, even the very first dollar.

Knowing the preferences of doctors and patients and that their costs will be reimbursed, hospitals purchase the newest equipment available in order to compete effectively with other hospitals. To protect themselves from the increased costs of these new services, consumers purchase even more insurance, and an ever escalating spiral of increased cost and more insurance results.

Feeding into this cost spiral is the continued development of medical care technology. Each year numerous diagnostic devices and therapeutic measures are created, such as computerized axial tomography (CAT scanner), coronary bypass surgery, kidney dialysis, and a variety of intensive care initiatives. Each of these new technologies requires new, more highly skilled personnel, further increasing the costs of medical care.

The key to controlling the rapid increase in medical care costs is to provide economic incentives to encourage physicians, hospitals, and patients to exercise more prudence in their use of medical care services. Mechanisms can be developed to encourage consumers and providers to make informed decisions about the purchase of medical care items and to evaluate whether such items are worth their real "costs."

One such mechanism would be the requirement that all Americans who could afford to do so pay the first dollar of their medical care (deductible) and some percentage of the costs of the remaining care (co-insurance). Such an arrangement would induce patients and their doctors to consider whether a given procedure was worth what the individual would have to pay. A number of health economists estimate that a policy of even modest deductibles and co-insurance for those who are not poor could substantially slow the rate of increase in health care costs.

Another appropriate step would be to change the incentives hospitals face under current third party systems, possibly by moving toward a system of "prospective" reimbursement. Under such a system, each hospital would have to function within a fixed annual budget, based on the number of patients expected in that year and the level of care those patients were expected to require. Such a system could encourage hospitals to deliver care more efficiently and refrain from frills for which they might otherwise have been reimbursed. "Prospective" reimbursement has been tried in a number of states with mixed results.

SOURCE: Edward F. X. Hughes, "The Nation's Health: Enlightened Reform May Hold Down Health Costs," Charleston (Illinois) *Times-Courier,* March 11, 1981, p. 20.

drawback of the health maintenance organization is that it provides an impersonal brand of medicine.

It is not widely known that over 45 percent of all Medicaid spending is for nursing homes. This proportion will surely rise as the country gets older (the median age of Americans is rising). In fact, there are now more people over sixty-five than there are teenagers. The Medicaid program has a strong bias in favor of institutionalizing people, even though medical professionals agree that many people respond better to treatment when they can remain at home among family and friends. The state of New York has responded to this problem with its Nursing Home without Walls program, which provides nursing-home-level care to people in their own homes. Not only does the program produce happier patients, it saves money by eliminating the need to build new long-term-care facilities. Michigan has experimented with alternatives to institutions (which are sometimes known as "medical warehouses"). Under its Chore Services program, friends and neighbors are put to work doing household tasks for homebound patients.[38]

Deinstitutionalization has also been tried in the mental health field, but with mixed success. Between 1955 and 1984, the population in state mental hospitals dropped from 600,000 to 130,000. The reasons are various, and include the following: psychotropic drugs were developed that proved helpful in controlling patients' symptoms; treatment was thought to be more successful in a community setting than in a long-term facility; courts have ruled that institutionalized persons have a legal right to treatment, not merely custodial care; and community release was believed to be cheaper.[39]

Deinstitutionalization is opposed by residents of the communities where aftercare facilities would be located, who fear deterioration of their neighborhood, and by labor unions representing health-care employees, who fear elimination of their jobs. In addition, there have been shocking stories of patients suffering "severe and chronic mental disorders cast adrift to live alone in squalid rooming houses with no psychiatric, social, or medical care other than drugs. Many were more isolated, forgotten, and miserable than they were in the crowded back wards of institutions. Two-thirds were readmitted to hospitals, some more than once, and became known as 'revolving door' patients."[40] Nevertheless, every reported study that compares adequately funded community care with state hospital care of the chronically mentally ill has shown that community care is as effective in rehabilitation as hospital care, if not more so.

Two other health-related activities of state and local governments are disease control and sanitation. Controlling communicable diseases, especially through immunization, is an important role of public health authorities. Local health officers also inspect grocery stores, milk suppliers, and restaurants for compliance with sanitation standards.

Two additional health issues need to be addressed: limited access to medical care by poor people, and the rights of nonsmokers. As indicated earlier in the chapter, poverty is becoming increasingly concentrated in large cities. Physicians, like many upper-middle-class people, are migrating to the suburbs (see Chapter 9). In addition, some doctors do not accept Medicaid patients. The result is that in many of the inner cities with the severest health problems, there is no regular source of care; people must rely on hospital outpatient clinics or emergency rooms.

Minnesota, Nebraska, and other states have given nonsmokers the legal right to breathe smoke-free air indoors. These states allow smoking only in designated areas of restaurants, stores, hospitals, buses, offices, and other indoor, enclosed areas used as places of work or serving the general public. (Bars are exempt.) Cities may also adopt such laws, and San Francisco has one of the toughest. Smokers reply that their rights have been infringed and that these laws are a reflection of overintrusive government.[41]

HOUSING

Housing policy is primarily a federal-local responsibility. The Housing Act of 1937 established local public housing authorities that build, own, and operate public housing for low-income people. The federal Department of Housing and Urban Development (HUD) supports these local agencies with grants and loans. Local governments are not required to provide for public housing programs, however.

HUD also runs mortgage insurance programs known as FHA or VA mortgages (because the programs were originally run by the Federal Housing Administration and the Veterans Administration). The beneficiaries of these programs are middle-class people, whose mortgages are insured against default; the savings and loan companies and lending institutions that loan the money; and home builders and realtors. Mortgage insurance, which has been spectacularly successful in promoting middle-class home ownership, has also greatly encouraged the movement of people out of central cities and into the suburbs (noted in Chapter 9). Also promoting home ownership in the suburbs is the fact that mortgage interest can be deducted from federal and state income taxes, a tax break of little practical benefit to low-income people.

In 1974, Congress passed the Housing and Community Development Act, which provides community-development block grants for eliminating slums and blight. Communities applying for the money must submit three-year community-development plans showing how the needs of low-income people are being met. Section 8 of the act also provides for rent subsidies to poor people: families whose incomes are less than 80 percent of the local median income are eligible for assistance. The federal government sends the subsidy to the local housing authority, which then pays the landlord. The amount of the subsidy is the difference between 30 percent (originally 25 percent) of the family's income and HUD's determination of fair market rent. Section 8 subsidies have been a means for dispersing public housing recipients into middle-class areas and out of slums.

Another federal policy, designed to achieve the twin goals of providing adequate housing and promoting integration, is the scattered-site public housing program described in Reading 11-4. In the same vein is Section 235 of the Housing and Redevelopment Act of 1968, which encourages home ownership by low-income people. Buyers are not required to make a down payment, but must only pay a small amount in closing costs. Since many of the homes turn out to need repairs the buyers cannot pay for, the homes are frequently abandoned. And because the purchasers have little equity in the home and the mortgage is insured by the federal government, the latter ends up owning the home. Section 235 (and its counterpart, the discontinued Section 236, whose goal was the construction of rental apartments) has made the HUD the nation's largest slum landlord. Because the program did not work as planned, Section 235 has been modified and greatly scaled down.

Such has also been the case with large, multistory public housing projects. Once a staple of federal housing policy, the projects became riddled with crime, vandalism, plumbing that does not work, faulty wiring, discarded garbage, and vermin infestation. The fifty-acre Pruitt-Igoe project in St. Louis became so uninhabitable that it had to be blown up with dynamite. Chicago's Robert Taylor Homes, in which twenty-thousand poor people are stacked up in high-rise buildings, has been criticized as a "human file cabinet." The environment is so dangerous that even police are reluctant to enter. Such projects are no longer being built for families with children.

Housing policy is surely not one of government's better examples of effective problem solving: not only has no really efficient means of housing large numbers of low-income people at reasonable cost yet been found, pervasive discrimination in housing still exists, more than twenty years after passage of the 1964 Civil Rights Act. Even in California—which had a civil rights law five years before the federal one, and with broader coverage—housing discrimination is still a significant problem.[42]

Perhaps in response to this checkered record, or simply to implement its own ideological goals, the Reagan administration is seeking to fundamentally alter U.S. public housing policy. Arguing that there is no nationwide shortage of rental housing but only spot scarcities curable by rehabilitation programs and targeted apartment construction, the administration would like to end subsidies for constructing new rental housing for poor people. Instead, low-income people would be given housing vouchers similar to food stamps with which to procure rental housing. The U.S. Conference of Mayors retorts that there is a serious shortage of housing for the poor in cities across the country.[43]

READING 11-4   SCATTERED-SITE HOUSING IN CHARLOTTE, NORTH CAROLINA

CHARLOTTE, N.C.—At first glance, the attractive two-story redwood structures on Florence Avenue in southeast Charlotte appear to be another of the many new apartment developments in this booming city.

But on closer inspection it becomes evident that most of the residents of these apartments are black, while people in the surrounding neighborhood are overwhelmingly white.

This is one of four new "scattered site" public housing projects built by the Charlotte Housing Authority in middle-class, predominantly white neighborhoods of the city.

Altogether, there are 165 units in four separate locations. An additional 173 units on four more sites are planned for the near future.

When all are built, they will account for less than 10% of the total public housing in Charlotte, but they mark a significant new direction for public housing generally.

The apartments, with their all-redwood or redwood and brick exteriors, have small balconies and patios, and there is plenty of play area for children.

The grounds are landscaped and well maintained. They were ablaze with color, recently, as Charlotte enjoyed the brief but brilliant blossoming of azalea bushes and dogwood trees.

Each site has 50 or fewer units. The density ranges from four to eight units an acre, which is lower than at most private apartment developments in the area.

All of this is a far cry from the overcrowded, crime-infested, poorly maintained buildings that frequently are associated with public housing.

"I think the gut reaction to public housing is 'Yes, it's needed but don't put it in my neighborhood,'" said Larry Loyd, assistant director of the Charlotte Housing Authority.

"We're trying to show people that we're not putting in junk, that these are attractive, well-designed units that provide a far better environment for the residents. We're hoping we can overcome the negative reaction to public housing."

Congress and the U.S. Department of Housing and Urban Development have been encouraging the "scattered site" approach to public housing for several years, but few cities have shown much interest. Why did the idea take hold in Charlotte?

The most important reason was a suit filed in 1970 by a group of black residents, represented by the NAACP Legal Defense Fund, against the city, the Housing Authority and HUD.

The suit charged that these agencies, by constructing thousands of public housing units on the west side of Charlotte in the 1950s and '60s, had unlawfully contributed to racial segregation and had deprived black residents of equal opportunity to obtain good housing.

The case was handled by Julius Chambers, the same local black attorney who won a school desegregation suit that produced a landmark U.S. Supreme Court decision upholding mandatory busing as a desegregation technique.

The case was heard by the same federal judge, James B. McMillan, who ordered the extensive countywide busing plan that was subsequently upheld by the Supreme Court. . . . The Charlotte Housing Authority agreed not to build any more public housing in "racially impacted" areas—those with more than 40% minority population—and to scatter future units on small sites throughout the city. (About 30% of Charlotte's population of 350,000 is black.)

Although the lawsuit, which was later dropped, served as a prod, local observers also give credit to Charlotte's business and political leaders for deciding to move ahead with "scattered site" housing even though it was strongly opposed by many residents.

"The city fathers here just took the bull by the horns," said Ray H. Wheeling, executive director of the Housing Authority. "They said, 'We'll take the flak on this' and they did."

The concept also was supported by the city's two major newspapers. . . .

When Charlotte Housing Authority officials set out to find and purchase new sites, however, they encountered stiff opposition.

To obtain the first four locations, it was necessary to use "many gimmicks to disguise the purpose," said Harvey Gantt, an architect who was the only black on the City Council at the time.

After sites were obtained, local homeowners' organizations sprang into action. They filed two suits in state court to halt construction but lost both.

Finally, last July, more than six years after the "memo of understanding" was signed, the first two sites were opened, followed by two more in September. . . .

Although the intent is to place public housing in all parts of the city, so far the locations have been in lower-middle-class or middle-class neighborhoods. At least two of the neighborhoods were already changing from predominantly white to racially mixed.

The only site selected in affluent South Charlotte required a zoning change, and that lost in the City Council by one vote—under pressure from prosperous homeowners.

There is a long-range hope that placing mostly black public housing in predominantly white neighborhoods will integrate the schools and make it possible to reduce the amount of busing required to carry out the desegregation plan.

The scattered-site projects have their flaws.

Because they are located in predominantly white neighborhoods, land costs more than sites for most public housing, sometimes more than HUD will pay.

The scattered sites tend to be far from jobs and public transportation there is poor.

More important, perhaps, the black families in the projects appear to be quite isolated from the whites living around them.

For these reasons, and because any public housing—no matter how handsome or well located—"tends to stigmatize the tenant," Gantt said he had his doubts about the new projects even as he was fighting on the City Council to have them approved.

SOURCE: William Trombley, "Scattered Sites—New Wrinkle in Public Housing," *Los Angeles Times,* May 7, 1980, p. I-30. Copyright 1980, *Los Angeles Times.* Reprinted by permission.

EDUCATION

Education once again became an important political issue in the 1980s as the presidentially appointed National Commission on Excellence in Education declared that "the educational foundations of our society are presently being eroded by a rising tide of mediocrity." Perhaps melodramatically, the commission went on to declare, "If an unfriendly foreign power had attempted to impose on America the mediocre educational performance that exists today, we might well have viewed it as an act of war."[44]

Reforms

The commission suggested numerous reforms. The average school day should be increased from six hours to seven, and the school year lengthened from 180 school days to 200. Teacher salaries should be increased in order to attract higher-quality people, and teachers should have an eleven-month contract. High school students should be assigned "far more homework." All high school students should be required to take four years of English, three years each of mathematics, science, and social studies, plus one-half year of computer science. College entrance requirements should be raised in these areas as well as in foreign languages.

The commission was particularly concerned about declining student test scores. In the federally funded testing program conducted by the National Assessment of Educational Progress, the top quarter of elementary and secondary students dropped the most between 1970 and 1980. (However, the greatest improvement was registered by the bottom quarter, especially black elementary school students.)

David Gardner, the president of the University of California, who headed the presidential commission, said that in the last fifteen years academic and vocational courses have been "systematically devalued" and replaced by remedial and personal development courses that "prepare young people for almost nothing." High school students are taking far fewer history, science, mathematics, and foreign language courses, but more health, physical education, remedial English and remedial math, and especially driver's education courses. Gardner was particularly critical of the latter, saying "My father went to a small, rural school in southern Utah, and the thought of substituting 'how to ride a horse' for English would never have occurred to him."[45]

Almost all of the commission's recommendations will cost a great deal of money, but no new money will be forthcoming from the Reagan administration. Whether state and local governments can, or will, fund such proposals will be discussed later in the chapter. Raising teacher salaries is a particularly expensive item, but the Carnegie Foundation for the Advancement of Teaching claims that "the teaching profession is in a crisis state because low pay and low morale are driving the most qualified young persons into other careers.[46] The foundation further contends that the caliber of those choosing elementary and secondary teaching as a career is low and getting lower. One hotly debated reform is merit pay for teachers. State and local governments adopting such a proposal have frequently given across-the-board merit raises to virtually all employees, thus negating the measure's "merit" aspects. On the other hand, if different merit raises are given to different people, the amounts had better be kept secret. Moreover, if school administrators select merit-pay recipients, there is the possibility of favoritism. California has adopted a modified form of merit pay called the *mentor-teacher program*. Teachers and school officials select outstanding instructors to receive extra salary for helping new teachers and developing curriculum; only 5 percent of the instructors can qualify.

Testing Laws

Over the last decade, the public has become increasingly concerned that many young people are graduating from high school without mastering basic skills in reading, writing, and mathematics. In response, almost all state legislatures have passed *minimum competency testing laws*. Legislators point to the fact that education is the largest item in the state budget, and that it is nearly twice as large as the second item (welfare)—is the public getting its money's worth? Opponents of minimum competency testing, who are usually liberals, argue that the exams do not test the instruction actually provided students, are unfair to students who are the victims of past racial discrimination (as in Florida), and are culturally biased against blacks and students who speak only limited English. One way for school districts to deal with the third objection (but not the first two) is to administer *functional skills tests*, which feature questions such as how to compute one's gas mileage or how to fill out an employment application. Other thorny questions concern the cutoff line for passing the test: Will educators set it so low that almost anyone can pass? If it is set high and many students therefore fail, will parents continue to support the program? Moreover, do school districts have the financial resources to provide the remedial instruction for students who fail the tests?

If the minimum competency of students can be tested, why not do the same for prospective teachers? Twenty states administer a basic skills test, a subject matter test, or a professional teaching skills test. The results have occasionally been startling. In Louisiana, less than two thirds of prospective teachers could pass the test developed by the Educational Testing Service (ETS); many are said to be moving out of the state to avoid the testing law. A recent poll of nearly two thousand experienced teachers by Louis Harris indicates that they prefer periodic testing of *practicing* teachers in their subject areas—a reform vigorously opposed by teachers' unions.[47]

The Expanding Role of the State

As we saw in Chapter 9, the Progressive reformers of the early twentieth century tried to take many areas of government, but especially education, "out of politics." Such a position could not be sustained in the 1980s, if for no other reason than the substantial amounts of public money involved. The issue is well summarized by Ellis Katz:

> For generations, the educational community struggled to remove education from the political arena. Behind a posture of professional expertise, it succeeded in having school board elections separated from general elections, giving local school districts independent taxing power, granting tenure to system professionals, and settling policy disputes among themselves. Today, however, the social and economic conditions that supported that image of professionalism and independence have changed so that education has become more of a political than a technical issue. Public dissatisfaction with the schools, the rapidly growing cost of education, and the development of special interest groups have combined to thrust education squarely into the political arena. Thus, solutions to educational problems will be more a result of general political leadership than of initiatives from a separate and independent educational community.[48]

Not only has education become political, it has become increasingly a matter for state, rather than local, concern. Frederick Wirt perhaps overstates when he writes that "local control is meaningless, . . . fully a myth," but his point is well taken.[49] Note in Table 11-6 that the states

TABLE 11-6   Estimated Revenue Receipts for Elementary and Secondary Schools,† Percentage Distribution by Level of Government, School Years 1970–1983

	1982–83ᵖ			1969–70		
	Federal	*State*	*Local**	*Federal*	*State*	*Local**
U.S. Average	7.4%	50.3%	42.3%	7.2%	40.9%	51.8%
New England	5.3	37.0	57.7	4.6	23.8	71.6
Connecticut	4.9	36.4	58.7	2.1	25.2	72.8
Maine	10.1	49.7	40.2	6.7	32.5	60.8
Massachusetts	4.8	39.4	55.8	6.0	20.0	74.0
New Hampshire	3.9	6.9	89.2	5.1	8.3	86.7
Rhode Island	4.7	37.0	58.3	5.9	35.3	58.8
Vermont	7.0	35.2	57.8	2.9	37.1	60.0
Mideast	5.2	42.0	52.7	5.9	41.6	52.5
Delaware	11.2	67.6	21.1	7.4	71.3	21.3
Dist. of Col.	15.5	n.a.	84.5	30.2	n.a.	69.8
Maryland	5.9	40.2	53.9	6.4	35.2	58.4
New Jersey	3.5	40.0	56.4	5.4	27.0	67.6
New York	4.0	41.9	54.1	4.7	46.4	48.9
Pennsylvania	7.5	45.2	47.4	6.2	46.2	47.6
Great Lakes	7.0	40.5	52.5	8.7	42.8	48.5
Illinois	8.5	38.0	53.4	12.8	41.2	46.0

TABLE 11-6 *(continued)*

	1982–83ᴾ			1969–70		
	Federal	*State*	*Local**	*Federal*	*State*	*Local**
Indiana	6.3	58.6	35.1	6.9	56.1	37.0
Michigan	8.1	36.1	55.8	7.4	42.7	49.9
Ohio	5.0	40.7	54.3	7.7	40.6	51.6
Wisconsin	5.4	37.4	57.2	5.5	37.6	56.8
Plains	6.5	42.4	51.1	7.7	42.7	49.7
Iowa	7.3	42.1	50.6	6.7	42.2	51.0
Kansas	4.8	44.4	50.8	6.9	43.3	49.8
Minnesota	4.7	48.9	46.3	6.1	56.6	37.3
Missouri	8.1	39.6	52.3	9.7	36.7	53.6
Nebraska	7.1	27.9	65.0	7.9	18.2	73.9
North Dakota	7.3	51.5	41.1	7.7	46.5	45.7
South Dakota	8.7	27.6	63.7	13.9	20.8	65.3
Southeast	11.2	56.8	32.0	12.9	54.0	33.1
Alabama	14.8	64.3	21.0	15.2	63.3	21.5
Arkansas	13.3	54.3	32.4	18.2	44.5	37.5
Florida	7.1	61.9	31.0	9.5	55.7	34.8
Georgia	10.2	55.6	34.2	10.5	58.3	31.1
Kentucky	10.7	70.5	18.7	13.6	56.2	30.2
Louisiana	9.4	55.9	34.7	11.9	56.4	31.7
Mississippi	23.0	53.3	23.7	21.4	52.4	26.2
North Carolina	16.1	61.5	22.4	15.6	65.7	18.7
South Carolina	13.6	57.1	29.3	14.0	59.5	26.4
Tennessee	13.0	47.2	39.8	11.9	48.0	40.1
Virginia	6.6	41.6	51.8	11.1	36.4	52.5
West Virginia	9.0	62.4	28.5	12.4	48.2	39.4
Southwest	10.2	53.2	36.6	10.1	47.3	42.6
Arizona	11.4	45.7	42.9	8.2	46.4	45.4
New Mexico	10.2	77.8	12.0	17.7	61.9	20.4
Oklahoma	10.3	60.2	29.5	11.8	43.8	44.4
Texas	10.0	50.6	39.5	9.3	46.4	44.3
Rocky Mountain	5.8	45.1	49.2	8.8	33.8	57.3
Colorado	5.4	36.9	57.7	7.6	27.9	64.5
Idaho	6.9	62.6	30.4	8.4	37.8	53.8
Montana	8.5	47.4	44.2	8.5	25.4	66.2
Utah	5.2	56.3	38.5	7.6	52.8	39.5
Wyoming	4.0	34.7	61.3	20.2	24.8	55.0
Far West	5.9	78.1	16.0	5.6	38.6	55.8
California	5.7	78.3	16.0	5.3	37.3	57.4
Nevada	5.3	85.8	8.9	8.8	36.5	54.7
Oregon	9.9	89.8	0.3	6.0	20.8	73.2
Washington	7.6	60.6	31.8	6.6	56.6	36.8
Alaska	8.8	36.8	54.4	27.1	53.3	19.6
Hawaii	5.4	75.2	19.4	9.7	87.2	3.2

SOURCE: *Significant Features of Fiscal Federalism, 1982–83* (Washington, D.C.: Advisory Commission on Intergovernmental Relations, 1984), p. 28.

* Local and other revenue.   p = preliminary.
† Revenue receipts were used as a substitute measure of education expenditure by level of government.

have now become the dominant fiscal partner in educational funding, supplying over half of the money. However, the average is greatly lifted by states in the Southeast and the Far West. Whatever the region, the threat to withhold state educational aid is enough to bring a local school district into line. The reasons for this centralization, some of which were noted in the last chapter, include court decisions in the area of school finance (to be discussed shortly).

Even without court decisions limiting the use of the property tax, the fact that this levy is overburdened would have increased the state's role. Not only did states change their funding formulas, but they expanded their role in curriculum, achievement testing, and accountability.[50] Federal government involvement in education (to be discussed later in the chapter) has stimulated state departments of education to become more active in educational planning, evaluation, and program development. Moreover, the "once monolithic education community has developed internal divisions, and state legislators are besieged by conflicting demands from teacher unions, local school boards, school administrators, community colleges, state universities, and a multitude of other special interest groups," such as taxpayers, parents, racial or ethnic or religious minorities, teachers, those who sell goods or services to schools (such as contractors who build schools and suppliers of sports equipment or textbooks), and students (especially if they are poor or handicapped).[51] In addition, as the roster of participants in educational policy making has increased, the "pie" of resources to be distributed or redistributed has grown smaller because of tax and expenditure limitations. These limitations have frequently forced the state to step in and bail out school districts or even to curtail its own expenditures.

Table 11-7 shows each state's spending per student and its ability to finance that spending. (See Chapter 10 for a definition of tax capacity.) The range is quite large, with Alaska and New York at the top and Alabama and South Carolina at the bottom. An interesting question is whether more spending leads to better results. The ten states whose college-bound students scored the highest on the Scholastic Aptitude Tests (SATs) or the American College Test (ACT) are California, Colorado, Delaware, Iowa, Minnesota, Nebraska, New Hampshire, Oregon, Vermont, and Wisconsin.[52] Four of these ten states are below average in spending according to Table 11-7, with New Hampshire being way below the average.

Court decisions in twenty-five states have required reforms in state and local school-finance patterns. Courts have declared that the manner in which the property tax was used to finance public schools in those states is a violation of the equal protection clause of the state constitution because a district with a higher tax *base* (one with highly assessed industrial, commercial, or residential real estate) could set a lower tax *rate* and still generate higher school revenue. The judicial reasoning is that the property

TABLE 11-7   Spending per Pupil and Tax Capacity

State	1982–83 School Year Spending per Pupil	1981 Tax Capacity	State	1982–83 School Year Spending per Pupil	1981 Tax Capacity
Alaska	$6103	$324	Washington	2706	99
New York	3888	89	Oklahoma	2629	127
New Jersey	3807	105	Ohio	2609	94
Delaware	3679	111	Missouri	2587	92
Michigan	3648	96	Virginia	2551	94
Connecticut	3464	110	Indiana	2530	91
Rhode Island	3463	80	North Carolina	2525	80
Oregon	3399	99	California	2507	115
Wyoming	3260	216	Maine	2498	79
Wisconsin	3216	91	Nebraska	2488	97
Maryland	3192	98	West Virginia	2480	90
Pennsylvania	3031	90	Louisiana	2321	117
Iowa	3022	102	South Dakota	2289	86
Minnesota	2987	100	Georgia	2243	81
Hawaii	2983	105	New Hampshire	2187	95
Illinois	2960	104	Nevada	2178	148
North Dakota	2933	123	Texas	2162	132
Kansas	2917	109	Idaho	2110	87
Colorado	2850	113	Kentucky	2056	82
Massachusetts	2803	96	Utah	2016	86
Montana	2793	114	Tennessee	2003	79
Florida	2768	101	Mississippi	1995	72
New Mexico	2759	114	Arkansas	1988	82
Total U.S.	2748	100	South Carolina	1892	75
Vermont	2741	84	Alabama	1507	74
Arizona	2727	89			

SOURCES: *National Journal,* October 15, 1983, p. 2106; and *Significant Features of Fiscal Federalism, 1982–83* (Washington, D.C.: Advisory Commission on Intergovernmental Relations, 1984), p. 92.

tax, as previously employed, made the quality of a student's education (defined in terms of the amount of money spent per pupil) dependent on the presence of nearby industry or high-priced homes. Although the U.S. Supreme Court has ruled that this method of school finance does not violate the U.S. Constitution, legislatures in these twenty-five states have shifted a greater responsibility for school funding to the state level (and state taxes).

The reasoning of the courts in these various states ignores some significant factors. Spending varies not only among districts in a state, but also among schools in the same district. Schools serving an upper-class clientele tend to receive more largess than schools with a lower-class student body. Moreover, since about three fourths of a school district's budget is for salaries and other personnel costs, the fact that one district spends more money than another district means primarily that teachers are better paid in the higher-spending district. The National Commission on Excellence in Education is correct when it says that teachers should be paid more money, but it does not automatically follow that better-paid teachers lead to better-educated students.

Finally, there is the question of whether school spending is the prime determinant of student learning. James S. Coleman, in a massive study of 600,000 students, their parents, and their schools done for the U.S. Office of Education, found that school resources are far less important in explaining student scores on standard achievement tests than are the student's home environment and the motivation he or she received from attending school with capable students.[53] School expenditures, facilities, and curriculum are much less significant than a factor beyond the reach of the school: early home environment.

Christopher Jencks and his associates set out to reanalyze Coleman's data and to refute him, but they ended up concluding that "the evidence we have examined does not suggest that doubling expenditures would raise students' performance on standardized tests."[54] On the other hand, one could argue that standardized tests do not measure such important aspects of schooling as appreciation of the arts, creativity, curiosity about other people and other cultures, good citizenship, and love of learning.

Federal Aid to Education

As Table 11-6 indicates, some states depend much more on federal education aid than other states. States in the Southeast and Southwest really seem to rely on this money. Federal aid to education is not intended to provide general support for elementary and secondary education, but is targeted for certain (categorical) purposes, such as for low-income or educationally deprived children, handicapped children, or bilingual education. The Elementary and Secondary Education Act of 1965 is particularly important legislation in this area. Ironically, some federal aid programs may have the inadvertent effect of harming the children they are intended to help. Teachers complain of the problem of *multiple pullouts:* children who are poor are temporarily removed from regular classes so that they may receive federally aided special instruction. If these children are also bilingual or handicapped, they are pulled out of class for additional assistance as well. The result is that these students miss out on their core courses of instruction. In a different vein, substantial amounts of federal aid also go to higher education.

Bilingual Education

In the area of bilingual education, school districts must comply with the U.S. Supreme Court's ruling in the 1974 case of *Lau* v. *Nichols*, 414 U.S. 563, that schools must provide extra assistance to children who cannot speak or read English. Reversing the decisions of previous administrations, President Reagan has decided to allow local officials to use "any effective approach" to teaching non-English-speaking students, including total immersion in English-only classes. Education officials in the Reagan administration have criticized previous bilingual guidelines as expensive and excessive regulation by which the federal government dictated to local schools what subject matter to teach.

Bilingual education is an intensely political issue, as are busing for purposes of integration, the teaching of "creationism," censorship of textbooks and library books, and strikes by teachers' unions. None of these are topics over which education professionals can claim that their expertise gives them the right to make a final decision. On one side of the bilingual education issue are those who say that pre-Reagan responses to the *Lau* decision overemphasized students' learning to speak their native tongue and that children were becoming dependent on that language. They frequently argue that children of previous generations, who may have spoken only Italian or Polish or Russian at home, were able to learn English fairly quickly. In vehement opposition are those Hispanic militants who want to maintain a distinct cultural identity based on a common language and who fear assimilation of their children. Complicating matters are the large number of people who have been trained, certified, and hired to teach bilingual classes and who fear loss of their jobs. However the bilingual controversy is finally resolved, school districts should proceed with caution if using the total-immersion approach, lest they traumatize children who speak little or no English and thereby increase the already high dropout rates among these students. Although students have a right to instruction in a language they can understand, a failure to learn English bars them from many later opportunities for well-paying employment.

Increased Enrollment

Yet another problem facing elementary and secondary education is how to accommodate enrollments swelled by the children of post–World War II "baby boomers." After many years of enrollment decline, schools must now provide more teachers, classrooms, and other facilities, especially in rapidly growing areas of the Sunbelt. Many of the children of this "baby boomlet" are minorities whose populations are growing faster than the white population. The existing shortage of science, mathematics, and bilingual education teachers is being severely worsened by this recent development.

Public Higher Education

Public higher education in the states is provided by three different types of colleges: flagship universities, state universities, and community colleges. The *flagship universities* are the most prestigious in the state

TABLE 11-8   Appropriations per Student

	1981–82 State and Local Appropriations per Student		Adjusted for System Cost	
	Amount	Rank	Amount	Rank
Alabama	$ 3,205	36	$ 3,186	31
Alaska	12,712	1	16,403	1
Arizona	3,193	37	3,305	27
Arkansas	3,441	26	3,070	35
California	4,087	11	4,797	4
Colorado	2,874	44	2,582	47
Connecticut	3,862	15	4,202	6
Delaware	3,129	39	3,236	30
Florida	3,547	24	3,959	12
Georgia	4,492	5	4,011	11
Hawaii	4,662	4	4,012	10
Idaho	3,643	20	4,039	8
Illinois	3,676	19	3,625	19
Indiana	3,377	29	3,141	33
Iowa	4,101	10	3,412	24
Kansas	3,587	23	3,130	34
Kentucky	3,975	13	3,715	17
Louisiana	4,017	12	3,619	20
Maine	2,886	43	3,025	38
Maryland	3,383	28	2,989	39
Massachusetts	2,764	45	3,177	32
Michigan	2,993	42	2,937	41
Minnesota	3,330	30	2,971	40
Mississippi	3,842	16	3,684	18
Missouri	3,008	41	3,057	36
Montana	3,257	33	3,533	22
Nebraska	3,773	17	2,801	44
Nevada	3,154	38	3,908	13
New Hampshire	1,943	50	2,028	50
New Jersey	3,207	35	3,369	26
New Mexico	4,320	7	3,874	14
New York	4,795	3	5,079	3
North Carolina	4,156	8	4,398	5
North Dakota	3,890	14	4,035	9
Ohio	2,745	46	2,523	48
Oklahoma	3,406	27	2,924	42
Oregon	3,320	31	3,239	29
Pennsylvania	3,613	21	3,584	21
Rhode Island	3,458	25	3,455	23
South Carolina	4,112	9	3,745	15
South Dakota	2,545	48	2,594	46
Tennessee	3,059	40	2,814	43
Texas	4,354	6	4,174	7
Utah	3,609	22	3,033	37
Vermont	2,403	49	2,205	49

TABLE 11-8 *(continued)*

	1981–82 State and Local Appropriations per Student		Adjusted for System Cost	
	Amount	Rank	Amount	Rank
Virginia	3,237	34	3,375	25
Washington	2,710	47	2,760	45
West Virginia	3,742	18	3,716	16
Wisconsin	3,314	32	3,259	28
Wyoming	6,608	2	7,552	2
U.S. average	$3,646		$ 3,646	

SOURCE: "How the Fifty States Rank,"*Chronicle of Higher Education,* February 24, 1982, p. 8. Copyright 1982 by *The Chronicle of Higher Education.* Reprinted by permission.

system, have the highest admission standards, and have a heavily research-oriented faculty. Examples are the main campuses of the University of Minnesota, the University of Texas, and the University of Washington. The *state universities* usually began as teachers' colleges, and they still perform that role as well as providing instruction in a broad range of fields, such as science, the liberal arts, and business. The *community colleges,* or *junior colleges,* have a two-year program in which students take courses in vocational education, courses for transfer to a four-year university, or courses for personal development. These colleges are usually locally funded and administered, but they receive substantial amounts of state aid.

The left-hand column in Table 11-8 ranks the states according to state and local appropriations per college student. However, such a listing can be highly misleading because some states, such as Hawaii and Iowa, have a large number of students in universities emphasizing research, which is an expensive endeavor. Florida and California, on the other hand, have emphasized community colleges, which are much less costly per student. The right-hand column shows how the states rank when *system costs* are considered. In addition to tax revenue, public universities receive substantial amounts of money from student fees, from research contracts, from endowments (especially the University of California, the University of Texas, the University of Minnesota, and the Massachusetts Institute of Technology), and from the sales of football tickets and television royalties (especially if the team is playing well).

Federal aid is particularly important in the form of such student-grants programs as Pell Grants, the Guaranteed Student Loan Program, and National Direct Student Loans. The Reagan administration has reduced funds for these programs and would like to end loans to students whose families earn more than $30,000 per year.

SUMMARY

According to one description, "three of the major functions of most states are the care of the insane, prisoners, and university students."[55] As we have seen, state and local governments provide these services and many more. The five policy areas considered in this chapter (law enforcement, welfare, health, housing, and education) are the focus of social services. In the next chapter, we will study services that are implemented less for the benefit of specific categories of people with particular needs, and more because these services are thought to benefit the state as a whole.

NOTES

1. V. O. Key, Jr., *Southern Politics in State and Nation* (New York: Knopf, 1949); and Key, *American State Politics* (New York: Knopf, 1956).

2. Thomas R. Dye, *Politics, Economics, and the Public* (Chicago: Rand McNally, 1966). See also Richard E. Dawson and James A. Robinson, "Inter-Party Competition, Economic Variables and Welfare Policies in the American States," *Journal of Politics*, 25 (May 1963), 265–89.

3. David R. Morgan, *Handbook of State Policy Indicators*, 4th ed. (Norman: University of Oklahoma Bureau of Government Research, 1982), pp. 10–11.

4. Ira Sharkansky, *Spending in the American States* (Chicago: Rand McNally, 1969), p. 147.

5. Mark R. Daniels, "Domestic Violence Policy and the American States" (paper presented at the annual meeting of the Western Political Science Association, San Francisco, 1980); Lee Sigelman and Roland E. Smith, "Consumer Legislation in the American States," *Social Science Quarterly*, 61 (June 1980), 58–70; Charles S. Perry, "Energy Conservation Policy in the American States," *Social Science Quarterly*, 62 (September 1981), 540–46; Michael Le May, "Expenditure and Nonexpenditure Measures of State Urban Policy Output," *American Politics Quarterly*, 1 (October 1973), 511–28; William Gormley, Jr., "Nonelectoral Participation as a Response to Issue-Specific Conditions: The Case of Public Utility Regulation," *Social Science Quarterly*, 62 (September 1981), 527–39; Lee Sigelman et al., "Social Service Innovation in the American States," *Social Science Quarterly*, 62 (September 1981), 503–15.

6. Sharkansky, *Spending in the American States*, p. 114. Sharkansky's findings are disputed in Gillian Dean and Kathleen Peroff, "The Spending-Service Cliche," *American Politics Quarterly*, 5 (October 1977), 501–16.

7. Jay Goodman, *The Dynamics of Urban Government and Politics*, 2nd ed. (New York: Macmillan, 1980), p. 250; see also "Fear of Crime 'Paralyzes' U.S.," *Chicago Tribune*, September 21, 1980, p. 1-1. Rape and domestic violence are especiallly underreported to police.

8. Clarence N. Stone et al., *Urban Policy and Politics*, 2nd ed. (Englewood Cliffs, N.J.: Prentice-Hall, 1986), p. 293.

9. James Q. Wilson, *Varieties of Police Behavior* (Cambridge, Mass.: Harvard University Press, 1968), p. 7. Emphasis added.

10. Joseph Wambaugh, *The New Centurians* (Boston: Little, Brown, 1970), pp. 170–71. Emphasis in original.

11. Alan Bent and Ralph Rossum, *Police, Criminal Justice, and the Community* (New York: Harper & Row, Pub., 1976), p. 77.

12. Arthur Niederhoffer, *Behind the Shield* (New York: Doubleday, 1967), p. 53.

13. Stone et al., *Urban Policy and Politics*, p. 304.

14. "Threat Posed by Career Criminals Rising," *Los Angeles Times*, March 4, 1985, p. I-11.

15. "Study Takes Aim at 'Intensive' Criminals," *Los Angeles Times*, September 6, 1977, p. I-3.

16. Peter W. Greenwood with Allan Abrahamse, *Selective Incapacitation* (Santa Monica, Calif: Rand Corporation, 1982). The prominent role of drugs in the scale can be attributed to the possibility that nearly half of all street crimes are related to the need of drug users to finance their expensive habit.

17. James Q. Wilson, *Thinking about Crime*, rev. ed. (New York: Basic Books, 1983), pp. 155, 158.

18. Extensive reviews of rehabilitation studies are presented in R. G. Hood, "Research on the Effectiveness of Punishments and Treatments," in *Crime and Justice*. Vol. III, *The Criminal in Confinement*, ed. Leon Radzinowicz and Marvin Wolfgang (New York: Basic Books, 1971), pp. 159–82; Walter C. Bailey, "Correctional Outcome: An Evaluation of 100 Reports," in ibid., pp. 187–95; Robert Martinson, "What Works: Questions and Answers about Prison Reform," *Public Interest*, Spring 1974, pp. 22–54; and James Q. Wilson, "'What Works?' Revisited: New Findings on Rehabilitation," *Public Interest*, Fall 1980, pp. 3–17.

19. Quoted in Deborah Bowditch, "State Prisons: Is Crisis a Way of Life?" *State Legislatures*, May 1980, pp. 7, 10. See also "Prison Overcrowding," *Editorial Research Reports*, November 25, 1983, pp. 885–86.

20. Radzinowicz and Wolfgang, *The Criminal in Confinement*, p. 141.

21. "Huge Disparities in Jail Time," *National Law Journal*, February 23, 1981, p. 1.

22. "Prison Industries: Factories with Fences," *State Government News*, June 1982, p. 18. The Kansas program is aided by the fact that Kansas is a "right-to-work" state, a very controversial issue noted in the next chapter.

23. Albert J. Reiss, Jr., *The Police and the Public* (New Haven: Yale University Press, 1971), p. 147. Jerome Skolnick has shown how it is possible for white police officers to be racially prejudiced yet carry out their work relatively evenhandedly. See his *Justice without Trial* (New York: John Wiley, 1966), pp. 84–86.

24. "Weaker Standards in Minority Arrests Cited," *Los Angeles Times*, July 1, 1983, p. I-3; "Blacks, Latinos Get Longer Sentences, Study Concludes," *Los Angeles Times*, June 30, 1983, p. I-1.

25. "25 Million Households Hit by Crime in 1982," *Los Angeles Times*, June 13, 1983, p. I-5.

26. Neil Peirce, "Corruption in the States," *Washington Post*, April 19, 1975, p. A-18; "A Critical Early Test Faces President Carter," *Los Angeles Times*, January 9, 1977, p. IV-1.

27. John Mikesell, *Fiscal Administration* (Homewood, Il.: Dorsey, 1982), pp. 62–64. This discussion of public-sector corruption is not intended to imply that such corruption is necessarily more common than private-sector corruption, or "white-collar" crime.

28. See the aptly titled "Oklahoma! Where the Graft Comes Sweepin' Down the Plain," *Time*, October 12, 1981, p. 31.

29. "Judge Convicted of Selling Justice 'Like Apples,'" *Los Angeles Times*, July 14, 1985, p. I-1.

30. John G. Peters and Susan Welch, "Political Corruption in America," *American Political Science Review*, 72 (September 1978), 976–81.

31. Barry Rundquist et al., "Corrupt Politicians and Their Electoral Support," *American Political Science Review*, 71 (September 1977), 961.

32. "Reagan's Polarized America," *Newsweek*, April 5, 1982, p. 21. The rise in poverty families headed by a woman can be attributed in part to an increasing divorce rate and an increasing rate of out-of-wedlock births that is characteristic of Americans in general.

33. James N. Morgan et al., *Five Thousand American Families* (Ann Arbor, Mich.: Institute for Social Research, 1974).

34. Robert Albritton, "Subsidies: Welfare and Transportation," in *Politics in the American States*, 4th ed., ed. Virginia Gray, Herbert Jacob, and Kenneth N. Vines (Boston: Little, Brown, 1983), p. 396.

35. Roy Bahl, *Financing State and Local Government in the 1980s* (New York: Oxford University Press, 1984), p. 23.

36. See for example, "Reagan's Polarized America," p. 20.

37. Steven D. Gold, "Recent Developments in State Finances," *National Tax Journal,* 36 (March 1983), 16.

38. Russ Hereford, "Controlling Health Care Costs," *State Legislatures,* March 1980, p. 21; "For States Squeezed by Medicaid Costs, the Worst Crunch Is Still to Come," *National Journal,* January 10, 1981, p. 49; Peter B. Levine, "An Overview of the State Role in the United States Health Scene," in *Health Politics and Policy,* ed. Theodor S. Litman and Leonard J. Robins (New York: John Wiley, 1984), p. 211.

39. "Deinstitutionalization: Does It Work?" *State Government News,* October 1980, p. 3.

40. *Health Policy* (Washington, D.C.: Congressional Quarterly, 1980), p. 84. See also C.K. Aldrich, "Deinstitutionalization," *University of Virginia News Letter,* 62 (September 1985), 4.

41. "Minnesota Clears Air for Nonsmokers," *Chicago Tribune,* October 20, 1980, p. 4-12. See also H. Jack Geiger, "The Nation's Health: Sideways Leap May Be a Step Backward," Charleston (Illinois) *Times-Courier,* March 18, 1981, p. 18.

42. "Housing Bias Remains Rampant in California and U.S.," *Los Angeles Times,* May 3, 1984, p. I-1.

43. "Vouchers Shift Thrust of Housing Policy," *Congressional Quarterly Weekly Report,* June 2, 1984, p. 1328; Neal Peirce, "Mini-Scandals Steal Thunder of Bold Strokes on Housing," *Los Angeles Times,* June 25, 1984, p. II-7; "U.S. Cities' Housing for Poor Scarce, Mayors' Study Says," *Sacramento Bee,* June 15, 1984, p. A7.

44. "Schools' 'Rising Mediocrity' Decried," *Sacramento Bee,* April 27, 1983, p. A1. The title of the commission's report is *A Nation at Risk.*

45. Quoted in "'Devaluation' of Traditional Education Hit," *Los Angeles Times,* March 18, 1983, p. I-3.

46. "U.S. Teaching in Crisis over Low Pay, Morale, Carnegie Study Finds, *"Los Angeles Times,* August 24, 1983, p. I-9. The title of the foundation's report is *"The Condition of Teaching: A State-by-State Analysis.*

47. "Poll: Teachers Back Reform," *Sacramento Bee,* June 28, 1984, p. A14.

48. Ellis Katz, "The States Rediscovered: Education Policymaking in the 1970s," *State Government,* 53 (Winter 1980), 32.

49. Frederick Wirt, "Institutionalization: Prison and School Policies," in *Politics in the American States,* ed. Gray, Jacob, and Vines, pp. 305, 320.

50. Katz, The "States Rediscovered," p. 31.

51. Ibid. See also Wirt, "Institutionalization," pp. 305, 308.

52. "New Federal Report Card Grades States' Education," *San Diego Tribune,* January 5, 1984, p. A1.

53. James S. Coleman et al., *Equality of Educational Opportunity* (Washington, D.C.: Government Printing Office, 1966).

54. Christopher Jencks et al., *Inequality* (New York: Basic Books, 1972), p. 93.

55. George C. S. Benson, Steven Maaranen, and Alan Heslop, *Political Corruption in America* (Lexington, Mass.: Heath, Lexington Books, 1978), p. 119.

chapter 12

Policy Areas: System–Maintenance Services

In this chapter we will study those state and local public policies intended to maintain the governmental and economic system in good working order: transportation policy, energy policy, environmental protection, water policy and the promotion of agriculture, and economic regulation. Because all of the states' residents are thought to benefit collectively from these system-maintenance services, they are sometimes termed *collective goods*.

TRANSPORTATION

Transportation-related services are an important state function: states spend more money on only two other services, education and social welfare. As an example, Missouri has over 110,000 miles of state-maintained roads, which is enough pavement to circle the earth at the equator four times.

Traffic from state to state is carried by the forty-thousand-mile interstate highway system consisting of freeways designated I-10, I-40, I-80, and so on. The system, now virtually complete, was built by the states, which matched every ninety dollars of federal funding for the project with ten dollars of their own. The interstate system constitutes only 2 percent of the nation's surfaced highways, but it carries more than 20 percent of all highway traffic.

Highway Expenditures

State spending on highways is conditioned not only by state wealth and population, but also by physical characteristics. Rural, spread-out states spend much more money on highways than densely populated small ones. Mountainous states literally face more obstacles than the flat prairie states of the Midwest. Weather also takes its toll: rain, snow, ice, the freeze-and-thaw cycle, and the use of road salt during winter vary from state to state. These factors are reflected in the state rankings shown in Table 12-1.

Note also that spending on highways has decreased in recent years, reflecting lower gas-tax receipts as motorists select more fuel-efficient cars. Since the characteristics of the motor fuels tax were described in Chapter 10, we might note here only that almost thirty states have no tax or a reduced tax on gasohol. Although it is a worthy conservation goal to promote this mixture of 90 percent gasoline and 10 percent alcohol, a small or nonexistent tax on it results in lower tax receipts. Motor vehicle registration fees (the license plate charge) are also an important source of road money. This fee can be based on either the horsepower or the weight of the car, which assumes that more powerful or heavier vehicles will do more road damage. Or it can be based on the cash value of the car, which makes it a personal property tax. States with a great deal of "through" traffic, such as Pennsylvania, New York, and New Jersey, also have toll roads. Finally, highways can be partially financed out of general revenues.

Whatever the source of the funds, it is a little-known fact that per-capita highway spending is the best predictor of a state's economic growth in terms of income, employment, and productivity.[1] It is an even more important predictor than state tax policy and whether the state is in the Sunbelt or Frostbelt.

The Politics of Highways

An important source of support for highway spending is the powerful highway lobby, which consists of a wide variety of interests: officials in the state highway department, automobile manufacturers, the United Auto Workers (UAW), tire companies and their unions, construction contractors and their unions, cement companies, oil companies and their unions, trucking companies and the Teamsters, bus companies and their drivers, outdoor advertisers, roadside restaurants and vendors, and state branches of one of the national automobile associations (A.A.A.). The breadth of this coalition is truly impressive, and it explains why state after state has a constitutional requirement that gas-tax revenues be used only to build and maintain roads.

Providing vital electoral support to the highway lobby are the state's rural residents, for whom roads are often *the* most important state political issue. For example, there is a large, isolated, rural area in western Illinois near where Illinois, Iowa, and Missouri meet; its residents refer to it as Forgotonia. People here want to know first what a candidate will do about getting better roads for the area before they hear how he or she views *any* other state issue.

TABLE 12-1   State and Local Highway Expenditures Per $1,000 Personal Income: 1970 and 1980

Rank	State	1970	Rank	State	1980
	U.S. Average	$22.06		U.S. Average	$17.25
1	Wyoming	69.47	1	Alaska	49.08
2	Alaska	61.06	2	West Virginia	43.45
3	Montana	54.10	3	Montana	40.47
4	West Virginia	51.31	4	Wyoming	40.24
5	Vermont	51.17	5	South Dakota	40.04
6	South Dakota	48.56	6	Kentucky	37.66
7	North Dakota	42.81	7	North Dakota	36.57
8	Idaho	39.63	8	Mississippi	32.84
9	Mississippi	39.38	9	Utah	28.39
10	Utah	37.93	10	Vermont	27.75
11	New Mexico	37.56	11	Iowa	27.41
12	Maine	34.36	12	Maine	27.33
13	Iowa	34.17	13	New Mexico	26.93
14	Kentucky	33.39	14	Arkansas	26.83
15	Louisiana	32.92	15	Nebraska	26.32
16	New Hampshire	31.89	16	Kansas	26.06
17	Nevada	30.76	17	Louisiana	26.05
18	Minnesota	31.61	18	Nevada	25.50
19	Alabama	29.68	19	Idaho	24.90
20	Oklahoma	28.80	20	Minnesota	24.79
21	Nebraska	28.52	21	New Hampshire	23.86
22	Arkansas	28.24	22	Wisconsin	22.91
23	Tennessee	27.21	23	Tennessee	21.41
24	Hawaii	27.19	24	Washington	21.36
25	Wisconsin	27.10	25	Georgia	21.02
26	Kansas	26.65	26	{ Oregon	20.95
27	Washington	26.43		{ Virginia	20.95
28	Oregon	26.37	28	Arizona	20.69
29	Arizona	25.82	29	Alabama	19.75
30	Virginia	25.79	30	Texas	19.44
31	Texas	24.40	31	Colorado	18.75
32	Delaware	24.39	32	Oklahoma	18.46
33	Pennsylvania	23.65	33	Delaware	18.29
34	Missouri	23.46	34	Maryland	17.55
35	Colorado	22.06	35	Missouri	17.47
36	North Carolina	21.67	36	North Carolina	16.97
37	Ohio	20.73	37	Illinois	16.71
38	South Carolina	20.24	38	Florida	15.87
39	Georgia	20.12	39	Hawaii	15.59
40	California	19.40	40	Indiana	14.97
41	New Jersey	19.24	41	Michigan	14.59
42	Massachusetts	18.10	42	South Carolina	13.85
43	Maryland	17.78	43	New York	13.44
44	Florida	17.61	44	Ohio	12.63
45	Connecticut	17.16	45	Massachusetts	12.02
46	Indiana	17.11	46	Connecticut	11.31
47	Rhode Island	16.97	47	Pennsylvania	11.24
48	Michigan	15.99	48	New Jersey	10.92
49	New York	15.73	49	Rhode Island	10.61
50	Illinois	15.03	50	California	10.14

SOURCE: David R. Morgan, *Handbook of State Policy Indicators,* 4th ed. (Norman: University of Oklahoma Bureau of Government Research, 1982), p. 91.

State legislators are often reelected to many terms in the expectation that increased seniority will lead to more clout and more road money for the region. For legislators, getting a new road or bridge is tangible evidence that he or she is working for the district. (In certain circumstances, *preventing* the construction of a highway in one's district is evidence that a legislator is working on behalf of the district. For example, Claremont, California, an upper-middle-class city east of Los Angeles, has successfully resisted for decades the completion of a freeway link that would pass through part of the city.) For governors, trading roads for votes is a time-honored practice.

It should also be noted that road builders are important campaign contributors, not adverse to augmenting the personal finances of friendly legislators and influential party leaders. Since contractors are often required to post a performance bond in the event a project of theirs is not completed, this lucrative bit of patronage can be handled by a legislator who also sells insurance.

Needless to say, states that spend more on highways also spend less on mass transit, and vice versa. Rhode Island, New Jersey, Pennsylvania, Massachusetts, New York, and Maryland—states near the bottom of Table 12-1—are relatively generous to mass transit. In states such as Illinois, which has serious urban-rural cleavages, bills for funding transportation (both roads *and* mass transit) will be package deals or else will never leave the legislature.

In recent years, both the federal interstate system and state highways have fallen into serious disrepair. As state road revenues have declined, maintenance costs have risen faster than the rate of inflation. Moreover, construction equipment is fueled by gasoline or diesel, and oil is one of the components of asphalt paving. Although the interstate system was built primarily with federal money, states are supposed to keep up the system; federal maintenance is provided only for the most heavily traveled routes. However, states have been unable or unwilling to honor their part of the bargain.

To make matters worse, Congress has opened the interstates to eighty-thousand-pound trucks; states that do not permit such trucks on their own highways will lose all federal highway funds. An "80,000-pound truck weighs the same as about 20 automobiles but hits the road with the impact of 9,600 autos." Moreover, 99 percent of the damage to pavement structure is caused by vehicles heavier than automobiles. Although truckers pay increased road-use taxes, these charges in no way approximate the amount of pavement damage inflicted by heavy trucks. This is why those little signs on the backs of big rigs saying "This vehicle pays $5000 in road use taxes" are highly misleading; the truck may have caused $20,000 of road damage per year. Furthermore, larger trucks are less safe. Although they constitute 1 percent of all vehicles, they cause 11 percent of all highway fatalities.[2]

Infrastructure Problems

The repair problems of the nation's roads are only part of America's crumbling infrastructure. A 1984 study done for the Joint Economic Committee of the U.S. Congress estimated that $1.2 trillion must be spent on roads, bridges, railroads, water and sewer lines, and dams before the end of the century—but only $714 billion is expected to be spent by federal, state, and local governments.[3] One quarter of the interstate highway system has exceeded its designed life and must be totally rebuilt. One out of every five bridges needs either major reconstruction or replacement. Half of Conrail's rails and roadbeds are seriously decayed. America's sewer and water systems, some of them made of brick, wood, or cast iron and many more than one hundred years old, have been described by *Newsweek* as "subterranean time bombs."[4] For example, more than 1 million gallons of tap water are lost each day through leaks beneath the streets of Berwyn, Illinois. The Army Corps of Engineers has inspected nearly nine thousand dams in highly populated areas and has found that about one third are unsafe—with 130 in danger of imminent collapse. The heart of the problem is that between 1972 and 1981, spending or infrastructure by all levels of government fell 25 percent in constant 1972 dollars.

There is little immediate political payoff for spending money on repairs: shining new facilities get much more attention. Besides, maintenance can always be deferred until after the end of one's term, when one's successors can worry about the cost. In any case, much of the infrastructure is underground (as in the case of sewers and waterlines) or out of sight (as are the undersides of decaying bridges). But because repair is postponed, it costs more later. Furthermore, there is a safety aspect to the problem: by spending $4.3 billion on the worst roads and bridges, it is estimated that 17,200 lives could be saved and 480,000 personal injuries prevented before 1998.

Mass Transit

Mass transit is becoming increasingly important for America's larger cities. Reliance on the single-passenger automobile has led to increasing energy costs, air pollution, and the saturation of roadways at peak commuting hours. Mass transit is clearly a more efficient means of transporting people.

When public transit systems are used at or near peak capacity, the energy savings can be dramatic. To move two hundred people ten miles, a fleet of five buses requires 1.7 million BTUs. In cars, even if all the riders carpooled, the same number would consume five times as many BTUs.[5]

Mass transit can take a variety of forms: buses, subways or rapid transit, light-rail systems, and commuter railroads. Buses currently carry about 70 percent of all mass transit passengers. They are more flexible than other forms of public transit because they are not attached to fixed, right-of-way routes. However, like the automobile on crowded city streets, they move very slowly. Moreover, driver salaries and fuel costs are an increasing part of bus service funding. Subways or elevated rapid transit can carry large numbers of passengers at high speeds, but the construction costs of such facilities, especially those underground, are enormous. These systems are especially appropriate for densely populated cities: San Francisco's Bay Area Rapid Transit (BART) is now operating well after a shaky start. Light-rail systems, the streetcars of sixty years ago, are now making a comeback. Whereas a bus can carry 70 passengers, streetcars can be strung together by a single operator-driver to transport 1100 people. Light-rail systems, which run on electricity, do not have the drawbacks of buses (slow speed, high personnel costs, petroleum dependency) or the high capital costs of subways. A successful use of light-rail system is San Diego's Tijuana Trolley, which runs the seventeen miles from downtown San Diego to the Mexican border. Commuter railroads are most appropriate for densely populated large cities; their main drawback is high fares. Still other forms of public transit are group taxis, dial-a-van, and jitneys (described in Reading 12-1).

READING 12-1   THE JITNEYS ARE BACK

Francisco Medinilla moved to California from his native Mexico 18 years ago. He is a rotund, genial and intense businessman whose 16-unit minibus "jitney" service is the soul of entrepreneurism and an immigrant's dream come true. But to the 2,000-bus-strong Southern California Rapid Transit District, private jitneys seeking patronage along the RTD's lines represent an abhorrent new form of competition. It fought unsuccessfully before the state Public Utilities Commission to deny start-up permission for Medinilla's "Express Transit District" and another applicant's "Maxi Taxi" vans.

Competition, however, may be precisely what city bus systems require if public transportation, faced by a cutoff of all federal operating subsidies, is to survive without prohibitively high fares or truncated service in the 1980s. And the private jitney, which was popular in America in the early 1920s and then regulated out of existence by jealous streetcar lines, may score a big comeback.

Jitneys—a colloquial expression for "nickel," the popular price of yesteryear—are small, shared-ridership vehicles, cruising for passengers along established transit routes. After their forced disappearance from most U.S. cities, they cropped up all over the world and today are a mainstay of transportation in such places as Manila, Hong Kong, Kuala Lumpur, Buenos Aires and San Juan. Juarez is where Medinilla got the idea for what has become his Express Transit Service. San Diego and Indianapolis approved jitneys in 1979 and 1981, but Los Angeles will provide the first "big time" head-to-head competition by jitney on major routes of a large public bus system.

That Los Angeles needs alternative transit, there should be little doubt. Population densities reach 50,000 a square mile along the Wilshire Boulevard corridor. The city has incredible capacity problems during peak hours, says Wendell Cox, a member of the Los Angeles County Transportation Commission; 40% of the 41- to 51-seat buses carry more than 70 riders at peak hours, Cox discovered.

In downtown Los Angeles, waiting passengers may see five or six buses go by that are so packed that not another rider can be crammed on board. Yet the RTD not only opposed Medinilla's application, but also assigned transit police to track his vans as soon as they started service Aug. 2, checking to see if they caused traffic blockages or any other problem.

Medinilla, his partner-brothers Aurelio and Manuel, and Maxi-Taxi's owner Boris Z. Gorbis found that they had a friend on the state Public Utilities Commission. Victor Weisser, director of the commission's transportation division, rejected the idea that jitneys operating at peak hours would "skim the cream" off public transit revenues. On the contrary, he said, "they would actually 'skim the deficit'" by reducing RTD's need to provide expensive peak-period services that involve buying buses and hiring drivers who are often idle the rest of the day.

Like almost every big U.S. public bus system, RTD labors under immense, red ink–generating disabilities—high union wages, large bureaucratic superstructures, lethargy from the knowledge that public subsidies will make up losses and political pressures to service unprofitable lines.

By contrast, Gabriel Roth and George Wynne state in a new report on alternative private transit services around the world ("Free Enterprise Urban Transportation," published by the Council on International Urban Liaison) that privately owned small transit operations have huge advantages. Owner-operators work harder over longer hours, handle more jobs and have less overhead. Their equipment, on a per-seat basis, is much cheaper than today's big buses, which cost up to $160,000 each. These owners often maintain the equipment personally or get family members to help. Smaller buses fill up quickly so that many of the regular bus stops can be skipped (and the ride speeded up). Often they make money on lines that big transit systems scorn.

Medinilla's operation reflects that kind of ingenuity. To avoid the huge capital requirement of buying a fleet of 15-passenger vans, he requires each would-be driver to put up $5,000 to become a limited partner of the firm. That capital goes to buying more vans; the driver gets $5 an hour in wages and shares in the profits at the end of the year. "The investors are my employees," says Medinilla, noting that many are ex–cab drivers.

Medinilla admits, "You have a helluva time getting people to use your service." But he is hustling to gain riders through advertising, pamphlets listing precise schedules for each of his four routes, and a fare of 75 cents—only 25 cents over the RTD's tax-subsidized 50 cents.

What the Medinillas and others like him represent, says C. Kenneth Orski, president of the recently founded Corporation for Public Mobility, is a sharp move away from the traditional view "that delivery of local transit services should be the exclusive domain of tax-supported public agencies, sheltered from competition by an array of protective laws and regulations." A better transit future, Orski predicts, will center around "principles of choice, competition and diversity."

Conflicts between jitneys and public buses are all but inevitable. In San Diego, the local transit authority is already complaining about jitneys swooping in ahead of its buses at certain stops to scoop up passengers.

But competition has great advantages. It may tame public-be-damned strikes in the big systems. In place of huge subsidies to monopoly systems, there could be subsidies for poor and elderly riders through transportation vouchers (like food stamps). And it should generate thousands of new jobs, especially for unskilled people, as private enterprise explores the frontiers of unmet transit demand.

SOURCE: Neal R. Peirce, "The Chips Are Down on Bus System Monopoly." © 1982, Washington Post Writers Group. Reprinted with permission.

The central problem of mass transit is that fare receipts seldom equal more than 40 percent of operating costs. Transit authorities could raise fares, but that would lead to decreased ridership. Hence, every transit system has huge operating deficits. Because of the politics of transportation discussed earlier, significant state aid is not likely to be forthcoming. In 1964, Congress passed the Urban Mass Transportation Act, which made relatively small amounts of federal aid available for capital improvements (such as new buses or subway cars), but not for operating expenses or deficits. The 1973 Federal Aid Highway Act allowed states to use federal highway trust fund money for mass transit purposes. In certain circumstances, these substantial sums of money can be used to reduce operating deficits. In 1982, Congress raised the federal gasoline tax by five cents a gallon (to a total of nine cents), with one cent specifically devoted to mass transit. The total amount of money appropriated for mass transit through fiscal year 1986 was over $17.7 billion. However, President Reagan intends to phase out federal mass transit operating assistance. The rationale for this change of policy is similar to those of other Reagan initiatives noted in Chapter 2: "In the past, the federal government has been involved in too many areas and has tried to do too much. . . . we must draw the line— determining where direct federal financing is in the national interest" and where financing should be the responsibility of state governments, local governments, or the private sector.[6]

Railroads

In recent years, railroads have been in serious financial difficulties. In the 1970s, more than one out of every three miles of rail track belonged to railroads involved in bankruptcy proceedings, including the Penn Central. In the early 1970s, Congress consolidated various bankrupt carriers into the freight line Conrail, and also created the intercity passenger line known as Amtrak, which receives federal subsidies. President Reagan would like to sell the federal government's stake in Conrail, cut off all federal funds for Amtrak, and reduce Amtrak mileage by 75 percent in the belief that the latter is inefficient. On the positive side for railroads are high fuel prices, which prompt truckers to put their trailers on railroad flatcars; increased coal demand, which leads to more coal traffic; and abandonment of unprofitable lines.

A surprising recent development is that states have gotten into the railroad business. West Virginia owns and operates a five-hundred-mile freight line that it believes is necessary to preserve chicken-feed sources for its vulnerable poultry industry. South Dakota, led by its very conservative governor William Janklow, was forced to engage in "survival socialism" when the Milwaukee Road went bankrupt and left half of the state's prime farmland without rail access to markets. South Dakota owns over 1300 miles of track, some of which is in *four other states.*[7]

ENERGY

Energy issues have been an important state and local concern since the Arab oil boycott of 1973, with some states being particularly innovative. Said one U.S. Department of Energy official, "We've stolen a lot of our legislation from the states."[8] For example, federal household-appliance efficiency standards were patterned after those first used in California. One study of state energy policy investigated seven policy measures that states have adopted on their own and that were not mandated by the federal government: state funding for research and development projects, comprehensive energy resource development plans, state-sponsored demonstration projects, tax incentives for industry, tax incentives for individuals, forecasting and modeling, and interstate energy resources development agreements. The most innovative states in the energy field are Arizona, New Mexico, New York, North Carolina, Oregon, and Texas; the least innovative are Alabama, Delaware, and New Hampshire.[9]

The amount of a state's energy consumption in the residential, commercial, and industrial sectors is the key predictor of its innovativeness. All states have state energy offices that perform tasks such as preparing forecasts of state energy supply, demand, and prices; presenting energy policy recommendations to the governor; devising fuel allocation plans; participating in the power plant facility-siting process; and administering federally funded conservation programs.[10]

We will discuss ten energy sources, plus a "source" frequently neglected—conservation. *Petroleum* is the source of about 45 percent of America's energy, but foreign supplies can easily be interrupted, and dependence on oil means that the U.S. could be blackmailed by a foreign power.

Natural gas provides approximately 27 percent of our energy needs. Since it is relatively nonpolluting, does not have the waste-disposal problems of nuclear power, and seems relatively abundant, one writer has described it as "the brightest prospect on a generally uncertain energy scene."[11]

Slightly more than one fifth of the country's energy needs are met by *coal*, which is so plentiful that the nation's coal reserve has an energy content twelve times that of all the crude-oil reserves in Saudi Arabia.[12] Much of the nation's coal is produced in the western states—for example, Wyoming—which leads to interregional antagonisms. Coal is either strip-mined (which scars the earth) or deep-mined (which is more expensive and is dangerous to the health and safety of miners). Coal-fired plants produce sulfur dioxide, a component of acid rain (discussed in the next section).

Water power (hydroelectric power) generates about 4 percent of the energy consumed in this country. In fact, the United States leads the world in the production of this source of energy.[13]

The remaining 4 percent of the nation's energy is provided by a wide variety of sources, some of which are controversial or currently experimental or even slightly exotic. Without doubt, the most controversial source of energy is *nuclear power*. Proponents argue that it is the cheapest way to make electricity and that its safety record is excellent compared with the numerous deaths associated with coal mining and the tens of thousands of deaths occurring each year from the sulfate particulates emitted from coal-burning plants. Opponents note that the radioactive wastes generated by nuclear plants remain toxic for 250,000 years and that no safe disposal process has yet been found.

The nuclear power industry is currently in serious difficulty, not only because of the political opposition it has prompted but especially because of its financial woes resulting from a leveling off of electricity demand. Since the Reagan administration favors nuclear power, antinu-clear activists have directed their efforts to state public utility commissions. Such activists received a powerful boost from the unanimous 1983 U.S. Supreme Court decision in *Pacific Gas and Electric* v. *Energy Resources Conservation and Development Commission*. The Court ruled that states can place a moratorium on the construction of new nuclear plants until state officials have decided that there is a safe means of disposing of nuclear wastes. It is important to note that the court did not issue its ruling on the basis of safety considerations. The federal Nuclear Regulatory Com-mission decides safety issues, but states may prohibit plants because of financial considerations. The lack of a demonstrated technology for satisfactorily disposing of high-level nuclear wastes increases the costs of nuclear plants and makes them economically risky. At the time of the Court's ruling, six states had such moratorium laws.

Solar energy is an excellent source of hot-water heating and swimming-pool heating. Because energy from the sun is nonpolluting (and cannot be interrupted by a foreign power), forty-four states provide property tax exemptions or income tax incentives or a sales tax exemption for the purchase of solar equipment. Since 1973, the federal government has provided financial assistance for the development of solar energy. Following a free-market approach, President Reagan is reducing such aid in the belief that the solar industry should sink or swim on the basis of its economic potential. In 1984, Congress ended all federal tax credits for installing solar and wind energy systems in an attempt to reduce the federal deficit.

Wind power has many of the features of solar: it is free and nonpolluting. But the wind does not always blow, just as the sun does not always shine. Hence, a large number of wind turbines must be concentrated in areas of high wind velocity. About one thousand giant windmills can equal the production of a single, conventional power plant. Unfortunately, many of the areas of highest wind velocity are scenic mountain passes, coastal bluffs, or river gorges.[14]

The remaining three energy sources are actually processes that make use of something that would otherwise be wasted and turn it into energy: resource recovery, biomass conversion, and congeneration. In the late 1970s, the city of Albany, New York, had a problem: its garbage landfill was nearly full. At the same time, the state government needed to heat and cool the state capitol and nearby state office buildings. Some creative New Yorker decided to kill two birds with one stone: burn the garbage to create steam to heat and cool the buildings. *Resource recovery* ("turning trash into treasure") not only saves money, it generates revenue: magnetic separators can recover iron, steel, aluminum, and glass from the garbage, and these can then be sold. It is important to note that half of the nation's mayors have reported that their cities will run out of disposal sites in the 1980s.[15]

Similar sources of energy are standing vegetation, aquatic crops (such as seaweed), forestry and agricultural wastes (such as bark and peach pits), and animal waste (for example, cow chips). The beneficial use of this refuse is known as *biomass conversion.*

Finally, waste heat can be save through *congeneration* (see Figure 12-1). This highly efficient process produces about one fourth of West Germany's electricity and about one fifth of England's, but it has the drawback of contributing to air pollution.

Although oil, natural gas, and coal will remain the "big three" of state energy supply, a wise energy policy—like a wise transportation policy—is multimodal. It is neither economically safe nor environmentally sound to rely on too few energy sources or transportation modes (such as excessive reliance on the automobile).

Another key goal in energy policy, as in transportation policy, is energy conservation. A report prepared for Congress has revealed that private residences, which consume nearly one fourth of the energy used in the nation, may waste half of that energy—an amount equal to 4.6

FIGURE 12-1

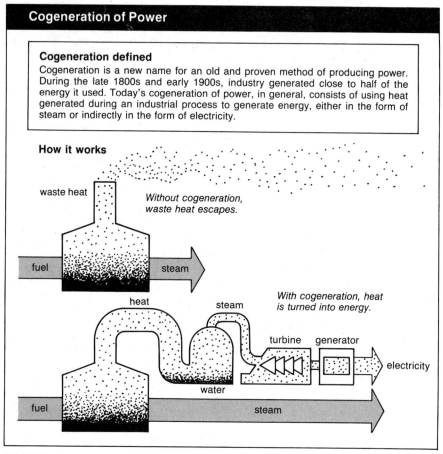

Cogeneration of Power

Cogeneration defined

Cogeneration is a new name for an old and proven method of producing power. During the late 1800s and early 1900s, industry generated close to half of the energy it used. Today's cogeneration of power, in general, consists of using heat generated during an industrial process to generate energy, either in the form of steam or indirectly in the form of electricity.

How it works

waste heat

Without cogeneration, waste heat escapes.

fuel   steam

With cogeneration, heat is turned into energy.

heat   steam   turbine   generator   electricity

fuel   water   steam

SOURCE: Copyright *The Sacramento Bee,* July 9, 1984, p. C-1.

million barrels of oil per day.[16] Such relatively simple alterations as improved insulation, weather stripping, storm windows and doors, and more efficient water heaters and furnaces are what are needed along with more stringent building codes. "Conservation is the only source of energy that can be rapidly deployed—in all consuming sectors—using existing technology and causing little or no environmental disruption."[17] Further examples of conservation include passive-solar building design (using a building's structure rather than mechanical means to collect solar energy), heat pumps, double-glazed windows, efficient air conditioning, electric-load management (decreasing electricity demand at high-use periods by transferring it to off-peak periods—by charging higher rates at peak periods), van pooling, and improved auto maintenance. State and local governments are in a particularly advantageous position to promote conservation because they control building codes and regulate public utilities.

Common Cause, the liberal reform group, has rated the states in energy conservation. It used all of the above measures and added a few of its own: mandatory lighting and thermal-efficiency standards for all new buildings, mandatory deposit laws for bottles and cans, declining block rates (to be discussed in the section on economic regulation), mandatory vehicle-efficiency inspections, and gasohol promotion.[18] According to this rating, the most conservation-minded states are California, Connecticut, Iowa, Michigan, Minnesota, New Jersey, Oregon, Rhode Island, and Wisconsin. Fourteen states were rated good or fair, and the remaining twenty-seven received an unsatisfactory mark.

ENVIRONMENTAL PROTECTION

Since the Reagan administration has not been particularly active in protecting the environment, this task is increasingly falling to state and local governments. At the same time, however, the administration is seeking to reduce federal aid for state-run environmental programs involving air and water quality, pesticides control, hazardous-waste control, and other fields.

Water Pollution

The landmark piece of federal legislation designed to eliminate the pollution of water is the Water Pollution Control Act Amendments of 1972 (sometimes called the Clean Water Act), which set a 1985 goal of eliminating the discharge of pollutants into navigable waters. (This deadline was later extended.) The act provided for $14 billion in waste-treatment construction grants. President Reagan, however, wants to reduce significantly such grants. The act also authorized the federal Environmental Protection Agency (EPA) to issue permits for the discharge of pollutants into water from any point-source of pollution. A *point-source* is an effluent discharge from a specific location, such as a factory or a city's sewers. Non-point-sources include runoff from fields, surface mines, timber harvesting, and so on, and can be very substantial.

Section 208 of the act provides for area-wide waste-treatment management planning. Governors designate area-wide planning agencies for those parts of their state with especially difficult water-quality problems. Applications for EPA waste-treatment construction grants and EPA pollution permits must be consistent with the area-wide plan. The state itself acts as the planning agency for portions of the state not covered by the area-wide planning agencies.

The Safe Drinking Water Act of 1974 requires the EPA to establish federal standards for drinking water and to protect underground sources of drinking water.

Air Pollution

Significant air pollution legislation also dates from the environmental consciousness of the early 1970s. The Clean Air Act Amendments of 1970 mandated national air quality standards and air quality control regions, emissions standards for new stationary sources of pollution, and stringent emission standards for cars, and provided for citizen lawsuits for violations of these standards. State and local governments were to bring air quality up to these national standards.

In 1977, Congress legislated delayed deadlines for meeting air quality standards and required states to revise their implementation plans. To maintain air quality in regions where the air was already clean, Congress required the EPA to propose regulations for the prevention of significant deterioration (or PSD) "in levels of nitrogen oxide, hydrocarbons, carbon monoxide, and photochemical oxidants. The PSD provisions were designed partly to prevent the nation's air from deteriorating to a mediocre national average, and partly to prevent industries from relocating facilities from exceptionally dirty to clean areas."[19]

In 1981, the National Commission on Air Quality, chaired by Senator Gary Hart of Colorado, issued a 643-page report that cost $9.5 million to compile. The panel recommended the elimination of 1982 and 1987 deadlines for state compliance with national standards. Instead, every three years the EPA would review states' progress in meeting the standards, and states would set their own deadlines. Other critics of air quality standards include the nation's ailing steel industry, which contends that such laws prevent it from being economically competitive; still other industries point to the billions of dollars they must spend on clear-air equipment. The coal industry would like air quality laws relaxed so that more coal can be burned. Amidst all the claims of industry on the one side and environmentalists on the other is the undisputed fact that there have been significant recent reductions in the amount of carbon monoxide, lead, ozone, and sulfur dioxide in the air.

Acid Rain

Not significantly reduced, however, is acid rain, which is formed when sulfur and nitrogen compounds emitted by power plants combine with moisture. The highly acidic droplets that are formed occasionally are as acidic as vinegar or even lemon juice. These acids kill fish, reduce crop and forest yields, and compound respiratory ailments in people.[20] Sulfur and nitrogen emissions can travel great distances and are a major source of conflict between the coal-burning Midwest (especially Ohio and Illinois) and the Northeast (especially New York and New England), which receives the acid rain, and between the United States and Canada. Coal burning can be made cleaner by *washing* the coal before burning or by *scrubbing* the emissions after combustion. Washing coal involves crushing it to remove pyrite, ash, dirt, and rock. Although the eastern U.S. receives rainfall that is twenty to forty times as acidic as unpolluted rain, the problem is nationwide: the western U.S. also receives rainfall twenty-five times as acidic as natural precipitation.

Remedying the problem is going to be expensive and politically difficult, which is why the Reagan administration would like to delay action as long as possible. If utilities in the Midwest are required to reduce their use of polluting high-sulfur coal, they will have to raise utility rates. Heavy industries relying on electric power, such as steel or automobiles or rubber, will pass their increased costs on to consumers. In addition, midwestern coal miners will lose their jobs, as will workers in related service industries. Industries installing smokestack scrubbers may face expenses in excess of $100 million per plant.

Toxic Wastes

Perhaps the key environmental issue of the 1980s is the safe disposal of highly dangerous toxic wastes. Examples of the problem include the following:

> Water wells in Toone, Tennessee, have been contaminated by pesticide wastes leaking from 300,000 fifty-five-gallon drums.
>
> A one-hundred-mile stretch of the Arkansas River has been condemned because of traces of dioxin—a chemical one hundred times as deadly as strychnine—from a chemical dump site.
>
> New Jersey officials ordered a landfill in Ocean County to be closed after toxic chemicals, including some suspected carcinogens, were discovered in nearby wells.

The amount of hazardous wastes generated each year is truly amazing: over 125 billion pounds, which is enough to fill the New Orleans Superdome from floor to ceiling every day. There are over 48,000 chemicals in use, but little or nothing is known about the effects on humans of 80 percent of these chemicals. Some have been shown to cause cancer, miscarriages, and birth defects. Hazardous wastes take the form of toxic chemicals, acids, caustics, solvents, pesticides, cyanide solutions, mercury and arsenic, explosives, and other materials. These dangerous wastes are produced by the chemical industry, metals production, electro-plating, textiles and petroleum refining, and other sources.

Hazardous wastes are supposed to be regulated by the 1976 Resource Conservation and Recovery Act (RCRA), which was intended to identify the characteristics of hazardous wastes; to require record keeping by generators of hazardous wastes; to set standards for transportation, storage, treatment, and disposal; and to provide guidelines for state hazardous waste programs. It took the Environmental Protection Agency four years to write the regulations implementing the RCRA, and these rules encompass over two thousand pages. For example, all companies generating, hauling, or storing wastes must notify the EPA of their existence; every shipment of wastes leaving a plant must be accompanied by forms identifying the firm producing the wastes, the transporter hauling them, and the company storing or disposing of them. If the company generating the waste has not received a copy of the form from the dump site within thirty-five days, the company must find out why and report any problems to the EPA. The purpose of this provision is to deal with the problem of "midnight dumpers," irresponsible persons who secretly dump dangerous wastes along rural roads or farmlands, or in woods and forests.

While the states were waiting for the EPA to issue its final regulations, some of them passed strict waste laws on their own. For example, Ohio has a 1978 law regulating wastes from "cradle to grave" and providing for ten thousand dollars per day in civil penalties; a 1979 Illinois law holds the operators of hazardous waste disposal sites liable for personal injuries for an unlimited period.

An especially dangerous aspect of the disposal of hazardous wastes is the contamination of groundwater. As we shall see in the next section, the nation is heavily dependent on groundwater for drinking. Most disposal sites are unlined, and when waste material mixes with snow or rainwater it forms a *leachate*—a liquid that moves downward through permeable soils and enters groundwater supplies. This contaminated water is impossible to clean.

Congress has recently closed numerous loopholes in the Resource Conservation and Recovery Act. For example, the original law exempted companies generating less than 2200 pounds of waste per month. Now, a company cannot dump more than 220 pounds without following EPA rules; dry cleaners, gas stations, and other small business are thus brought under coverage of the act. Moreover, the recent revisions now define petroleum and other refined products as chemical wastes that must be disposed of safely. The EPA is now required to control leaks from millions of underground storage tanks, many of them corroding and containing highly toxic chemicals, which may pose a threat to drinking water supplies. Companies also cannot dispose of wastes by blending them into fuels to be burned in industrial boilers.

Complicating the whole waste disposal problem is the fact that no community wants to be the home of a waste disposal site. See Reading 12-2. However, there are some disposal methods that do show promise:

Secure Landfill. This method requires a nearly impermeable bottom, such as a 30-foot-deep layer of clay, underneath the landfill. But the landfills must

READING 12-2   NOT IN MY BACKYARD

It was drizzling and cold at 4 A.M. Feb. 21 in Curtis Bay, Md., but about two dozen residents were carrying protest signs and chanting "Take away PCBs."

They were waiting for a 15-vehicle caravan that was transferring thousands of gallons of PCB-contaminated waste oil to a federal storage facility in their town. The oil had come from nearby Sharptown, where residents had demanded removal of rusting, abandoned tanks containing the cancer-causing chemicals.

But Curtis Bay residents wanted no part of Sharptown's problem. They had gathered before dawn to let government officials know they wanted the chemicals removed as soon as possible.

This was just one in a series of recent skirmishes in the battle over where to put toxic chemical wastes. It's a battle that has to stop, says the Environmental Protection Agency (EPA).

EPA Administrator Douglas M. Costle says the country is suffering from "the backyard syndrome."

"Everyone wants these wastes managed, but not in his backyard," Costle said. "And our entire nation is someone's backyard."

The residents who live near waste sites fear ground water contamination, air and land pollution, fires, explosions, spills and reduced property values.

SOURCE: "Solutions Sought to 'Backyard Syndrome,'" *Congressional Quarterly Weekly Report*, March 22, 1980, p. 802.

---

be constantly monitored to make sure the wastes are not leaking into the air or underground water supplies.

Deep Well Injection. One of the cheapest disposal methods is to inject toxic wastes into underground pockets or abandoned mines located deep in the earth—sometimes several miles below the surface. But there are many uncertainties. It is difficult to make sure the cavities are below the water table. And the behavior of wastes under pressure is uncertain. Built-up pressure has caused wells to erupt, sending gallons of waste gushing hundreds of feet into the air. Geologists fear the process may cause earth tremors. But it is safer than land dumping and cheaper than neutralizing or detoxifying chemicals.

Chemical Fixation. This method, successful in Great Britain, is used primarily with metallic wastes, which do not decompose. They are mixed with inert fly ash or silicate chemicals and then harden into a harmless cement-like material that can be dumped in unlined landfills or used for land reclamation.

Microbiological Treatment. Industry can neutralize much of its organic waste by feeding it to special strains of microbes that break the chemicals down into carbon dioxide, water and sludge.

High Temperature Incineration. Although it is expensive and requires a lot of energy, this method is probably the wave of the future, according to the Chemical Manufacturers Association. It involves burning wastes at temperatures as high as 2,400 degrees Fahrenheit to convert highly toxic substances like kepone and PCBs to harmless gases and salts. Because landfills require long-term monitoring and liability could last forever, many companies are planning to switch to incineration.[21]

In 1980, Congress passed the Comprehensive Environmental Response, Compensation and Liability Act (usually known as the Superfund), which provided $1.6 billion for cleaning up abandoned waste sites or for use in the event of spills. The Superfund is financed 87.5 percent by a tax on generators, and 12.5 percent by federal funds. Although this money is supposed to fund cleanup of approximately four hundred sites, only six were completely cleaned up during the first five years of the act's implementation; the task is turning out to be much more difficult than originally anticipated.

Noise Pollution

Every year, the U.S. Department of Housing and Urban Development (HUD) conducts a survey of city residents to determine what they dislike the most about their living environment. The annual "winner" is not crime, not air pollution, not traffic congestion—but noise pollution.[22] Prolonged exposure to high-decibel noise (for example, air-raid sirens or rock music) can lead to permanent hearing damage. Fairly continuous exposure to noise in excess of seventy decibels leads to hearing loss. See Figure 12-2. Moreover, noise causes physical and psychological stresses that lead to high blood pressure, insomnia, migraine headaches, ulcers, digestive disorders, and other maladies. To make matters worse, unborn children experience many of the responses to stress of their mothers.

To deal with these problems, Congress passed the 1972 Noise Control Act, which authorized the Environmental Protection Agency to impose noise-emission standards on major sources of noise, such as trucks, buses, and power lawnmowers. The Quiet Communities Act of 1978 provided the EPA with funds to assist state and local governments in noise control. Fourteen states and ninety localities have programs receiving such money.

An interesting by-product of the latter program is that noise control can also promote energy conservation: storm windows not only keep out the cold, they reduce sound by one half. President Reagan would like to turn all noise-enforcement responsibilities over to the state governments, and he would like to eliminate funding for the EPA's role in this field.

Reform of Traditional Environmental Regulatory Techniques

The standard approach to protecting the environment is the *command-and-control technique*, in which regulators devise detailed rules governing private activity in an attempt to protect the public interest. Hence, there must be a regulation to cover every possible circumstance. As we shall see

FIGURE 12-2

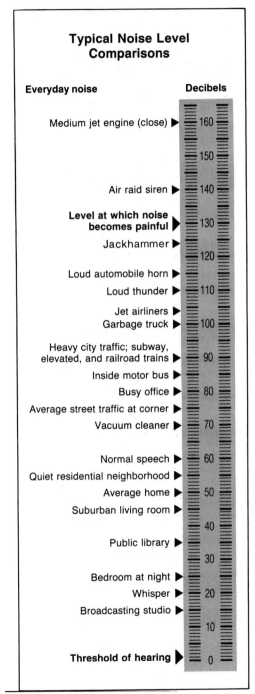

SOURCE: Copyright *The Chicago Tribune*, September 7, 1980, pp. 3-4. Reprinted by permission of Tribune Media Service.

later in the chapter, state Occupational Safety and Health Administrations (OSHA), in dealing with on-the-job safety, have issued pages and pages of regulations precisely covering the use of ladders and toilet seats.

Charles Schultze, former chairman of the Council of Economic Advisers under President Carter, has written that this conventional approach is too cumbersome and complex, and that the job of policing over fifty thousand major corporations is too difficult and expensive for bureaucrats.[23] Schultze suggests a *pollution tax*—a tax on firms according to the amount of pollution they emit. This far simpler system is keyed to economic self-interest: the less you pollute the less you pay or, it pays to be clean! The plan would rely on an extensive metering system that can accurately gauge the amount of a firm's pollution. Not only is the metering system cheaper than the present corps of regulators, it would actually make money for state treasuries. The current command-and-control system relies on someone bringing suit against polluters; a pollution tax would lessen the need for lengthy litigation. Those who favor the conventional system ask if sufficiently accurate meters have been developed. And what if the pollution charges were too low, so that it would be cheaper for a firm to pollute than not to pollute?

Another interesting concept in federal and state environmental regulation is the *bubble idea*. This idea assumes the existence of a giant bubble over a region: as long as total air pollution under the bubble does not increase, various pollution adjustments within the bubble may be made. For example, in order to get regulatory approval for a project that will generate a certain amount of pollution, a corporation agrees to pay for abating *at least* an equal amount of pollution caused by *somebody else*. Such *offsets* allow for both environmental protection and industrial growth. The argument here is not for less pollution control, but less expensive pollution control. However, the sources of pollution that are the easiest and least costly to clean up will be dealt with first. What happens when all the easiest ones are gone?

Another policy is known as *banking*. If a corporation cleans up existing pollution, it can build a new facility that creates as much *but not more* pollution. By cleaning up more pollution than is required, a corporation can "bank" the extra amount for future projects or sell it to other corporations. Critics question whether banking implicitly recognizes a right to pollute the environment.

WATER AND AGRICULTURE

Clean water, like clean air, should be considered a scarce resource to be preserved. However, water use is increasing much more rapidly than population growth: there was a 22 percent increase in the 1970s alone. The movement of population, jobs, and political power to the Sunbelt, noted in previous chapters, is in fact dependent on water.[24] Water waste is, therefore, a particularly significant problem.

> Many cities—most notably New York—do not require homeowners to install meters to keep track of their water use, which would encourage conservation. The EPA has funded dozens of sewage treatment plants that dump treated waste water into the ocean rather than recycling it.
>
> Because water has been treated as a limitless resource, cities have not replaced or repaired their aging water pipes. In New Jersey, for example, old water mains lose 20 to 50 percent of their water through leakage.
>
> Cheap irrigation water—sometimes priced 50 times less than what it actually costs—is provided to Western farmers by Congress, which does not require conservation. Because the water is so inexpensive, Western irrigators often waste the water by flooding open fields rather than using sprinklers. The General Accounting Office found in 1976 that more than 50 percent of the country's irrigation water was wasted.[25]

Since 83 percent of the nation's water is used by agriculture, conservation is particularly appropriate in this sector. Flooding open fields uses up to six times as much water as does spraying water. Drip irrigation is especially efficient because it applies small amounts of water directly to plant roots with hardly any evaporation loss.

In addition to questions of water quantity are questions of water quality. As shown in Table 12-2, some states, such as Florida, Idaho, Iowa, Mississippi, Nebraska, and New Mexico, are heavily dependent on ground-water. Samples of groundwater regularly reveal toxic and nontoxic contaminants such as "hydrocarbons and chlorinated hydrocarbons, minerals from irrigated fields, nitrates from sewage and fertilizers, road salt, bacterial contaminants and toxic residues from pesticides."[26] A 1985 report prepared for Congress revealed that only about 40 percent of the operators of toxic-waste landfills are complying with a federal requirement that they monitor their dumps for leaks into underground water supplies.

Some states are taking vigorous steps to protect groundwater, while others are sitting back and waiting for federal leadership. Connecticut has adopted a classification system for aquifers, assigning water-quality goals for each and providing the controls necessary to assure that the goals are met. Wisconsin identifies substances already in the groundwater or that are likely to enter it, then establishes groundwater-protection standards for each.

State water policy is inextricably intertwined with state policy toward agriculture. One fact the nearly every state must confront is that the number of farms is going down. In 1983, there were 2.3 million American farms, which was 475,000 less farms than only ten years before. Average farm acreage increased from 383 acres to 437 acres during the same period. Farmland is being converted to nonagricultural uses, especially in New England and the Mid-Atlantic states, but the nation is not running out of farmland, as some have feared. The farm population is approxi-

TABLE 12-2 **Dependence on Groundwater as a Source of Drinking Water**

State	Percentage of Total Population Relying on Groundwater	State	Percentage of Total Population Relying on Groundwater
Alabama	59	Montana	47
Alaska	63	Nebraska	86
Arizona	71	Nevada	64
Arkansas	67	New Hampshire	61
California	46	New Jersey	53
Colorado	23	New Mexico	92
Connecticut	37	New York	32
Delaware	65	North Carolina	60
Florida	91	North Dakota	66
Georgia	70	Ohio	40
Hawaii	87	Oklahoma	40
Idaho	88	Oregon	56
Illinois	38	Pennsylvania	30
Indiana	58	Rhode Island	33
Iowa	82	South Carolina	61
Kansas	62	South Dakota	79
Kentucky	39	Tennessee	51
Louisiana	62	Texas	58
Maine	37	Utah	58
Maryland	30	Vermont	56
Massachusetts	31	Virginia	34
Michigan	38	Washington	44
Minnesota	67	West Virginia	53
Mississippi	90	Wisconsin	64
Missouri	31	Wyoming	61

SOURCE: Veronica Pye, Ruth Patrick, and John Quarles, *Groundwater Contamination in the United States* (Philadelphia: University of Pennsylvania Press, 1983), p. 39.

mately 5.6 million persons, or 1 out of every 41 Americans. In 1950, 1 out of every 6 Americans was living on a farm; in 1916, it was 1 out of every 3. Table 12-3 provides information on farm income, farm acreage, and real estate values.

Every state has an agricultural agency responsible for checking the spread of insect pests, controlling plant and animal diseases, enforcing food inspection laws, and grading farm products. At the local level, almost three thousand special districts known as *soil conservation districts* employ approximately 5500 people. Over four fifths of these employees are paid by state and local funds, the rest by the federal government. In order to improve soil fertility, soil conservation district technicians work with farmers to rehabilitate eroded soil, and provide the latest information on rotation, terracing, ridge planting, crop drainage, contour plowing, and other agricultural improvements.[27]

TABLE 12-3   Farm Income, Acreage, and Real Estate Values

State	Total Income	Acreage		Real Estate	
		Number of Farms	Total Acreage (in thousands)	Total Value (millions)	State Rank
All states	$148,043,274	2,400,370	1,038,530	$816,556	
Alabama	2,303,044	56,000	12,300	11,341	30
Alaska	16,900	420	1,530	—	—
Arizona	1,716,829	7,200	39,000	11,466	28
Arkansas	3,535,880	57,000	16,400	18,106	15
California	14,455,276	80,000	33,700	64,198	2
Colorado	3,072,388	25,800	35,800	15,000	18
Connecticut	309,595	4,300	490	1,291	43
Delaware	405,287	3,400	660	1,095	44
Florida	4,257,740	41,000	13,000	18,616	13
Georgia	3,239,045	58,000	15,200	12,798	26
Hawaii	484,791	4,400	1,960		
Idaho	2,153,717	24,200	15,100	11,370	29
Illinois	7,552,565	104,000	28,700	55,678	4
Indiana	4,643,923	88,000	16,900	29,155	7
Iowa	10,559,214	117,000	33,800	60,908	3
Kansas	6,089,587	76,000	48,500	28,372	8
Kentucky	2,916,342	102,000	14,500	14,442	21
Louisiana	1,926,847	37,500	10,200	15,412	17
Maine	410,719	7,900	1,560	992	46
Maryland	1,057,171	18,000	2,750	6,644	36
Massachusetts	341,716	5,300	630	1,075	45
Michigan	2,903,037	65,000	11,500	13,708	23
Minnesota	6,855,057	103,000	30,400	36,389	5
Mississippi	2,535,224	53,000	14,500	14,500	19
Missouri	3,753,300	118,000	31,400	27,381	9
Montana	1,749,858	24,000	62,100	15,773	16
Nebraska	7,364,328	63,000	47,600	29,798	6
Nevada	240,768	2,900	8,900	2,510	41
New Hampshire	104,697	3,200	540	587	47
New Jersey	517,063	9,500	1,030	3,212	40
New Mexico	692,229	13,500	47,400	10,001	33
New York	2,601,519	50,000	9,500	7,467	34
North Carolina	4,128,767	88,000	11,100	14,252	22
North Dakota	2,910,567	38,000	41,700	18,181	14
Ohio	3,716,204	93,000	16,200	23,879	10
Oklahoma	3,258,753	71,000	34,300	23,873	11
Oregon	1,805,935	36,000	18,200	11,181	31
Pennsylvania	2,998,392	60,000	8,800	11,722	27
Rhode Island	32,793	750	80	224	48
South Carolina	1,173,097	33,000	6,100	5,600	38
South Dakota	2,680,121	37,000	44,500	12,949	25
Tennessee	2,140,585	95,000	13,400	13,025	24
Texas	10,323,263	185,000	138,400	79,718	1

TABLE 12-3 *(continued)*

State	Total Income	Acreage		Real Estate	
		Number of Farms	Total Acreage (in thousands)	Total Value (millions)	State Rank
Utah	550,816	12,900	12,300	7,257	35
Vermont	409,137	7,500	1,700	1,328	42
Virginia	1,687,072	60,000	9,800	10,192	32
Washington	3,099,832	39,000	16,300	14,474	20
West Virginia	227,877	20,600	4,300	3,565	39
Wisconsin	5,293,626	92,000	18,500	19,850	12
Wyoming	540,772	9,100	35,300	6,001	37

SOURCE: *Book of the States, 1984–85* (Lexington, Ky.: Council of State Governments, 1984), pp. 465, 466, 471.

The loss of topsoil through wind and water erosion remains a serious problem. In fact, such loss is one-quarter *greater* than it was during the Dust Bowl era of the 1930s. Some areas particularly hard hit are the southern Mississippi Valley; the area where Washington, Oregon, and Idaho come together; and the area where Iowa, Missouri, and Illinois meet. For example, Illinois loses over 180 million tons of soil each year, which is two bushels of dirt for every bushel of corn produced.

ECONOMIC REGULATION

State regulation of economic activity has a long history in the United States. In fact, extensive state regulation preceded federal regulation: many midwestern farm states regulated railroads in the nineteenth century in an attempt to lower farm-to-market costs. Other states established child-labor laws, maximum hours, and worker-safety laws before the federal government did.

In a federal system, the overlapping of federal and state regulation of the same economic activity is bound to be extensive, especially since the federal government has *plenary* (complete) power to regulate "interstate" commerce, which the courts have interpreted to mean virtually all economic activity in this country. However, the federal government may choose not to exercise this power because of deference to states' rights, or because it wishes to further the concept of free enterprise, or because powerful interest groups oppose the exercise of that power. Because the Reagan administration seeks less government control over business and is shifting regulatory activity to the states, efforts by the latter in this field are becoming increasingly important.

Emmette Redford has noted four patterns of federal-state relations in the area of economic regulation.[28] First, the states may exercise original powers of legislation because of the reserved powers granted to them by the U.S. Constitution, or because of inaction by Congress. State and local governments have the police power, which, as noted earlier, is the power to pass laws promoting the health, safety, welfare, and morals of the people. For example, states define the rights of property ownership and how property may be transferred; they exercise regulation of trades, professions, and labor unions, even though such initiatives may affect interstate commerce. Second, the national government may provide for state service or regulation. After the U.S. Supreme Court ruled that the federal government had the power to regulate the insurance industry, Congress passed the McCarran Act of 1945, which provided for continued state regulation of the industry. Section 14(b) of the Taft-Hartley Act of 1947 allows states to ban the union shop (discussed near the end of this section). The services, rates, and finances of hydroelectric projects are regulated by the Federal Power Commission only in states without a regulatory commission of their own. The third pattern of federal-state relations is parallel action. For example, both levels incorporate and service banks and regulate railroads. Finally, national and state levels cooperate in many areas: coal mines are inspected jointly by national and state inspectors; the soil conservation districts mentioned in the previous section are a federal-state-local endeavor; unemployment compensation programs are administered in cooperation with a national agency; and state courts sometimes serve as courts of original jurisdiction for interstate civil suits involving lesser amounts of money.

In addition to state activity, 82,000 *local* governments pass many ordinances affecting economic interests. For example, cities and counties zone land (an action that has major effects on property rights); license trades, businesses, and amusements; and maintain health standards in restaurants. Special districts supply power, water, and other services.

Public Utilities

Public utilities provide such essential services or commodities as water, electricity, natural gas, telephones, railroads, and buses. Because the public is so heavily dependent on these services or commodities, there is a danger that the providers will attempt to take advantage of the public. Hence, providers are either heavily regulated private corporations or government agencies. Neither of these arrangements guarantees that the public will be protected.

Rates charged by providers are set by a public utility commission, and if the providers are private corporations, the amount of profit is also determined. Many providers are monopolies and may have the power of eminent domain. The public utilities commission, which is sometimes called a public service commission, usually consists of three or five members, although Oregon has a single commissioner. Twelve states elect their commissioners, and the rest use gubernatorial appointment, usually with state senate confirmation required. According to one study, electing utility commissioners rather than appointing them leads to *higher* electricity rates for both residential and industrial customers.[29]

The setting of utility rates is a complex process and one that affords commissioners a great deal of discretion.[30] First, the rate base and the *rate of return on investment* (the maximum amount of utility profit) must be determined. This return must be high enough to allow the company to attract sufficient capital. After the rate base and the rate of return have been determined, *expected capital outlays* must be calculated. The utility's revenue needs are a reflection of the projected demand for the service or commodity, fixed costs, fuel, labor, and other factors. Finally, a *rate schedule* for different classes of customers (industrial, commercial, residential) must be computed.

As the reader has no doubt determined, the rate-setting process has an immense amount of room to maneuver and is highly political. Appointed commissioners, even though their terms may be six years and therefore longer than the governor's term, do not want to embarrass the person who appointed them. Besides, they may have political ambitions of their own. Elected commissioners do not want to anger ratepayer-voters, but they also like the campaign contributions and organizational support provided by utilities and large utility customers.

The importance of rate structures must be stressed since nearly every person pays directly or indirectly for electricity, water, telephone service, and so on. In years past, the rate structure was *declining block rates,* which means that as more electricity or natural gas is used, the per-unit price decreases. The policy favored high users. Many utilities are now promoting conservation by increasing unit costs as consumption increases. "Lifeline rates"—extremely low unit charges (below the cost of generation) for residences using little electricity, gas, water, and telephone service—have been established to aid low-income people. Electric-load management was discussed earlier in this chapter.

The rate-making process, like state and local government in general, is one in which various interests are intensely active. William T. Gormley, Jr., notes four different models of regulatory-policy making: the capture model, the interest group model, the organizational model, and the surrogate representation model.[31] He finds that each has some truth to it, but that full truth is found in none. In the *capture model,* the regulated industries dominate the process. In the *interest group model,* different groups with conflicting objectives compete with one another: utilities, business groups other than utilities, citizen groups, labor unions. The *organizational model* emphasizes the role of regulatory agency staff members. The staff, with expertise in such fields as engineering, economics, accounting, and law, has the function of educating commissioners. It analyzes all proposals submitted to the commission and interprets the position of their authors, offers recommendations to commissioners, develops its own policy proposals, and finally writes the actual opinions rendered by the commission. The *surrogate representation model* highlights the public officials who intervene in regulatory agency proceedings as surrogates for the public: the state attorney general and the consumer counsel. Gormley's study of twelve states prompts him to rank (from top to bottom) the following actors as influential (after the commissioners themselves): utility commission staff members, utility companies, surrogate advocates, business groups, citizen groups, municipalities, labor unions, individual citizens.

Regulation of Business

States regulate a wide range of economic institutions, including banks, savings and loan associations, credit unions, and finance companies. These institutions can be state-chartered (or federally chartered), with the state auditing their books and prescribing levels of reserves. Through usury laws, state legislatures set the maximum interest rates lenders may charge. In 1980, Congress passed a very peculiar law (the Depository and Monetary Control Act) that "permanently" removed state limitations on interest rates for first-mortgage loans and interest ceilings on business and agricultural loans of $25,000 or more. However, Congress gave the states three years to override this *preemption* of their usury laws if they so chose. Although Congress could have irrevocably preempted the state usury laws, its "permanent but removable" preemption presented the states with a murky legal issue and prompted lender-versus-consumer struggles in many states. Should Congress employ its power to force states to reconsider their policies on a broad range of other issues, state legislatures could be plunged into continuous turmoil.

State agencies also regulate insurance companies, but they have not usually gotten into the rate-setting field. As we noted in the chapter on state legislative politics, the members of the legislature's Insurance Committee are frequently insurance salespersons. Insurance companies may have a similarly friendly relationship with the state Department of Insurance and the insurance commissioner. However, the state tax on insurance premiums can produce substantial amounts of revenue: in California, it generates about $700 million per year.

States license (and presumably require some demonstration of competence from) a very wide variety of occupations and professions: for example, barbers and beauticians, embalmers, real estate agents, plumbers, boxers, physicians, veterinarians, optometrists, nursing home operators, and certified public accountants. Many of these practitioners, and especially the last three, must undergo mandatory continuing education, but the benefit to either the public or the licensees of such programs has not been conclusively established.

State regulation of business plays a prominent role in the closely watched rankings of states in terms of *business climate*. The two most prominent surveys are conducted by Alexander Grant and Company, a Chicago accounting company, and *Inc.* magazine, which studies small businesses. The Grant study is used by corporations considering relocation to a new site and includes such factors as unemployment taxes and benefits (which are usually paid entirely by employers); state and local tax rates, expenditure policies, and debt; unionization rates and wages; labor productivity; and energy costs and environmental controls.[32] States with low taxes, low levels of spending, less unionization and lower wages, and low energy costs do well in the Grant survey. As Table 12-4 indicates, these are usually Sunbelt states. Officials of states doing poorly on the Grant ranking attack it vigorously, noting that it omits cultural amenities, recreational opportunities, weather and climate, proximity to markets,

TABLE 12-4   Business Climate Rankings

	1984 Grant & Co. Manufacturing Climate Ranking	1983 Inc. Small-business Climate Ranking		1984 Grant & Co. Manufacturing Climate Ranking	1983 Inc. Small-business Climate Ranking
Alabama	19	41	Montana	20	14
Alaska	—	46	Nebraska	4	39
Arizona	5	38	Nevada	23	42
Arkansas	9	36	New Hampshire	26	17
California	30	2	New Jersey	29	10
Colorado	18	3	New Mexico	28	8
Connecticut	34	9	New York	39	4
Delaware	36	16	North Carolina	10	30
D.C.	—	N.A.	North Dakota	3	19
Florida	1	6	Ohio	46	29
Georgia	13	23	Oklahoma	21	33
Hawaii	—	31	Oregon	47	21
Idaho	17	47	Pennsylvania	41	15
Illinois	44	11	Rhode Island	45	20
Indiana	25	18	South Carolina	15	50
Iowa	31	34	South Dakota	2	43
Kansas	11	25	Tennessee	14	24
Kentucky	24	22	Texas	6	1
Louisiana	16	27	Utah	8	37
Maine	37	45	Vermont	35	26
Maryland	27	35	Virginia	12	13
Massachusetts	33	7	Washington	38	12
Michigan	48	28	West Virginia	40	48
Minnesota	43	5	Wisconsin	42	49
Mississippi	7	40	Wyoming	32	44
Missouri	22	32			

SOURCE: Jerry Hagstrom and Robert Guskind, "Playing the State Ranking Game: A New National Pastime Catches On," *National Journal*, June 30, 1984, p. 1270.

and supplies of raw materials. If we assume that top corporate leaders rely on the Grant study, what is at stake for states are jobs, tax revenue, economic growth, population increase, and even political power.

The *Inc.* ranking relies on different criteria since it is concerned with small businesses. The most important criterion is availability of capital and state support for small business (direct loans, venture capital programs, state management advice to small businesses). Next in importance are labor costs, population change, and number of fast-growing small businesses. Taxes are not a particularly prominent factor. The *Inc.* rankings also appear in Table 12-4.

Despite popular misconceptions, most plant relocations do not involve crossing state lines or moving from the Frostbelt to the Sunbelt. A study of 410 large manufacturing companies with 18,000 plants revealed that only 14 percent crossed state boundaries.[33] Most relocate in their local area, especially suburbs and rural areas. The employment growth in Sunbelt areas has resulted from the establishment of new branch plants and from the fact that these areas started from a lower industrial base with fewer manufacturers. As we saw in Chapter 9, much of the Sunbelt job gains are in service industries. Neal Peirce argues against the ill-advised state policy of "smokestack chasing" and noted that the overwhelming majority of new jobs come from the birth and expansion of independent local corporations.[34] Small firms are the nation's most important job generators. (Hence, the *Inc.* column in Table 12-4 may be more significant than the much-discussed Grant ranking.) The reason southern and western states are growing faster than northeastern and midwestern ones is that the former have done a better job of expanding existing firms and starting new ones.

The most important consideration in business location decisions is extent of unionization. Companies feel that labor unions circumscribe their management prerogatives, and hence they favor right-to-work states (to be described shortly). Another significant consideration is proximity to markets, which reduces transportation costs. Other factors about equal in importance are: attractiveness of the area as a place to live (high-technology industries want to keep their engineers happy), proximity to suppliers or resources (paper mills must be near trees and water; petrochemical companies need to be near oil pipelines), and low labor rates (highly competitive industries such as apparel or leather or furniture place more importance on this than do capital-intensive operations).

What is most striking about these calculations is the absence of concern over state and local taxes.[35] Tax breaks of every conceivable kind have been used as "carrots" to lure employers: outright exemptions on property taxes, revenue bond financing, sales tax forgiveness on new industrial equipment, inventory tax exemptions, lower corporate or personal income taxes, lower unemployment compensation fund payments. Since so many governments are offering these inducements, they can cancel each other out. Moreover, they miss the main point: for many companies, labor costs are twenty times as large as state and local tax payments. Not only does the beggar-thy-neighbor approach lower the local tax base, it angers local companies that have remained in the area for years because it subsidizes their competitors. In addition, tax breaks are seldom directed at small businesses, which are often owned by local entrepreneurs, not distant stockholders.

Some states have eagerly sought foreign investment, which can provide an important boost to lagging state or local economies. State farm income is also increasingly tied to overseas markets. States seek to expand existing in-state industries, attract out-of-state industry, and diversify their economic base by encouraging specific industrial sectors. The benefits to a state's economy from increased exports go beyond the immediate production of jobs and include indirect or *multiplier* effects in areas such as transportation, finance, insurance, and tax revenues.[36]

A variant of the lower-taxes-to-lure-business approach has been adopted in twenty-four states and is known as the *enterprise-zone concept*. Congress is considering similar action. The idea is to attract employers into depressed, high-unemployment areas of large cities by means of reduced state and city taxes, streamlined business regulations, and increased public expenditures for neighborhood cleanup and anticrime efforts. Firms once considering leaving these decaying areas are reported to be expanding their operations instead. Connecticut claims that the approach has been very successful in spurring investment, saving existing jobs, and creating new ones.[37] Critics of the approach argue that taxes are not an important factor in business location decisions, especially for small businesses whose foremost need is capital. Furthermore, they contend that large corporations, which do not need tax breaks, will receive them and that states and cities will lose tax revenues while having to provide added services.

During the economic recession of the late 1970s and early 1980s, many states considered plant-closing legislation, and a form of this legislation was enacted in five states. Although the content of the various bills was different from state to state, they generally provided that firms significantly reducing their work force or closing or relocating must give advance notice ranging from sixty days to two years; must give severance pay to both workers and the community; must offer the employees comparable employment and pay at the new location: must continue health insurance for displaced workers; and must give employees the opportunity to purchase the closing establishment. Although such laws help to relieve a community's anger at the departure of a major employer, they do not address the problem that most relocations are from one community to another, not across state lines.[38] Moreover, they can actually make matters worse because they appear to be the vindictive, rear-guard action of a declining region, and they send a very poor signal to corporations considering a move to that region.

Employer-Employee Relations

States have long regulated working conditions in order to promote worker health and safety; every state now has some version of an Occupational Safety and Health Administration (OSHA). Long before the national government legislated working conditions, states had established child labor laws, maximum hours, and minimum wages. A recent example of state activity in this area is *right-to-know laws*, which require that employees be informed of and given training in the use of toxic substances found in the workplace. California was the first state to pass such a law, and it did so over the stiff opposition of chemical manufacturers. California's director of industrial relations determines which chemicals are hazardous, and the manufacturer of the chemical must send a Material Safety Data Sheet to purchasers of the product. All employers using one of these chemicals must inform all employees who work with the chemical of proper handling methods. In the words of the author of the bill, "If a guy has his hands in a bucket of something eight hours a day, he has a right to know what it might do to him."[39]

In the field of labor law, states can provide for the union shop, the agency shop, or the open shop. In the *union shop*, new employees must join the labor union chosen by a majority of employees within a certain length of time after being hired. The agency shop requires workers either to join the union or pay a service fee equal to union dues and assessments. The fee is intended to deal with the problem of "free riders"—workers who receive the benefit of the contract but do not pay for the cost of negotiating it. *Right-to-work laws* outlaw both the union shop and the agency shop, and establish instead the *open shop*, in which employees may or may not be union members; no union is the exclusive bargaining agent for employees. Twenty states, generally located in the West, the upper Plains, and the South, have these laws.[40] Right-to-work states are not heavily dependent on unionized labor, but this characteristic both led to the enactment of such laws and has been intensified by them.

In order to provide economic security for unemployed workers, the states and the national government have established the unemployment compensation program, financed by a payroll tax on employers. (A few state unemployment compensation systems levy a tax on both employers and employees.) The 1985 rate was 5.4 percent, up to a maximum of seven thousand dollars per year. To be eligible to receive benefits, a person must have worked from three to six months, depending on state law. Benefits are determined by each state and vary widely, but are at least half of the person's weekly wage. Benefits can be received from twenty-six to thirty-six weeks, and even longer in states with unusually high rates of unemployment.

SUMMARY

Many of the public services discussed in this chapter, although provided by different government departments, are highly interrelated. Transportation cannot be provided without energy, which should be produced in an environmentally responsible manner. Water, so vital for agriculture, is a resource to be conserved and protected. The pursuit of private economic gain must proceed within governmentally established rules that protect the public interest. As American society becomes increasingly complex and interdependent, state and local public agencies must avoid the kind of bureaucratic tunnel vision that prompts its employees to say, "I work for the state Department of Transportation, and my job is to move people—somebody else can worry about energy conservation."

NOTES

1. Thomas R. Dye, "Taxing, Spending, and Economic Growth in the American States," *Journal of Politics*, 42 (1980), 1098–99, 1101.

2. "Old Battle Erupts Once Again on Longer, Heavier Trucks," *Congressional Quarterly Weekly Report*, April 12, 1980, p. 991. See also California Assembly Transportation Committee, *California Transportation Today* (Sacramento: California Assembly, 1979), p. 38; and "Interstate Highway System at Twenty-five," *Editorial Research Reports*, October 9, 1981, p. 738.

3. "The Nation's Repair Bill: $1.2 Trillion," *U.S. News & World Report*, March 5, 1984, p. 12. See also "The Repairing of America," *Time*, January 10, 1983, p. 12; and Pat Choate, "New Federalism and Old Facilities," *Society*, July-August 1982, p. 66.

4. "The Decaying of America," *Newsweek*, August 2, 1982, p. 15.

5. Julian Weiss, "Public Transit: On Track at Last?" *State Legislatures*, June 1980, p. 16. See also "The Decaying of America," p. 15; Jay Goodman, *The Dynamics of Urban Government and Politics*, 2nd ed. (New York: Macmillan, 1980), pp. 242–46; and Neal Peirce, "San Diego's Trolley Is Right on Track," *Los Angeles Times*, July 6, 1980, p. IV-5.

6. Former Reagan transportation secretary Drew Lewis, quoted in "Administration Proposals for Transportation Signal Reduction of Federal Role," *Congressional Quarterly Weekly Report*, March 14, 1981, p. 483.

7. "States Resort to 'Survival Socialism' in Bid to Preserve Vital Rail Lines," *Los Angeles Times*, April 11, 1982, p. IV-1. See also James Runke, "Transportation," in *Book of the States, 1980–81* (Lexington, KY.: Council of State Governments, 1980), pp. 386–87.

8. Quoted in "Tail Wags Dog as States Lead U.S. in Energy Programs," *Los Angeles Times*, May 18, 1980, p. VI-1.

9. James Regens, "State Policy Responses to the Energy Issue," *Social Science Quarterly*, 61 (June 1980), 44–57.

10. Ron Smith and Gail Prostrollo, "Energy Policymaking in the States," *State Legislatures*, November-December 1980, pp. 3–8.

11. Reo Christenson, *Challenge and Decision*, 6th ed. (New York: Harper & Row, Pub., 1982), p. 11.

12. Jennifer Stoffel, "Coal: What Cost?" *State Government News*, February 1981, p. 4.

13.   Editorial Research Reports, *Energy Issues* (Washington, D.C.: Congressional Quarterly, 1982), pp. 103, 114.

14.   Christenson, *Challenge and Decision*, pp. 7, 12, 17; Editorial Research Reports, *Energy Issues*, pp. 67–73; "U.S. Again May Tilt at Windmills," *Los Angeles Times*, July 28, 1979, p. I-1.

15.   Jennifer Stoffel, "Garbage: A Growing Resource?" *State Government News*, August 1980, p. 5. In the same issue of this periodical, see Gould Hagler, "Biomass: The Backyard Oil Well," p. 7.

16.   Conservation Begins at Home," *State Legislatures*, May 1980, p. 4.

17.   David Nemtzow, "Energy Conservation: Are the States Responding?" *State Legislatures*, July-August 1980, p. 14.

18.   *The Path Not Taken* (Washington, D.C.: Common Cause, 1980), p. 22. It can be detected that despite its "liberal" reputation, Common Cause has a strongly "mandatory" thrust.

19.   Editorial Research Reports, *Environmental Issues*, p. 26. See also "National Commission Report Starts Congressional Debate on Renewing Clean Air Act," *Congressional Quarterly Weekly Report*, March 7, 1981, p. 424.

20.   Editorial Research Reports, *Environmental Issues*, pp. 63–78. See also "The Nation," *Los Angeles Times*, April 23, 1984, p. I-2; and "The Bitter Politics of Acid Rain," *Newsweek*, April 25, 1983, p. 37.

21.   "Solutions Sought to 'Backyard Syndrome,'" *Congressional Quarterly Weekly Report*, March 22, 1980, p. 802. Other information sources for this section are Jon Steeler, "In Whose Backyard?" *State Legislatures*, April 1980, p. 23; "Handle with Care: Hazardous Waste," *State Government News*, December 1979, pp. 3–4; "U.S. Sets New Rules in Toxic Waste Fight," *Chicago Tribune*, November 17, 1980, p. 1-1; "Chemical Wastes: A Buried Bombshell," *U.S. News & World Report*, September 29, 1980, p. 39; and Jon Grand, "Environmental Management, in "*Book of the States, 1984–85* (Lexington, Ky.: Council of State Governments, 1984), p. 452.

22.   Editorial Research Reports, *Environmental Issues*, p. 83. See also pp. 84–93..

23.   Charles L. Schultze, *The Public Use of Private Interest* (Washington, D.C.: Brookings Institution, 1977). See also Allen Kneese and Charles Schultze, *Pollution, Prices, and Public Policy* (Washington D.C.: Brookings Institution, 1975).

24.   "War over Water: Crisis of the 1980s," *U.S. News & World Report*, October 31, 1983, pp. 57–62.

25.   "Water Crisis Is Predicted Unless Congress and States Get Together on Water Policy," *Congressional Quarterly Weekly Report*, April 18, 1981, p. 677.

26.   Jon Grand, "Groundwater Protection Lacing," *State Government News*, June 1984, p. 12; See also Jon Grand, "States Protect Groundwater," *State Government News*, July 1984, p. 12.

27.   Neil Sampson and Eugene Lamb, "Soil and Water Conservation," in *Book of the States, 1984–85*, pp. 482–84. See also "Is U.S. Paving over Too Much Farmland?" *U.S. News & World Report*, February 2, 1981, p. 48.

28.   Emmette S. Redford, *American Government and the Economy* (New York: Macmillan, 1965), pp. 112–14, 151–54.

29.   Thomas Pelsoci, "Commission Attributes and Regulatory Discretion: A Longitudinal Study of State Public Utility Commissions" (paper presented at the annual meeting of the American Political Science Association, New York City, 1978), pp. 22–23. In Virginia, the utility commission—called the State Corporation Commission—is appointed by the legislature.

30.   Ibid., pp. 5–6; public lecture delivered by Charles Teclaw, staff member of the Illinois Commerce Commission (Illinois's public utility commission), Eastern Illinois University, Charleston, Illinois, November 5, 1981.

31.   William T. Gormley, Jr., "Alternative Models of the Regulatory Process: Public Utility Regulation in the States," *Western Political Quarterly*, 35 (September 1982), 297–317. See also Gormley's *Politics of Public Utility Regulation* (Pittsburgh: University of Pittsburgh Press, 1983).

32. Jerry Hagstrom and Robert Guskind, "Playing the State Ranking Game: A New Pastime Catches On," *National Journal,* June 30, 1984, pp. 1268–84.

33. Roger Schmenner, *Making Business Location Decisions* (Englewood Cliffs, N.J.: Prentice-Hall, 1982).

34. Neal Peirce et al., *Economic Development: The Challenge of the 1980s* (Washington, D.C.: Council of State Planning Agencies, 1979), p. 17.

35. Ibid., pp. 21–22, 42–43; Neal Peirce, "Tax Breaks to Attract Business Glitter Like Fool's Gold," *Sacramento Bee,* July 9, 1979, p. B11. The attractiveness of lowering state and local taxes is offset by the fact that they can be written off from federal taxes.

36. John M. Kline, *State Government Influence in U.S. International Economic Policy* (Lexington, Mass.: Heath, Lexington Books, 1983), pp. 35–53.

37. Neal Peirce, "Enterprise Zones: Successful in States, but Blocked in Congress," *Sacramento Bee,* January 15, 1984, Forum p. 3.

38. David L. Birch, *The Job Generation Process* (Cambridge, Mass.: MIT Program on Neighborhood and Regional Change, 1979); Robert Leone and John R. Meyer, "Can the Northeast Rise Again?" *Wharton Magazine,* 3 (Winter 1979), 21–27.

39. Quoted in "California Leads the National Again," *Sacramento Newsletter,* September 15, 1980, p. 2.

40. Alabama, Arizona, Arkansas, Florida, Georgia, Iowa, Kansas, Louisiana, Mississippi, Nebraska, Nevada, North Carolina, North Dakota, South Carolina, South Dakota, Tennessee, Texas, Utah, Virginia, and Wyoming.

Epilogue

Change and reform have been the themes of this book. The rate of their introduction can be expected to increase. Predicting the political future is always hazardous, but it is safe to say that change will be incremental, that it will maintain continuity with the past.

As state and local governments have modernized and professionalized, they have become more activist and interventionist. Is this a liberal development that spells defeat for conservatives? Activist subnational governments of the future will probably use their taxing and spending powers to redistribute income from the wealthier to the have-not segments of the population, intervene more vigorously to regulate economic activities, and promote liberal social goals. On the other hand, activist governments can also use the power of government to achieve conservative goals, as the Reagan administration has done. We noted in Chapter 1 that the moralistic political culture is gradually replacing the individualistic one in many parts of the country. Because of the "politics of issues" that accompanies a moralistic political culture, state and local politics will clearly see more confrontations between liberalism and conservatism in the future. These battles will be fought out not only in legislative bodies but in the direct democracy arena through the use of the initiative. Also, Chapter 3 indicated that normative incentives to political activism are becoming more important than material ones; state and local governments may be in for some stormy days.

A few developments worth monitoring as state and local governments look toward the 1990s are the following. Population movement from the Frostbelt to the Sunbelt is expected to continue; the South will become more similar to the rest of the nation in terms of income. The South is also slowly losing its sectional distinctiveness in politics as the Republican party, perhaps aided by national party committees, becomes stronger. For structural reformers, the modernization of state government structure—for example, longer state legislative sessions with higher salaries and more professional staff assistance for members, and more simplified and centralized state court systems—is an important issue. For policy reformers, local government land-use decisions are a key concern, as is the "aging of America." With people living longer, the national median age is rising; health care costs for state and local governments will increase dramatically. Older people are also becoming very important politically on issues of importance to them. As for federalism, the huge deficits incurred during the Reagan administration will lessen future federal aid, even if President Reagan is followed by a liberal, Democratic administration. A liberal president might also want to broaden the regulatory-federalism techniques of crosscutting requirements and crossover sanctions, but state and local officials would be determined opponents.

The 1990s will have untold challenges and opportunities. The author is reasonably confident of one thing: the men and women selected for elected and appointive positions in state and local governments are more competent and better prepared for these challenges and opportunities than in the past. State capitals are seeing fewer "good-time Charlies" and more people who look at themselves as men and women who can solve state problems and meet the needs of their people. Since it is becoming more difficult to win election to subnational office, it is more likely that those who do win will use their office to accomplish something of substance. The 1990s belong to this kind of state and local official, and to the college students of the 1980s who will become those officials.

Suggested Readings

ANDERSON, JAMES E., et al., *Texas Politics*, 4th ed. (Harper & Row, Pub., 1984).

ANDERSON, LEON, *To This Day: The 300 Years of the New Hampshire Legislature* (Phoenix Publishing, 1981).

BACKLINI, ABDO, and DAWSON, CHARLES S., *The Politics of Legislation in New York State* (Comparative Development Studies Center, State University of New York at Albany, and the New York State Assembly, 1979).

BEDICHEK, WENDELL M., and TANNAHILL, NEAL, *Public Policy in Texas*, 2nd ed. (Scott, Foresman, 1986).

BEERS, PAUL B., *Pennsylvania Politics Today and Yesterday* (Pennsylvania State University Press, 1980).

BELL, ROGER, J., *Last among Equals: Hawaiian Statehood and American Politics* (University of Hawaii Press, 1984).

BENTON, *Texas Politics*, 5th ed. (Nelson-Hall, 1984).

BEYLE, THAD, and BLACK, MERLE, eds., *Politics and Policy in North Carolina* (MSS Information Corporation, 1975).

BLANK, ROBERT, H., *Regional Diversity of Political Values: Idaho Political Culture* (University Press of America, 1978).

BOLNER, JAMES, ed., *Louisiana Politics* (Louisiana State University Press, 1982).

BONE, HUGH A., et al., *Public Policymaking, Washington Style* (University of Washington Institute of Governmental Research, 1980).

BRYAN, FRANK, *Yankee Politics in Rural Vermont* (University Press of New England, 1974).

CHARTOCK, ALAN S., and BERKING, MAX, *Strengthening the Wisconsin Legislature* (Rutgers University Press, 1970).

CHEN, STEPHEN, *Missouri in the Federal System*, 2nd ed. (University Press of America, 1983).

COLBY, PETER, ed., *New York State Today* (State University of New York Press, 1984).

COMER, JOHN C., and JOHNSON, JAMES B., *Nonpartisanship in the Legislative Process: Essays on the Nebraska Legislature* (University Press of America, 1978).

CONNORS, RICHARD, and DUNHAM, WILLIAM, *The Government of New Jersey* (University Press of America, 1984).

COOPER, WELDON, and MORRIS, THOMAS R., *Virginia Government and Politics* (University Press of Virginia, 1976).

CORNWELL, ELMER, E., JR., et al., *The Rhode Island General Assembly* (American Political Science Association, 1970).

CRAFT, R., *Strengthening the Arkansas Legislature* (Rutgers University Press, 1972).

CRAIN, ERNEST, et al., *The Challenge of Texas Politics* (West Publishing, 1980).

CRANE, EDGAR, P., ed., *Illinois: Political Processes and Governmental Performance* (Kendall-Hunt Publishing Company, 1980).

DAUER, MANNING, ed. *Florida's Politics and Government* (University Presses of Florida, 1984).

DAVIS, J., WILLIAM, and WRIGHT, RUTH, *Texas: Political Practice and Public Policy*, 3rd ed. (Kendall, Hunt, 1982).

DOYLE, WILLIAM, *The Vermont Political Tradition* (Northlight Studio Press, 1984).

DRURY, JAMES, W., *Government of Kansas*, 3rd ed. (Regents Press of Kansas, 1980).

GANTT, F., et al., eds., *Governing Texas*, 3rd ed. (Harper & Row, Pub., 1974).

GARCIA, F., CHRIS, and HAIN, PAUL, eds., *New Mexico Government* (University of New Mexico Press, 1981).

GARGAN, JOHN J., and COKE, JAMES G., *Political Behavior and Public Issues in Ohio* (Kent State University Press, 1972).

GIESKE, MILLARD L., and BRANDT, EDWARD, eds., *Perspectives on Minnesota Government and Politics* (Kendall, Hunt, 1977).

GREENE, LEE, et al., *Government in Tennessee*, 4th ed. (University of Tennessee Press, 1982).

HANSEN, GERALD, *Arizona: Its Constitution and Government* (University Press of America, 1979).

HARDER, MARVIN, and DAVIS, RAYMOND G., *The Legislature as an Organization: A Study of the Kansas Legislature* (Regents Press of Kansas, 1979).

HARDER, MARVIN, and RAMPEY, CAROLYN, *The Kansas Legislature* (University Press of Kansas, 1972).

HEPBURN, LAWRENCE, *State Government in Georgia* (University of Georgia Institute of Government, 1980).

HERZIK, ERIC, and TEATER, S. B., eds., *North Carolina Focus* (Center for Public Policy Research, 1981).

HEVESI, ALAN G., *Legislative Politics in New York State* (Praeger, 1975).

HOJNACKI, WILLIAM, *Politics and Public Policy in Indiana* (Kendall, Hunt, 1983).

HORAN, JAMES F., et al., *Downeast Politics: The Government of the State of Maine* (Kendall, Hunt, 1975).

HOWARD, THOMAS W., ed., *The North Dakota Political Tradition* (Iowa State University Press, 1981).

HYNEMAN, CHARLES S., et al., *Voting in Indiana* (Indiana University Press, 1979).

JONES, EUGENE W., et al., *Practicing Texas Politics*, 5th ed. (Houghton Mifflin, 1982).

KARSCH, ROBERT, *The Government of Missouri*, 14th ed. (Institute of Public Administration, 1978).

KELLEY, ANNE E., *Modern Florida Government* (University Press of America, 1983).

KENNEY, DAVID, *Basic Illinois Government*, rev. ed. (Southern Illinois University Press, 1974).

KESSLER, JAMES B., *Empirical Studies of Indiana Politics* (Indiana University Press, 1970).

KIRKPATRICK, SAMUEL A., *The Legislative Process in Oklahoma* (University of Oklahoma Press, 1978).

KRAEMER, RICHARD, and NEWELL, C., *Texas Politics*, 2nd ed. (West Publishing, 1983).

LAMARE, JAMES, *Texas Politics*, 2nd ed. (West Publishing, 1984).

LAUNDRY, DAVID, and PARKER, JOSEPH, *Mississippi Government and Politics in Transition* (Kendall, Hunt, 1976).

LEHNE, RICHARD, and ROSENTHAL, ALAN, eds., *Politics in New Jersey*, rev. ed. (Eagleton Institute, 1979).

LLOYD, A. Y., and SINGLETON, J. ALLEN, *Kentucky Government* (Kentucky Legislative Research Commission, 1980).

LOPACH, JAMES, et al., eds., *We the People: The Workings of Popular Government* (Montana Press Publishing Co., 1983).

LORCH, ROBERT S., *Colorado's Government*, rev. ed. (Colorado Associated University Press, 1983).

MCCLESKEY, CLIFTON, et al., *The Government and Politics of Texas*, 7th ed., (Little, Brown, 1982).

MARTIN, CURTIS, and GOMEZ, RUDOLPH, *Colorado Government and Politics* (Pruett Press, 1976).

MARTIN, DAVID L., *Alabama's State and Local Governments*, 2nd ed. (University of Alabama Press, 1985).

MASON, BRUCE B., and HINK, HEINZ R., *Constitutional Government in Arizona*, 6th ed. (Cliber Publishing Co., 1979).

MAY, JANICE C., et al., *Texas Government*, 8th ed. (McGraw-Hill, 1980).

MIEWALD, ROBERT, ed., *Nebraska Government and Politics* (University of Nebraska Press, 1984).

MILBURN, JOSEPHINE, and SHUCK, VICTORIA, eds., *New England Politics* (Schenkman, 1981).

MILEUR, JEROME, and SULZNER, GEORGE, *Campaigning for the Massachusetts Senate* (University of Massachusetts Press, 1974).

MILLER, TIM R., *State Government: Politics in Wyoming* (Kendall/Hunt, 1981).

MITAU, G. THEODORE, *Politics in Minnesota*, rev. ed. (University of Minnesota Press, 1970).

MOREHOUSE, THOMAS, et al., *Alaska's Urban and Rural Governments* (University Press or America, 1984).

MORRIS, THOMAS R., and SABATO, LARRY, eds., *Virginia Government and Politics*, 2nd ed. (University of Virginia Institute of Government, 1984).

NICHOLS, GLENN W., et al., ed., *State and Local Government in Idaho: A Reader* (University of Idaho, 1970).

OGLE, D. B., *Strengthening the Mississippi Legislature* (Rutgers University Press, 1971).

PETTUS, BERYL, and BLAND, RANDALL, *Texas Government Today*, 4th ed. (Dorsey, 1986).

ROSS, MICHAEL J., *California: Its Government and Politics*, 2nd ed. (Brooks/Cole, 1984).

SCALES, JAMES, and GOBLE, DENNEY, *Oklahoma Politics* (University of Oklahoma Press, 1982).

SCARROW, HOWARD A., *Parties, Elections, and Representation in the State of New York* (New York University Press, 1983).

STOLLMAN, GERALD H., *Michigan: State Legislators and Their Work* (University Press of America, 1978).

SWANSON, WAYNE R., *Lawmaking in Connecticut* (American Political Science Association, 1972).

WALTON, ROGER A., *Colorado: A Practical Guide to Its Government and Politics*, rev. ed. (Publishers Consultants, 1983).

WILSON, RICHARD L., *Tennessee Politics* (Kendall/Hunt, 1976).

WISE, SIDNEY, *The Legislative Process in Pennsylvania* (American Political Science Association, 1971).

ZIMMERMAN, JOSEPH F., *The Government and Politics of New York State* (New York University Press, 1984).

Author Index

Subject Index